ALSO BY BILL BARICH

Laughing in the Hills

Traveling Light

Hard to Be Good

Bill Barich

BIG DREAMS

Bill Barich is the author of *Laughing in the Hills,*
Traveling Light and *Hard to Be Good.* His writing
has appeared frequently in *The New Yorker.* He
lives in the San Francisco area.

BIG

DREAMS

Into the Heart of California BILL
BARICH

VINTAGE DEPARTURES
Vintage Books
A Division of Random House, Inc. New York

To Patsy and Nora
Girls of the Golden West

FIRST VINTAGE DEPARTURES EDITION, APRIL 1995

Copyright © 1994 by Bill Barich

All rights reserved under International and Pan-American Copyright
Conventions. Published in the United States by Vintage Books, a division
of Random House, Inc., New York, and simultaneously in Canada by
Random House of Canada Limited, Toronto. Originally published in
hardcover by Pantheon Books, New York, in 1994.

Parts of *Big Dreams* have appeared, in a different form,
in *The New Yorker*, *Volt*, *Zyzzyva*, and the *San Francisco Examiner*.

Grateful acknowledgment is made to the following for permission to
reprint previously published material: •*Hal Leonard Publishing Corp.*:
Excerpt from "All the Gold in California," words and music by Larry
Gatlin, copyright © 1979 by TEMI Combine Inc. and Songs of All
Nations. All rights for TEMI Combine Inc. controlled by Combine Music
Corp. and administered by EMI Blackwood Music Inc. All rights reserved.
International copyright secured. Reprinted by permission of Hal Leonard
Publishing Corp. • *New Directions Publishing Corp.*: Excerpts from *The
Day of the Locust* by Nathanael West, copyright © 1939 by The Estate of
Nathanael West, copyright © 1966 by Laura Perelman. Reprinted by
permission of New Directions Publishing Corp. • *Rondor Music
International*: Excerpt from "California Girls," words and music by Brian
Wilson, copyright © 1965 by Irving Music, Inc. (BMI). Copyright
renewed 1993 by Irving Music, Inc. (BMI). All rights reserved.
International copyright secured. Reprinted by permission of Rondor Music
International. • *Sony Music Publishing*: Excerpt from "Kern River" by
Merle Haggard, copyright © 1985 by Tree Publishing Company, Inc.
All rights administered by Sony Music Publishing, 8 Music Square
West, Nashville, TN 37203. All rights reserved. Reprinted by
permission of Sony Music Publishing. • *University of California Press*:
Excerpts from *Up and Down California in 1860–1864* by William H.
Brewer, translated and edited by Francis Farquhar, copyright © 1949 by
The Regents of the University of California. Reprinted by permission of
the University of California Press.

The Library of Congress has cataloged the Pantheon edition as follows:
Barich, Bill.
Big Dreams / Bill Barich.
p. cm.
ISBN 0-679-42151-3
1. California—Civilization—20th century. 2. Barich, Bill—
Journeys—California. I. Title.
F866.2.B37 1994
979.4'05—dc20 93-43213
CIP
Vintage ISBN: 0-679-76035-0

Book design by Fearn Cutler
Map design by Vikki Leib

Manufactured in the United States of America
10 9 8 7 6 5 4 3 2 1

I tried hard to imagine another earth and could not.
I tried hard to imagine another heaven and could not.

Czeslaw Milosz, "From the Rising of the Sun"

I love you, California, you're the greatest state of all
I love you in the winter, summer, spring, and in the fall
I love your fertile valleys, your dear mountains I adore
I love your grand old ocean and I love your rugged shore

Where the snow-crowned Golden Sierra
Keep their watch o'er the valley's bloom
It is there I would be in our land by the sea
Every breeze bearing rich perfume.
It is here nature gives me her rarest. It is
    Home Sweet Home to me,
And I know when I die I shall breathe my last sigh
For my sunny California.

—*F. B. Silverwood and A. F. Frankenstein*
California State song

STATE FLOWER: California poppy
STATE BIRD: Valley quail
STATE TREE: Giant redwood
STATE REPTILE: Desert tortoise (endangered)
STATE FISH: Golden trout (endangered)
STATE INSECT: Dog-faced butterfly (endangered)
STATE ANIMAL: Grizzly bear (extinct)

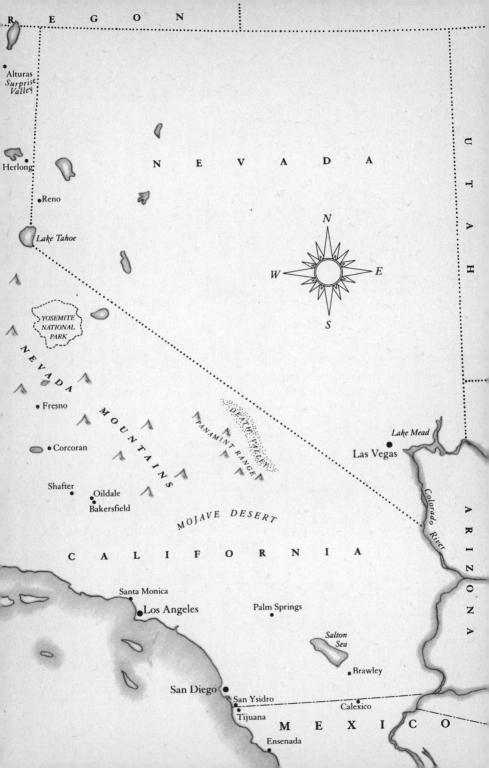

CONTENTS

PART ONE

AWAY

In California, if you go out to take a sunbath, when you wake up
you're middle-aged.
—*Ludwig Bemmelmans*

In 1957, a boy on my Long Island block stopped me after school one afternoon and told me that the Brooklyn Dodgers, my favorite baseball team, were definitely moving to Los Angeles. The shock to my system was extreme. I was thirteen years old and had never been betrayed before.

Those first, rare ball games from the Coast were watched closely at our house. I remember being awestruck by the billowy palm trees and the perfect weather. I thought, It never rains out there! Everything looked fresh and clean, spared from the urban grime of Brooklyn's Ebbets Field. Even on our midget TV screen, I noticed an appealing absence of tension, as if everyone in the pastoral West were granted enough space at birth to satisfy each wish.

At that instant, my perception of the universe altered subtly. No longer was California just a musical name at the far edge of a map in my geography book. Now it was real instead of imaginary, a place that anyone could go to, where people actually lived. Here was the start of an obsession.

All winter, as I walked dejectedly over our frozen playground diamonds, I pictured myself transported to the Dodgers' tropical stadium for some batting practice. The fantasy had a healthy radiance, an aura of well-being. My own neighborhood, a subdivision of almost identical Levitt tract homes built on some plowed-under potato fields, seemed threadbare by comparison. The landscape had no glamour. Snow fell and then melted, and slush slopped into your boots.

In high school, I listened to the Beach Boys' records and went to the Meadowbrook Theater near no meadow or brook to see B-grade beach-party movies shot in Malibu, wherever that was. The atmospheric blend of sand, surf, and blondes in bikinis spoke profoundly to my teenage narcissism, and I began to ache for some contact with California and all the bright, sexy, untarnished things it represented.

But how to get there? It took a stroke of luck. After graduating from college, I joined the Peace Corps and was dispatched by dint of miracle to the University of California in Los Angeles for ten weeks of training before being shipped to Nigeria for a tour of duty.

Our group of volunteers was quartered at a rundown, pink-stucco apartment complex not far from the UCLA campus. We loved it beyond reason. Bougainvillea grew in jungles along the crumbling garden paths, while tiny hummingbirds sipped nectar from the scarlet bristles of some bottlebrush trees. In the unaccustomed February heat, we swam laps in a decrepit pool and reclined on ratty loungers to elaborate our tans.

Every letter we wrote to our families struck the same chord. "Dear Folks," we bragged. "It's February, and I'm sitting by the swimming pool...."

Paradise, we thought.

In L.A., the sun really did shine every day. It lent an elevated status to our lives that we preserved by snapping photos. We posed on ocean bluffs, flexed our biceps at Muscle Beach, and stood with our toes touching the stars embedded in the Hollywood Walk of Fame. The city itself was held in an eternal soft focus—hazy, loose, and easy on the senses.

On Alvarado Street, we discovered Mexican food and fell to

worshiping the avocado, an exotic fruit none of us had tasted before. Avocados became an emblem of what we were experiencing, the rough skin of existence peeled back to reveal the succulent, green flesh hidden within.

For our Saturday night gatherings, we fixed guacamole in big bowls and licked the pulp from each other's fingers. Music blared from radios, and the gentle air caressed us. Our seduction was complete. Late in the beery evening, I would retire to a corner and take a private vow to return to California someday, buoyed up on the usual pilgrim's dream, the seed dream of all westward migration, a dream of starting over.

In 1969, at the age of twenty-five, I did start over, forsaking a hapless career as a teacher of New Jersey seventh-graders to cast my lot with the hippie tribe in the Haight-Ashbury. I had no job or profession in mind, but in an intuitive, quasi-mystical way I believed that something was waiting for me in San Francisco, a new self whose shape I could barely discern. Everyone in Levittown thought I was crazy.

Then came the spectacular drive across America. Cut loose from my roots, I felt both guilty and thrilled, scared and ultra-confident. The industrial ravages of the East dropped away behind me, followed by the countless farms of the Midwest, cow after cow after cornfield, but in Wyoming the scenery turned panoramic and filled me with optimism. I swallowed the broad vistas whole, in great gulps, simultaneously expanding my lungs and my consciousness.

Outside Cheyenne, I picked up two hitchhikers from Nebraska. They had infant beards and pretended to be older than they were. I guessed that they were runaways, and they owned up to it in Utah. They were escaping from pigs and haystacks, they said, and aiming themselves toward salvation in their own personal Eldorado.

Nevada was a blur of sagebrush and desert scrub. At dawn on a pearly August morning, tired but elated, we crossed over into California shouting *Yes! Yes!* and ascended into the Sierra Nevada.

As we approached Donner Pass, at an altitude of about 7,200 feet, one of the hitchhikers brought forth a recollected grade-school lesson about the emigrants from Illinois who had got trapped in the mountains during the winter of 1847–48. Those who'd survived had cannibalized their comrades.

"I'd never eat anybody," the other hitchhiker said.

"Then you'd be eaten," his partner grimly replied.

The tale of Donner Pass put a damper on our mood. Its moral appeared to be that not every trip to California would ultimately be rewarded.

So we rode on in silence and brooded about our fate until the vegetarian hitchhiker pulled out a harmonica and noodled a backwoodsy rendition of a dumb pop song about going to San Francisco and wearing flowers in your hair. We couldn't help singing along, and soon we were laughing as we winged our way over a bridge into a magical city cloaked in a dense summer fog.

In the Haight-Ashbury, I rented a cheap flat and furnished it à la mode with a massive stereo and a mattress on the floor. Something new and exciting seemed to enter my orbit almost daily—seven-grain bread, Zen meditation, the pungent smell of eucalyptus leaves. There was an earthquake, 4.7 on the Richter scale. Objects broke and were never mended. And one night at the Fillmore Auditorium, while Janis Joplin was wailing on stage, a girl in a see-through blouse ran up and kissed me without any warning at all.

O, man. California.

THAT MAGICAL CITY VANISHED IN TIME, of course blown away like a thistle, but I stayed on in San Francisco. I worked and married and bought a house. Always I harbored a naïve belief that I was only a temporary resident who would be going back to New York someday soon, but I never did.

Twenty years slipped by before I knew it. Slowly, without willing it, I'd been transformed into that curious thing, a Californian, and on the brink of middle age, as the century was about to turn, it occurred to me to demand an accounting.

If I hoped to take stock of my life out West, I reckoned that I should also take stock of some other lives and visions, listening to my fellow dreamers while I explored our common bonds. So I decided on an ambitious journey, even a metaphysical investigation, allowing myself six months to wander from the Oregon border in the Far Northwest all the way down to Mexico.

Every true California story, I would learn, begins in yearning and ends in transformation.

At the public library, I found two writers to accompany me on the road, Edwin Bryant and William Brewer. They had embarked on similar journeys in the mid-nineteenth century, but the reports that they had compiled were different in tone and in kind and were separated by the yawning chasm of the Gold Rush. Whereas Bryant had traveled west from Kentucky in 1847 to a little-known territory still wreathed in myths, Brewer had made his tour after the first great cycle of boom-and-bust, and his writing was sometimes tinged with the initial stirrings of loss.

A stiff, formal, frontier portrait of the youthful William Brewer served as a frontispiece in his posthumous book, *Up and Down California in 1860–1864*. He was handsome and bearded and had a high-minded look.

Brewer had come to the West from Poughkeepsie, New York, to join Josiah Whitney's geological survey team as its chief botanist. His wife and infant daughter had recently died, and he was starting over. He put in long hours in the field and was known for his honesty, his tact, and his genial good humor. At every opportunity, he wrote richly detailed letters to his brother Edgar back east—the clear-eyed letters of a naturalist—leaving behind the raw materials that would later be edited into a narrative.

Edwin Bryant had bequeathed us no picture in his *What I Saw in California.* He was a journalist of bold temperament, and he couldn't resist a trip to the Coast to examine all the curious rumors that he'd heard about "the countries bordering the Pacific." He believed, too, that the milder climate along the ocean might help to improve his failing health.

Opinions about California were divided, Bryant noted. Some Kentuckians were certain that it sheltered "the condemned and abandoned of God and man," while others claimed that its attractions were "scarcely inferior" to those of Eden. Gossip had it that five thousand Mormons were stationed in Kansas to prevent any emigrant parties from reaching "the reputed El Dorado." Bloodthirsty bands of Indians were also supposed to be there, robbing and murdering innocent victims.

Bryant wasn't sure what to think about such talk. As he saw it, his job was "to give a truthful and not an exaggerated and fanciful account of the occurrences of the journey, and of the scenery, capabilities, and general features of the countries through which we shall pass"—a worthwhile goal, I agreed, and one that I would try to live up to in my own report.

ON THE MORNING OF MY DEPARTURE, a Sunday in mid-April, an unexpected storm swept into San Francisco and began drumming against our bedroom windows at dawn. I heard thunder, saw streaks of lightning, and thought about omens as I slipped into my clothes and bent to kiss my sleeping wife good-bye, not knowing what a good-bye it would prove to be.

The night before, we had stayed up late over a bottle of wine, trying to convince ourselves that my impending absence would be good for our relationship. We had been happily married for almost fifteen years, but in the last few months we had foundered in a new place that baffled us—a distasteful place where our needs were in competition. We seemed to be growing in opposite directions, and the torque of it had left us drained and frightened.

Whenever we had hit a rough patch in the past, we'd been able to wait it out. Always the confusion and the negative emotions would dissipate after a while. This time it felt different, but I left the house still clinging to the hope that being apart for a few weeks might break the deadlock between us. Things would be back to normal, I told myself, when I came home for a rest at the midpoint of my journey, in early July.

Midpoint, midlife, middle age: I walked blindly into the future and boarded a little United jet to Eureka, a port city on the North Coast about three hundred miles away. The pilot took us up through some bruised-looking thunderheads, and soon we were suspended in that up-in-heaven space, where the world appears to be made of pure light and every trouble is insubstantial.

An hour later, we dropped toward some spring-green fields that were strewn with yellow mustard flowers and sloped toward the sparkling scallop of Humboldt Bay. The earth was keenly alive after the rain, refreshed and replenished and vibrant with energy.

At the airport in Eureka, I claimed a rental car and drove straight to Brookings, the first town on the Oregon side, where I checked into a motel and provoked a small commotion. The old man behind the motel desk eyed me with suspicion, as though he were making a mental inventory of my person to describe me to the police. I couldn't figure out why, but then I caught him staring at my license plate—at the blue letters on a white background that spelled *California*.

The old man was suffering from a peculiar anxiety that I'd witnessed before in Oregonians. Those afflicted with it were nervous about the empire to their south, worried about the nearness of sushi and acupuncture, and downright phobic about the prospect that Californians might someday take over their state and ban the use of chain saws and the wearing of flannel shirts.

Brookings was a fishing town that was turning into a retirement colony. Perkiness was rampant in the streets as the elderly swapped bowling scores and funny anecdotes from sermons. At a central grocery store, they stocked up on generic goods in feedlot sacks, fifty pounds of dog kibble or oat bran, and I began to wonder if the millennium might be even closer than I imagined.

ON THE CHETCO RIVER IN BROOKINGS, with a light fog burning off and a smell of sun-warmed bay leaves rising, I stood knee-deep in the stream casting flies to invisible steelhead, the big, sea-run rainbow trout that return to their natal waters to spawn. The stream had a flat, neutral color from the rocks and pebbles lining its bed, and I looked across it to a ridge where some silvery-green Douglas firs arched toward the sky.

No fish, the meditative motion of casting, the sun roaring in my bones. Happiness, for a moment.

Tomorrow, I thought. Tomorrow I'll cross the border.

Daydreaming, I imagined Edwin Bryant and his party getting ready to leave for California. I could see his ox team pawing the ground and sending clouds of breath into the air, could see Bryant tightening the cinches and wondering if he were about to make a foolish mistake or a glorious one.

A contingent of his fellow Masons gave him a send-off. Grandmaster Reese, their potentate, delivered a joking speech that consigned him to the grave or to perpetual exile. Bryant found it "rather overstrained in pathos" and much preferred an original hymn that the Masons and their wives sang with great vigor to the tune of "Old Rosin the Beau." Prayers were offered, and a benediction.

Then Bryant mounted his horse in the full bloom of spring. He must have felt the adrenaline racing through him. He must have felt his heart beating for fair as he set out to address the continent in its ceaseless variety. On horseback he rode away from the Midwest toward the Rocky Mountains, scribbling notes on scraps of paper and reducing the broad beauty of the moment to electric syllables, a poetry of the actual:

Remarkable Butte
Terrific Storm
A Good Supper
Cold Nights
Human Skull
Desert Plain.

PART TWO

FAR NORTH

Trees down
Creeks choked, trout killed, roads
—*Gary Snyder, "Logging"*

My back has become like a mountain ridge,
so thin,
so hungry
—*Karok coyote saga*

CHAPTER 2

COMING INTO CALIFORNIA, I passed a sign that welcomed visitors to the state while issuing no warning of its perils, and then an agricultural inspection station where uniformed agents were on the lookout for criminal bugs, the medflies and the gypsy moths trying to hitch a free ride to paradise on an Oregon apple or a Washington pear. Less than a mile away, I saw another sign that laid out some particulars.

Smith River   6
199   16
Crescent City   19

The landscape hadn't changed much since Brookings. To the west, in fenced pastures along the ocean, herds of dairy cattle were grazing. Blackbirds and starlings fluttered about them in nervous arcs. There were yellow acacias in farmhouse yards, clapboard barns covered with a yellowish moss, and some wilted plumes of pampas grass that had once been ornamental but now seemed merely tired.

To the east, some fields planted with Easter lily bulbs pressed up against hills that were studded with a diversity of trees—tan oaks and red alders, chinquapins, incense cedars, and a tall stand of Douglas firs that gave way at last, on the hilltop, to ponderosas and fleecy-needled digger pines. Almost the entire crop of Easter lilies in the United States came from the Brookings–Smith River area, about $4 million worth of flowers annually.

Pelican Beach was a strip of sand on a quiet inlet a mile or two down the road. The Knottical Inn, a curious building on a bluff above it, caught my eye. It had the merry nonchalance of a folk-art piece. The entrance was festooned with multicolored fishing floats and almost blocked by old wooden barrels. A battered dinghy sat landlocked near the front door. Dogs barked with menace when I pulled into the parking lot, but once I got by them, I was in a beautifully situated restaurant that offered grand views of the limitless Pacific, a vivid aquamarine.

At a small redwood bar, an elderly couple were having a quiet cocktail before dinner. The restaurant's cook sat on a stool next to them, taking a break before the evening crunch. He had robust, gray sideburns that flowed in cottony columns from under his toque. He was watching *Coal Miner's Daughter* on the bar's TV and vetting it for any possible deviance from his notion of reality.

"That's the original Grand Ole Opry, all right," he said approvingly when Sissy Spacek, as Loretta Lynn, began to sing. He finished up his coffee and retired to the kitchen, leaving the rest of us in charge of the facts.

From the bartender, an open-faced, thirtyish woman, I ordered a beer. Her name, I discovered, was Penny Knott. Her family owned the restaurant—hence, The Knottical—and everybody pitched in to run it. Penny greeted the customers, her brothers worked as waiters, and her mother was the general overseer, responsible for the decor and making no apologies about it.

The Knotts had come to California from Colorado in 1964, so that Penny's father, a carpenter, could take a job helping to rebuild the town of Klamath after the Klamath River had destroyed it in a major flood. Her parents had never been especially comfortable in the freewheeling California atmosphere, Penny said. They thought the state was "debauched." She wasn't dissatisfied herself, she went on—just feeling restless and in need of something new, a change of some kind. She was considering a move to Phoenix or Tucson.

I asked Penny what it was like to straddle a border between states, and she told me that she noticed a difference in her customers from either side.

"The people from California are more graceful, and they tip better," she explained. "Oregonians are much more careful. They're legalistic—you know what I mean? They always want to be sure they're getting full value for their dollar."

Apparently, we'd hit on a controversial topic around Pelican Bay because when Dusty, the cook, and his sous-chef overheard us through the open kitchen door, they played their own variations on the theme until Dusty felt compelled to emerge again to offer a good-natured defense of Oregon and Oregonians. He let it be known that he was a native Californian, Sacramento-born, but that he would never live there again, not even if hell froze over.

"What do you pay for your car's license fee?" he inquired.

I could sense a trap being set. The gears in the cook's finely tuned brain were spinning. "A lot," I answered.

Dusty nodded vigorously and almost sent his toque flying. "In Oregon," he said, "we pay almost nothing." He described a house he was renting, a lovely, tranquil, Oregonian house that he could never have afforded on the other side of the great divide.

"Doesn't Oregon bore you sometimes?" I asked, remembering all those chain saws and flannel shirts.

The cook smirked and laid down his trump card. "You can always *drive* to Sodom and Gomorrah," he said, putting an abrupt end to the debate.

In the fading evening light, customers were filtering into The Knottical and engaging in the eternal struggle for the prize tables by the windows. Penny would seat them and then return to talk some more. Her current restlessness had to do with searching for a vision of her future, she said. She had recently attended a meeting at a grange hall nearby, where Billy Mills, the famous Olympian who was half Sioux, had given a speech about how Indians of all tribes lacked representation in Congress and needed to band together. The speech had inspired her to do some thinking.

It dawned on me that the Far North was still Indian country in California, and that Penny might have some Indian blood herself.

"Are you part Indian?" I asked, feeling foolish as soon as the words were out of my mouth.

She looked at me as if I ought to know better, pinching an arm and glancing quizzically at a leg. I was getting an object lesson, the first of many.

"It's not so simple, eh?" Penny said, with a knowing smile.

CIRRUS CLOUDS AND A SMOKE-HUNG SKY. A ship appeared on the horizon, an ocean liner plunked down by the highway. The Krupps had built it in Germany years ago as a yacht for a New York millionaire, who had christened it *Caritas.*

When the navy requisitioned the ship in the 1940s, it became the U.S.S. *Garnet,* but the *Garnet* fell into private hands after the war, and tugboats towed it from Oakland to the mouth of Smith River. Twelve tractors dragged it from there to its present position, where its job was to lure tourists like me to Ship Ashore Resort.

After a late supper in the dining room, I took a stroll along the river. The tide was low, revealing mud flats and shell debris. A great blue heron stood on its long, spindly legs by the timbers of a rotting pier, waiting patiently for its evening meal. Surfbirds, black-and-white, waddled over rocks that little breakers kept washing clean.

In a region that had once boiled and spilled over with water, the Smith was the last big, free-flowing stream—the last anywhere in California, really. On the North Coast, the Klamath, Eel, Trinity, Mad, Van Duzen, and Russian rivers had all been dammed for flood control, to supply irrigation to farmers, or to fuel suburban development.

Like the U.S.S. *Garnet,* the Smith belonged in a museum. It showed how bountiful the coastal rivers used to be. It still supported large runs of spawning salmon and steelhead, and they were often of legendary size, with a few thick-bellied chinook weighing in at almost sixty pounds each year. Because the stream had no impoundments, it cleared quickly after a winter storm, but its uniqueness was also its curse. If the fish were thick, so were the fishermen, jammed in elbow to elbow.

Jedediah Smith, fur trader and mountain man, had lent his name to the river. In prints and sketches, he was always dressed in fringed buckskins, but he was actually born in New York and didn't see the other side of the Mississippi until, in his early twenties, he signed on as a hunter with General William H. Ashley of Saint Louis, who advertised in newspapers for "enterprising young men."

In 1828, while on a beaver trapping expedition, Smith passed along the North Coast on his way to Oregon, eager to be gone from California. The Mexican authorities had created difficulties for him since his arrival, pestering him for detailed papers and even for a passport bearing the seal of Mexico, so he was bound for the relatively unpoliced Willamette Valley, where he could set his traps without interference.

Smith had great skill as a mapmaker. On the maps that he drew of the area, he labeled a stream that emptied into the ocean at Requa as the "Smith River," but subsequent explorers corrected him. That stream had its headwaters in Oregon and was already known as the Klamath River, so "Smith River" got bounced from one place to another by cartographers until it stuck to the next river to the north, where it remained.

Word of the change never reached Jed Smith. Some Umpqua Indians ambushed his party in Oregon and killed most of his men, and he died himself three years later in a battle with some Comanches on the Santa Fe Trail. His associates in Saint Louis mourned his loss and honored him with a hyperbolic eulogy in the *Illinois Monthly Magazine*.

"And though he fell under the spears of savages," it said, "and his body has glutted the prairie wolf, and none can tell where his bones are bleaching, he must not be forgotten."

An evening mist, cool and damp, settled onto my skin. The mist, the smoky sky, the spiraling trees, the spooky quiet—they were a signature of the Far North, its essential elements. While gulls whirled and piped, I watched a blood-red sun sink into the ocean and saw two dusky shapes at the river's edge, a teenage girl with a ponytail and a young man who was being enterprising.

"You're going to be something when you grow up," he told her in a syrupy voice.

"I already am grown up," she said.

"No, you're not. You're already just pretty."

She could have been tiptoeing on a log. I imagined all the girls on all the beaches in California who were trying to keep their balance as the sun went down.

SMITH RIVER TOWN WAS A SPECK in the enormous greenery of the Far North, a relic of the nineteenth century. Two roads converged at the town's center before running by some shops and winding past dilapidated migrant shacks into open country. The buildings on Fred Haight Drive, the main street, were old and shabby and in need of paint. They looked much as they must have when settlers had hammered together Smith River in the 1850s, chopping down ferns that were sometimes knotted and tangled to a height of ten feet.

Nothing much was happening on the morning I stopped to visit. I found a transients' hotel, a video store, and, unbelievably, a tanning parlor that was defunct and shuttered, its radiant appliances collecting dust. Who would ever pay for a tan in Smith River? I wondered. Farmers got brown by working outdoors in the fields. The parlor was like a seed that had blown up from Beverly Hills and had failed to germinate, withering and dying in alien soil.

Dust had collected elsewhere in town, as well. Smith River seemed to be in the process of dismantling itself. At Hollie's Market, fixtures were ripped from the walls, and the shelves were toppled. Goods of every kind were tossed randomly into shopping carts, aspirin bottles mingling with candybars and bottles of Pepto-Bismol.

Mrs. Hollie, a short, dark-haired woman, was counting greeting cards at a check-out stand, scratching numbers on a brown paper bag. I bought a bag of peanuts, her only customer.

"Are you about to open or about to close?" I asked.

"We're closing," she said. "It's been twenty-five years!"

"So you've had enough?"

"Enough? Why, *yes!*"

Mr. Hollie joined us from the rear of the market. He wore a John Deere tractor cap and had a friendly, ruddy, country face. In his manner, I saw another old-fashioned thing, a gentlemanly urge to be around while a stranger was talking with his wife. We chatted about blameless subjects, about how the lily bulb growers were pushing out the last dairy farms and how 120 inches of rain might fall in Smith River during a wet winter.

"Will you be moving on?" I wanted to know.

Mrs. Hollie was a native of the town. She wouldn't consider leaving. "It's too late to start over in a new place," she said.

Mr. Hollie laughed and said, "We'd be getting a pretty late start."

Some Indian men were lounging on the front steps of an old house not far from the market. They fell silent and turned to stare when I drove by. They did the same thing to other cars, but if an Indian driver passed, usually in a scruffy pickup or an antique V-8 sedan, they would raise their arms to wave. It was as if an Indian driver afforded them some relief from an ongoing monotony that only they could feel. They were acknowledging the presence of an Indian world that was ordinarily concealed within the white one.

The men were probably from the Tolowa tribe, I thought. Once, the Tolowa had dominated the land around Smith River, controlling a territory that stretched from Crescent City, just to the south, all the way to the Rogue River in Oregon. They were efficient hunter-gatherers and had feasted on the rich resources of the North Coast— the game, the berries, the fruit, and the waterfowl.

In 1872, Stephen Powers, a reporter with a gift for ethnography, had set down his impressions of the tribe for the *Overland Monthly,* then the premiere journal in the state. The Tolowa, Powers wrote, were tall, haughty, aggressive, bold, and altogether forceful. They were in the habit of marching down to Requa, a Yurok village, rounding up a few captives, and holding them for ransom. They liked gambling and card games and had a superstitious reverence for the dead, never speaking their names, even by category, as in "father" or "mother," so as not to insult them.

For the Tolowa, Powers said, heaven was somewhere behind the sun. This belief was a natural outgrowth of their coastal climate, he maintained, since they had to suffer through "chilling, dank, leaden fogs" all summer and dreamed of bathing in "warm, soft rays" through eternity.

That afternoon, I took a back road out of Smith River, and it led me by chance to a neatly kept Indian cemetery enclosed by a white picket fence. Little ovals of rust had bled into the wood from aging nails, and the gates were held fast with twine.

For some minutes, I stood at a gate deciding whether or not to go in, but then I did and walked carefully among the headstones and the gravestones and read the chiseled inscriptions. I looked out at the ocean, so near, and at Prince Island, an uninhabited rock where seabirds were flocking.

Most of the Indians buried in the cemetery had not lived very long, but I came across some exceptions, such as Joe Seymour, who'd lived to be a hundred. A vase of plastic flowers on Seymour's grave had toppled over, so I set it right. The only sound I could hear was the crying of the seabirds.

*   *   *

A LIGHT RAIN WAS FALLING when I got to Crescent City the next day, and everything in sight was gray. The sky, the streets, the dogs, the cats—all gray, as gray as flophouse linens. The grayness had an inordinate strength and seemed to suck the brilliance out of other colors, leaching them of their substance. Here was a primal gray that could not be appeased with coffee, tea, brandy, or flames, a gray so clammy and relentless that prolonged exposure to it threatened to sever your ties to the universal oversoul.

The doldrums, then. April twentieth, noon, and the thermometer was bottlenecked at forty-six degrees. I took a room at American Best Motel, a confident establishment if ever there was one, and discussed the weather with the manager, Bob Young, who advised me that there would be no change until early evening, when the mercury would drop a few more notches to add another dollop of misery to the prevailing chill.

For with the grayness, the abiding gray, came a weird sort of cold that couldn't be measured reliably on any gauge. No matter how you tried to resist it, it got to you sooner or later, seeping through your clothing to reside in the marrow of your bones. It felt as if a steady clatter of miniature ice cubes were being released into your bloodstream. You shivered, stiffened, and stamped your feet, but your metabolism refused all entreaties.

Crescent City was a famous fishing town. Touring the harbor, I could see some boats out on the ocean and pitied the poor crewmen aboard them. Say, for example, that they were into the twelfth day of a two-week voyage, at a point in nautical time when the cramped quarters of an old trawler became almost unbearable—the decks slick with slime, the heater broken, the head a holy nightmare, and the stink of bait, entrails, and dead fish permeating every inch of enclosed space.

At sea, in frigid weather, every metal surface seemed to stick to

the crewmen's skin. They had to keep clenching and unclenching
their hands to prevent their brittle fingers from breaking. Their noses
dribbled and their sinuses impacted. The only escape from the debilitating elements was down below, where a fellow could lie on a
hard bunk beneath a thin, gray blanket and flip the bilge-swollen
pages of an ancient copy of *Playboy* from which his brethren had
surely torn the centerfold.

Even when the boats returned to shore, the poor men would
find precious little to distract them. Crescent City might be the largest
town in Del Norte County, but it had less than four thousand residents. Only twenty thousand people were scattered over the entire
county, an expanse of some 641,290 acres. That worked out to about
one person per 30 acres. The state and federal governments owned
three-quarters of the land and preserved it in parks and forests. There
were no metropolitan areas nearby.

An economic depression stalked Del Norte County. Fishing and
logging, the traditional industries of the Far North, were both battling
to survive. The locals complained about too much government reg-
ulation, but the ocean and the forests had been attacked with a
vengeance over the years, and their dwindling resources were in need
of protection. An era of Wild West–style plundering that had always
supported the area was drawing to a close.

In Crescent City, the powers-that-be were looking to tourism to
patch the holes in their economy. Every tackle shop in the harbor
was piled with fliers and pamphlets advertising such stellar attractions as the annual Dungeness Crab Festival, but there was still the
problem of the weather to be surmounted—a bleak, damp grayness
in the spring, and in the summer a dizzying, gray fogbank that lifted
for just two hours each afternoon.

Throughout the long day I felt the forlornness of Crescent City.
Young men cruised absently around the harbor in their trucks, smoking dope and popping the tops on half-quart beers. They were tough
kids raised to work in mills or on boats, and they wouldn't stoop to
being waiters or clerks—they weren't servants. They'd been cheated

of a future, really, so they behaved recklessly and acted out their anger, getting into fights and copping DUIs.

Outside the canneries in the harbor, workers stood around in bloodstained aprons. Trucks pulled up to chutes that fed into the cannery buildings and disgorged butchered fish in pieces—heads, tails, and guts in a roaring gush. On one pier, some fish buyers were huddled in shanties to cut their deals.

By the Seafarer's Hall and the Commercial Fishermen's Wives Association, I paused at a drinking fountain inlaid with a plaque that said, In Memory of Steve Williams, Lost at Sea, March 6, 1970, and then these words:

> They that go down to sea in a ship
> That do business in great waters
> These see the works of the Lord,
> He maketh the storm a calm,
> Then they are glad
> Because they are quiet
> So he bringeth them into
> Their desired haven.
> > Psalm 107, Verses 23–30.

MORE RAIN FELL ON MY SECOND DAY in Crescent City, buckets of it, so I took shelter at the Visitor Center of Redwood National Park. The park covers about 106,000 acres in California's redwood country, a strip of land that extends from the Monterey Peninsula into Oregon.

Children were stretched out on the floor of the center reading books, while their parents bought postcards and quizzed the rangers on duty, who wore uniforms and Smokey-the-Bear hats and sometimes showed a humorous grace-under-pressure when they responded to questions.

"What did Lady Bird Johnson plant in the grove that's named for her?" somebody asked.

"Her feet," came a ranger's response.

I studied the exhibits and learned that Spanish explorers had called our *Sequoia sempervirens "palos colorados"* on account of their reddish color. An average redwood lived for about two thousand years. The same watery, gray climate that chilled the blood of human beings helped the trees to stay alive so long and grow to such an impressive size. The damp soil kept their roots moist, and their trunks and branches didn't lose much water through evaporation or transpiration.

Passing through Crescent City in 1863, William Brewer had spent some time in a redwood grove and had recorded his wonderment.

"The bark is very thick and lies in great ridges," he wrote, "so that the trunks seem like gigantic fluted columns supporting the dense and deep mass of foliage above. . . . A man may ride on horseback under some of these great arches." There was a special tree down the coast in Trinidad, he said, that a speculator proposed to cut down and turn into a schooner.

It was December, and Brewer mentioned that the grove had an "almost oppressive effect upon the mind." In summer, a redwood forest with its slanting light can be likened (and, too often, *was*) to a cathedral, but the same forest in winter is a cold, dark, hostile environment. Already the redwoods were under siege, Brewer implied. "A man will build a house and barn from one of them, fence a field, probably, in addition, and leave an immense mass of brush and logs as useless."

The ravaging of virgin redwood groves had continued unabated for more than a century, and now the few remaining old-growth forests were increasingly off-limits to the timber companies that had harvested them for ages. Around Crescent City, the bitterness toward organizations like the Sierra Club ran deep and played itself out in such bumper stickers as Stamp Out Spotted Owls. Loggers took it hard when they perceived that a bird's life mattered more to society than a man's did.

The rain kept falling. One of the rangers removed her hat

for a minute to take a breather, and we got to talking. Linda lived with her husband and her daughter near Lake Earl, on the outskirts of town. She was completely at home on the coast and could hike, camp, fly-fish, and even make a meal off the land if it came to that.

Although Linda held redwoods in high esteem, she wasn't sentimental about them. Her appreciation for the trees was strictly botanical. She marveled at how unique they were and what they meant to the ecology of the planet. Logging had always been part of life in Del Norte County, she said, and she only objected to the cutting of irreplaceable, old-growth stock.

Linda told me a parable about the redwoods. A friend of hers who was broke and without hope had once accepted a job as a logger to feed his family. Everything went well until he was ordered to top an old-growth stand behind his grandmother's house. She ragged him about it, and so did the neighbors. The logger felt guilty and couldn't sleep. He'd try to scale a tree, and down he'd slide, wedging splinters into his face and his hands. He thought to himself, Those redwoods are fighting back!

"So what happened?" I asked.

"He quit and got a job driving a bulldozer where the prison's going in," Linda said. "Out on Lake Earl Drive."

I had heard about this prison, Pelican Bay, a maximum-security institution, in town. It was supposed to have beds for 2,200 inmates, but it would doubtlessly hold many more than that. Prisons in California were in short supply and always exceeded their carrying capacity. Since 1984, the state had been constructing them as fast as it could after a hiatus of twenty years.

It surprised me that a little place like Crescent City would welcome a prison, especially one for murderers, kidnapers, rapists, and gang members, all the rottenest apples in the barrel. I was even more surprised when I saw that it was being built in a residential neighborhood close to a school.

That evening, I remarked on Pelican Bay to Bob Young at

American Best, and he set me straight by telling me that the prison had a projected annual payroll of about $42 million.

ON MY THIRD DAY IN CRESCENT CITY, the sun miraculously began shining, and the town became its ideal Chamber-of-Commerce self, all salt air and sparkling sea. My thoughts turned to fishing again, so I phoned Bob Dearth, the president of Del Norte Fishermen's Marketing Association, to indulge in some talk of hooks and down-riggers and the ocean brine.

I had it in mind to ask Dearth to show me his boat, but his wife intervened. He had promised to paint their house that morning, and she meant to hold him to it. After some hushed bargaining, though, he was granted a grace period of one hour, and I went to meet him at his berth in the harbor. In a while, a little Japanese pickup came steaming toward me. It stopped abruptly, and Mrs. Dearth released her husband to my custody.

Bob Dearth was a solid man in his fifties. He had the chafed skin of a seafarer and spoke gently and with respect for words. He had twinkly eyes behind glasses and enjoyed a joke. Pens and pencils were jammed into the front pocket of his Big Mac overalls as a tribute to his presidential rank.

"Time to switch on the bilge pump," he said cheerfully, stepping onto his boat, the *Vilnius,* a twenty-five-foot-long salmon trawler equipped with a 160-horsepower outboard engine, more juice than such boats usually had. The skipper was a speed jockey.

Dearth had built the *Vilnius* from scratch in his backyard, starting with a fiber-glass hull that had cost him seven hundred dollars. He'd intended it to be the first rung on a ladder leading him to a bigger craft, but times were rough, and he had decided to hang onto it instead of going into debt. Age had taught him caution and forebearance.

"See that over there?" He pointed across the harbor to a nice, big, all-weather shrimp trawler, the *Catherine Marie,* that was about forty-five feet long. "That's *my* boat. I bought that boat down in Texas, but I lost it here in a bad year."

Dearth hailed from a fishing family. His father and his two brothers had all fished commercially. His home port was in the Department of Fish and Game's Klamath Management Zone, and he shared the zone with two other groups of users, sports anglers and Indians.

In the KMZ, the salmon runs were so depleted that a "season" might only last for a day or two, he said. The season changed from year to year, but regardless of *how* it changed, there were never enough salmon for Dearth to earn a living on them. He ran the *Vilnius* as a transit boat, traveling around to more fertile waters. He went down to Fort Bragg in early April, a trip of about two hundred miles, and up to Coos Bay, Oregon, in July, where he remained until autumn. He was always back in Crescent City by Halloween, mending his gear for Dungeness crab season, which could still be rewarding in the KMZ.

The traveling caused him difficulties. Dearth missed his wife while he was away in Oregon, and he missed his two sons all the time. The boys had crewed for him on the *Vilnius* since they were just out of diapers, but they were adults now and had left home to see what they could of the world. That was often the case around town, Dearth said. The children felt a tug when they were in their teens. There were no jobs to hold them, so they took off.

As president of the Marketing Association, a co-op, Dearth was adept at reciting the troubles confronting fishermen in the Far North. The decimated salmon fishery was the most serious problem. In the past, the fleet had contributed to it by taking too many salmon, but Dearth felt that the Department of Fish and Game was overcompensating by unspooling too much red tape and creating regulations that were too harsh.

Logging companies had also caused some of the wreckage

through negligent practices that had ruined many spawning streams, poisoning them with silt and pollutants. Then there were the boats that pursued hake, a cod, in the mid-water fishery and caught incidental salmon in their nets—27,000 incidentals in a recent year. The hake had no real value in the United States. Mother ships from Russia, China, Korea, Poland, and Japan processed it offshore and readied it for export. Abroad, it was used in synthetic crab and shrimp products.

Fishermen also paid exorbitantly for their disaster insurance, Dearth said, and they had to compete with fish dealers who sold pen-raised salmon from Norway and giant sea bass from Chile. There was a bottom line to all this. It used to be that any lout with a boat could survive, but now you had to be smart. You had to sweat and be willing to work the debilitating hours.

"You get out of it exactly what you put into it, and nothing more," Dearth asserted. The slack was gone.

Above us, the sun was arching toward noon. Dearth shut off the bilge pump, smiled, and stretched his arms over his head. Troubles aside, he still loved being a fisherman. He loved the freedom, the independence, and the ocean in its many moods. He was glad to come home tired from doing some physical labor and didn't think he would last very long in an office building where the air was stale and nobody knew the meaning of happiness.

The *Vilnius* might not be a stellar craft, but she pulled her weight at sea. Her name had emerged during a brainstorming session during which the skipper and some friends aspired to bless the boat with a touch of magic, believing that something cosmic would do, maybe Pluto or Saturn or, better yet, *Venus!* But somewhere between the filling out of forms and their bureaucratic shuffling, a spelling error had occurred, and when Dearth got his papers back he had a *Vilnius*, not a *Venus*. Being someone accustomed to the operations of fate, he had let the error stand.

Mrs. Dearth was barreling toward us across the harbor, a sure sign that our hour together was up. As Dearth opened a truck door,

I asked him if he had decided what color to paint the house. He had.

"I'm going to paint it gray," he said.

THE ROLLING GREEN HILLS OF POINT SAINT GEORGE, northwest of Crescent City, marked the break between the open ocean and the sheltered cove of Pelican Bay. Here the Tolowa had chipped flint and had worked with antler bone to fashion arrowheads and simple tools. They had done their heavy butchering and had cleaned their fish, counting on the sea breezes to carry away the blood odor and the gulls to police up the offal.

When the first ranchers and prospectors began carving into the coastal scrub and chopping at the great tangle of ferns, there were about 1,500 men, women, and children in the Tolowa tribe. By 1856, only 316 of them were still alive. By 1910, only 150 Tolowa remained.

Sometimes the breeze at Point Saint George turned into a gusty wind that pushed the fishing boats from Saint George Reef back to land. A Tolowa myth had it that an Indian boy had caused offense long ago by climbing a forbidden hill to pick some sweet, ripe salal berries. To punish him, North Wind swept down and grabbed his grandma, tearing her apart with an awesome force and scattering her limbs on the water, where they were transformed into a string of rocks that is now found on marine charts—Seal Rock, Whale Rock, Star Rock.

I walked around Point Saint George for a long time and then returned to Crescent City, where lights were glowing all along the crescent-shaped bay. In the harbor, I saw an old Portuguese fisherman, his hair still inky black, grip his wife graciously by an elbow as he escorted her up some stairs to a restaurant, whispering to her in their native tongue.

Chalkboards in restaurant windows listed the daily specials, crab and cod and shrimp in batter, clams steamed and chopped and served over linguine, salmon from Norway poached or broiled. The odor

of cooking oil masked the cannery stink. I could feel a cloaklike
dampness around me, a fetid moistness from which the redwoods,
the skunk cabbage, and the mushrooms were all drawing breaths.

There was a ghostly quality to the night, something sad and
otherworldly. It had to do with the climate and the isolation of the
Far North, but also with the slow passing of the old means of survival—the trades, the crafts, and the industries that were losing their
ability to support and sustain a way of life tailored to the specifics
of a certain place. I thought how removed I was from anything
remotely associated with the popular image of California. Even our
symbolic sun had to struggle for a purchase.

CHAPTER 3

Up over the klamath mountains I went in the last week of April, through some redwoods and past Trees of Mystery, where "authentic Indian artifacts" were for sale. The Klamaths were draped with clouds and had a soulful presence. They were home to the usual array of firs, pines, and oaks rising in tiers but also to such rarities as Alaska and Port Orford cedars and the Engleman spruce, indigenous to the Rockies. The weeping spruce grew here, as well, and nowhere else in California, rooting itself to the ridges of north-facing slopes at altitudes above 7,500 feet.

The Klamaths were intimidating. They dwarfed human beings and made us seem like an afterthought in the master plan of creation. Starting in southern Oregon, they ran for about 130 miles between the Coast and the Cascade ranges to the east, falling into several subgroups—the Siskiyou, Salmon, Marble, Scott Bar, and Trinity mountains. All through the Klamaths, there were alpine streams and lakes, and the forests were thick with black bears, cougars, mountain lions, feral pigs, and blacktail deer by the thousands.

The Klamath River was no less imposing. It carried more water than any other river in California, except for the Sacramento. It was big, wide, and deep, the color of coffee mixed with cream.

From an overlook in Requa, the ancient Yurok village, I watched it dumping tons of mud and silt into the ocean. Sea lions were swimming in the murky wavelets at its mouth, swatting at salmon and steelhead. They held fish between their teeth and barked like mutts. Cormorants were perched on the rocks around them with their wings spread, as still as totems.

No fishing boats were in sight, even though the ocean was as flat as the surface of a skillet.

Trees and water, water and trees: that was the mantra to be chanted on the North Coast. There were ghosts in the mountains, too, just as in Crescent City, the spirit lives of old Klamath town hovering above the floodplain by the river, where the water had swelled in raging tides to sweep away houses, buildings, and automobiles, all the structures and interdependencies of three hundred and fifty people, repeating a historical cycle.

A new Klamath town, the one that Knott the carpenter had helped to build, was on the other side of Highway 101, far from danger. At the town gate, a salmon carved from wood was suspended in a heart. Two stone bears prowled the ramparts of a bridge, and a little tombstone peeked out of the long grass by the main road, inscribed thusly, Bigfoot, R.I.P.

Nothing seemed to be moving in Klamath, nothing but the river. William Brewer had observed a similar emptiness in 1863. The gold-mining fever was over, he said, but some forty-niners had switched to mining copper up Del Norte way. Brewer found them lodging fecklessly around potbellied stoves in filthy barrooms, where they played cards and railed at each other all night. Unable to sleep, he checked into a tidy Dutch tavern, but his stay was spoiled again, this time by a drunken miner who was determined to enlighten him on the subject of geology.

Along the river, Brewer saw evidence of flooding. He saw devastation. Some miles inland from the coast, he came to the town of Hamburg, where only two years before, there had been three hotels, three stores, two billiard emporiums, and many miners' cabins. Now all were gone.

> The placers were worked out, the cabins became deserted, and the floods of two years ago finished its [the town's] history by carrying off all the houses, or nearly all. . . . A camp of Klamath Indians on the river bank is the only population at present! Their faces were daubed with paint, their huts were squalid. . . . In contrast with this was a sadder sight—a cluster of graves of the miners who had died. . . . Boards had once been set up at their graves, but most had rotted off and fallen—the rest will soon follow.

At the Beehive Cafe in Klamath, I paused for a cup of coffee. It was almost noon, but again, as at Hollie's Market, I was the only customer. The only waitress, a welcoming woman with gray hair, seemed glad for the company and was eager to exchange a bit of gossip.

The Beehive used to hum and buzz with loggers from dawn until suppertime, she told me, but not anymore. The last mill had shut down a while ago, and its rusted, scrappy remains lay behind the local Mobil station. The logging around Klamath was done by gypos now, small companies with low overheads. The big timber firms had cut too much too quickly, the waitress believed, snatching what they could and never thinking about the future. Did I know that it took sixty years for a redwood to reach a harvestable height?

"They were piggish," she said.

I laughed and said, "Like the rest of us," sliding some coins under my saucer.

Upstream from Klamath town, the river wound through a steep canyon. Deadfall, stumps, and the scars of clear-cuts interrupted the smooth, green flow of the mountains. Across the water, on the opposite bank, the Hoopa Valley Indian Reservation began. Junker cars were distributed among the trees, hauled in from body shops and accident sites. The road ended in Klamath Glen, a hamlet of trailers, drift boats, and rental cabins for visiting anglers. Two young loggers were leaning against a truck and handing a pint of whiskey back and forth.

"Too muddy even for the gypos to be out," one of them shouted to me when I waved. He seemed far away from the world, out of touch with it, like a pebble cast at the moon.

It started raining again. An Indian family stood fishing by the river, four kids and a mom and a pop, all oblivious of the weather, as if they'd been bred to the damp. They let the drops roll off them, casting and reeling in their lures. The rain drummed against my windshield and spattered on the ground. I heard a symphony of liquid sounds around me—the river, yes, but some creeks, too, and the water dripping from leaves and branches into rills, and the rills running into puddles, and the puddles seeping into the secret wellsprings of the Klamath, replenishing its subterranean reserves.

AT THE BUREAU OF INDIAN AFFAIRS (BIA) IN KLAMATH, I met an agent, Norman McLemore, who had come down from Fairbanks, Alaska, to take over the office just a month before. Fairbanks was in the grip of a big freeze when McLemore had left, with temperatures to seventy-below, so a new post in California had seemed like a godsend. He had expected lots of sunshine, some good beaches, and lots of pretty blondes. That was how the state had always looked to him on TV.

When McLemore got to Klamath, it was raining, and it had been raining a little ever since. He had visited the coastal beaches a few times, but the sun was weak there and the water was too cold for swimming. As for the blondes, they were nowhere to be found.

"You have to go south for that," he advised me. About California, he had become a wiser man.

McLemore was half Navajo. He wore a silver bracelet, a flashy ring, and a belt buckle in turquoise and silver. He had grown up in

Arizona, on the Navajo reservation around Window Rock, and had worked on it as a peace officer with the Navajo Division of Public Safety as a young man, but the job wasn't leading him anywhere, so he got an urge to travel and joined his parents in Bethel, Alaska, where his father had a job with the BIA.

He passed his first few months in Bethel trying to join the Alaska State Troopers. He scored a 94 on his exam and did well on all the agility tests, but he was never hired. Later, in Juneau, he tried again under an affirmative action program, and once more, in spite of doing well on his tests, he failed to be hired. He attributed it to prejudice. So, instead, he worked as an assistant to an Alaskan tribe and became involved in some disputes over land allotments, and after that he joined the BIA.

The Klamath office of the BIA was small and cramped and a little difficult to find, tucked into a plain building near the police station. California had a Native American population of more than two hundred thousand, the largest in the nation, with about 130 tribes that spoke some twenty-four separate languages, but the bureau spent less money in the state than in any other of its administrative regions. I thought it must be due, at least in part, to the invisibility of Indians in most cities. Only in the Far North did a white Californian feel their presence so strongly.

The lack of resources weighed on McLemore because he had a tricky, laborious situation to resolve. The Yurok tribe was at the center of it. They had shared the 93,000-acre Hoopa Valley Indian Reservation with the Hupa—the tribe's name was spelled differently from the place's name—for over a century. The two had always managed to coexist and had always done business, with the Hupa traditionally trading such inland food as acorns and fruit for the Yuroks' canoes and fish.

In the past few years, however, there had been some feuding and litigation between the tribes, and they were about to be partitioned by an Act of Congress. The Yuroks would get their own reservation, but anybody who wanted to live on it and partake of the benefits had to be certified as a Yurok Native American by the BIA, submitting a complicated application form. Yuroks who had some Hupa blood could apply to stay on the Hoopa Reservation. A Yurok, once certified, could also forsake his or her claim and accept a buy-out of fifteen thousand dollars.

McLemore had received about seven thousand applications so far. He figured that he could dismiss about a quarter of them out of hand, but the rest demanded his attention. He would not enjoy the task, either, because he was against any partitioning and suspected that it merely amounted to a strategy of divide-and-conquer. Partitioning diluted the power of Native Americans, he felt—it had done that to the Navajo and the Hopi. He believed that Indians ought to consolidate, but that they would need a unifying vision to lead them. There was no such vision at present.

Above all, McLemore hoped to be fair in dealing with the Yurok. Indians had already suffered enough in California. Theirs was a history of brutality, violence, and murder that had genocidal implications.

When Junípero Serra had established his first mission in what was then known as Alta California, in 1769, the Native American population had totaled about 350,000, but disease and armed attacks soon reduced it by half. During the Gold Rush, miners stole Indian land and reduced the population to about 50,000 through random slayings. In 1851–52, the federal government agreed to give California tribes some provisions, some cattle, and some tracts of land—about 7 million acres, or 7½ percent of the state—but the U.S. Senate, in a secret session and under pressure from business interests and the legislature in California, refused to ratify the necessary treaties.

Congress did pass a law in 1860, though, that allowed for Indians to be held as "apprentices," or chattel, and many of them were still in slavery long after the Emancipation Proclamation.

About one-third of California's tribes currently had no legal standing, said McLemore, and hence no access to federal benefits. He told me that the commerical fishing season would begin on the

Klamath River in late May or early June. The Yurok would need their official IDs from the BIA by then. If they didn't have them, they'd go ahead and fish, anyway—more trouble, not less.

McLemore sighed. He had too much to do. He had to find a house to buy in town, but here again California had pitched him a curveball. There was a crazy real estate boom in and around Klamath, and sellers were demanding premium prices for dumps. A crummy trailer home on a straggly, weed-burdened lot back in Klamath Glen could cost upwards of fifty thousand bucks.

"Why is that?" I asked.

"Pelican Bay State Prison," he answered. "Everybody thinks it's going to make them rich."

McLemore shook his head. California, it was not to be believed.

On my way to the hoopa valley reservation, I ran into a problem of my own, several monstrous motor homes and trucks pulling trailers that were creeping along the pavement of Highway 101. You could practically hear the vertebrae cracking as necks craned for a view of some treasured aspect of Redwood National Park.

California had given birth to these suburbs on wheels, of course. In the 1920s, Wally Byam, an advertising man in Los Angeles, started publishing a magazine that catered to the do-it-yourself craze that was sweeping the country, and he printed some plans for building a trailer in one issue. When readers wrote to complain that the design was faulty, he felt obliged to improve it and kept tinkering until he came up with something better.

By 1936, Byam had a new business venture. That year, he introduced a sleek, silvery, riveted-aluminum trailer, the Clipper, that became the flagship of his Airstream Trailer Company. Because of its contours, which were based on aircraft principles, it glided along, said the old copywriter, "like a stream of air."

The Clipper had a tubular-steel dinette, its own water supply, electric lights, a chemical toilet, a galley, and an air-conditioning system that used dry ice. It slept four and carried a steep price tag of $1,200, but consumers were undeterred. The fledgling company couldn't fill all its orders.

Here was a purely American moment. In one fell swoop, Byam had tamed the thrill, the terror, and the sheer adventure of the open road, vanquishing it with backyard technology while simultaneously turning the last wild places in the state into potential venues for domestic sitcoms. Soon caravans of Airstreams were roaming the globe, mutating and spawning replicants, showing up for confabs in Uganda, at the Leaning Tower of Pisa, at Saint Basil's Cathedral in Moscow, and at the Jami-i-Masjid mosque in Afghanistan, but Byam never realized his grandest dream of putting a circle of trailers around the Great Pyramid in Egypt.

The back road into Hoopa Valley, Bald Hills Road, broke off in an easterly fork a few miles from Big Tree, a landmark redwood some three hundred feet tall. As soon as I turned off the main highway, the trailer people were left behind, and I was alone in the landscape, the only car around.

The Bald Hills were a spring-green color, ripe with juice, but the outlying mountains were still capped with snow. The road turned rough and potholed in places, but I made it over Schoolhouse Peak and French Camp Ridge and dropped down toward Weitchpec, a town at the confluence of the Klamath and Trinity rivers, at the southern border of Yurok territory, where tension was in the air. Graffiti were sprayed on walls, bridge stanchions, and boulders: Yurok Power and Hoopa Stoners and Fuck the Police.

At the Weitchpec store, a large display of handguns was arranged in a glass case, next to shelves crammed with liquor. The clerk behind the counter had a look of suspicion on her face, and she was short with me when I bought a soda.

Around Klamath, there was talk about the tribal split. Most everyone seemed to think that the Yurok were getting the short end of the stick. One rumor had it that the Hupa were anxious to have the Yurok gone, so that they could strike a bargain with a timber company to harvest more trees from the virgin forests on their land. The rumor couldn't be pinned down and proved, but many people subscribed to it, anyway.

A road ran from Weitchpec through the pinched-in granite walls of the Trinity River canyon. Scarlet larkspur was blooming in the foothills. The coastal damp was gone, and the sun was very hot. In the town of Hoopa, poppies were strewn along the playing fields at the high school, home of the Hoopa Warriors, and at the edges of pastures. White butterflies were floating in clouds.

The river was deep green and almost clear, and in the shallows a woman was wading, her white dress hiked up to her thighs. A man was putting in a rowboat upstream from her. I thought he might be her lover or her husband, but he just drifted by.

THE ONLY MOTEL IN HOOPA, a Best Western, brand new, still smelled of the freshly laid carpeting. My room had a sliding-glass door that gave me a view of the Trinity River. After a light supper in town, I went to the community center near the motel for a Bingo game that had drawn a big crowd.

About a hundred people, more than half of them Indians, sat at folding tables in a smoky room where teen-age waitresses dashed around dispensing Pepsis and nachos. A noisy popcorn machine provided a soundtrack, echoing like an old popgun being shot. I had bought a ten-dollar Bingo packet at the door, but the cards made no sense to me. The Bingo I'd known as a child was easy to play, but now there were a dozen different games, Red Cross, Black-Out, and others, and no rules to explain them anywhere in the packet.

As I stood there bewildered, a man, Wayne Kinney, approached and said in a kindly voice, "You need some help? I'll help you. Go sit at my table."

Wayne Kinney was about forty. He had a round, almost moon

face and dark brown eyes. His yellow polo shirt was as chipper as a crocus, and he wore a snappy little hat pushed back on his head. He spoke so softly that I had to listen closely to hear him. He was sharing his table with two cousins, both daughters of his mother's sisters, and with a fleshy, broad-beamed woman everybody called "Auntie," who did not say a word the entire night, preferring to chainsmoke Pall Malls, mark her Bingo cards, and knit her brow in frustration.

Wayne sat across from Auntie. He looked excited. "I feel lucky tonight," he declared, drumming his fingers and grinning. Bingo had been good to him lately. In the past few weeks, he had won three hundred dollars, but, alas, the money was gone.

A Yurok, Wayne had been living in Hoopa Valley for three years, up by Weitchpec. Before that, he had worked as a hairdresser in San Francisco and had owned a shop. Without actually stating it, he let it slip that he'd fallen on hard times. His wife and his daughter were still in the city, and Wayne was laboring to support himself by cutting hair and doing perms at Margaret's House of Beauty, in Hoopa.

The Best Western fascinated Wayne. He had stayed there once with a friend after a Bingo victory, and he seemed to fear that the experience might never be repeated. "How much does your room cost?" he asked.

"Thirty-nine dollars."

He did some private calculating. "But it's nice," he said with authority, as if trying to convince himself that he hadn't been foolish to blow his winnings on a motel. "The room has a radio. It has a good TV."

Wayne's cousin, Marcia, who was visiting from Milpitas, near San Francisco, was busy with her Bingo cards. When I asked what had brought her to the valley, she told me that she had needed to see some people. She had ridden up on a Greyhound and would go home by bus in a few days.

"I ran away," she said, without a trace of humor.

During the evening, I came gradually to understand that it wasn't unusual for some Yuroks to go out into the white world and stay in it for a long time—years, even decades—and then to arrive at a moment in life where only some contact with friends and family, with ancestors, with all the specificities of being a Yurok, could quell an ache. Not every Yurok felt that way, surely, but Marcia and Wayne and their clan did.

The Bingo games began, one after another. At our table, the women were playing two or three cards each. It was a simple matter to lose fifty dollars on a Wednesday or a Friday night. You could lose even more on the weekend, when the pots and the buy-in were more substantial. The little balls churned in their cage, an announcer called the numbers, and the numbers flashed on a board, like bolts of hope.

Late that night, an old woman won a special prize—a black 4 × 4 Nissan truck that was parked in the hall. There was a smattering of polite applause, but nobody whooped or blushed or giggled uncontrollably, as they did on television game shows. I was reminded of something that I'd once read about the Pit River tribe. Jaime de Angulo, a gifted amateur anthropologist, had described a peculiar, "passionless," Indian state of being that was removed from all desire, beyond all expectations, outside the scope of ordinary time, and unaffected by the notion of change.

After fourteen games, I threw over my cards to Wayne. My eyes were burning from the cigarette smoke, and I was ready for bed.

"I didn't know there were so many ways to lose," I said to him, and he smiled and watched me go.

In my motel room, the phone rang ten minutes later. It was Wayne. He wanted to borrow eight dollars, so that he could play the final Bingo games. He proposed to give me a haircut in exchange.

The call upset me. How did he get my room number? But then I remembered how small Hoopa was, and how few guests were at the Best Western, and I saw, too, that the request might seem natural and even logical to Wayne, particularly after he had invited me into his family circle. So I met him at the motel desk and made the loan. He acted sheepish.

"Business was real slow today," he said, in apology. "Not many customers."

"That's all right," I told him.

He studied the bills in his hand, and his round face brightened. "Now I can play the last two games. The big money games!" He gave me a business card with the address of Margaret's House of Beauty. "Stop by tomorrow for your haircut, okay? Any time is fine with me."

BEFORE THE COMING OF THE WHITE MAN, the Hupa and the Yurok used Dentalium shells for money. Dentalia are mollusks that inhabit the sand in deep water along the Pacific Coast. Their shells are small, whitish, opalescent, and delicate.

The Indians in California seem not to have harvested the mollusks themselves. Professor Alfred Kroeber, in his classic of anthropology, *Handbook of the Indians of California* (1925), suggested that each shell probably traveled many miles from Oregon or even Vancouver Island to be traded as currency among "a series of mutually unknown nations."

Dentalia were kept on strings, often long ones of more than three yards. They were strung by size and graded by length—the fewer shells to a string, the higher its value. In the animistic universe of the two tribes, dentalia were viewed as living beings that had free will, entities that could be talked to, or argued with, or implored. The Yurok thought the shells were difficult to get along with, hard to seduce, even snobbish. Dentalia chose their associates with care.

If a Yurok gained some wealth, he frequently traded it for other things, all rated on a scale. A large boat was worth two 12-shell strings, but it could also be bought for ten big woodpecker scalps, soft and brilliantly scarlet. A small boat cost one 13-shell string or three big woodpecker scalps, but if you had two deer hides sewn together and painted, you could get the boat even up.

Desirable brides were expensive, fetching at least ten strings of various types, plus, say, a headband of fifty woodpecker scalps, some black obsidian, a boat, and so on. Doctors' fees were steep, too, but not as steep as the price you paid if you killed a man—fifteen strings, some rare red obsidian, some deerskins, a boat, and, in most cases, a daughter.

Once the Hupa took possession of their reservation in 1864, they started leading a regulated, orderly, Western-influenced life. The Yurok had always been less organized, more prone to chaos, and maybe more poetical. The tribe had no chiefs in the usual sense. A person's status in each village was determined by his wealth, or sometimes by his age.

To Kroeber, Yuroks appeared cautious and fearful, "touchy to slight and sensitive to shaming," quick to anger, and capable of hating "wholeheartedly, persistently, often irreconcilably." They were also perceptive, courteous, and affable, he said.

Stephen Powers, who visited the two tribes in 1871, was much less critical. The Yurok were lively, he reported, and they were monogamous and excelled at social dancing. Often they dressed in "civilized suits" and were mounted on horseback.

Of the Hupa, Powers was positively admiring. He considered them the Romans of northern California. Their language was as rigorous as Latin, he felt, "rude, strong, and laconic." They were politically adept, skilled in relations with other tribes, and so "fatally democratic" that they had no leaders during a war. Every man fought according to his own lights, in a way that seemed good to him.

Both the Hupa and the Yurok were profoundly interested in the supernatural. Instead of confronting an enemy, for example, the Hupa liked to hire a sorcerer to avenge an insult or score a victory. Sorcerers brewed poisonous potions; fired invisible arrows at their victims; collected hair, spittle, feces, and pieces of clothing for casting spells; and performed incantatory chants to do harm.

An Indian devil, a *kitdongwe,* was the most horrible type of Hupa sorcerer. He painted his face black, carried a weapon made of human bones and sinew, and did his prowling at night. A *kitdongwe* could change into a wolf or a bear and could travel at blinding speeds, almost flying. He hoped to keep his secrets from his relatives, hiding his weapon under a rock or in a tree hollow, but it betrayed him sometimes by shooting out sparks and flashes.

Shamanism was sorcery's benign counterpart. A shaman dealt in healing, not in harming. Among the Yurok, shamans were ordinarily women. Guardian spirits came to them and bestowed power while they were in trances. The spirit took the form of a dead person—often a dead shaman—or an animal, such as a hawk or a whale. It had the job of putting a *teloget,* or a "pain," into the dreamer.

The pain allowed a shaman to cure some diseases. It could be sought after as well as bestowed, but it needed to be paired with another pain to become active. So a shaman would climb to a stony, sacred spot in the mountains, and there she would dance alone until her guardian spirit put another pain into her. That caused her to lose her senses.

After recuperating in a sweathouse, the shaman was ready to begin. In her body, the pains became a slimy substance capable of sucking the actual, corporeal pains from a sick person. She would then stick her fingers down her throat and regurgitate the illness.

The Yurok felt that illnesses were the result of many things. Sometimes a spirit took a person's soul, requiring a ritual to set matters straight. Sin could also make a Yurok sick, and only a full confession could heal him. Maybe the sick person had robbed a grave or had kept a monster as a pet. A shaman listened to the confession and judged whether or not it was pertinent. If it wasn't, the patient died, but a pertinent confession blew away the disease, like a righteous wind.

Some illnesses had nothing to do with *teloget* or spirits and couldn't be treated by a shaman. Among them were cuts, bruises, a wound from a bullet or an arrow, and a slipped disc.

◆   ◆   ◆

MARGARET'S HOUSE OF BEAUTY was indeed a small house off Highway
96 in Hoopa. When I arrived, Wayne Kinney jumped up from the
barber chair where he was relaxing and, with a sweep of his arm,
gestured that I should take it. The gesture seemed to say, Here is
your magic-carpet ride to hair perfection.

Wayne's boss, Margaret, a Hupa who had once run for a seat
on the Tribal Council, was giving a woman a perm in a chair across
the room. There were mousses, sprays, and gels spread on counters,
and they gave off an aroma of innocence, part bubblegum and part
floral perfume, that was an ideal complement to the entire adventure
of hairstyling, with its devoted but largely unsuccessful attempts to
turn an ordinary head into the item of wonder that rested on the
necks of handsome men and glorious women in fashion magazines.

Wayne was glad for the chance to pay off his debt, but when he
touched my hair and wondered aloud how much to trim, I became
nervous and made some excuses. It wasn't that I didn't trust him,
although, heaven help me, the notion that I might be misunderstood
as in my boyhood days, when militant barbers always reduced my
crew cut to a field of quarter-inch nubbins regardless of instructions,
did cross my mind. I was just experiencing the tiny panic that every
vain Californian feels in the presence of an unfamiliar stylist.

California, after all, was the capital of hair in the United States.
The shampoo flowed like water and the sales of Rogaine were off
the board. If you went to the movies or a concert or a ball game,
you had to be amazed at the shiny, silky hair all around you, great
masses of it, every strand washed and conditioned and brushed to a
luster—so different from the oily, greasy, matted, Vitalised and Bryl-
creemed hair I used to see at Ebbets Field.

At first, Wayne didn't know what to do about being rejected.
Had he offended me? He was so gentle I couldn't imagine him
raising his voice. After some deliberation, he solved his dilemma by
insisting on buying me coffee in town. That cheered him up, and he

grabbed his snappy hat and waved good-bye to Margaret. On the
way out, he said that it didn't bother him to work for a Hupa. He
had no animosity toward the other tribe. There were good Hupa
and bad Hupa, the same as with the Yurok.

As we drove to a restaurant Wayne liked, the only sit-down spot
in Hoopa, he scouted the roads for people he knew. "There goes my
cousin," he said, waving when another car went by.

Wayne enjoyed riding in a new Taurus, even though it marked
him as a bit of an outsider, somebody who was comfortable with the
possessions and the rewards of the white world. Other Indians on
the reservation sometimes took him to task for acting *too* white, he
confessed. His interest in tribal affairs was recent, in fact. Until the
past year or so, he hadn't paid much attention to being a Yurok, but
he'd been in a couple of ceremonial dances lately and had a dawning
pride in his ancestry. He told me that he had been reading the ancient
myths and tales.

"At the museum in Golden Gate Park, there's a big display of
Yurok culture," he said, and then he added, so as not to sound cocky,
"I don't know why they chose us."

In the restaurant, Wayne's outgoing nature flourished. A very
old white man entered, tottering along on the arm of his wife. A
surgeon had done something to his ear, which was scarred, bandaged,
and a little bloody, as if a dog had chewed on it. Wayne offered his
condolences.

"You be sure to take care of that," he instructed the old man.
"Soak the ear or whatever you're supposed to do." His concern was
genuine. I could see the worry on his face.

When our waitress came, Wayne urged me to have a pastry with
my coffee, or a sandwich or a slice of cake. He had the sort of
generosity that could get a man in trouble, the makings of a soft
touch.

He spoke for a while, almost wistfully, about his parents, who
were childhood sweethearts and had lived on opposite sides of the
Trinity River, in Weitchpec. His mother still lived there, and so

did his brothers. One of them taught school, and another had lost a leg in a motorcycle wreck. Wayne's own talents tended to be artistic. He loved to paint and draw, and that had motivated him to enroll in a beauty college in San Francisco and seek a career as a hairdresser.

Out of the blue, he asked, "Do you like to travel? Where have you been?"

I reeled off a list of foreign cities and countries that I'd visited, including London. At the mention of London, Wayne leaned forward, and his soft voice grew even softer and more intimate. He had been there, too, he said, a few years ago, hanging around in pubs and playing darts. The game became his obsession. Back in California, he had started searching for pub-type taverns that had dartboards, wasting too much of his time.

I was curious about whether Wayne planned to go back to the city someday.

"I'm not ready yet," he said flatly. "I need more confidence in myself. Maybe I'll go back or maybe not."

In a way, it seemed that he was suspended between worlds, the white one and the Indian one, with a foot planted in each. I felt that he might be waiting for a sign, feathers blowing in a breeze, to show him which direction to go.

For now, the reservation served Wayne as a haven, but he saw its hazards, too. Unemployment could run as high as 70 percent. If you had no money, you fell below the poverty line and were just another statistic on the county rolls. When he had first moved to the Far North, he said, he had rented a nice trailer at a park in Hoopa, but burglars kept breaking in. He knew who they were, stoner kids in their late teens who came from bad homes and ran in packs, stealing to buy liquor and amphetamines.

Wayne had got tired of the break-ins and had moved to another trailer, in Weitchpec, but he didn't like it as much. He wanted to give me a tour of Yurok country, he said, but his difficult circumstances prevented him from doing it. They reflected nothing of his status as a man who had once operated a beauty salon in San Francisco, so we sat where we were, drank our coffee, and talked of distant places.

ONE AFTERNOON IN HOOPA VALLEY, while I was driving around to no purpose, I crossed over a bridge and went down a dirt road to a bluff by the Trinity River. On the bluff, there were some wood structures, the remnants of an old Hupa village. The tribe still used such sites for its rituals and its dances.

The main dwellings, or *xonta,* were almost hidden in thick grass and clumps of bluish lupine. They were made from cedar planks and built partially underground. The entry holes were just big enough to admit an adult and just small enough to keep out a bear. The *xonta* measured about twenty square feet from one end to the other, and the space inside looked cozy and inviting. It must have been wonderful, I thought, to be so tightly connected to a human community that you could sleep on the ground in the unbroken circle of your family.

In the old days, the Hupa had gathered acorns from the oaks on the bluff, leached them of their tannic acid, and turned them into a porridge. The river had given them salmon, eels, and candlefish, and there were ducks and geese to be harvested from the sky. Hunters brought back elk and deer from the mountains, while women and children picked the wild berries.

I sat on the grass in the sunshine and let the moment wash over me. Hoopa Valley still had an immense serenity. The Hupa and the Yurok must once have carried it within them, a peacefulness beyond our understanding.

HUPA SOVEREIGN DAY, the official day of partitioning, was a grand event. Private jets began flying into town early in the morning with the key political allies of the tribe, along with some dignitaries and some honored guests. At the Hoopa Neighborhood Facility, eighth-graders were serving a chowline breakfast, and you could watch a video about Public Law 100-580. On a lawn outside, TV cameras were drawing a bead on a banner-and-flag-draped stage, where the important speeches were to be delivered.

The two stars of Hupa Sovereign Day were Senator Daniel Inouye of Hawaii, the chairman of the Senate Select Committee on Indian Affairs, and U.S. Congressman Doug Bosco, who was from northern California, had authored the partitioning bill, and had married into a wealthy timber-industry family.

Their speeches were as dull as such speeches always are, but they sounded especially queer in Hoopa Valley. The speakers, too, seemed odd. In their pancake makeup and their crisp, dark suits, they resembled ill-at-ease ambassadors from a foreign country, which, in essence, they were.

There were protests against Public Law 100-580 in town. At Mike's Auto Body Shop, four figures were hung in effigy out front, dummies representing Inouye, Bosco, Senator Alan Cranston of California, and an unidentified perpetrator. The shop was owned jointly by Mike McConnell, a Hupa, and Herb O'Neill, a Yurok. They had posted a sign near the dangling bodies that said, "Welcome to Yuropa," an imaginary land where the tribes would still live together in harmony.

McConnell and O'Neill had worked with each other for years, a couple of Indians with Irish names who enjoyed banging on fenders and trading quips. O'Neill, at seventy-four, had a face that was creased everywhere. When I asked how old he was when he came to Hoopa Valley, he held his hands about sixteen inches apart, the size of a newborn infant.

He smiled and said, "I was an orphan."

Someone had dispatched him to an orphanage in Santa Rosa, in Sonoma County, and from there he enlisted in the army and fought in Germany. After the war, he returned to the reservation because he had nowhere else to go.

O'Neill wasn't sure who had won what in the partitioning. Did it have to do with water rights? With logging interests? He just didn't like the idea of the tribes being separated.

A customer pulled in while we were talking, attracted by the lynched dummies. He looked at them for a time and said, "Did you know that Inouye has only one arm?"

"Sure," O'Neill told him. "That's why they call him the 'One-armed Bandit' in Hawaii."

McConnell, the artist responsible for the figures, had never heard about the lost arm before, so he went over and ripped one off the Inouye dummy.

THE BEST WESTERN IN HOOPA was scheduled to be transformed into the Tsewenaldin Inn at a dedication ceremony on Hupa Sovereign Day, so I had to check out. I looked through my sliding-glass door while I was packing and saw a woman come out of the bushes by the river, her hair matted with leaves and twigs.

I realized that it was the same woman I had seen on that first afternoon in town, but she no longer wore a white dress. Instead, she had on a rose-colored sweatsuit, and her feet were bare. She was not young and beautiful, as I had naïvely assumed, but middle-aged and in some kind of mental distress.

As I observed, she rolled the sweatpants to her knees, waded into the river, and stood at the same spot where I'd noticed her before, staring into the water for about ten minutes without moving a muscle. Then she got out of the river, stripped off her sweatpants to reveal a pair of blue gym shorts, and waded back in. Again, she stood absolutely still in the same spot for about ten minutes, staring, before she stumbled up the bank and walked off toward town.

As I was leaving the motel, I asked the desk clerk, an agreeable white woman, if she knew anything about the woman in the river.

The woman's mother had drowned about a year ago, the clerk said, and since then, on almost every day, even in the coldest winter months, the woman had waded into the Trinity to stare into the water and search for her mother's body.

CHAPTER 4

DOWN THE ROAD FROM HOOPA VALLEY, at the base of the Trinity Mountains, lay the town of Willow Creek, where everyone was involved in the annual rite of preparing for tourist season on the day that I arrived. As a fisherman mends his nets in anticipation of salmon, so, too, did the proprietors of motels, gift shops, and sporting goods stores in the Far North get ready for their customers, whitewashing walls, hosing bug corpses from screens, and practicing their smiles before a mirror.

Willow Creek drew its inspiration from the Old West, from buckboards, grizzled prospectors, and weathered barn siding. It had a rustic, no-nonsense atmosphere, a quality of being literal that came as a relief after the slippery sadness of Hoopa. The businesses in town pointed up a country person's distaste for anything fancy.

Bob's Shopping Center
Hodgson's Department Store
Chris's Forks Lounge
Wyatt's Motel
Hansen's Logging Supply

The simple, forthright names suggested a smalltown responsibility, as well. If you were offended by the service somewhere, you could look up Bob or Chris or Old Man Hodgson in the phone book and cuss them out. They might cuss at you in return, but that was the way of discourse in the West, although insults had replaced sixguns as the weapon of choice.

At Big Red's Cafe, a hungry crowd had gathered for lunch and gossip. The menu guaranteed that everything was fresh, except for the help. Like Red, many of the patrons were big, really big—big in the bones and big in the stomach. The daily special, a pork tenderloin sandwich, sounded good, so I took a stool and ordered it.

A gigantic man in a logger's plaid shirt walked in and sat down next to me. He said to the waitress, who was wiry, feisty, and skilled at riding herd on the regulars, "Mary, is that pork tenderloin a pretty good-sized sandwich?"

"It's better than nothing," Mary answered.

"Aw, hell. I'll have a cheeseburger and fries."

"Same as you did yesterday."

The giant grunted and snatched absently at a circling fly, a sure harbinger of summer. He began telling anyone who'd listen about his morning at the history museum over in China Flat. He'd swept the floors and had sorted through the new T-shirts, which featured a crosscut saw as part of the museum's logo.

In the Far North, you found museums everywhere. History had become an exercise in nostalgia, maybe because the past with its vision of gainful employment for all was more intelligible and had more resonance than the tapped-out present or the imponderable future.

Willow Creek was once an important timber center, just as it had once been a Gold Rush settlement, but its loggers were confronting the same rigid restrictions and protests that currently prevailed elsewhere in California, and layoffs were common. Although the loggers were surrounded by trees in Trinity National Forest, they were often kept from cutting any down, so the folks in town were counting on tourism as a quick fix for their economy, like the people in Crescent City.

It seemed to me that they had a chance of succeeding. They had some good campgrounds, and better hiking, fishing, and weather, but their window of opportunity was still brief. Snow could start falling by early October, and it would certainly fall in November, and Trinity County was not known for its skiing. The county was even emptier than Del Norte, four times as large but with fewer residents—about fourteen thousand of them on more than 2 million acres.

Mary brought my pork tenderloin sandwich. Big Red had breaded and deep-fried the meat to infuse it with even more calories and cholesterol and give it some greasy-spoon oomph. When I took a bite, hot oil poured down my chin, as in a medieval torture, and gave me a nasty burn. The oil left a raw, red blister below my lip that scabbed over and finally turned into a scar. It was still there when I crossed the border into Mexico.

That evening, I camped on the Trinity River. Beneath some pines and some Douglas firs, on ground tinted a burnished red by iron ores, I staked my tent, as diligently attentive as I had been as an eight-year-old, when camping meant a night in a Long Island backyard. I smelled the pine needles and watched the scrub jays and the sparrows and the crazy little chipmunks scooting around like wind-up toys.

It was tremendously satisfying to be alone by the Trinity River. There was something magisterial in the sensation, something opulent and restorative. I consulted my maps and atlases and plotted a route for the next day that would take me back over Highway 96 to Yreka, in the north-central part of the state. From there I would travel east through sheep and cattle country to Alturas, the last frontier, where the earth froze six feet deep in winter. Or so I'd been told.

♦   ♦   ♦

HIGHWAY 96 FROM WILLOW CREEK to Happy Camp ran parallel to the Klamath River and its many tributaries, offering a dream of abundant water come true—muddy water dripping, spilling, and trickling down from the mountains, water in such quantity that it demanded a whole new set of gerunds to keep pace with its apparently infinite outpouring.

What a cosmic tease this gushing would have been to a farmer in the dusty, dry San Joaquin, or to a developer of the hard-baked, desert flats beyond Los Angeles, in all those places where the land was like an old washcloth that you had to wring for hours to squeeze out a few drops of juice.

In California, water was destiny, the lifeblood of empire. It had been the star player in a series of melodramatic thefts, kidnappings, and reroutings that had started around the turn of the century, when San Francisco's water barons conspired to build a dam at the Hetch Hetchy Gorge of the Tuolumne River, in Yosemite National Park.

At about the same time, William Mulholland, an Irish immigrant who'd worked his way up from the position of ditch-tender to run the Los Angeles Water Company, had embarked on a plan to tap into the Owens River, in the Sierra Nevada, building a conduit of some 250 miles. His project was second only to the Panama Canal in its scope.

So precious and competitively sought after did the mountain rivers become that in 1945 Governor Earl Warren established a State Water Resources Board to study and control the distribution of water. The board kept absorbing other agencies, inflating itself from within, until it turned into the Department of Water Resources, in 1957, and formulated a new master plan.

The plan incorporated the already existing Central Valley Project, an intricate, hopscotching network of dams and diversions that borrowed water from one stream, only to replace it with water from another. The CVP dated from 1935. It was a federally backed, public-works project under the auspices of the Bureau of Reclamation, and its first phase of construction was finished in 1955. At its hub were four dams on three rivers—Shasta and Keswick on the Sacramento, Folsom on the American, and Friant on the San Joaquin.

The Trinity River was impounded at a shocking cost and joined to the system, its flow channeled under the Klamath Mountains, into the Sacramento, and finally into the CVP. All this siphoning, this immense restructuring of natural arterials, this surgery being performed on the body of California, was due to end in 2020 with virtually every drop of "surplus" northern water recycled to the south.

Water, ever more water. Ikes Creek, Slide Creek, Bluff Creek, and Slate Creek. Outside Somes Bar, the Salmon River flowed into the Klamath, glittering like an emerald. A few whitewater rafters, the first of the season, could be heard hollering as they splashed through the spume, whacking madly at the river with their paddles.

Toward Happy Camp, the Klamath started to clear. My map was littered with the names of mines, Independence, Buzzard Hill, and Kanaka in the shadow of Frying Pan Ridge. There were still hopeful souls who worked the water with pans, sluice boxes, or hydraulic dredges, believing that it had not yet surrendered all its treasure. They could be seen wading in the shallows and searching for one last big-time strike in this region of last things, before epic California vanished forever.

THE NEW 49'ERS STORE in Happy Camp had a coin-operated sifting jig out front that customers could use. You hauled up some dirt or sand from the Klamath, poured it in, deposited a quarter, and watched the machine rumble for a few minutes as it purportedly separated valuable gold from mere earth. Never in a million years would I have trusted it. What if the jig really stole your gold, hiding it in a secret compartment? The annals of mining history were filled with tales of human greed.

True New 49'ers would not share my suspicions. They had a

positive outlook and belonged to a club that held claims to mining property in California, Arizona, Idaho, and Oregon. Club members claimed to have recovered an estimated $300,000 in gold from the Klamath River alone. The club literature did not say who had done the estimating, but only someone like me, a paranoid, would ask such questions.

For a New 49'er, it was enough to know that the club offered training sessions, campgrounds, fraternity, success, and a 10 percent discount on such mining equipment as Diablo Gold Demon metal detectors, Gold King placers, and Weasel goldspinners. The club's initiation fee was not cheap, but you could parcel it out at $35 a month until you'd submitted the complete payment of $3,500.

Inside The New 49'ers Store, there were handsome dredges fitted with pontoons and fired by Honda engines. A clerk told me that miners working around Happy Camp could clear ten or fifteen ounces of gold in a summer. She had done some prospecting herself and marveled that no two pieces of gold were ever alike. She'd found nuggets that had reminded her of a Rorschach blot, a monster with fangs, E.T.'s head, and a map of the United States, minus Florida.

In a back room, Geneva Sanchez and her friend Dee were sitting on a bench and viewing a New 49'ers video about famous gold discoveries. The women were gold gypsies camped on the Klamath with their husbands. They'd just paid a dollar each to take a shower at the store, and their hair was still a little wet. They smelled wonderfully soapy and scrubbed and were not at all discouraged that they'd missed the real Gold Rush. Optimism was their boon companion.

Geneva Sanchez was a Modoc from Oregon. She was a powerhouse, short, stocky, and bright-eyed. Existence for her was a constant series of electrifying thrills. Her grandfather was an herbalist in Portland, she said, and she had met her husband, Fernando, through him.

Ah, Fernando! He was the flame burning at her emotional core. She spoke of him with such passion that he seemed to materialize in the video room, a handsome prince off the cover of a Harlequin romance.

At the age of ten, Fernando had run away from his home in Mexico to look for work over the border. He drifted north to Portland, where Geneva's grandfather found him hanging around the bus station and hired him to do some farm labor. Geneva fell for him immediately. She and Fernando had grown up together and then had married, and now they were on the road to Eldorado together, gold gypsies, living on their savings and the jewelry and the Indian beads that Geneva sometimes sold.

Fernando couldn't read very well, so Geneva had taken it upon herself to read to him aloud. At night, by the campfire, she read to him from books about gold and gold mining. Her own favorite was a book about The Lost Cabin, a renowned but mysterious spot somewhere in the West where a huge stash of gold was reported to be buried. She was stunned that I'd never heard about The Lost Cabin and set matters straight by reciting, with appropriate gestures and sound effects, the entire story.

"The Indians killed him!" she exclaimed. "They torched the cabin! But the man wasn't really dead!"

She and Fernando were trying to locate the cabin, Geneva confessed, but if she thought about it too much, she got excited and couldn't sleep. Fernando was also prone to losing sleep over gold. The whopping nuggets displayed at the courthouse in Yreka had almost turned him into an insomniac.

"Have you ever actually found any gold?" I asked Geneva.

"Oh, yes!" she cried, clapping her hands together.

The gold, in dust and in flakes, was still in her possession. She was a pack rat and a hoarder, she said. As an example, she brought up the time when she was about to go into the poultry business. She had enough land in Oregon for some hens and a rooster, but the more she mulled it over, the more she realized that she would get attached to the chickens and would wind up knitting them little hats and sweaters instead of butchering them.

Geneva laughed about the chickens. When the video was over, she toweled her hair again and invited me to drop by for a New 49'ers potluck dinner on Sunday. She hated to rush off, she said, but she had to get back to camp soon—Fernando would be missing her! She had to fix their dinner and make their bed, a four-poster that they had bought in Mexico. They hauled it with them wherever they went and slept on it under the stars.

FROM HAPPY CAMP AND THE KLAMATH MOUNTAINS, I descended to the broad plateau of the southern Cascades. Lilacs were blooming in the fields near Hamburg, where William Brewer had observed those Gold Rush ruins.

Hamburg had a population of eighty. Drift boats were up on trailers in front yards, marking a season's end for the local fishing guides. The air had lost its last trace of coastal moisture and had become dry and desertlike, and the landscape colors had changed from dominant greens to earthier tans and browns.

Highway 293 was a two-lane road to Yreka. There was a spareness to California now, a hardscrabble quality. I saw clumps of sagebrush and circling buzzards. Soon I was driving through some splendid, craggy rock formations like those in the American Southwest. The rocks had a reddish cast. The sun was low in the sky, really roaring, and it seemed to set them ablaze.

The scenery was so warm and rosy that it affected me like a glowing hearth, so I pulled over to bask in the beautiful twilight. In all that barrenness, I expected to be alone, but I wasn't.

A man was pitching his tent in a nest of wood chips on the side of the highway, ignoring the big-rig trucks whistling by. He had on a red deerstalker's cap, a railroad shirt, red suspenders, gray pants, and some black hiking shoes that were torn and frayed and looked like the spent rubber tread that comes flying off tires. He was so intent on the job that he jumped when I approached him, blinking at me and yanking at his pointy, gray beard.

"Bob Burnett," he said, shaking hands. "From Medford, Oregon."

"It's a gorgeous sunset, isn't it?" I threw an arm wide to gather in the emberlike rocks.

Burnett chewed on the notion for a second or two. "It *is* gorgeous!" he agreed. "Thank you for calling my attention to it. I was so busy with my tent I forgot to take a picture."

He retrieved a camera from a backpack that was lashed to the frame of his ten-speed bike and began snapping photos of the rocks. The bike was his sole mode of transportation. A mini-trailer on wheels was hitched behind it. Burnett's pots, pans, film, and sundries were stowed in it and protected by a plastic tarp. He had a tattered orange pennant on his handlebars as a safety precaution.

After returning his camera to the pack, Burnett confided that he was on a special mission. He was trying to visit every Lions Club in his Lions Club district, which stretched from Coos Bay in Oregon to Mount Shasta in California. He'd made the same journey a year ago, but he hadn't planned it well enough and had failed. This time, he said, he had mapped his route with precision and had sent a letter to all the clubs along the way announcing his impending visit and his goal of attending a meeting.

He had also sent a letter to every sheriff's department because fellows who rode their bikes alone were always getting their heads bashed in. If that happened to Burnett, he wanted his body to be identified and the bastard who did the bashing to be caught and sent to prison.

"How old are you, Bob?" I asked.

Grinning and blinking, he said, "I'm on the far side of twenty-eight."

Burnett explained how he had come to be on the road. He was a pollinator by trade, who worked in the Medford orchards. One morning a while back, he had got out of bed too swiftly and had suffered a dizzy spell. He thought it might be a stroke or a heart attack, but his doctor told him that it was a natural result of aging.

Old age wasn't something that Burnett looked forward to, so he had embarked on his trip before it was too late.

He had set out riding from Medford in November, in an autumn chill, and would be home in Oregon by late May. He showed me a map on which the route he'd taken was marked in yellow ink. He had survived rain, snow flurries, and a hailstorm, and felt none the worse for wear. The handlebars of his bike were patched with electrical tape, though, and his front-wheel rim had dents in it from his hammering at it to straighten it.

Bob Burnett, I said to myself, you have the right spirit. You would have made it as a pioneer.

For some reason, the question of money came up, and Burnett let it be known that he was a little short of it. He had just two bucks in his pocket, in fact. When I offered him a ten-spot as a sort of sponsorship, he accepted it reluctantly. He kept insisting that it was a loan, not a donation, propounding a mystical theory whereby it would be repaid to me down the line by another pilgrim in our straggly brotherhood, passed on in one form or another, whether as greenbacks, tools, equipment, or even some sage advice at the exact moment when I needed it most.

Yes, Burnett said, it would happen that way. Without another word, he shook my hand again and walked over to fiddle with his camp site, smoothing out the wood chips where his bedroll would rest as the big rigs went zooming by.

AFTER THE GLOOMY DAMP OF THE NORTHWEST COAST, its deep and yearning greens, its isolation and its vast distances, Yreka looked like a metropolis to me, alive with human energy. There were more than five thousand residents in the city, a mob scene compared to Happy Camp. The evening was mild and almost summery, and as I wandered the streets I felt elated to be around so many people, experiencing the same bloodrush of possibility that must have affected the miners who used to blow through town on a Saturday night.

At the county courthouse, I studied the gold that had bedeviled poor Fernando—mega-nuggets like asteroids—and in A. J. Bledsoe's *Indian Wars of the Northwest,* I came upon an official telling of The Lost Cabin story that did not differ much from the version that Geneva Sanchez had performed for me.

In Bledsoe's rendering, an adventurous miner strikes it rich "in the foothills near the sea-shore" and buries his fortune by his cabin "on the northern Coast of California." Some Indians attack him and believe that he's dead, but they can't find the treasure and burn the cabin down. The lucky miner regains consciousness—but he's gone crazy! Somehow he makes it back to his hometown in the East, where, on his deathbed, he suddenly turns rational again. Summoning his friends, he gives them a detailed description of the cabin's site, but, to this very day, *the gold still has not been found!*

Yreka was not a corruption of *Eu*reka, as I'd guessed. It was derived instead from an unidentified Indian tongue and probably meant "north mountain," a reference to Mount Shasta, a volcanic cone that was the central landscape feature of Siskiyou County. At 14,612 feet, its peak was always snowcapped. It had a younger twin, Shastina, that had reached a height of 12,336 feet. All through the southern Cascades, there were such cones. The range had incurred more volcanic activity than any other part of the state, resulting in a dissected tableland of basaltic sheets, mudflows, and ash.

Foothills were strung between Yreka and Shasta Valley, an area of about five hundred square miles. The valley's eastern half was raw, rocky, and short of water, a scabby territory of sagebrush and volcanic debris, but its western half tolerated farming and ranching. Native grasses had once covered it, but the settlers had plowed them under to plant wheat. In time, livestock was introduced—horses for the mining camps, sheep, and cattle, both dairy and beef.

Alfalfa was grown in Shasta Valley now, enough for three cuttings a year, and so was barley, all of it dry-farmed without any irrigation. Dairying didn't matter much anymore, but there was still some wheat. The cattle grazing in pastures were usually beef cattle, either Herefords or Aberdeen Angus, and I passed small herds of them as I made my way, slowly, toward Alturas.

THE CATTLEMAN'S CLUB IN GRENADA, in Shasta Valley, was established in 1917. The building didn't look that old, any more than it looked like a private club. What it looked like, really, was a roadhouse where a man could get a decent burger and a cold beer on a warm afternoon in early May. The jukebox was playing some Randy Travis, and when the bartender brought my Bud and asked if I wanted a glass, I knew instinctively that the correct answer was "No."

The bartender, Jim, conducted himself convivially. He was new to the job and hoped that it wouldn't last forever. By trade, he was a millworker, he said, but his union, the International Woodworkers of America (IWA), had been on strike against Roseburg Forest Products, which operated a mill in nearby Weed, for about four months. The strike was mainly over wages and benefits. Jim had run through his savings and needed some cash to pay his rent.

Roseburg was a huge corporation, he told me, one of the largest in the timber industry. Its home offices were in Oregon.

A couple of Shasta Valley cowboys were sitting to my right. They were working men in dirty jeans and scuffed boots, and they carried on a muted conversation, parceling out their sentences with deliberate care, as if an auction-yard foreman of the English language might hold them to account for anything they uttered. Chuck Pearce, who was sitting on my left, had no such fear. For him, talk was like breath, a gusher compounded of gossip, anecdotes, jokes, and opinions.

Although Pearce had no ties to Roseburg, he still had strong feelings about the strike. It had crippled the economy in Weed so badly that he couldn't sell his mobile home there and move to Blythe for the bass fishing, as he wanted to do.

"When I can't catch a fish, I just hook some old girl in the ass," he remarked with a wink, reaching over to give his wife, Juanita, a sexy pinch.

Pearce was definitely a ladies' man. At the age of seventy-two, he kept his stomach flat and his figure trim. If a song he liked came on the jukebox, he hopped up and danced to it alone, hooking his fingers through the loops of his jeans. Juanita watched him with bemused affection. She was a Cherokee about fifteen years younger than her husband, but he was her wayward boy.

He poked me with an elbow after one of his dances and whispered, "There'd be no damn divorce courts if all the women were like her."

He knew whereof he spoke. Juanita was his third wife. They'd been together for twenty years, while his other marriages had lasted eleven and six years respectively. Pearce had a thing about numbers. He believed in their potency and proved it by taking off his straw cowboy hat and showing me how he'd written the date of purchase on the sweatband. He'd bought the hat in La Paz, Mexico, on a fishing trip.

Pearce was from Madisonville, Kentucky, but he'd earned his fortune in the Golden State like the Argonauts before him. The army sent him to California, and when he finished serving, he opened a dry-cleaning business in Chula Vista, south of San Diego, in 1946. The navy threw him a contract to clean its uniforms, and soon he was pushing sailor blues through his shop at a blizzard clip, running the machines around the clock.

He had retired to Weed in 1981 to be closer to his sons. One of them, a contractor, was even more successful than he had been, Pearce claimed.

"That boy's got a house with nine bedrooms," he informed me, counting away. "He owns thirteen cars."

Jim had the Weed *Press-Herald* with him and pointed out two ads that Roseburg had placed. They were there to hurt the strikers, he thought.

In a full-page ad, the company had printed some tables indicating that the average Roseburg worker in Weed earned $32,096 a year, which was a heap of money in a poor town. Jim felt that the statistic was misleading because it included such extras as health and unemployment insurance, workers' comp, social security, pension benefits, and vacation and holiday pay. The figure for regular wages was only $19,106.

"If we were really making $32,096," he asked, "would we be out on strike for four months?"

One line in the ad went, "These yearly earnings are equal to or certainly better than our competitors and are certainly better than other jobs in this community."

There was a time in the lumber trade, I was told, when small, independently held firms had treated their employees as family, seeing to everything from their housing to the schooling of their children, but that time had passed. Now corporate giants ruled the forests of California—Weyerhaeuser, Georgia-Pacific, Louisiana-Pacific, Roseburg—and they were strictly profit-driven. Often they depended on clear-cutting, a practice that the *California Forestry Handbook*, a government publication, describes as "a drastic treatment." Clear-cuts reduce the forest cover so much that soil damage can result, unless appropriate erosion control procedures are undertaken.

A Waylon Jennings tune started playing, and Chuck Pearce hopped up to do his unique, personal-type dance. He wanted me to join him and Juanita on an excursion to The Dugout, a bar over in Black Butte, but I had an intuition that The Dugout was only a stop on a caravan that might roll on for hours, so instead I escaped into the fine spring day and pushed on toward Weed, hoping to get there before evening.

WHEN ABNER WEED, a former soldier from Maine who was at Appomattox with Robert E. Lee, came to California in 1869, about 17 percent of the landmass was given over to forests. The most prominent tree species were fir, redwood, Douglas fir, and pine. The Spaniards and the Mexicans had mostly ignored the resource, and it was only when some ambitious Americans took matters in hand that an embryonic timber industry started to develop.

In 1834, J. B. R. Cooper built a water-powered sawmill on the Russian River, in Sonoma County. Within the next decade, there were mills at nearby Bodega Bay and in Santa Cruz, south of San Francisco. In 1848, James Marshall, a carpenter, built a sawmill for John Sutter on the South Fork of the American River, not far from Sacramento—a mill that became the most notorious in history when flecks of gold were seen flashing in its tailrace.

The Gold Rush sparked a big increase in the demand for lumber. Miners needed wood for sluices, flumes, dams, and cabins. By the time Weed headed for the Siskiyous, the finest, most accessible redwoods and pines had been cut, but the forests were so rich that the harvesting had scarcely affected them.

The pressure accelerated, though, as loggers on the eastern seaboard laid waste to the last virgin stands of white pine. Timber companies began exporting lumberjacks and materials to strip the western forests, sometimes breaking down an entire mill, loading it onto a ship, and sending it around Cape Horn. There were few restrictions in the timber business then, and blocks of trees could be bought reasonably from homesteaders, who'd been deeded them by the government.

The forests in Siskiyou County where Abner Weed established his Weed Lumber Company had some towering groves of Douglas fir. The tree grows in every western state, and it was destined to replace white pine in terms of importance and would eventually account for about one-quarter of all the standing saw timber in the country.

A Scottish botanist, David Douglas, had identified the trees while on a scouting trip in the United States for the Royal Horticultural Society. He was astounded by their size—one tree he measured was 227 feet long and 48 feet around—but the size also worked against his attempt to gather specimen seeds. He couldn't fell a fir with his hatchet or hit any of the high-up cones with his buckshot.

Douglas fir proved to be ideal for lumbering. It grew rapidly, was long-lived, large, and yielded a wood that had superior physical properties. It could be used in many ways—for railroad ties, telegraph and telephone poles, structural beams and trusses, and as a sturdy form for pouring concrete. Carpenters liked it for its nice grain and its ability to withstand warping. When the technology evolved for making plywood, the Douglas fir became a principal element in its composition.

The captains of the timber industry in the West had apparently learned very little from the leveling of the eastern forests. They practiced clear-cutting, but they rarely did any reseeding. Their unwieldy donkey engines damaged sprouts and seedlings and killed off the future crop.

So outrageous were their abuses that in the 1890s a Board of Forestry was instituted in California to exercise some control. The first forest rangers went to work in 1919, but they were in the hire of individual counties, and the counties were often too broke to meet the rangers' paychecks.

Gradually, the U.S. government acquired more and more western timberland, preserved it as national forest, and accorded it some protection under the law, but the Forest Service did a poor job of enforcing any safeguards on the public's behalf. Its record in timber sales was equally abysmal. In a recent year, 76 out of 123 national forests lost money in their dealings with the timber industry. A tourist could buy a Forest Service map for a dollar, the same price that a timber firm paid for a hemlock one hundred feet tall.

As for Abner Weed, his timing was perfect. He had access to the Scott Bar, Trinity, and Klamath mountains, and to all the trees on Mount Shasta. He created an economy in the wilderness, and a town sprouted around it and showed its appreciation by taking his name. Weed went on to be a county supervisor and later a state senator. He quit the timber business in 1913 and severed ties with his businesses—a box factory, a sash and door mill, and a plywood plant, the second on the West Coast.

Long-Bell Lumber acquired the complex in 1924 and owned it for about thirty years before merging with International Paper. In 1981, International Paper sold everything to Roseburg Forest Products, the largest privately held timber corporation in the nation.

THE MILL IN WEED STILL STOOD AT ITS ORIGINAL SITE, on a hill at the edge of town. Its founder had chosen the location for the breezes that blew there most afternoons and helped to dry the freshly cut wood. Some scabs were operating the plant at half-capacity when I pulled up in the late afternoon, and I could smell a characteristic odor in the air, a sharp, bitter, chemical stink of pulp and sawdust that defines the processing of lumber, just as a billowing smokestack defines the processing of coal.

The IWA pickets were hanging around a shed across from the main gate of the plant. An old Chevy with a cracked windshield was parked by the shed, and the black millworker at its wheel was talking to his daughter through an open window. She was playing in the dirt with a wigless Barbie that somebody had donated to the cause. There were other donations, too—stacks of canned goods, some firewood, and some paper for printing leaflets. The strikers had also held two rummage sales for families in need.

About six men were on duty. They had none of the distress that comes at the start of a job action. Four months was a long time to be out—a long time to have your hands idle—but they seemed to have adapted to their situation, much as they'd adapted to the stink of the mill.

Rich Fulkerson was trying to make the best of things by relaxing in a lawn chair in the sun. He was a big redhead from Michigan, and his face was as bright as a firetruck. He had fallen in love with a woman from Weed after he'd got out of the army in Los Angeles, but life was too hectic for them in the urban south, he said, so they had come back to her hometown. Now they owned a house, and though Fulkerson knew he could lose it to the bank, he wasn't worried.

"You can bring up a family on the minimum wage if you have to," he asserted, in the happy-go-lucky way of big, freckled redheads. "I'm thinking of trying a more artistic line of work, anyhow."

"What might that be?" I asked him.

"Oh, I don't know. Maybe writing stage plays or scripts for the movies."

Robin Styers, a shop steward, sat on a log near Fulkerson. He was shy but intense, and his jaw had the firm set of a person given to moral convictions. He was a Weed boy, born and bred—his father had driven a logging truck there. In his only foray away from town, he had gone to college in Chico, but Chico didn't suit him and he'd left without graduating. He understood the timber business inside out and probably had always suspected that he'd wind up in it someday.

Styers was not the type to instigate a strike, but there was an outrage simmering in him, a pain at being slighted. He gave me an overview of the conflict. The old International Paper mill had been shut down when Roseburg had bought in, he said. That mill was outdated and harkened back to an era when most mills handled lots of old-growth timber. It had saws capable of cutting a log that was ninety inches in diameter, and equipment that could debark a log that was eighty feet long.

Roseburg had retooled the mill, installing new machinery for dealing with smaller logs from clear-cuts. The machines were speedy and efficient. Clear-cutting was more common than ever, Styers said, since the timber industry had gone corporate. When companies were independent and often family-owned, they tended to manage their holdings for a sustained yield, guaranteeing both wood and work.

Sustained-yield forestry was not as profitable as clear-cutting, though. By Styers's estimate, it might bring you a profit margin of 16 percent annually, while clear-cutting—taking all the trees from

a stand in one fell swoop, without much thought for tomorrow—
could net you a margin of between 25 and 40 percent. Roseburg had
earned a profit of about $6 million the previous year, he said.

Styers didn't hold the profit against Roseburg. He was not unsympathetic to the problems that a corporation faced. The devastated
forests were overly protected now, he believed. Lumber companies
had to deal with so many regulations in California that some of them
were looking to the American South instead, where the laws were
more lenient and there were plenty of softwood trees to harvest.

"Those environmentalists, they're too pure," Styers complained.
"They haven't read their Darwin. It's natural for some species to go
extinct. Even spotted owls."

What angered the strikers about Roseburg was that so little of
the $6 million profit had trickled down to them. They felt that their
employer was being greedy. Everything for Roseburg and nothing
for them—that was how they saw it. When the IWA first tried to
organize at the mill, in 1985, management had begged for a chance
to prove its sincerity, but the effort had apparently not satisfied the
millworkers, who had voted in favor of a union shop two years later.

The current job action had arisen when Roseburg had demanded
an across-the-board rollback in wages, arguing that the employees
had to share in the losses that it was supposedly absorbing. But the
mill in Weed had a very good record of productivity, Styers told me,
and a very low rate of absenteeism. If Roseburg had really taken
some losses, the losses had to do with a bigger picture and not with
the performance of the men in Weed.

In all, fourteen Roseburg mills were out in Oregon and California, Styers said. He pushed his cap back on his head and tossed
a wood chip at the ground in frustration. There was nothing the
men could do, regardless of how disgusted they might be. Roseburg
had them by the balls. Good jobs were as rare as prima ballerinas
in Weed. You couldn't make a new start elsewhere, either, because
you couldn't sell your house. Every block in town was cumbersome
with realtors' signs.

The men hoped that the strike would end soon. It had to end soon, they felt, because spring was a busy season at the mill with lumber needed for new construction.

In the meantime, they would sit around the shed and rail about the MBA accountants who didn't know diddly-squat about millwork, and about the Japanese ships anchored in the ocean that were milling trees that could have been milled in Weed. Then, when their shift was done, they would get up to go home, brushing the dust from the seat of their pants as Robin Styers did. He smiled for the first time that afternoon.

"Damn!" he said, touching his butt again. "That was a *hard* piece of wood."

IN THE EVENING GLOW, I climbed into the bleachers at a playground in Weed to watch a tee-ball game of baseball. Two half-pint teams, the Mets and the Astros, were contending on a gritty diamond absent of all grass and echoing the rough, intractable, bare-bones character of their town. Millworker families applauded the boys from the stands, cheering pop-ups and triples with equal enthusiasm. The men sipped from beers in paper sacks, while the women munched on popcorn that was not store-bought but brought from home.

The families had the cheerful camaraderie of people who are down but not out, who have lived through difficulty more than once and rest assured that they will live through it again. I took from their ragged, assembled presence a memory of my own Little League days, when the world and all its importance was confined to a ball field three blocks from our house.

The ball park had a PA system, and a droll announcer, Weed's own Red Barber, doled out comments and statistics with an orotund grace. To the plate came Marcus Applewhite, whose batting stance was fierce but peculiar. He had no pitcher to face, just a tee with a baseball perched on it. He took a mighty swing and smacked a grounder that skittered through the arched legs of the shortstop into left field, where it once again eluded capture, and here was Marcus Applewhite rounding third, digging for the dish, and easily avoiding the tag of the catcher, who, in point of fact, had not yet received a throw.

"Way to go, Marcus!" a father-manager shouted, patting the lad on the back. "Now pull up your pants."

While Applewhite followed orders, I looked toward the outfield with Mount Shasta looming regally behind it and saw that among all the advertisements pasted to the ball-park fence—the courtesy gestures of cafés and optometrists and auto-body shops—none had been placed by the leading employer in Weed, Roseburg Forest Products.

CHAPTER 5

When josiah whitney's geological survey team arrived at Mount Shasta in September of 1862, William Brewer was filled with expectation and noted that climbing the mountain had come to seem the "grand goal" of the expedition. His camp at Strawberry Ranch, a sort of public house where hay was sold to travelers, gladdened him. The site abutted a cold, clear stream and backed onto a slope with tall pines, and cedars almost as tall.

So little was known about Mount Shasta then that even its height had yet to be fixed correctly. The guesses ranged from thirteen to eighteen thousand feet. Its name was assumed to be of Indian origin, but a case could also be made that it came from the Russian *tshastal*, meaning white or pure, or from the French *chaste,* also meaning pure. Locals just called it "the Butte" as an understated, western way of appreciating its grandeur while appearing to be unimpressed.

Brewer got conflicting reports about a possible ascent of Shasta, hearing from one source that the hike was easy and ended with a view of all creation, and from another that nobody had ever scaled the summit because the conditions were too harsh. The team engaged a guide, Mr. Frame, who convinced them that the climb could be done. Mr. Frame had done it once himself. His only caution to the men was that they would have to provide their own muscle.

It was a bit late in the year to be starting out, but the team had no problems on their first leg and camped for the night at 7,400 feet. As the terrain became steeper, however, the party had to alter its pace. Professor Whitney's fingers were frostbitten, while Brewer's had turned deep blue, as had his lips. The men wore colored goggles to protect them from the sun glaring off the snow and trudged panting through drifts, sometimes slipping on hardened lava and loose rocks, until they reached the summit at last.

Once they were there, they complained about being sleepy. Some of them got sick after lunch and vomited severely—an effect, said Brewer, of the "rarified air." The day was cloudy, so the team didn't have an unobstructed view. They looked out upon a "perfect wilderness of mountains" in every direction, stretching to the Pacific Ocean. Their descent went smoothly, although Brewer passed a rough night wrapped in blankets, still in his heavy clothes, sleeping in the snow and noting "ugh! how cold it was."

Snow would not have bothered John Muir, who climbed the mountain more than once, the first time in the spring of 1875. He seemed to relish extremes, to be drawn to the *wild* in wilderness. One November, as he curled up at his base camp on Shasta and got ready to enjoy a big storm, he had the misfortune to be rescued by some do-gooders, and he saw in this, rather bitterly, how difficult it was becoming for anybody to evade the embrace of civilization.

Another writer, Joaquin Miller, a Hoosier who came to California in a covered wagon, had also celebrated Mount Shasta in his work. Born with the unlikely name of Cincinnatus Hiner, he changed it on the advice of a friend after he had published a poem about Joaquin Murietta, the Mexican bandit. The only person he disappointed was his mother.

Miller was slow to develop his talent. His initial effort was a diary that he kept while he was slaving in the gold mines around the mountain. After that, he sojourned among the Modoc tribe for five years and later practiced law in Oregon, but the desire to write still dogged him, and in 1870 he jumped into the lap of literature by traveling to London via New York, a city that gave him the willies.

"I have fought many battles with Indians," he confided to his journal. "I have seen rough men in the mines, but such ruffians as assailed me on landing from the Jersey ferry I have never encountered before."

In Nottingham, Miller left a laurel wreath on the tomb of his hero, Lord Byron. He met no success with English publishers and had to print and distribute his book of poems, *Songs of the Sierra,* himself. It earned some marvelous reviews and made its author a literary darling, who dined with Robert Browning and Dante Gabriel Rossetti and frequented salons in buckskin-and-leather outfits crowned with a sombrero.

Miller became known as the "Byron of the Rockies." His *Life Among the Modoc,* a prose memoir, appeared in 1873 and immortalized the Butte in its very first line, which read, "Lonely as God, and white as a winter moon, Mount Shasta starts up sudden and solitary from the great black heart of Northern California."

Although Miller truly loved the mountain, he chose to spend his royalties on a rambling estate in Oakland hills, where he passed his declining years as a white-bearded, bohemian sage, who drank, caroused, and championed the cause of free love. He died at the age of seventy-seven, in 1913, another dreamer who'd struck it rich in California.

MOUNT SHASTA HAD A REPUTATION as a holy place among certain Indian tribes, so it made sense that the Order of Buddhist Contemplatives should have an abbey on Summit Road, even though they had landed there by chance.

A dust of fresh snow covered the ridges of the mountain down to an altitude of about six thousand feet on the cool, sunny morning that I drove up there. Manzanita bushes were growing along the abbey's walls. The crisp air and the moisture had brought out the streaked marbling of the wood, and the branches were clustered with tiny, white, bell-shaped flowers.

At the main gate, I picked up a security phone and spoke to a person inside. About ten minutes later, a monk came forward to admit me. She wore a Russian-style winter hat and a brown robe sashed at the waist with a purple cincture. She was in her forties, although the bright focus of her presence made her look younger. Her hair was shaved to a graying stubble. She had ruddy cheeks from working outdoors, and eyes that were alive to nuances, very clear and blue and open.

All over California, religious communities such as the abbey were still cropping up, as they had been for centuries, taking advantage of the space, the freedom, and the notorious receptivity of people in the state to new ideas—or, in the case of Buddhism, an old idea newly translated. I had been attracted to the apparently simple Buddhist canon from the moment I'd moved to San Francisco, but I soon learned how complicated simplicity could be. Balancing a book by D. T. Suzuki on my lap, I would wrench myself into a near-full-lotus position and fail miserably at the task of trying not to think and trying *not* to not think.

From my efforts, though, I gained the smallest glimmer of what a Buddhist might be hoping to accomplish, and discovered, too, that out West it was easier to incorporate a spiritual dimension into my life than it had been in the East.

I didn't know why that should be so, whether it had to do with the glory of the land or with a renewed interest in nature and the very idea of creation, but it was also the case with the monk who was my guide. She was from a Methodist family in Nebraska. Her grades were so good in school that she had followed an academic career path without thinking much about it, but she also had a spiritual longing that wouldn't go away.

As a child, she had discovered a shelf of books about world religions at her neighborhood library and had read them with enthusiasm. After graduating from the University of California at Berkeley, she moved to Eugene, Oregon, where she did typing and secretarial work. She was in a phase of shopping around for some kind of spiritual discipline when she began investigating Soto Zen, the form of Buddhism practiced at Shasta Abbey.

As her thirtieth birthday approached, she decided to attend one of the retreats that the abbey offers to outsiders. It held enough interest for her that she became a lay Buddhist, but after only a few years in such a role she found it in herself to enter the monastic life and train as a Buddhist priest. She knew by then that she was on the right path, and that Soto Zen was the correct practice for her.

There were about forty monks in training at Shasta Abbey, she said, about half of them men and half of them women. The abbess and spiritual leader was P. T. Jiyu-Kennett, an Englishwoman who was certified as a priest in Japan and had started the abbey in 1970. D. T. Suzuki had introduced her to Mahayana Buddhism in the 1950s, and she later wrote a classic about Zen training with the wonderful title *Selling Water by the River,* a business I had conducted far too often.

The abbey owned sixteen acres near the mountain. The grounds had once been a resort, and the stone buildings were the work of an Italian mason. A walkway, roofed against the heavy winter snows, connected one building to another. As we strolled around, monks kept circulating, greeting each other with a bow and clasped hands while they went about their chores.

We paused to look at a Kanzeon garden that was used for teaching Sunday school classes to children. In Soto Zen, Kanzeon is the *bodhisattva* who represents compassion and mercy. The garden was an elaborate rock formation that the kids had populated with toys—miniature plastic cowboys, rubber snakes, dinosaurs, even transformers.

Next, we saw the Ceremony Hall, a dark, quiet room with stained-glass windows. The monks meditated in a Meditation Hall adjacent to it four or five times a day, for thirty to forty-five minutes each time, from their wake-up call at six in the morning until lights-out at ten. They meditated while they worked, too, and in the evening there was a period of walking meditation. The opportunities to meditate were endless, really, because the monks were charged with the duty of recognizing the Buddha nature, or spiritual value, in the most ordinary activities.

The notion—or so it seemed to me—was to make yourself an entirely conscious being, aware of every passing tick of life, and aware, too, of all the lives that were ticking by around you. And the trick, of course, was not to be attached to any of it, but to consecrate its transience instead—a transience that included your own few fleeting seconds of enlightenment.

Little wonder, then, that the Buddha smiled.

At the abbey, the monks grew most of their food. The head gardener was a lanky man in khakis and a blue flannel shirt, who had a goofy-looking, flapped hat on his head to protect him from the sun. I have never met an unhappy gardener, not ever, and this monk did nothing to break that streak.

The monk's spring crops were just sprouting. His snow peas, lettuce, chard, and fava beans were all coming in, but it was the favas that turned him on. He leaned on the handle of his pitchfork, just as a gardener should do, and spoke of how the beans would be harvested and dried, articulating the procedure so tenderly on their behalf that each fava seemed to be a unique organism of considerable worth.

My visit to Shasta Abbey ended in a little gift shop, where I bought some books and pamphlets and asked my guide what it was like for her to live on Mount Shasta, with its snowy peak constantly in evidence. The mountain flowed in and out of her thoughts, she said. It would disappear in clouds, or in fog, or in gray weather, only to appear again.

◆   ◆   ◆

FROM MOUNT SHASTA, I took Highway 89 toward Fall River Valley and cattle country, going through some more lumber towns on the brink of disaster or already fallen. McCloud had a cluster of by-now familiar For Sale signs on the houses around a working mill that was just limping along. The town once had its own railroad, the McCloud River Railroad, that connected the Southern Pacific line to the Great Northern line. McCloud's mills, even into the 1960s, had cut a million board-feet of wood every year.

Pondosa, down the road, was in much worse shape. It had gone to dust and pine needles, the rot of the earth devouring the abandoned company houses on the fringe of a defunct mill. The windows in the houses were all busted out, leaving shards of glass stuck in the frames. The doorknobs had been jimmied free, and the doors were nailed shut to keep the floorboards from being stolen. The trees, great firs and pines, had all been slashed and toppled, and they lay on the ground bleaching and decomposing, their fibers consumed by termites.

Beyond Pondosa, I turned onto A-19, the McArthur Road, traveling southeast and watching as the forests began to open onto the valley. There was more light, and the dark greens and browns of thickly timbered land were replaced by more alfalfa fields and the blues of lakes and streams.

Fall River, a spring-fed creek as lovely as any in the state, ran by the road at Glenburn, and I remembered how I had once met John McArthur, a cattle rancher, at the bar of a lodge where I was staying on a fishing trip. His family was the family of McArthur Road and the town of McArthur, emigrants from Scotland who'd been in the valley for ages. When I showed an interest in seeing his spread, he told me to give him a call in advance, any time, at home or at The Buckhorn, his saloon of choice.

The fishing was too good, though, and I couldn't tear myself away from the river, but I thought that I might call McArthur this trip.

Fall River Valley was among my favorite spots in California. The sense of space, the broad vistas, the fenced pastures dotted with cows, they all took me back to a primal image of the West that I had formed as a boy, relying on comic books and movies. I liked the streams flowing through the valley, and the flocks of ducks and geese flying by overhead, their bodies framed against a big sky that was sprinkled at night with a million stars.

On the horizon, there was the craggy shape of Mount Lassen, another cinder cone, and when the weather was clear Mount Shasta, too, was visible in the distance. The trout also gratified me, fat browns and rainbows lying in the slack current, little monarchs of a watery, food-rich kingdom. Above all, it was the calm of Fall River Valley that appealed to me, a feeling that I would never be cramped or invaded or pushed up against by others, that there was, in the end, quite enough room for everybody.

So I started having fantasies—ranch fantasies, middle-aged cowboy fantasies. I imagined myself on the porch of my spread, picking my teeth with the stem of a wild oat and dreaming about the evening rise, when feeding trout would surface to dimple the river. The fantasy was captivating enough that I stopped at a real estate office in Fall River Mills, the largest town in the valley

The realtors on duty were Hoss and Georgie Bader. As his name implied, Hoss was a very sizable fellow. He looked as if Ben Cartwright had raised him on the Ponderosa, but he was really a refugee from Los Angeles. Georgie came from Fall River Mills. Like the McArthurs, her family went way back. Her grandfather was the first white baby to be born at Fork Crook, a military outpost nearby that had been built in 1857 as a shelter against Indian attacks.

"I'm thinking about buying a ranch," I said, surprised by my own boldness. "Have you got one to sell me?"

Hoss and Georgie reeled off some properties. There was a tract ranchette on one-and-a-half acres that went for $69,000. There was a huge, clapboard fixer-upper farmhouse on twenty-five acres for

$187,500. But an actual ranch? There weren't many big ranches anymore. They'd been parceled off and subdivided to provide homes for all the retired people who were coming to the valley, golfers who played on the links at Fall River Country Club, over by Fort Crook. Farmers had also grabbed some of the ranchland, to grow such exotic crops as garlic and wild rice.

"People are retiring here?" I asked, stunned by a vision of arthritic duffers in tam-o'-shanters chipping and wedging where the cowpies used to be.

"Yes, sir," Hoss said. "More and more of them. Our own young people don't stay around. There's no jobs for them."

The Baders were singing a song I'd heard before, from Crescent City to Weed. They gave me some tourist newspapers that had copious real estate listings. The entirety of northern California, it seemed, was up for grabs.

As I was going out the door, I asked if John McArthur was still around, thinking that he might have sold out, as well, but Georgie laughed and said fondly, "Oh, that John McArthur! Did you know that he still gets up on horseback and drives his cattle home right down the middle of Highway 299?"

THINGS HAPPEN ON A CATTLE RANCH, unexpected things. The cows in their lazy grazing create an illusion of placidity, but accidents are always lurking beneath that deceptive surface to keep a rancher on his toes—a horse bursting free from its corral, machinery quitting, a hired hand getting served his divorce papers and peeling into the next county on a four-day drunk, or, for John McArthur, a valve breaking on an irrigation pipe and spewing precious water in every direction.

There was no way in hell that McArthur had time to see me. He had no recollection of ever meeting me and no inclination to rectify that. He was wet, tired, and cranky, and suggested that I call his friend, Albert Albaugh, if I wanted a short course in the cattle business. Albaugh was the goods, McArthur said, plus his irrigation pipes were all intact.

At the Albaughs' house, Mrs. Albaugh answered the phone. "Why doesn't John McArthur talk to you?" she wanted to know, a perfectly sensible question.

"Broken valve."

"Can't he talk to you tomorrow?"

"He isn't sure."

The Albaughs lived a few miles from town on Pittville Road. Their house overlooked Fall River Valley and had a good view of Mount Lassen. Some wash was hanging on a clothesline behind the house, flapping in the breeze and smelling fresh and soapy, and there were a few head of cattle, Herefords again, in a pasture.

Two pickup trucks were parked by the back door, which is usually the front door on ranches. It lets you stamp the mud off your boots and wash your hands in the kitchen sink. The front door was for social visits. The minister came through it, and so did stiff-necked relatives, those far-flung aunts and uncles.

Mrs. Albaugh checked me over before opening the door all the way. Albert Albaugh was in the living room, sitting in a lounger and gazing out a picture window. He was in his seventies. He had a strong-featured Germanic face and wore red suspenders over a blue work shirt. His shoes were off.

There was the most incredible smile on Albaugh's lips, a smile of utter contentment, as if all his passions had been played out, the light and the dark, leaving him without a single grudge against existence.

"They tell me things are changing in Fall River Valley," I began.

The smile didn't budge. "More people than cows now," Albaugh allowed.

That was all he had to say to me about the cattle business. He wasn't being curt. It was just all he had to say.

Mrs. Albaugh snatched up the conversation. She was a proud,

intelligent woman, the mother of three grown children, all college graduates, a fact that seemed important to her. I thought she might have mentioned it so that I wouldn't mistake her family for country bumpkins, an assumption that city folks sometimes make about anybody who lives in rural California. Farmers and ranchers are sensitive to such slights, and Mrs. Albaugh was no exception.

The Albaugh family had worked their ranch since the turn of the century, she told me. They had 550 acres, but they were gradually phasing themselves out because of Albert's age. They were down to about 20 head of beef cattle, all Herefords, but in their prime they had run 450 head northwest of Big Valley.

The cattle had grazed on a spring range starting about April fifteenth and had been transferred to a summer range in June. In the autumn, Albert and his hands would round up the fattened cattle and bulls and drive them home. The best steers and heifers were sold at local feeder sales in and around Fall River Valley, while the old cows and other stock had to be transported to the big auction yards in Cottonwood, near Redding, in Sacramento Valley.

During the years when the Albaughs had been serious ranchers, the game had become much more difficult and complex, Mrs. Albaugh said. In order to hold on to the pasture land that they leased, they had to pay fees to four separate parties—the Bureau of Land Management, two private timber companies, and the Pit River Indians. Their costs kept rising, particularly feed costs, and they kept losing stock. The cows got hit by trains and by cars. Predators killed them and rustlers even stole a few.

You had to be smart and hardworking to succeed as a cattleman now, Mrs. Albaugh asserted. That was another song I'd heard before.

One of the Albaughs' sons had bought them out and still did some fairly large-scale ranching, while another boy was growing wild rice, garlic, and mint in the valley. The Albaughs' daughter lived up in Oregon, and when Mrs. Albaugh started describing a trip there and praising the state, I said, "But it's not California, is it?"

"Sometimes I'd rather not be from here," she said heatedly.

"When I travel and say I'm from California, everybody thinks it means Los Angeles. Los Angelés! That's nine hundred miles from here. There's more to California than Los Angeles."

Her outburst puzzled me. I guessed that there must be something beneath it, something as yet unsaid, so I asked her, "What else don't you like about California?"

"The political thing gets to me," she answered. "People in rural areas like this one, our votes hardly count."

Mrs. Albaugh thought that the state government discriminated against farmers and ranchers. Its policies were formulated to serve urban and suburban constituencies, she believed. She had no kinship with such people, no political bonds, no shared interests. The issues that *were* of concern to her, such as water rights—water for pastures, for alfalfa—were seldom properly addressed at the state level. She felt disenfranchised from the political process, virtually unrepresented.

A schoolbus stopped on the Pittville Road, its red lights blinking, and the Albaughs' grandson, who was about six or seven, dashed up the path and through the back door to join us in the living room. He had some ghoulish, plastic vampire teeth in his mouth and ran around trying to scare us, but we were too old.

When Mrs. Albaugh left to make us some coffee, I glanced over at Albert Albaugh, who was wriggling his toes inside his socks, looking out the picture window with a pair of binoculars, and scanning the horizon. He was still smiling his incredible smile, the soul's sweet rising into flesh, and still had nothing else to say.

"More people than cows now." Those were Albaugh's final words on the subject of change in Fall River Valley.

SPANIARDS HAD BROUGHT THE FIRST CATTLE TO CALIFORNIA, the missionaries initially, followed by the explorers Gaspar de Portolá and Juan Bautista de Anza. Their herds ranged freely and consumed all the native grasses, a sea of grass reduced to stubble. Around the practice of ranching there developed a class of people, Californios, who were of Mexican or Spanish descent, and whose lifestyle combined an air of ease and grace with a sensual appreciation of their plentitude.

Californios were terrific horsemen, dancers, and singers, and they loved to throw lavish fiestas at which they slugged back wine, performed steamy fandangos, and disconcerted straightlaced tourists from abroad. Sir George Simpson, the governor-in-chief of Hudson's Bay Company, put it this way in his *Narrative of a Journey Round the World* (1843):

> The population of California in particular has been drawn from the most indolent variety of an indolent species, being composed of super-annuated troopers and retired office-holders and their descendants. . . . Such settlers were not likely to toil for much more than the cheap bounty nature afforded them, horses to ride, beef to eat, with hides and tallow to exchange for such other supplies as they wanted. . . . The children improved upon the example of the parents through the influence of a systematic education . . . which gave them a lasso as a toy in infancy and a horse as a companion in boyhood. . . .

It was the hides and the tallow that kept the Californios and their *rancheros* going. They were exporting enormous quantities of both by the mid-1830s, primarily from San Diego, where the cargo was loaded onto ships bound for the newly industrialized East, for Boston. The hides were used in the manufacture of leather goods, and the tallow for soap and candles. As many as a million hides may have been traded during the era.

For a time through the 1850s, ranchers controlled most large parcels of land in the state and dictated their use. Farmers had to fend for themselves. If they didn't care to have cattle grazing on their farm, they were responsible by law for putting up fences.

There were about 3 million head of cattle in the state at the peak

of the ranchers' power, in 1862, but the count dropped swiftly after
that as the rancheros went bankrupt, done in by taxes, mismanage-
ment, and loss of title to their land. The railroads also encroached,
as did federal grants to homesteaders. Only about 630,000 cattle were
left in California a decade later.

Eventually, it became essential for some agency to address the
question of pasturage rights on public property and what to charge
for them. The job was assigned to the Bureau of Land Mangement
(BLM) under the Taylor Grazing Act of 1934.

In administering the use of government land, the BLM had to
walk a very thin tightrope. For instance, it had to offer habitat to
such threatened species as desert tortoises, bald eagles, bighorn sheep,
and wild burros, while also dealing with (and hoping to profit from)
the companies that were pursuing timber, minerals, oil, natural gas,
and water.

Of all the activities that the BLM supervised, it earned the least
from grazing rights. The federal government owned about 61 percent
of the land in California, but its 225 or so livestock allotments made
only $370,000 a year, three times less than the agency got for granting
simple rights-of-way. The BLM had been pressured for ages to up
the ante, but a block of U.S. senators from the West, some of whom
sat on pertinent committees at the Department of the Interior, had
deflected any such legislation, as well as most attempts to minimize
the damage that cattle did to public lands.

A grazing allotment from the BLM was typically overstocked
with cows. The cows soon stripped it of vegetation and layered it
with manure. The manure washed into rivers and creeks, inflating
the nitrogen and the coliform bacteria levels and harming the fish-
eries. Other animals felt the effects of overgrazing, too, especially
wildlife such as the mule deer, whose survival range in California
had been turned into a cheatgrass barren that could support only
jackrabbits, horned larks, and cattle.

But it was the cattle ranchers' sponging of water that caused the
greatest controversy. Californians went through about 11 trillion gal-

lons of water each year, and about 85 percent of it was reserved for agriculture. The biggest agricultural users were cattlemen, whose irrigated pastures drew off more than 4 million acre-feet of water per annum—about as much as 21 million people might use at home.

Irrigated pastures sucked up one-seventh of all the water in the state, but the cows fattened on the grasses accounted for only one five-thousandth of the economy. After irrigated pastures, alfalfa—food for cows—was the second most water-intensive crop. Some of the cattle ranches in places like Fall River Valley and Big Valley were in near-desert environments that could not have sustained even a tiny herd without irrigation.

A statistic that critics of the BLM often cited put everything in perspective. If you were to eliminate irrigated pastures and alfalfa from California's agricultural profile, along with such thirsty crops as rice and cotton, you'd save enough water to accommodate 70 million new residents—music to a developer's ears.

Despite such controversies, the business of cattle-ranching went on pretty much as it had always done. There were still buckaroos who rode the range, a pinch of Skoal between lip and gum, and remained faithful to upholding the rituals of the mythic West. The beef cattle still got sold in Cottonwood at roundup time, at Shasta Livestock Auction Yard, where Ellington Peek presided over the bovine transactions.

Peek's weekly auction was the fanciest this side of Amarillo. Buyers came from every western state and purchased about 140,000 cows annually. A sale of about 250 head could gross Peek about a million dollars. His corrals were usually packed with steers and heifers ripe for the slaughter, the stuff of T-bones and Big Macs, but he also handled the stringy old bulls whose fate it was to end up as an ingredient in Oscar Mayer bologna.

AH, THE WEST IN CALIFORNIA, its dying gasps! At a variety store in Fall River Mills, while I was ransacking the bins for a new notebook, there came parading through the door a fellow in an off-the-rack suit of no particular flair, who carried a sample case and had the abject manner of somebody still fumbling to find his purpose in life. A drummer he was, a poor traveling salesman advanced into the wrong century and covering a territory that probably stretched all the way to Boise.

In the past, our drummer might have dabbled in a welcome commodity, gingham or lace or Dr. Headbanger's Magic Elixir, three parts diluted molasses to one part grain alcohol, but now he was selling oilcloth shades, an item whose continued manufacture was a mystery to me. Opening his case, he pitched his wares to the store's buyer by saying, "The Latin type of people enjoy these in their homes."

She looked at him doubtfully, parsing "Latin type" and translating it into "Mexican fieldhand."

Later, I went by Sportsman's Liquor, where the marquee advertised Beer, Boats, Bullets, and Booze, an afternoon's entertainment anywhere in America.

At the Fall River Hotel, a half-timbered, Tudor-style building that surely was once a home away from home to countless drummers, all of them carefully attending to their rooms at night, setting out the framed photos of the wife and the kids, I ran into a nasty little man behind the grill, who, without provocation, called me a "flat-lander" to my face, another city person who was spoiling a previously unspoiled corner of Shasta County.

The little man had been a musician and a bronc rider and might have broken something in his head. He said that I must be one of those post–World War II sissies whose misguided parents had brought him up on Dr. Spock, that Communist.

"You didn't get punished enough, is all!" he yelled. "Nothing else is wrong with you!"

In the morning, getting ready to leave Fall River Mills, I turned on the motel TV and listened as Pat Robertson, the evangelist, encouraged his audience to support more prisons and harsher penalties for criminals.

"There weren't many repeat offenders in the Old Testament," he said, with a chuckle.

By Fort Crook, on the irrigated, green links of Fall River Country Club, I saw a battalion of electric carts conveying elderly duffers over the front nine.

CHAPTER 6

MODOC COUNTY was the last frontier in California, almost 3 million nearly empty acres tacked onto the far northeast corner of the state. The earth was so rocky, porous, and strewn with lava that only a tenth of it could be cultivated, although sagebrush grew lavishly and gave the local ranchers fits. They believed that it crowded out the bunchgrass that was supposed to nourish their cattle, so they burned it, drowned it in herbicides, or chopped it down.

A rancher in Modoc County could be a lonely man. He had to know how to control things, how to get around things. He had to value action. If some government ecology scientist–type person told him to quit shooting the ground squirrels that were tearing up his pastures, he had to walk on the dark side for a while and kill the scroungy bastards by stuffing some poisoned lettuce down their holes. It came out the same in the end.

Alturas, the county seat, was a town of about three thousand. It sat on the North Fork of the Pit River at an altitude of about 4,500 feet. It was tough, bare-knuckled, and not a little mean. In its rawest neighborhoods, it looked as though it had been the site of a colossal demolition derby whose promoters had skipped away without bothering to clean up the wreckage. All manner of metallic waste, from mufflers to hubcaps, was slowly disintegrating on the perimeter of the Great Basin Desert.

An undercurrent of savagery seemed to swirl through the streets of the town. Almost every public phonebooth was trashed, the glass broken, the directories ripped apart, and the receivers yanked from their wires, as if the very idea of communication were somehow ridiculous on the frontier. You could feel the frustration of the many midnight calls that had never got answered, all the furious venting of steam that had followed in the wake of perennial misunder-standing.

Alturas was built on extremes. To live there, you needed a healthy dose of self-reliance. The climate was a deadweight on the notion of California as one big garden spot, a near match for Cheyenne, with the temperature in winter dropping at times to twenty below. You could count on just seventy-six frost-free days a year. The cold weather started in September, and the ground could still freeze hard in late spring.

Escape from Alturas was almost impossible. The Sierra Nevada and the southern Cascades cut it off from the rest of the state. When you couldn't find something special in town, you went to Oregon to buy it, to Klamath Falls, more than a hundred miles away. Somebody itchy for adventure—a cowboy, say, who was sick of punching cows—thought nothing of highballing it to Reno on the spur of the moment and turning around to speed home the same night, a round-trip of some four hundred miles.

True Alturans didn't mind the loneliness or the harsh weather. Their landscape satisfied them the way an ocean satisfies a sailor. They spoke readily of its beauty—a beauty all the more valued because most outsiders failed to see it. A true Alturan had a wide streak of pride, the hallmark of a survivor.

Basques had first come to Modoc County to tend sheep, as they had done in other regions of the state, and there were old Basque hotels and restaurants in most settled places. At a Basque restaurant one night, I had a long, haranguing talk with a rancher who'd been running stock in Alturas for twenty-nine years. He and a pal had been making the rounds of bars, downing vodka since noon.

The rancher had icy blue eyes and a scar or two from barroom brawls. With each new vodka, he would lean over and say to me, enunciating the words precisely, "You have got to . . . get your ass . . . over the Warner Mountains . . . to Surprise Valley."

Surprise Valley was his personal temple. He went there often for solace and to be even more isolated and alone.

"If you don't do anything else here," he'd say, "get your ass . . . to Surprise Valley. Just do it!"

The rancher had an honest affection for the natural world, but he despised those who drooled and gaped and were sentimental about it. He despised anything sentimental and hated people who painted rosy pictures of all God's creatures, those Sierra Clubbers who stooped to protecting such lowlife animals as the coyote.

"They ought to see a young sheep that's been torn apart!" he railed, stirring his vodka with a pinkie. "Or a colt with its legs and its bowels chewed up, left on the range to die!"

He believed that it was foolish to poison ground squirrels, though, because eagles and hawks ate them, and the poison spread through the food chain. He knew of a much better solution.

"We've got all these goddam deadbeats in town, why not put 'em to work? Give 'em all twenty-twos, pay 'em the minimum wage, and let 'em shoot the furry little sons-a-bitches." He glared at me with those icy blue eyes. "Man *is* a killer by instinct, you know."

Although Modoc County was one of only two California counties where the population had declined in the last decade, the rancher still felt put upon. The deadbeat newcomers were not true Alturans and didn't understand a single principle of ranching. They lived in low-income housing units and worked at service-related jobs or merely collected food stamps and welfare benefits.

Sometimes the sense of being put upon got so bad for the rancher that he considered selling his land and leaving California altogether to start fresh in a Nevada town near Winnemucca that was still western and wild, where the horses were broken properly, in the old style, and the cattle still had rights.

"Yes, sir, I might just move the whole operation to Denial," I heard him say, but when I looked at my atlas later, I saw that he had meant *Denio*.

IN THE MORNING, I got my ass to Surprise Valley. It was a level expanse of ground shimmering with salt flats, lakes, streams, and some wavery sand dunes that leaped out and surprised you as you came down from the forested slopes of the Warner Mountains.

To the weary emigrants who had baptized it after a trek across the Nevada deserts, it had resembled an oasis. Their log cabins still stood in Cedarville, arranged in a semicircle like Conestoga wagons as a barrier against Indian attacks. The tillable land, a verdant strip about fifty miles wide, was all ranches and pastures now.

In a Cedarville park, I read an issue of the Modoc County Historical Society's journal that was devoted to Surprise Valley. It carried excerpts from settlers' writings and afforded a painfully honest account of nineteenth-century wilderness life that my rancher friend would have approved of.

Jan. 29, 1887—Last evening about 5 o'clock the wind was blowing a perfect gale. The chimney caught fire and if it had not been for Papa's, Dan's, and George's hard working the house would have been burnt.

February 1, 1887—Papa would not let us attend school today. The boys heard yesterday that Mary Hickerson has scarlet fever....

February 12, 1887—Mr. Fee was very unfortunate yesterday. His team of four nice horses got frightened and ran away and while they were jumping a fence one of the horses broke a leg and they had to kill it.

Diary of Dot Munroe

In October 1864 we moved to Surprise. . . . But we was happy until
the Indians began to steal our stock and kill men. I could hardly
bear to see any of our folks go out of sight and still they had to be
gone. Many a time I could not work I would be so uneasy I would
stand in the Door and look and look to see if I could see them and
some times I expected to see the Indians coming too. . . .

                                         Reminiscences of Amanda Boyd

It was good to remember that the Indians had some murder in
them, that they hadn't simply rolled over at the first approach of
white men. So much harm was done to them collectively that histories
sometimes glossed over the fury of certain tribes and how they had
lashed out against settlers, even the innocents among them. They
could put their fury to advantage, turning it into a psychological
weapon that let them fight valiantly when they were outnumbered,
as the Modoc did during the Modoc War of 1872–73.

The conflict had its origins in governmental stupidity. The
United States had pushed the Modocs from their ancestral land in
1864 and forced them onto a reservation in Oregon, where they had
to live next to their traditional enemies, the Klamaths. Trouble was
bound to occur. A Modoc subchief, Kintpuash, killed a Klamath
shaman and absconded from the reservation with fifty-three men
and some women, children, and elders, fleeing to the lava beds by
Tule Lake, northwest of Alturas.

Kintpuash was "Captain Jack" to the whites. He and his men
used the rocks of the lava beds to build defensive walls. The ensuing
battles were fierce and bloody. Although the Modocs had no real
firepower, they held off more than a thousand federal soldiers
for about six months before surrendering. Captain Jack was in
hiding, but some of his men betrayed him, and he was caught and
hanged.

The Modoc defeat came at a moment when the spiritual un-
derpinnings of Indians everywhere in California were being de-

stroyed. One Modoc would tell later about how the war had cost
him his faith. A tribal doctor, a visionary, had drawn a boundary
around Captain Jack's camp with a long cord painted red and had
insisted that if the soldiers tried to cross it they would all die, but
the soldiers did cross it, and the Modocs had died.

"This is the last time we will believe in doctors," John Sconchin,
another Modoc, would say. "We'll ask them no more."

The Modoc tribe had unraveled after its losing battle, and some
members went back to Oregon while others wandered obliviously
into Oklahoma.

AFTER GETTING MY ASS TO SURPRISE VALLEY, viewing a Drinker-Collins
Duplex Respirator iron lung at the town museum, and eating too
much roast lamb and drinking too much raspy red wine with ranchers
and Basques, there wasn't a lot to do in Alturas, except to stand on
a corner and watch the fleet of beleaguered automobiles that were
sure to disassemble in the desert someday. The cars seemed to be
held together by the will of their drivers, whose faces, passing on
parade, had a lean and hungry look, both sad and threatened, a
record of abuses given and abuses received.

The word was that Alturas got lively and even madcap when
the goose and duck hunters were around, but hunting season was a
long way off.

So many drifters, the flotsam of the frontier. At the California
State Employment Development Corporation, three clerks were shuffling paper in an antiseptic environment at odds with the very fabric
of Alturas while they waited for a client, any client, to walk in. It
happened to be me. I asked what kind of jobs were available in the
county.

The head clerk had a deadpan manner. "Well, let's see," he said,
peering down at some index cards and rifling through them. "We
got two yardwork jobs tomorrow, three and four hours apiece. We

got a minimum-wage job pouring concrete for six hours. That's about it."

Another clerk yelled from his desk. "Hey, Ralph, you forgot about that construction job! Four to six months, putting back together an apartment building that collapsed."

"So when somebody moves to Alturas, where do they work?" I asked.

"They don't work," Ralph said calmly. "They eat up their savings, and they go home or they go on welfare. We've never had any industry here but for a mill. It's always been seasonal jobs, ranch jobs."

"Nothing steady in the cattle business?"

He shook his head. "The ranchers are just starting to recoup from bad times. We had three big ranches go under last year. The banks wouldn't carry them."

The money budgeted for Modoc County's general relief fund seldom lasted for an entire month, Ralph told me, but that wasn't uncommon in rural California. Most counties were broke and couldn't provide the public services that were mandated by the state. They were resentful about being held to account, too. People expected services, and when they brought their expectations to agencies where the door was locked, they sometimes got a little overheated and kicked at the door.

Every service in the county was stretched to its limits, from mental health to transportation, but Ralph seemed proud that at least the Alturas library was still open on occasion.

"Mount Shasta," he said, "they just closed theirs."

The other clerk yelled again, "Hey, Ralph! Tell him about Redding. Redding *is* booming!"

"That's all subdivisions. Houses going up. Same thing in Anderson. All around there, north of Sacramento."

I recalled the golf course in Fall River Mills and sketched a scenario for Ralph whereby second homes and golf links might transform the sagebrush. He rejected it with blithe disdain.

"Lot of miles between here and Fall River Mills," he said and laughed. "But if it came to that, I guess we could build us a Modoc wall, like Captain Jack."

Spoken like a true Alturan.

BIRDS. At the Modoc National Wildlife Refuge, a series of manmade sloughs, ponds, and canals outside Alturas, there were birds by the thousands, flocking, nesting, and flying about, creating with the flap of their wings the crackly sound of a tarpaulin rippling in a gust of wind.

All alone in the refuge, I looked toward an overcast sky and watched Canada geese take to the air. They rose awkwardly at first and then, higher up, acquired a graceful symmetry as they shaped themselves into a V and became a pattern of dark spots against the clouds.

In the ponds, ducks floated and bobbed, red-breasted mergansers, blue-winged teal, and a pair of ruddy ducks in mating plumage. The male's beak was an extraordinary blue, all the fibers of pigmentation boiled down and concentrated in a little piece of bone.

Coots were everywhere, plain-feathered and acting dumb, seemingly the most plodding of waterfowl but maybe the most cunning, always foraging inoffensively, their heads pumping like cartoon characters, too ugly and banal to ever attract a shotgun shell.

The distant hills were a blackish purple. There were lush pastures and wispy grasses in light-colored tufts. The birds sang and sang, a dissonant chorus of trills, honks, and arpeggios. In my solitude, I saw what it must have been like to stand on the Modoc plateau before the settlers and the railroads came, when the Far North was still a virgin wilderness, its amplitude undiminished in any way.

Elegiac feelings swept over me. The state had once been covered with 5 million acres of wetlands, but they were almost gone now, and with them would go the birds.

A spring shower in the desert. A mild fragrance of sagebrush, and the silver and gray-green of its leaves.

◆   ◆   ◆

HIGHWAY 395 OUT OF ALTURAS ran along the spine of the Sierra Nevada down to Mojave town in the southern desert, hundreds of miles away. It ran through many different types of terrain, but the terrain it ran through on the way to Susanville was definitely *out there,* yet more dusty, tufted, sagebrushy, disconnected land, the sandy earth much whiter now and the snow banished from the mountains.

Far back from the road, almost far enough to be invisible, I saw solitary, tin-roofed houses that seemed not so much to have been constructed from the ground up as lowered intact from a spaceship. The owners put a premium on privacy and even secrecy. Their only neighbors were jackrabbits, grouse, and kangaroo rats, other critters surviving on the margin.

Termo was *really* out there. It had a gas pump, a general store that was for sale, probably in tandem with the Brooklyn Bridge, and a gaggle of rough-hewn cabins that appeared not to have been occupied since the Gold Rush. A hand-painted sign said, Johnston's Video Rental and Indian Gift Shop, Cabin #3 Behind Store.

By Cabin #3, there was another sign, above a caked flowerbed where the droopy, frost-damaged stems of some dying plants were taking a nap. Caution, it said, Flowers Growing.

Through a screen door I heard some Texas swing on a radio, the hillbilly skitter of Bob Wills. Inside the cabin, a slender woman, her hair pulled back in a bun, was making some bead earrings at a table. The earrings were a jubilant yellow.

"Are you Mrs. Johnston?" I asked.

"No, I'm Jessie. A friend of the family." She was minding the store while the Johnstons were in Reno. Mrs. Johnston was a Sioux medicine woman, who went by the name of Tears-in-the-Wind and had been on a vision quest for twenty years. Still another sign attested to it: Vision Quest, Twenty Years with No Drugs or Alcohol. It hung by a shelf of Bruce Lee kung-fu videos.

Jessie didn't belong to the Sioux tribe herself. Instead, she was

a member of a loosely knit fellowship of Indians whose tribal an-
cestries were murky. Although she didn't look much older than fifty,
she had six children and twenty grandchildren and lived with her
husband in a double-wide mobile home in a location that she wouldn't
disclose, somewhere around Termo, *way out there.*

It was pleasant in the cabin. A warm, dry, desert wind was
howling outside, but it didn't penetrate through the well-chinked
walls. While Jessie strung her beads, I listened to the radio and made
a mental count of all the Indians that I'd met at random in the Far
North. Again, I thought about the separate and hidden Indian universe, a skeletal world that only an Indian could know about intimately or could touch.

Jessie talked about her compound. She had a propane tank and
a generator for electricity, but there was no phone and she didn't
want one. It was peaceful that way. Her adult children lived in other
states and wrote letters and visited during the summer, lodging in
other trailers on the property, and they all stayed up late at night to
gossip about things.

"It's not like in a city, where you live in a duplex and have to
worry about waking up somebody," she remarked, stringing beads.

In Oregon, Jessie's husband had owned a backhoe business, but
the stress of it had bothered him, so they came to California looking
for an easier life. That hadn't really worked out, she admitted. Jessie
had done some stints as a waitress and had picked some crops as a
fieldhand. Her attitude toward the state was mixed. She loved the
physical beauty and particularly the serenity of the desert, but she
thought that the taxes were too high.

Jessie said that she had learned for certain that the myth about
California magically being able to solve a person's problems was not
true.

Tears-in-the-Wind did paintings on cow skulls, going Georgia
O'Keeffe one better. Three skulls were on the floor, bright and
colorful, and I would have bought one if she had charged a little
less. You have to pay for inspiration.

"She never knows what she's going to paint," Jessie declared, with respect. "She has to wait for it to come to her. There's no plan. That's the way I do it with my earrings. It takes a little longer, of course, but I couldn't do it any other way."

SUSANVILLE, THE SISTER CITY TO FLORA, ILLINOIS, was boiling hot, with late May doing an impersonation of mid-July, so I went right into the Susanville Hotel as soon as I hit town and ordered a tall glass of iced tea. I had a second glass and took my tab to the cash register, where the cashier was eating a late lunch, chewing studiously on a big chunk of charred cow that flopped over the edges of his plate.

He was a heavyset Basque in his forties and had the torpid capaciousness that Basques sometimes have, a slow-moving, in-gathering quality. They were prone to melancholy, too, and the shepherds among them sometimes sang of their woe as they roamed the womanless mountains with their sheep.

Susanville had once been Rooptown, after Isaac Roop, a timber baron from Maryland, but Roop had changed the name as an homage to his only daughter, Susan, in 1854. There was still a sawmill in town, but it was having no better luck than the other mills around. The Susan River had already been reduced to trickle by the heat, and the streambed was chalky and dry. Cattle ambled through the desert searching for bunchgrass.

On the surface, Susanville looked like another economically depressed place of the Far North, a town that had not yet broken with its past to invent a future, but if you stayed for a while, you felt a buzz in the air, the shock of something happening.

Old Susanville, Roop's town, still existed, but it was confined to Main Street. Its spirit lingered in the Pioneer Saloon, a cavernous joint with the brands of cattlemen burned into a back wall. Old Susanville was a hair salon where two women were wondering what to do with the buffalo meat that their husbands had brought home from a hunt. It was E Clampus Vitus, a fraternal organization that had started in Sierra City in 1857 to parody all the other fraternal organizations in the state.

But while the Clampers were listening to their leader, the Noble Humbug, speak at their Hall of Comparative Ovations, a new Susanville was taking shape. Instantly identifiable California guys and gals formed its population, tanned and aerobicized and aglow with an odd conviction. They ate oat-bran muffins and drank smoothies made from organic bananas and had smart clothes and flashy cars and did the odd line of cocaine. They did not seem to be living *in* Susanville but rather in an idea *about* Susanville, in the California depicted on TV.

On a balmy Friday night, I watched Main Street turn into a boisterous cruising strip for kids of high-school age and a little older. Cars, trucks, and vans were strung along the avenue as far as the eye could see. The kids came from all over, from Termo, Big Valley, and Fall River Mills, driving for hours past ranches and cows to be part of the action.

As they inched forward with their windows rolled down, I could feel their tremendous yearning for romance, excitement, and sex, for all the grand experiences that they assumed to be available in a real city, in Reno, just ninety miles away.

In the new Susanville, the once-great distances of the Far North were being eroded. The sprawl of Reno, where tract houses were going up in a frenzy, had crept closer. There were people moving into Susanville who didn't know a band saw from a chain saw. They commuted to Reno for work and returned to such subdivisions as Susan Estates—an estate in ranch country!

Susanville was becoming a new kind of western suburb. Money was greasing the wheels, all the bucks being spent on real estate and new construction, but none of it fell into the hands of the millworkers, the wranglers, or the men who drove the lumber trucks. Money had torn a hole in the town's dynamic, and now rancor and alienation were afoot.

Crime in Susanville was increasing, for instance. Drug-related arrests and violent offenses were way up. The jail could hold forty-one inmates, but the average daily count was fifty-five. According to the local paper, the Lassen County Municipal Utility District Board "was facing grand jury accusations of willful, corrupt misconduct." The Salvation Army, short on donations and long on demand, had already shut down its grocery giveaway program for the month.

As part of its "Take Pride in America" campaign, the Bureau of Land Management had requested some civilian help in cleaning up Bass Hill, where residents were illegally dumping more and more junk—garbage, yard clippings, mattresses, old appliances, and the rotting corpses of deer, dogs, pigs, and cattle.

I gathered that the California prison system would be the ultimate beneficiary of the Susanville boom. The correctional center in town was currently oversubscribed and had recently been under a tight lockdown because of a war between two rival Hispanic gangs whose members would never have been in the Far North without the state springing for their fare. Almost 5,000 men were jammed into a facility that was supposed to contain 3,102 of them.

Alturas might have no work to offer, but at least you could sign on as a correctional officer in Susanville. It paid the highest hourly wage in the county, a flat $10.00, which compared favorably to $8.65 for a millworker, $8.12 for a truckdriver, and $5.75 for a secretary.

GOOD-BYE, SUSANVILLE, AND GOOD LUCK! Better to build yourself a squatter's cabin in the Diamond Mountains, I thought, and live on squirrel stew and blackberry pie.

Honey Lake, southeast of town, floated like a *fata morgana* in the ripply heat, its waters a puddle resting in a bowl of cracked and whitened alkaline soil. The entire Honey Lake basin was part of the Sierra Army Depot now. The U.S. military had many such installations in the state's wastelands, hidden from public view.

In the spirit of curiosity, I figured I'd take a look at the depot and left the highway for a two-lane road into Herlong, where the

tattered homes of army personnel were congregated. From the condition of the place, I deduced that Herlong most be very low on any
soldier's priority list, a duty station with all the plusses of a bus
terminal in Waco.

Ahead, there was a heavy-duty fence separating the depot from
ordinary human concerns. A woman in a guard booth informed me
that it was against military regulations, depot policy, and virtually
every tenet in every army security manual to admit an unauthorized
visitor wishing to see nuclear warheads, antiballistic missiles, and any
other pertinent hard- or software on the base.

I turned around. Herlong, I was thinking, what a pitiful town
you are, just blistered sand and G.I. rules, so far from the big picture
that the concept of "middle-of-nowhere" doesn't even apply, but then
I passed a plain house and there, sitting on what would have been
a lawn if lawns grew easily in the desert, was an elderly black couple
who looked as contented as people on holiday. They waved as I
slowed down, so I parked the car and walked up to them and saw
that the house was really a store of some kind, though I couldn't
guess what it might be selling.

Emma Brown rose from her lawn chair and gave me some
instructions. "You go on in and browse," she told me firmly. "Take
your time in there. Go on ahead."

Inside, the house/store was brimming with merchandise that I
would never need, not in an eternity, lots of metal trays and plastic
goblets, lava lamps and gurgling babydolls, toy trucks and paper
cocktail napkins printed with silly jokes, the sum of it made in
Taiwan, Hong Kong, and Sri Lanka. Nothing in the store was
singular. Every item came by the dozen.

I was fondling an Apollo moon-shot commemorative tumbler
when Mrs. Brown came in. "You've got some of everything in here,"
I said to her.

She laughed and explained how her husband used to go on
shopping sprees at wholesale outlets in Reno and Las Vegas every
now and then. The store was his hobby. The Browns had lived in

Herlong for thirty-eight years, long enough to feel as if they owned the town, and though they were retired at present, they liked to keep busy.

They had originally moved to California from Louisiana so that Mr. Brown could work at the army depot, and he had stayed with the work through the decades, while Mrs. Brown had raised their children, all eleven of them, nine girls and two boys, who were between twenty and forty-two. She was as proud of them as a mother could be. They were dispersed around the San Francisco Bay Area now and had solid, professional careers. There was even a Correctional Officer Brown.

Mr. Brown was still sitting quietly in his lawn chair, keeping to the shade. He studied the desert scrub and the electrified fences and listened to the cars going by and to the scream of military jets as they streaked through the sky. He'd had a stroke, Emma Brown said, and she hated to leave him alone. I was reminded of how we make up our world from what we have at hand, from the things that drop into our laps from the junkyard of existence.

Herlong wasn't my idea of paradise, but it had done all right by the Browns, yet I wondered if they didn't miss Louisiana.

"No way!" cried Emma Brown. "We love it here in California. I don't care a heap if I never see Louisiana again."

"Why is California so special for you?"

"Better opportunities," she replied. Then she added emphatically, "For black people! Down home, we lived in the country, and it was always hard times for us. We could *never* get ahead."

California, the land of opportunity: here it was again, the familiar refrain, but for the Browns the transformative possibilities of life on the Coast had less to do with geography than with an attitude, an openness. They had found a freedom that was unavailable to them elsewhere, and they had cherished it even in the raggedest desert, laboring to compound their accrued benefits and passing them on to their family, as did all good tenants on earth.

"How is it that your children have done so well?" I asked Mrs. Brown.

She deliberated for a time. "Well, I was around for them," she said. "That was one thing. I was there in the morning and after school. It was a lot of work for us, you know? But they never got away with *anything*. If they did something wrong, they heard about it. That's about all you can do, isn't it?"

"I guess so."

Mrs. Brown patted my arm. "That and saying your prayers."

So THERE I WAS IN RENO ON A SATURDAY NIGHT, across another border, lost in the pink palace of Circus Circus and gaping at some trained chimps as they rode their little motorcycles around a ramp inside the casino. *Bing, pop, ka-pow,* the casino was one big echo chamber of noise. Matrons from the hinterlands were plunging quarters into the slots, while croupiers in bargain-basement toupees kept a close eye on the dice rattling across the green felt.

On South Virginia Street, in the heart of downtown, the Susanville cruising scene had been magnified and pushed to its logical conclusion. Traffic was at a standstill as the young people conducted a rollicking gala on wheels, shouting at one another and trying desperately to score a phone number or a motel room number where the night's hot party would be going on.

They were in rebellion, I now understood, against the country through which I had just traveled—in rebellion against the shuttered mills and the crippled ocean, the distances and the wilderness and the difficult frontier. They wanted no more of forests, streams, or mountains and craved instead to be linked to another California, the one in which gratification was instant and orgasms were titanic.

A case could be made that the Far North really didn't belong in the state. As a distinct bio-region, it had more in common with its neighboring regions in Oregon and Nevada. In the past, there had actually been some attempts to dignify its apartness by granting it a new independence.

The Siskiyou Plan, for example, although it was never implemented, had yoked together seven northern counties as the state of Siskiyou. In 1941, Del Norte, Trinity, Siskiyou, and Lassen counties had merged with Josephine and Curry counties in Oregon and, as the state of Jefferson, had indeed seceded from California. There might still be a Jefferson if the Japanese hadn't bombed Pearl Harbor right after Secession Day. The brand-new Jeffersonians felt so bad and disloyal that they quit their bid for sovereignty and rejoined the United States.

I thought about the duffers of Fall River Mills and had a vision of the Far North's future. In the absence of any logging or commercial fishing, when the water was tightly rationed and the big cattle ranches were all but gone, other golfers might well be marching north and scaling any Modoc walls in their path to buy second or retirement homes and play on courses where the mills and the canneries had been. There would be more suburbs, and more prisons. The realtors would have a field day.

Ah, well. Cheer up, I told myself as I watched those dynamite chimps go round and round. In my hotel room, long past midnight, I unfolded my maps again and picked a road that would take me into the Central Valley, where I planned to begin the second stage of my wandering. May had turned into early June, and I'd been gone from home for about six weeks.

PART THREE

ELDORADO

I reached my hand down and picked it up; it made my heart
thump, for I was certain that it was gold.
—*James Marshall*

Buy land. They're not making it anymore.
—*Will Rogers*

CHAPTER 7

DAWN IN YOLO, CALIFORNIA, northwest of Sacramento. I was parked by a wheatfield to watch the landscape come alive. All along County Road 194, the earth was as flat as a Kansas prairie, and there were farms large and small. The first seasonal planting of corn was sprouting, row upon row of green seedlings that rustled whenever a rare breeze blew. The wheat tassels rustled, too, a grainy whispering. The sun blazed.

In the heat and the stillness, every sound stood out for me to hear—the hum of a powerline, the hiss of a sprinkler, the coughing chug of a tractor starting up.

Redwing blackbirds, dots of scarlet and shiny black, dipped into the fields and crooned some courting music in their electrical way. Driving slowly, looking, I saw tomatoes growing, then some strawberries and some beans. Sloughs and irrigation ditches cut through the farms. The oaks were hung with Spanish moss.

I passed old cars carrying fieldhands to work, Mexican men crammed in tightly, their faces stoical in the morning light. The cars were from out of state sometimes, from Texas or from Oregon. The men had on baseball caps or cheap straw hats and marched into imposing walnut orchards, where the trees stood in dignified columns, and into scrappier orchards of peaches and pears. In the distance, grain elevators climbed toward a sky that was a curious agricultural color, not blue or gray or bluish-white but a soft, hazy, brownish shade that echoed the tilled and furrowed soil.

In Yolo, I stopped for breakfast at a country store. It didn't have a coffee machine, so I grabbed a Diet Coke and a donut wrapped in cellophane. A teenage clerk quit sweeping the floor to ring up the sale. He was a snuffly boy who was putting in some time at work until he had to leave for school. It was early June, and he had to last through a couple more weeks of painful education before he would be free to lean on his broom all day.

"Can you tell me what's growing across the road?" I asked him, curious about a crop that I didn't recognize. I was in the Central Valley now, a new part of California, and I had new things to learn.

This boy was no help, though. He didn't know the answer and didn't want to know the answer. Talk of farming bored him. He moped by the cash register and hung his head, as if I'd caught him out at class, and finally he called to his boss, who was busy stocking shelves with canned goods—the Jolly Green Giant's processed version of the vegetables that were harvested from the fields around us.

"Customer has a question!" he shouted.

The boss was an overweight man with an apron tied around his ample waist. He had a bum leg and dragged it a little, and that caused his breathing also to be heavy. The twenty-foot walk was a nuisance to him, and when he got to the counter he fixed me with a baleful glare, implying that I had made a very bad mistake to disrupt his life so early on a Monday morning.

I was afraid that he might yell at me, but when I put my question to him, he relaxed, and the fierce energy flowed out of him.

"Why, it's barley, I believe," he said sweetly, as though he, too, were a schoolboy, the classroom expert stepping forward to claim a prize. It made him happy to be asked about the place where he lived and probably had lived all his life, to be posed a question that he *could* answer, something about Yolo and not about the huge world beyond it. Ask me another one, his grinning face was saying.

Outside, I unwrapped the donut. It had the texture of something you could bury for a few decades, then dig up and find in the same condition. I tapped it with my fingers—solid stone—before tossing it into a slough, fodder for the birds.

A pickup rolled by carrying two Sikh farmers, their hair coiled in turbans. They were staring intently at the heat vapors rising from the road. Already my car was sizzling to the touch. It was going to be the sort of day when careless girls in shorts got stuck to polyvinyl seats. The valley could be oppressively hot from spring right through until late fall. The horizon at dawn often turned a ruinous orange, as in the aftermath of a conflagration.

The Central Valley lay in a trough between the Sierra Nevada and the Coast Range, running for about 450 miles from Redding to a point just south of Bakersfield, where the Tehachapi Mountains began. Even in its widest sections, it was no more than 50 miles across. It had about 25,000 square miles of mostly level land and an ideal growing season that could last for up to ten months in some spots. The harvest months were almost always free of rain.

Before the first farms were plowed, the Central Valley was a grassy wilderness and home to five Indian tribes of the Penutian language family—Wintun, Maidu, Miwok, Costanoan, and Yokut. The Sacramento River used to seep up from its headwaters in the Klamath Mountains every winter and swamp its banks to form an inland sea. As the river receded in the spring, it left behind marshes cluttered with bulrushes and tule reeds. Oaks, willows, sycamores, and cottonwoods took root in the floodplain forest, and some of their descendants could still be found along creeks and streams.

Geographers often separated the Central Valley into distinct regions. The Sacramento Valley was the northernmost. It could be subdivided roughly in two. In its upper half, towns such as Orland and Corning were known for their almonds and their olives. The lower half, where Yolo was, had marshes and wetlands that were perfect for rice. Prunes, clingstone peaches, sugar beets, melons, and a host of other fruits and vegetables were also grown, along with wheat and barley.

The Sacramento Valley came to an end at the confluence of the Sacramento and the San Joaquin rivers below Sacramento. The rivers formed a crude delta where the farmland had been reclaimed at a considerable cost—the Delta region. Everywhere you saw dikes and levees to prevent flooding. The soil was a rich mixture of river silt and peat. Delta farmers brought in the most asparagus in the nation. They also grew celery, corn, tomatoes, potatoes, and Bartlett pears. There were some islands sown densely with corn.

Below the Delta was another region, the San Joaquin Valley, which was hotter, drier, uglier, and yet more fertile than its counterparts. Three of its counties ranked among the top-five farming counties in the United States, and the region as a whole ranked first among the nation's agricultural areas. Drop a seed anywhere and it would germinate, as long as the farm where you dropped it had received an appropriate share of irrigated water.

Irrigation was vital to the Central Valley, but it was especially vital to the San Joaquin. Its survival as a farming community depended on the Central Valley Project and the California Water Plan, a similar public-works operation of dams and aqueducts that the state had authorized and had begun building in 1947. The key dam in the CWP scheme was on the Feather River in Oroville, in the Sierra Nevada foothills. Without the water from both projects, the San Joaquin would revert to a subtropical desert.

As I pulled away from Yolo on County Road 194, I came upon a common sight in the valley, two shirtless men sitting on the bank of a slough and angling for catfish, enjoying the shade of some cottonwood while their magical stinkbait, spoiled chicken livers or aromatic cheese, worked its wonders down below. They were a California version of good ole boys, red in the neck and beefy in the arms. One of them would own a pit bull, I thought, and keep it on a short leash in a side yard of his tract house.

"That's a *baaad* dog," he'd say affectionately, if you asked him about it.

IN NEARBY MARYSVILLE, a Gold Rush town on the Feather River in Yuba County, I had a room near a gracious, leafy park. The motel owner was a former San Franciscan who'd left the city because the fog had stiffened his joints and had given him arthritis. He told me that with a straight face. He allowed that there was also some fog in Marysville, a soupy, ground-hugging layer of air born in the tule marshes in winter, but he claimed that it didn't affect him in the same way.

To bolster his case, he trotted out the example of a friend in San Francisco, another man so severely crippled by fog that he could barely walk.

"So he moved away, too?"

"He didn't have to. He cured himself with aloe vera pills."

I had driven to Marysville from Reno along a route that many pioneers had taken in the nineteenth century, around the northern tip of Lake Tahoe with its steely-blue depths and down through the Sierra Nevada. Along Interstate 80, the Truckee River had looked enticing, but I had ignored it because never, not ever, had I hooked a decent trout there in twenty years. It gladdened me to know that Edwin Bryant had also been skunked on the Truckee, back when nature was practically required by law to be bountiful. He had fished it twice in August of 1846.

"Not even a nibble compensated my patient perseverance," he wrote, in a little ode to dejection.

Bryant and his party had only recently pierced "the settlements of California." Their journey from Missouri had been momentous. They had kept up a rapid pace, covering at least twenty miles on

most days and forty miles on a few. The men had met various Indians
and had smoked tobacco in peace pipes. They had seen antelope in
herds of three and four hundred. They had shot deer, ducks, a wolf,
and a sandhill crane. Grizzly bears had disturbed their camp, and
they had eaten a puzzling stew containing some shellfish that Bryant
called "muscles." An insane man had leaped on them from his wagon,
and they had dosed him with an emetic.

Lastly, they had trekked across the great Salt Lake Desert in
Utah—"utter sterility"—and had rested by the Truckee before starting their descent from the mountains. On August 30, they paused
on a summit to view "the spacious valley of Sacramento" for the first
time. Said Bryant:

> A broad line of timber running through the centre of the valley
> indicated the course of the main river, and smaller and fainter lines
> on either side of this, winding through the brown and flat plain,
> marked the channels of its tributaries. I contemplated this most
> welcome scene with such emotions of pleasure. . . . I shouted to him
> [Jacob, a member of the company] that we were "out of the
> woods"—to pull off his hat and give three cheers, so loud that those
> in the rear could hear them. Very soon the huzzas of those behind
> were ringing and echoing through the hills, valleys, and forests. . . .

The Bryant party didn't dally on the summit. They were eager
for some civilized company and pressed on toward Sacramento.

Marysville was about forty miles north of the capital. The Feather
River formed a boundary between it and its neighbor, Yuba City, to
the west, a short drive across a bridge. The Feather could be an
impressive stream as it tumbled out of the mountains, but in the
valley it ran slow and green. To the Spaniards, it was *Rio de las
Plumas* because of the waterfowl feathers that were always swirling
on its surface.

There were eleven thousand people in Marysville, but it wasn't
likely to get much bigger. Developers were inhibited by the dikes

and levees on the Feather. They had to do their speculating in Yuba City instead, where many parcels of farmland were available.

Already Yuba City was twice the size of Marysville. It was habitable, but you'd never praise it for its beauty. It had once finished last in a poll ranking American cities on their virtues as a place to live. It had traffic, congestion, and every franchise under the sun. Among its famous citizens was Juan Corona, a farm-labor contractor and a mass murderer, who had hacked up twenty-five migrant workers and buried them by the river.

Subdivisions had started devouring the farms in Yuba City as early as 1924, when Jake Onstott had gone to a local bank with an idea to circumvent foreclosure on his spread. He carved the land into lots and sold them to some employees of the Pacific Gas and Electric Company. Onstott's farm became Garden Acres. Now there were Orchard Estates and Vintage Court and South Wind and Lincoln Park and Wildewood East. Commuters to the capital bought the houses in them, government clerks and petty bureaucrats, and so did military personnel from Beale and Mather air force bases, which were close by.

In Yuba City, you could drive down a suburban block, turn right, and wind up in an orchard. Marysville's streets were not so informal. The town was quieter and more conservative, Republican rather than Democratic. In the 1850s, it had been the state's third-largest city, a center for supplies that were sent to the gold miners in the foothills of the Sierra Nevada. From San Francisco, ships sailed up the Sacramento River to the Feather River, then docked and unloaded.

In the evening, I walked around the old downtown and admired the handsome brick buildings from the Gold Rush era. I imagined it in its prime, with brimming poker parlors and dance halls, and the spritely cadences of an upright piano for a soundtrack. A miner might treat himself to a bath in a claw-footed tub, washing away the dust of his camp, knock back some whiskey, stop in at a bordello, and top off the night with dinner at a fine Chinese restaurant.

The Chinese section of Marysville was once so thriving that it

rivaled the big Chinatown in San Francisco. Some of its buildings
were still standing, marked by aging signs or palimpsests on the
bricks—a Hop Sing Society and a temple dedicated to Bok Kai, the
River God of Good Fortune. Before the dikes and the levees were
built, Bok Kai was charged with the job of flood control. He had
handled the task successfully in China, along with averting famines.

IN CHINA, IN THE 1850s, California was known as the Golden Mountain. Immigrants from Kwangtung Province in Canton were the first
foreigners to enter the state in any number, running away from an
economy in shambles. They were packed onto ships and transported
in hideous filth to San Francisco.

A middleman frequently paid for the immigrants' passage and
indentured them to miners. They repaid the loan out of their minuscule earnings, often at a scandalously high rate of interest. In the
mining camps, the Chinese did pickax work. They broke rocks and
dug tunnels with such serene composure, never complaining, that
the miners called them "celestials."

When the boom phase ended in the gold mines, some Chinese
remained in the foothills and bought up claims cheaply. They were
able to scratch out a living where less diligent men had failed. Other
laborers moved south to the Chinatowns in Marysville and San Francisco, taking jobs in laundries, restaurants, and factories, and as ped-
dlers and domestics.

Pig-tailed Chinese houseboys were a vogue among city swells,
and most cigars in California were rolled by Chinese hands. In 1865,
Charles Crocker, a railroad baron, hired a fifty-man, all-Chinese crew
to lay track for his Central Pacific line and was so pleased with the
result that he soon had ten thousand celestials in his employ.

The Chinese advanced themselves by jumping at every opportunity. They worked on farms, in the shipping trade, and at lumber
mills, accepting abysmal wages that few white men would even

consider. By the 1870s, their secrecy, their numbers, and their willingness to do almost anything had the state in the grip of a Yellow
Peril. One popular book predicted that they would take over California by the end of the century. The Chinese were villified and
subjected to mob violence. Some were lynched, while others had their
houses burned down.

In the midst of the hysteria, the California State Senate convened
a committee of seven senators to gather testimony about the "social,
moral, and political effect of Chinese immigration." From its witnesses and self-styled experts, the committee heard that the average
immigrant paid between forty and fifty dollars for his steamer passage; that the average laborer in China made between ten and twenty
cents a day; that Confucius encouraged ancestor worship; that many
Chinese marriages were arranged by contract; that prostitution in
China was regarded as a profession, not as a sin; and that boys as
young as twelve had contracted syphilis and gonorrhea from Chinese
prostitutes in San Francisco.

A Mr. W. J. Shaw, who had spent either three or four months
in China—he couldn't remember for certain—alerted the senators
to the fact that Chinese children with bad habits were drowned by
their parents. The Chinese had no literature, Shaw said, and their
architecture was primitive.

James Galloway, a lawyer and a forty-niner, painted a black
picture of Chinese life in the mining camps, where, he insisted, the
men smoked opium, ate dog meat, stole from one another, consorted
with lewd women, and showed no moral concern of any kind.

"I am not much prejudiced against them," Galloway averred,
although under questioning he confessed that he'd written some
inflammatory articles about "coolie labor."

Some well-intentioned ministers testified that the Chinese could
be saved only through Christian education. Reverend J. H. C. Bonte
veered slightly off the subject to make some prescient remarks com-
paring the Chinese to the Japanese. He said:

They [the Japanese] seem to have an instinctive understanding of our institutions. I have read essays by even young Japanese girls, and they seem to have an instinctive insight into things as they are. . . . In dress and appearance, Japanese coming here try to imitate Americans. They stop at hotels . . . and live like Americans. I am utterly amazed at the difference between the Japanese and the Chinese.

Statistical tables brought before the senators indicated that immigration was on the rise again, with 16,085 Chinese going through the port of San Francisco in 1874, and 18,021 in 1875.

A clipping from the *San Francisco Journal of Commerce* was read into the record. It suggested that after the Chinese had overrun the Pacific Coast, they would spread their rule around the world, just as Attila, Tamerlane, and Genghis Khan had done.

Finally, some Chinese who resided in California were summoned to testify. They were reluctant witnesses, often tough guys and petty criminals in the employ of the tongs that worked as enforcers for various family associations. They sold opium, operated gambling dens, and ran girls. They had a bravado about them and knew how to stonewall.

Take Billy Holung, a saloon worker at the Pony Exchange. Senator Hayward interrogated him.

Q: How do these Chinawomen come here—the women who are prostitutes?
A: I don't know.
Q: Who owns them?
A: I don't know.
Q: Did you ever see any rewards offered for killing men?
A: Never heard of that.
Q: Do you know anything about Ah Quong being killed?
A: Yes, sir.
Q: What was he killed for?

A: I don't know.

Q: Who killed him?

A: I don't know.

Sometimes there was a bantering quality to the interrogation, as when Senator Donovan questioned Hong Chung, an inspector for the Sam-yup Company, a family association, who was becoming a legal citizen after twenty-four years in the state. Senator Donovan asked if other Chinese would follow suit.

A: Yes, sir.

Q: A great many?

A: Yes, sir.

Q: Will all become American citizens?

A: Yes, sir.

Q: And stay here?

A: Yes, sir.

Q: Will they become candidates for the office of Governor of the State as soon as they are citizens?

A: May be. I don't know. They are going to become citizens. I like to be citizen. American man make no good laws for Chinaman. We make good laws for Chinaman citizens.

Q: Would you like to be Governor of the State of California?

A: Of course. I like the State of California a long time; I like a free country.

Q: Would you like to be Governor?

A: I cannot be Governor. I like the State of California, and like to be a citizen of the American man's people.

When the committee had finished its deliberations, it put forth a mild, unenforceable recommendation that no more than ten Chinese should be permitted to emigrate on any ship. It had no effect on the swelling tide. Although the federal government passed a prohibitive Exclusion Act in 1882 that forbade Chinese laborers and their wives from entering the country and denied them the right to become citizens, the sphere of Chinese influence kept expanding.

The tongs, which were first formed in San Francisco in the 1850s, still rule every Chinatown in the United States. Anyone can join one by paying about thirty dollars. Each tong has a gang that does its bidding. A Chinatown is carved up block by block, and everybody knows which street belongs to which gang. The tongs' pursuits are the traditional ones of gambling, prostitution, extortion, illegal immigration, and drug dealing.

Among the Chinese in California today, there are pockets of immense wealth, but outsiders seldom see any evidence of it. All the gangsterish maneuvering in a Chinatown is invisible to them, deliberately so. Even the Chinese-language newspapers seldom report on Chinatown crime because too many people, including pillars of society, would be implicated.

Over the years, the fears expressed at the committee hearings have proved to be unfounded, though, particularly those of Senator Donovan. The Chinese account for almost one-fifth of the state's population, but there are only a few prominent Chinese politicians, and no person of Chinese ancestry has ever run for governor.

THE DREAM OF STRIKING IT RICH IS ENDEMIC IN CALIFORNIA, and those devoted to agricultural pursuits are not immune to it. For Carlos Zambello, the possible ticket to the moon was wild rice. Although consumers in the United States bought a pound of it about as often as they bought a new car, Zambello was not deterred. He knew that more and more Californians were wising up every day, turning health-conscious, and forsaking red meat for grains that were high in fiber.

Zambello, an Argentine by birth, operated the Wild Rice Exchange with some partners on Highway 99, outside Yuba City. He was a stocky man of almost forty whose brisk manner blended the scientific and the entrepreneurial. He presented himself as a busy executive with a full docket of appointments, but he had the social grace that came from good breeding and made a little time to talk with me when I got curious about his business.

In his office in a trailer, he sat me down and gave me some complimentary wild rice that he packaged under the Gourmet Valley label, along with some pamphlets filled with recipes. Another pamphlet offered history and anecdotes and explained that wild rice was not a true rice at all but rather the seed of a tall, aquatic grass.

Zambello was from the farm country north of Buenos Aires, at the edge of the Wet Pampas. The soil there had been exploited for over a century without being fertilized, he said, and it held no promise, so when he traveled to the United States as a foreign exchange student to complete his high-school education, in 1971, he became intrigued with his new country and its many possibilities.

Wild rice was among them. Indians harvested it on Leech Lake Reservation near Grand Rapids, Minnesota, the town where he was staying, but he learned that the traditional farmers of the region were seldom tempted to try it as a crop. They worried about the yield— it could never be predicted exactly because the variables were too great. Humid summers in the Midwest could ruin the rice with damaging funguses, and harsh winds caused it to shatter. In addition, the seeds were three times as expensive as ordinary seeds.

The wild-rice picture, then, was not very bright unless you transposed it to California, as Carlos Zambello had done.

On the Sacramento River floodplain, ordinary rice grew handily. The crop was simple to manage and clockwork in its cycles. Seeds were sown from planes in the spring, and farmers released water from dikes and wells to make shallow paddies. Mosquitoes were the bane of the paddies. Thirty-seven different subspecies could be isolated, including a malarial strain, but they were no bother to the rice. The harvest was in late summer. Special harvester combines built to slog over wet ground did most of the work. The rice was dried and stored in silos, and water birds ate the chaff.

Since the 1940s, when a professor from the University of California began growing a domesticated strain as a potential food for ducks, farmers on the floodplain had been experimenting with wild rice, banking on the mild climate and the virtually pest-free environment. Their efforts increased through the 1970s, and Zambello had joined them in 1986 by purchasing and refurbishing a dilapidated rice drier and a cobwebby warehouse.

His partners, who did the actual farming, stuck to a strict routine, he told me. Seeds were air-dropped from February through May, and they had a growing season of about ninety days. Wild rice couldn't tolerate any weeds or chemicals and germinated at a lower temperature than white or brown rice. Sometimes rice midges attacked the crop in the early stages, but there wasn't much to fret about after that. Once the wild rice was harvested, it had to be dried and carefully roasted. The precious seeds were stored in water at a temperature close to freezing.

The first year that Zambello was in business, he had made a killing on a bumper crop. He and a friend, Daniel Maohs, had devised a means to ship wild-rice seeds without damaging them, and he had sold about 7 million pounds of green, field-run product to marketers and processors in Minnesota—he had harvested 19 million pounds in all. Unfortunately, some competitors soon hit on the same innovation, and things were never quite so good again.

Zambello sometimes sounded frustrated when he talked about the obstacles facing him. Wild rice was costly and had an exotic reputation. In general, he said, Asians wouldn't touch it, and neither would Hispanics. People were confused about how to cook it, and about what to do with it once it was cooked.

Still, Zambello had his fantasies. Someday, he thought, the Wild Rice Exchange might be a tourist destination on the order of a Napa winery. He would call it the Old Rice Mill. It would have a tasting room for wild rice and a gift shop with T-shirts and the entire line of Gourmet Valley products. He had even gone so far as to hire an architect to draw up the plans, and he pulled out the sketches to show me. The Old Rice Mill resembled a Moorish palace crossed with a sand castle.

In 1986, that banner year, Zambello had believed that construction on the mill might soon begin, but he knew now that he would have to wait. He would have to be patient, as well, yet he was not without hope. He was in California, after all, where the transformations were always imminent and continuous and many a left-field scheme had turned to gold.

THE CHINESE WERE DISAPPEARING FROM MARYSVILLE, but new immigrant groups continued settling in the Sacramento Valley to take their place. Sikhs from the Punjab were among them. On Bogue Road one afternoon, I had to blink when in the midst of tract houses I passed a blue-and-white temple with minarets. It had the effect on me of seeing a mosque in Levittown. Christmas lights were strung about it, as though every day brought a reason to celebrate.

The head priest at the temple was called "Bengal," or so I heard his name when we talked on the phone. Bengal's English was heavily accented and hard to decipher. He agreed that I could visit the next day, but he neglected to tell me where to meet him, so I wandered about peering through doors until I came to one that opened onto a glossily waxed corridor. Some old men were sitting on the floor of a room at the end of it and drinking tea.

Bengal stood out from the others. He was still young. He had an intelligent face and eyes that burned. He wore a gold-orange turban and a silk pajama suit. He looked regal. Some kernels from a Chico-san rice cake were clinging to his scraggly, black beard, but he paid no attention and comported himself with great dignity. He had the proud, stiff-spined strut of a British colonial officer and paced a few steps before putting his hand softly in mine by way of greeting.

An old man fetched me a cup of tea. It was rich and sweet,

thickened with condensed milk, and I drank it in throaty gulps, following the example of the elders.

"That is how we do it!" Bengal said. His voice was both musical and exclamatory. He smiled brilliantly, as if the sight of me, a visitor from another planet, would never fail to delight him.

Sikhs had been migrating to such valley towns as Yuba City and Nicolaus for many years, Bengal told me, fleeing from the bitter turmoil of their homeland. They were often farmers, so they farmed in California, but poets and novelists were among them, too, as were turbaned gas station owners and proprietors of 7-Elevens.

Sikhism was known as a tolerant religion, I learned. Its founder, Gurū Nānak, was said to have lived first from 1469 to 1539, then until 1708 reincarnated as ten different gurus. His Alphabet of Teachings had a finely wrought humility. It taught that faith and contentment were the food of Angel-Beings, and that the world was a passing vanity. Sikhs didn't fast or believe in penances, and they didn't worship images, statues, or idols.

"How many Sikhs are there in the area?" I asked.

"Well, let me see. About six or seven thousand?" Bengal replied. Sometimes he tilted his head at an angle when he spoke and put an index finger to his chin, as if he were going to recite some verse.

He took me to visit the temple, leading me into a simply furnished bedroom and instructing me to remove my shoes. I prayed that my socks would be clean, and the prayer was answered. Next, I had to wash my hands at a sink. I held them under the tap for a minute or so and dried them on a towel that dangled from a child's pegboard, where the hooks for clothing were little plastic ducks.

"Ducks," I said, amused that they'd been incorporated so easily into an ancient ritual.

Bengal seemed to get a kick out of this. His eyes burned and flashed. "Yes, ducks!" he repeated with a laugh. "Really! They *are* ducks!"

"Is the weather here in the valley like the weather in the Punjab?" I asked.

"Yes!" he cried. "Exactly the same!" And did the Sikhs grow the same crops here? "Yes, yes! Same everything!"

At the temple door, a carton spilled over with orange kerchiefs.

"Cover your head, please," Bengal instructed, but he didn't show me how to wear the kerchief, whether to tie it like a babushka or fashion it into a turban, which I couldn't have done, anyway. So I just let it rest lightly on my head, rearranging it now and then to keep it from falling off. The kerchief smelled of incense.

Bengal pushed open the door, and we entered a large space that was like a high-school gym without the athletic gear. Tinsel and ornaments hung from the ceiling, but they had no special meaning. There were no chairs. During the prayer services, the congregation sat on the brown carpeting. Men and women were always kept apart. A throw rug was spread out before the altar, and a holy book was on it.

With a respectful gesture, Bengal directed my attention to the pictures of gurus on the walls. They came in neon colors, as if they'd been electrified from within, pierced by divine light. Their expressions were intimidating, and their features seemed exaggerated—ears, noses, and hunks of flesh. Bengal counted them off as we passed them.

"Number One, Number Two, et cetera," he said.

I ran the gauntlet of gurus holding the orange kerchief on my head. I had done stranger things in California, many times.

For a moment, Bengal turned serious and impressed on me that the temple and all its facilities were available to *any* person, Sikh or not. *Any* person could come to Bogue Road and be housed and fed for seven days, as long as he or she refrained from tobacco and alcohol. That was the only point that Bengal felt compelled to stress—not a religious point, surely, or an item of dogma. He had none of the zealot's urge to convert.

For emphasis, he said again, "*Any* person!"

The old men were still in the tearoom when we returned. I was curious about when the Sikh migration to Yuba City had begun, so

Bengal put the question to the eldest of the elders, who was about one hundred and twenty. The man's skin was as dark as a filbert and some of his teeth had gone to heaven. He had accessorized his turban with a brown Harris tweed sport coat.

"Ah, ah, 1906," he responded, though not with much conviction.

I was struck by how uninterested the old men were that a stranger was around. The way they sat and conversed, the subtle chatter and argument, the tea and the rice cakes—it was as if their sole mission in life were to perpetuate the texture and the traditions of a Punjab village in the new freedom of California, far from Hindu threats.

The old men slurped their tea. Not a head lifted as I put on my shoes. I considered staying on to talk some more, but Bengal seemed to be getting impatient, so I thanked him instead.

"I won't keep you any longer," I said.

Such bliss! Sublime! A transcendent grin! Bengal was glowing like one of the gurus.

THE SMALLEST MOUNTAIN RANGE IN ALL CREATION, the Sutter Buttes are the most significant landmark around Marysville and Yuba City. Although they rise to jagged peaks of only about two thousand feet, they dominate the level fields and farms of the Sacramento Valley.

In a Maidu myth, the buttes were said to be the result of an accident, dropped by the Great Spirit in his haste to build the Coast Range of mountains as a bulwark against the stormy Pacific Ocean. The Maidu believed that the souls of the dead came back to dwell here, at *Histum Yani,* and they revered it as a holy place.

Itinerant painters used to travel through the valley to do portraits of homesteads, and farmers almost invariably insisted that the Sutter Buttes be incorporated into the scenery, even if the mountains were not technically anywhere nearby.

A sink of twenty thousand acres fell along the northern and western fringes of the buttes. Waterfowl had always wintered in its permanent and seasonal marshes. The sludgy, poorly drained soil of Butte Sink made it worthless for farming, so the Department of Fish and Game managed it as an artificial wetland, filling it with well water and the water that ran off from the rice fields. That made for superior duck hunting, and the private hunting clubs of the valley were indebted. A proprietary membership at the most exclusive one could cost a million dollars.

I had hoped to hike around the Sutter Buttes, but a barbed-wire fence kept out people and cattle. I tried to imagine what the buttes would look like with a subdivision at their base. A proposal would soon go before the voters in Sutter County that would permit construction, if approved, of 625 houses on 1,172 acres. Cal-Ontario, the developer, had already started on a golf course. Its master plan called for a second course and also a resort hotel.

AS I WAS LEAVING TOWN ON HIGHWAY 99, I noticed a little farm stand by the road that looked so pure and unspoiled that I had to stop and restore my faith that all of rural California had not yet lost its flavor.

A woman was selling baskets of pretty strawberries that she had grown herself on a small plot of ground. For twenty years, she had been growing her special berries, she said, tending them with what I assumed to be a gardener's love of the earth instead of a craven agribusiness person's desire for profit, and with that belief in my heart I paid for a basket and buried my nose in the rich, up-floating scent of ripening fruit.

And the taste? Cardboard mixed with sawdust.

CHAPTER 8

WHAT A SWEET LITTLE TOWN Colusa was, all red-brick storefronts and creaky wood-frame houses with porches, a farming town still intact. Everybody was riding out a storm on the afternoon I drove through, waiting for the mottled thunderheads in the big sky above to break apart and deliver their blessing. A strong breeze had the leaves of the oaks and the black walnut trees along River Road rattling like castanets. The road was an old route to the gold mines and ran clear to Mount Shasta.

Down Main Street, ever Main Street, came a farmer crawling home on his tractor, its wheels caked with mud from the fields. Nobody pushed to pass him or gave him the finger. Colusa had good manners. There was a good quiet in town, too, a peaceful feeling that seemed to obtain in farming communities that hadn't yet lost their traditions.

Behind a supermarket, a Chinese man sat on an inverted blue-plastic, milk-carton box and blew smoke rings, perfect ovals, while the young woman beside him busied herself with her hair, re-arranging her new permanent every time the wind undid a few strands. All the stools inside the Sportsman's Club were occupied by sports who could be counted on to peek out at the purplish sky and decide that another round was in order, yes, indeed.

At the center of Colusa was a courthouse square, the kind of formal public space that you saw in Frank Capra films, those crazy American movies in which justice was always triumphant. The courthouse had been built between 1860 and 1861 in a deliberately antebellum style, with a portico held up by columns. So many of the town's early settlers had come from the southern states and had expressed such earnest, pro-Confederate sentiments during the Civil War that Colusa had earned a nickname, "the Little South."

Just as the thunder started crackling, a mother raced by with her baby swaddled in a blanket. She looked like a running back headed for the end zone and trying hard not to fumble. I took shelter in a gazebo where an old man was sitting with his two granddaughters. The girls had on light cotton dresses and were at an age when they seemed to be composed entirely of elbows and knees.

The wind was really whipping. It snatched the old man's Stetson from his head and threw it down, but he was on it in an instant and snatched it back.

"Funny how you can smell rain," he said, and it was true. I *could* smell the rain, an odor like no other.

The first drops fell then, and the sky burst open and dumped a ton of rain all at once, fat, nickle-sized drops falling down in a tumble. The girls were shy and giggly and didn't know for sure what came next, if the storm would end soon or whether it might never end and we would all be trapped in the gazebo forever.

The sensation was bracing. It made me remember thunderstorms out of the past, in other places, drenching downpours in the Tuscan countryside and incredible gulleywashers banging on the tin roof of my Peace Corps house in the Nigerian bush.

A good, hard rain stopped the world for a while. Somehow it put tender emotions into the heart, maybe because it scared us a bit and trimmed back our wishes to the basics—shelter, warmth, food, and human company. Storms were sexy, too, galvanizing the nerves and setting a kinetic energy to roaring through the vitals. The rain made you want to connect, to be joined to another as you were joined to the furies.

A taste of rain. Now I understood. After only a week in the heat and the torpor of the Sacramento Valley, I had a craving for something liquid, for the ocean and the coast.

THE RAIN SLOWED ME DOWN ON MY WAY TO MENDOCINO. Highway 20 was not a road to make any time on, not during a storm. Twilight found me unhappily holed up in Clearlake Oaks, in Lake County, in a cottage on Clear Lake. The towns on the lakeshore could be as isolated and depressing as any in the Far North. Work was just as scarce. Apple and pear orchards, some vineyards, a handful of cattle ranches, downtrodden resorts—that was Clear Lake.

Like the rain, Clear Lake held memories for me. Somebody had told me long ago, when I was an infant Californian, that the bass fishing at the lake was unbeatable, so my brother and I once made an excursion to it in a 1951 Hudson that he'd just bought. The car was the color of a dill pickle and had enough room inside for the Brady Bunch. The woman who'd sold it to him phoned every month to be certain that it still ran. The Hudson had belonged to her grandfather, and she seemed to feel that his soul had transmigrated to it.

How California, we thought.

Later, a robber in the Haight-Ashbury stole the seats from the Hudson, and we would drive it around sitting in armchairs. The slipping and sliding could be entertaining, but that was another story. As for the bass in Clear Lake, we never caught any, hooking instead such slum-dwelling species as carp and catfish.

The decline of Clear Lake was another chapter in the ongoing saga of California's fall from its princely place in nature. In the 1920s, the lake gained popularity as a family resort, but overfishing killed off many of the bass. Others were killed by the chemicals that were sprayed to control festering clouds of gnats. The water needed for households left the lake choked with weeds and deteriorating from the effects of a sewage system that was built as an afterthought. By July, Clear Lake was often awash with algae blooms.

Trailer homes were concentrated in the lakeside towns now, and that was the first thing you noticed—trailers everywhere, some dandy ones and some gross ones, their yards patrolled by an army of ceramic jockeys, gnomes, trolls, and sleepy Mexicans astride their predictable burros.

Retired people owned many of the trailers. They moved to Clear Lake because the living was cheap and the climate was fairly mild, but the isolation often drove them away. They left the care of their trailers to local realtors, who rented them to tenants on welfare or with substance-abuse problems, or those who were hiding out from a bad marriage, a bounced check, or the law. Bikers also favored the trailers and operated a prosperous methamphetamine trade out of labs in the woods.

In California, someone was always getting rich, even Hell's Angels and Satan's Slaves.

My cottage at Clearlake Oaks was a masterpiece of its kind, the 1950s preserved. It had knotty-pine walls decorated with framed, paint-by-number canvases of boats, kittens, and flowers. The kitties made you want to reach for your .357 magnum. The refrigerator was a Kelvinator. In the living room, a wicker couch was arranged invitingly next to an endtable scarred with cigarette burns. Two ashtrays appropriated from Harrah's Casino in Reno were set on it, along with a box of matches.

Relax, pal, the cottage seemed to say. Take off your shoes and light up a Chesterfield. Do a crossword puzzle, scratch yourself idly, or flip through the evening paper—but the paper only made me more tense. The lead articles were devoted to a teenager who'd been assaulted, illegal sewage spills into the Lakeport water system, and some lawsuits that had been settled on behalf of thirteen diners who'd contracted hepatitis at a Wendy's.

The log of the Clear Lake Sheriff's Department was mere lagniappe.

7:20 P.M. Lucerne woman reports a subject has been shot and is bleeding badly. Sergeant reports subject is en route to Lakeside Community Hospital.

7:28 P.M. Lakeport caller on 911 reports a possible suicide attempt using razor blades.

10:57 P.M. Clearlake 911 caller reports hearing what he thinks are gunshots fired next door.

11:07 P.M. Lakeport man reports two young abandoned children belonging to a known woman. Children placed with Child Protective Services.

The cottage. A fishy odor and the sound of water slapping against a dock. I bolted my door and went to bed at nine o'clock.

CHARLES STONE AND ANDY KELSEY were pioneer ranchers in Lake County. In 1847, they bought some land at the southwestern tip of the lake from General Mariano Vallejo, who controlled many big parcels in northern California and fathered sixteen children to help populate them. Stone and Kelsey hired some Pomo Indians to build them an adobe house and subsequently treated them like slaves.

The Indians and their families were subjected to sadistic bullying. The men were beaten, whipped, tied up, and hung from trees. The women were raped. The Pomo slaves were often denied any food. About twenty of them starved to death in the winter of 1848.

There was a tale about a young Indian whose starving mother had sent him to Stone's house, where her sister worked, to get some wheat. The boy's aunt gave him five cups wrapped in an apron, but

Stone ran down the boy on horseback, took away the wheat, and shot him.

The Pomo finally rose up in 1849. Five Indians went to the adobe house after the servants had secretly stripped it of weapons. They put an arrow through Stone's gut and stabbed Kelsey in the heart with a spear.

A party of soldiers from the federal government was sent to Clear Lake the following year to avenge the murders. The only Indians that they could find lived on some islands far from the site of the massacre, at the other end of the lake. The troops decimated them, anyway, using cannons, bayonets, and whaleboats. About a hundred Pomo died on Bloody Island.

A few Pomo still lived on a small reservation by the lake. I toured it in the morning. They, too, had trailers, and their yards were piled with the junk that Indians seemed to collect everywhere in the state—old tires, rusty auto parts, batteries in need of juice, stove flues, broken TV sets, and so on.

When I had first seen such yards up in Smith River and in Hoopa Valley, I had thought the Indians identified with the junk and viewed themselves as outcasts and castoffs. Now I believed that the Indians knew something that we didn't—something about the white man's world coming slowly undone—and that they also knew that the demand for, say, a 1952 Kelvinator refrigerator freezer coil might someday be worth its weight in gold.

The most logical explanation, of course, was poverty. The lives of the poor were miserable, even in California.

I left the Pomo and Clear Lake and drove over the Mayacamas Mountains to Hopland. The fields along Highway 101 were once planted with hops that were sold to breweries, but the hops were gone now and vineyards had taken over. Hopland was in the throes of a wine-grape craze. It had fancy wineries, trendy shops, and effete bed-and-breakfast inns—California as interpreted by a set designer, precisely the sort of place that Bruce Anderson railed about in his *Anderson Valley Advertiser,* the most controversial little weekly around.

•　•　•

BRUCE ANDERSON HAD NOTHING AGAINST GRAPEVINES, but he didn't like what they stood for. They carried connotations about class and privilege that went against his proletarian grain. Anderson was a throwback to the Old Left. He joined hands across the centuries with such other fly-in-the-ointment California journalists as Mark Twain, Bret Harte, and Ambrose Bierce.

Not for nothing did the *Advertiser* have a quote from Vladimir Lenin on its front page: "Be as radical as reality." Lenin's words were a bookend to a quote from Joseph Pulitzer on the other side of the page. "Newspapers should have no friends," Pulitzer counseled.

The *AVA* was widely read in Mendocino County and in hip enclaves around the state, but it also had subscribers in such far-flung liberal parishes as Greenwich Village, Minneapolis, and Madison, Wisconsin. Its approach to the news was literate, muck-raking, opinionated, and frequently off-the-wall, mixing high-school sports with gossip ("Shirley MacLaine's *Inner Workout* videotape, the latest New Age rage, is a hot item locally") and with slams at timber companies, politicians, and tourism.

Anderson was not related to the Walter Anderson who'd settled the valley in 1851. He worked out of Boonville, on Highway 128. The town had been a way station for New Age dropouts since the 1960s, when marijuana growers, midwives, dope casualties, psychics, artists in macramé, genuine organic back-to-the-landers, and others moved in and took the loggers, sheep ranchers, and apple farmers by surprise.

Bruce Anderson liked to pay tribute to Boonville's eccentricity. He would tell you that Charles Manson had lived there for a time, and that Jim Jones of the People's Temple had taught sixth-grade in Anderson Valley for two years.

Even the old-timers in the valley were a trifle strange, Anderson would suggest. Some of them could still speak Boontling, a language that the kids in Boonville had invented more than a hundred years ago so that they could talk freely in front of adults. Ed "Squirrel" Clements and Lank McGimsey were instrumental in spreading Boontling. They did their best creative work in the hop fields and at the swimming hole.

Boontling drew its inspiration from the town's actual life. A doctor, for instance, was called a "shoveltooth," because the valley's first resident doc had a protruding set of choppers. To be embarrassed was to be "charlied," after Charlie Ball, an Indian who was bashful. The Boonville constable affected a unique, high-heeled boot because one of his legs was shorter than the other, so if you got arrested, you were "high-heeled." Anybody who'd been thrown from a horse was "bluebirded," after the lad who'd once said, "I got bucked so high that a bluebird could have built a nest on my ass."

As an occasional reader of the *AVA*, I had formed an image of Bruce Anderson as a pugnacious fellow, but in person he was considerate and self-effacing. I thought he might have developed a gentle manner so as not to be physically intimidating. He was a big, strapping man closing in on his fiftieth birthday, and he looked as though he earned his living felling trees, not sitting at a computer.

I met him at his house outside Boonville. He and his wife, Ling, were saying farewell to a Norwegian foreign exchange student who'd been with them for the school year. Ling was a tiny woman about five feet tall. Anderson towered over her by more than a foot. They had been together nearly thirty years.

Bruce Anderson was a native Californian and had grown up in a large, struggling family in Marin County. His adolescence was so tumultuous that he got farmed out to the U.S. Marines for character adjustment. Afterward, he won an athletic scholarship to Cal Poly in San Luis Obispo, but he was more interested in history and the liberal arts than in engineering, so he transferred to San Francisco State, where he earned his degree.

In 1963, Anderson entered the Peace Corps in Malaysia. The job pleased him so much that he continued teaching there after his tour ended. He and Ling met and married there, and they had the first

of their three children, but soon Anderson got in trouble with the
authorities for agitating against the Vietnam War. He was accused
of associating with a clandestine Communist organization, had his
passport revoked, and was expelled from the country.

Anderson had remained an idealist. He and Ling had moved to
Boonville from San Francisco, where he worked as a cabbie after he
got home, so that they could buy a big, inexpensive house and take
in foster children. They'd taken in about seventy of them to date,
mostly black teens from the inner city. Anderson felt that they had
done more good than harm, but it bothered him that so many of his
wards wound up in prison. They were maimed in early childhood,
he said, beyond any attempt to heal them.

In 1984, Anderson bought the *AVA*, which was an ordinary
country paper, as an experiment to see what would happen if he told
the truth—*his* truth—in print. His editorials were often satirical or
sarcastic, and he loved to prick the balloons of pompous officials.
Babbitry he skewered with glee, but he tried not to hit anybody who
couldn't fight back.

The *Anderson Valley Advertiser* had a circulation of just 2,500
copies, but its clout in Mendocino County was significant. For example, Anderson had attacked the quality of public education in the
county with such bite that the superintendent of schools once confronted him at a public meeting. A scuffle broke out, and Anderson
ended up doing thirty-five days in Mendocino County Jail. He hadn't
minded so much, he told me, because he was in there on principle.

Vineyards were a recent crusade for the *Advertiser*. The price of
land in Napa and Sonoma counties, the choice wine-grape regions
in the state, had skyrocketed, so grape growers and vintners were
spilling over into Anderson Valley. In the past year, Louis Roederer,
the French giant, had set up shop to make a champagne-style sparkling wine, and other wineries were buying the last orchards along
the highway. The Navarro River, a salmon and steelhead stream
used to irrigate the grapes, was going dry.

Anderson worried that the wine crowd would have the same

effect on Boonville that they'd had on Hopland. The ranchers, the farmers, and the loggers would go. There would be tourists and a social scene. Land values would escalate, and the children of valley families would be priced out of their home territory. The valley would be transformed into another Hopland.

All is flux, the philosopher said, but I sympathized with Anderson. The next thing he knew, he'd have a bunch of shoveltooths on holiday messing with his beer. He might be hot-tempered and sometimes bullheaded, but he seldom lost his ability to laugh. I liked an editor who was bold enough to publish a Boonville kid's report about the annual marijuana harvest. The kid was his son, Robert Mailer Anderson.

Young Anderson, a dope neophyte, had happened on a moonlit group in the woods, who were listening to a Grateful Dead tape and inhaling the vapors from a pink ceramic bong. He had joined them tentatively.

"Anybody burns incense or gets naked," he wrote, "and I'm leaving."

HIGHWAY 128 TOOK ME OVER HILLS and through redwood groves along the vanishing Navarro River toward the coast. There I picked up Highway 1 and followed it north, enjoying the ocean air and watching the sky go dusky.

Albion, Little River, all the coastal villages on the highway had been connected to the timber industry at their inception. Every mile or so, on every creek, there was a mill and sometimes a narrow-gauge railway. Trains chugged up into the mountains and were met by ox teams hauling logs. The logs were milled and delivered to ships anchored below the ocean bluff through big chutes—a cascade of lumber, forests tumbling down to the sea.

Mendocino was Hopland intensified, rife with gingerbread Victorians and gay little shops, a Cape Cod imitation where the primary business was tourism. Most rooms were expensive or booked, so I drove on to Fort Bragg, a blue-collar town where Georgia-Pacific had a working mill, among the last around.

In Fort Bragg, it was simpler to find a tattoo parlor than a bunch of arugula. At one parlor, I studied the designs on display—a snarling panther, astrological signs, Jesus Christ in his Crown-of-Thorns—and wondered who bought them. The religious imagery sold to the Hispanics who worked at Georgia-Pacific, I was told.

I heard in town that the timber companies were cutting smaller and smaller redwoods, debarking them, and chipping them for waferboard, a material that was often used in tract-house walls. Along the highway, you didn't notice any clear-cuts, but if you drove along a logging road into a forest, you saw the scarred hillsides and the stumps and the deadfall.

Fort Bragg also had a commercial fishing fleet that was based in Noyo Harbor, at the mouth of the Noyo River. The fishermen were voluble activists, who were trying to save what they could of the fishery. They had lobbied successfully against a proposal to license offshore oil drilling, a major issue on the North Coast, and not so successfully against the sale of salmon habitat—water from spawning streams—to farms in the Central Valley.

The times were hard for working stiffs, really. They, too, were becoming an endangered species in California.

Some fishermen were making ends meet by donning wet suits and diving for abalone. Others were selling sea-urchin eggs to the Japanese, who prized them for sushi. The fisherman hired Mexicans to do the picking, because Mexicans were the only ones who *would* do it. The hours were weird, subject to the tides, and the rocks were slippery. The spiny urchins and barnacles could slash a picker's hands.

In the harbor, the trailers and the shacks of the Mexicans were sprinkled among boat dealers and some businesses retailing nautical gear. It was astonishing to think of some bloody-fingered kid from Guadalajara dozing there between shifts, while the *uni* he had gathered were being packed in ice for the long flight to Tokyo, and the redwoods were sleeping in the walls of tracts.

• ◆ •

MIKE KOEPF CAME FROM A FISHING FAMILY and knew the Mendocino coast as well as anyone. He was an old acquaintance of mine and met me for dinner at The Wharf, a waterfront restaurant, where the bar was jammed with fishermen drinking shots and beers and carrying on about the fish that were missing from the empty, blue sea.

As a child, in the early 1950s, Koepf had spent his summers in Noyo Harbor. His father had fished commercially out of Fort Bragg and Half Moon Bay, south of San Francisco, and had docked his boat at Noyo for the salmon season. The salmon were so plentiful then that Koepf could remember them stacked up three and four feet high on the floors of the fish-packing houses. He had slaved on the boats himself for eighteen years, but he was a confirmed land-lubber now and had written a few novels. Twice he'd run for a congressional seat in the county as an environmental activist, and had surprised himself by almost winning once.

Koepf had the Germanic temperament and was no stranger to brooding. A former Green Beret, he sat in a slump-shouldered way and gave off an aura of acute physical power. Ordinarily, he could be found at his old stomping grounds in Elk, another little town farther south on the coast, but he confided that he'd just got married again and had moved in with his new wife, Anne-Marie, in Fort Bragg. He was happy about the turn of events, but he had to shake his head shyly over the wonder of it all.

In California, the domestic permutations must be infinite, I thought. I doubted that Koepf had ever imagined that he'd have more than one wife, just as I had never imagined that my own marriage might end someday. How poorly prepared we were for what happened to us when we finally gave in to our yearnings.

We ate some fish and chips while talking about timbering and fishing, and Koepf was feeling so expansive after the meal that he invited me home to meet his bride. They lived in a quiet neighborhood on a hill above town that showed them a sliver of the ocean.

The houses down the block were workers' houses, older, compact, and unadorned.

Koepf had told me that Anne-Marie was a gypsy, but I didn't know whether or not to believe him. I would only recognize a gypsy if she were dressed in flowing silks and shuffling some fortune-telling cards, which Anne-Marie was not. She introduced me to her children from another marriage—marriages, ghostly and otherwise, were everywhere that night—and then Koepf and I went outside to watch the sunset.

I noticed immediately that something odd was going on at the house next door. On the lawn, a compact, burly, squat little man was pacing around and muttering to himself, while he kicked at some fallen leaves and snatched at the shrubbery. He seemed to be having an intense experience of some indescribable kind and was about to spontaneously combust.

"Hello, Joe," Koepf yelled to him through cupped hands.

Joe trotted over barefoot in a soiled white T-shirt and khakis. He had muscular arms and a broad peasant's back. He was a Portuguese from the Azores. In Fort Bragg, there were lots of Portuguese, Italians, and Finns whose ancestors had fished or worked in the forests. Joe himself worked for Georgia-Pacific and earned nine dollars an hour. He had been at the mill for fourteen years, but his English still wasn't very good, except for his swearing.

The stew he was in had to do with a formal letter that he had just received from Georgia-Pacific. He'd gone over it several times, but he couldn't read well enough to understand it.

"I bring it to you, Mike," he said urgently. "You read it for me. Okay, Mike?"

"Okay, Joe."

Joe dashed to his house and was back in a flash with the letter. It was typewritten on letterhead stationery in corporate legalese, but Koepf was able to decode it. In essence, a government watchdog agency had ordered Georgia-Pacific to inform Joe that he'd been exposed to some asbestos fibers around his work station.

"What it mean, Mike?" Joe asked, his brow knitted. He figured that he'd been fired.

Koepf held the letter at arm's length and looked at it in disgust. "You know what it means, Joe?" he said. "It means that you're screwed."

"What you telling me, Mike?"

"It means you should get a lawyer, Joe." Koepf was angry. He had seen such things before. "Get yourself a fucking lawyer and a fucking doctor. Get yourself a chest X ray."

Joe looked both stunned and anxious. "You shitta me," he said.

"No, Joe, I'm not shitting you."

"You shitta me, Mike."

"No, Joe." Koepf sighed in commiseration and counted wearily on his fingers. "One, get yourself a lawyer. Two, get yourself a doctor. Three, get yourself a chest X ray."

Koepf drew Joe into his house and poured him a shot of whiskey. We all had a shot of whiskey.

After the initial blow, Joe seemed remarkably calm. It was as if he'd been kicked in the head by a mule he knew was going to kick him. He'd been waiting for the kick all his life.

Koepf tried to apprise him of his rights, but Joe had no access to the world of doctors and lawyers and appeared to be frightened of it. The only news he had ever heard from a doctor or a lawyer was probably bad news, so he poured himself more whiskey, made a fist, and punched himself in the palm, over and over again.

"You shitta me," Joe said, pacing in circles. "You shitta me, you shitta me! What I gonna do?"

THE GEORGIA-PACIFIC MILL offered tours to the public, so I joined one in the morning, thick-headed from the whiskey and curious to see what life at the mill was like. Our guide was an emotionally restricted youth who had us sign a waiver absolving the company from all blame if we should be injured or killed on the premises. He handed out hard hats and earplugs and recited some statistics in a voice absent of inflection.

Georgia-Pacific had 650 hourly workers and 100 salaried workers. The company owned about 200,000 acres of redwood-type timberland in Mendocino County. The mill ran for eighteen hours a day.

In the millyard, a cogenerator was burning sawdust and bark, throwing off thick clouds that blocked the light. A truck stopped to dump a load of cedar logs. We entered the mill proper and walked up a catwalk to a big room where the debarking was done. A worker seated in a control booth enclosed in Plexiglas used a computer and robotics to do the job. Such new technologies had cut the workforce in most mills by about 30 percent.

A log dropped into a chute, and the worker pressed some buttons to maneuver a hose into place. It fired a stream of water that spun the log and stripped it of its bark. Chips of wood tore free and stuck to the Plexiglas. Under our feet, the platform rumbled. The noise was deafening, even with earplugs.

Another log dropped into the chute in a few seconds, and the worker repeated the process. He did this all day, every working day, and no doubt considered himself lucky. He had one of the highest-paying slots at the mill. A saw sharpener was at the top of the heap, and next came the chief sawyer.

The faces of the workers showed no feeling. They worked with precision, ceaselessly repeating the same tasks. The mill was far too noisy for them to carry on a conversation or to lighten the boredom with a joke. The saws and the machinery were a constant danger, so they had to be alert. In some ways, the mill was not unlike a minimum-security prison, except that you were released at the end of your shift. But as Joe had sagely said, "What I gonna do?"

BOATS ON THE OCEAN BLUE. I watched the fleet set sail from Noyo Harbor on my final morning in Fort Bragg. The fishing might be poor, but the calvacade remained commanding and imperious, an act of optimism in dark times. It needed an anthem, the tonal riches of a Sibelius. *Blue Horizon, Blue Pacific, Lydia, Janie W., Christina Marie,* the fleet drew your eyes away from the floating cigarette butts and the trailers with sheets and bedspreads pinned up to cover the windows.

Scruffy guys in rubber boots circled the harbor looking for a day's work as a deckhand—twenty bucks, twenty-five bucks, they'd go out for fifteen or even ten—and at night they'd blow their earnings at The Wharf and howl about the wealthy bastards who were buying up Mendocino County from Anderson Valley all the way to the coast, planting their vineyards, designing their fancy wineries, and building their mansions.

In the sky, real clouds, and clouds from the Georgia-Pacific mill.

CHAPTER 9

DEPARTING from San Francisco on October 18, 1846, Edwin Bryant, who had worked his way from the Sacramento Valley to the city, set sail for Sonoma in a cutter that belonged to the Portsmouth, a sloop-of-war. He was impressed by the little islands in the bay, Yerba Buena, Bird, and several others, not so much because they stung him with their beauty but because they were a snowy white from the copious droppings of waterfowl.

Bryant and his party reached the mouth of Sonoma Creek that night, and after a supper of salt pork and bread the men bedded down in the marshes. At daybreak, with a favorable wind and tide, they navigated the creek, landed at an embarcadero, and started hiking the four miles to town. Although it was early autumn, they experienced an intense heat as they walked. The hills framing the valley were overgrown with dry, brown wild oats and other grasses on which free-ranging cattle grazed.

In Sonoma, Bryant came upon the remains of a mission, its buildings reduced to a shapeless mud. The buildings—what was left of them—were grouped around a plaza that looked "dull and ruinous" in contrast to the picturesque countryside. The walls of the plaza had crumbled, and its fences had been trampled or burned for firewood. Its chief ornaments were the skeletons and skulls of butchered cows.

Securing rooms in the half-finished adobe house of a Mr. Griffith, a North Carolinian, Bryant tried to console himself with a good night's sleep, but fleas and vermin hounded him mercilessly. He thought that they were the result of Indian filthiness.

"Smallpox, erysipelas, measles, and scarlet-fever combined could not have imparted to my skin a more inflamed and sanguineous appearance," he declared.

His mood took a turn for the better when he paid a visit to General Mariano Vallejo, the town's most honored resident. Vallejo was a gentleman of superior taste and acumen, and his house was "scrupulously clean"—no fleas or vermin. It had sofas, mirrors, paintings, engravings, and even a piano. Moreover, Senora Vallejo was a knockout, possessing "in the highest degree that natural grace, ease, and warmth of manners which render Spanish ladies so attractive and fascinating to the stranger."

Later in the afternoon, while talking with a Mr. Leese, who had a vineyard, Bryant was given some grapes "as luscious, I dare say, as the forbidden fruit that provoked the first transgressions. Nothing of the fruit kind can exceed the delicious richness and flavor of the California grape."

The grapes were a special treat. Vineyards were not yet a fixture in the Sonoma and Napa valleys. Cyrus Young had probably planted the first, in 1838, on his Napa rancho, but the grapevines were just a hobby and had no commercial impact. Not until Agoston Haraszthy de Mokesa, an affable, idiosyncratic Hungarian count, arrived in Sonoma County did wine grapes have a true advocate.

Haraszthy came to California in a roundabout way, stopping first in Wisconsin, where he grew hops to make beer and got into trouble by trying to start a colony dedicated to free love. He fled to San Diego with his four sons, Attila, Arpad, Bela, and Geza, and reinvented himself, becoming the county sheriff and then a member of the state legislature in 1852.

When Haraszthy later accepted a post at the U.S. Mint in San Francisco, he planted some vines at Crystal Springs in San Mateo County, south of the city. They did badly and so did he. His superiors at the mint charged him with embezzlement, and though the charges were false, he had to move again and chose to settle in Sonoma because the soil and the climate seemed perfect for wine grapes.

He bought some property on the east side of town in 1857 and planted it with such select foreign varietals as tokay and zinfandel. In two years' time, he had 85,556 vines growing at his Buena Vista Winery. Chinese laborers had dug a tunnel into a hillside, and five thousand gallons of wine were stored there, some of it in redwood barrels. Later, the winery added real stone cellars that were constructed with the rocks excavated during the tunneling.

For the State Agricultural Society, Haraszthy wrote an article about practical viticulture that made him famous. Such information was difficult to come by, especially pertaining to non-native grapes. Readers from around the country besieged him with letters, pamphlets, cuttings, and vines, and, in a short while, Sonoma went from being a cattle boneyard to a clearinghouse for grapevines and viticultural information. Its nurseries were the primary suppliers of vines to farmers elsewhere in the state.

Traveling to Europe as an emissary of the governor, in 1861, Haraszthy sent home about two hundred thousand cuttings, a sample that included every major species of rootstock still found in California today. His luck went sour again after the trip, and he lost his land due to business reversals and escaped to Nicaragua, where he planned to grow sugarcane. He endured his last bit of misfortune there, drowning while he tried to ford a river.

Two of Haraszthy's sons, Attila and Arpad, had stayed behind in Sonoma, and they married two of General Vallejo's daughters, reaping the benefits of the superior breeding whose praises Edwin Bryant had sung.

In Haraszthy's global exchange of rootstock, there was a hidden menace—phylloxera, an aphid indigenous to the United States east of the Rockies. Phylloxera devastate grapevines by sucking on the new roots and inhibiting growth. Some phylloxera were accidentally sent to France with a shipment of cuttings in 1860, but they were not discovered for eight years and had entrenched themselves so completely by then that they decimated the wine industry. Many of the very best vineyards were lost, and the French were still recovering at the turn of the century.

Growers in California were hurt, too, but they also reaped some benefits from phylloxera. The bugs killed off any inferior vines that had been imported from Europe and did in the old mission grapes that the Spanish padres had brought with them. Farmers adopted a generic rootstock that was aphid-resistant and grafted varietals onto it, and the quality of their crop (and the wine pressed from it) started to improve.

To Robert Louis Stevenson, a visitor to the Napa Valley in the 1880s, phylloxera was an "unconquerable worm." He bemoaned the situation in France and cursed the fates that had deprived him of a chance to taste a great Châteauneuf-du-Pape or a true Rhône. He had been interested in wine all his life, he said, even in the raisin wine that a childhood mate had kept in his toybox.

Stevenson observed the farmers in and around Napa Valley and saw the same assiduous experimentation that had put Haraszthy on the map. They were always switching their vines from one spot to another, giving them more light or less water, searching like alchemists for the secret formula that would create a noble vintage. That would take time, Stevenson thought, but he felt confident enough about it to make a prediction.

"The smack of California earth," he wrote, "shall linger on the palate of your grandson."

IF, AT THE TURN OF THE CENTURY, Agoston Haraszthy were to come into Sonoma County as I did, following Highway 101 to Cloverdale, he would have been overwhelmed by the spread of vineyards. Along the Russian River, grapevines covered every inch of ground and were putting out a tendrilly tangle of lush, green leaves that had begun to obscure the trellises that supported them. They had crept up from the flatland onto the hillsides, capturing territory where sheep had always grazed. Prune, pear, plum, and apple orchards, once the agricultural mainstays of the county, were almost gone. Grapes had taken over.

This was a landscape I knew well—the pungent bay laurels and the smooth, reddish-trunked madronas, the many seasonal creeks almost dry now in mid-June, the pink-gilled mushrooms that sprouted each winter in a meadow on Chalk Hill Road, and the pair of Bullock's orioles, bright yellow, who used to set up housekeeping in a big black oak tree on our property at the start of every spring.

For five years, early in our marriage, my wife and I had lived cheaply in Alexander Valley, not far from Cloverdale, so that I could try to write. For two hundred dollars a month, we rented a double-wide mobile home on a fourteen-acre estate that was for sale. It had shag carpeting and walls so thin that twice I punched holes in them after being rejected by yet another editor impervious to my genius, but it sat on a hill above the Russian and often gave me, curiously, a feeling of peace such as I'd never had before.

In the valley, I felt that new eyes had been sunk into my skull. The processes of the natural world were inescapable, unfolding all around us in vivid slow motion. I saw things in brilliant outline, in Technicolor, and learned the names of plants and wildflowers and kept logs and diaries and lists that could be embarrassing in their simplicity when somebody stumbled on them. A friend once turned the pages of a birding guide, looked at the checklist at the back, and said, "It must have taken a lot of nerve to check off 'Robin.'"

I was not dismayed. To address the yawning gaps in my education was a gratifying experience. I understood that I would never be able to buy a piece of the valley, so I took to owning it in the only way I could, letting it penetrate my being and become an integral part of my California, of what California meant to me.

As for the writing, it went slowly, slowly, but I had lucky days when I was patient. Something of the calm, nurturing rhythm of farming sustained me, I think, and it didn't seem so terrible, while surrounded by grapes whose growth was barely perceptible, to work on a paragraph all morning, crumpling up page after page. My patience ran out sometimes, though, and when I reached my limit I would step outside for a head-clearing trip to the river. I walked its margins so many times that you could no doubt find my footprints imbedded somewhere, the fossil remains of a novice.

The Russian, too, had its moods. For much of the year, it ambled at a leisurely pace, but the winter rains made it swell in tumult and brought it to the tips of its banks. Flooding was not uncommon, and the land below our hill, an untended orchard where a few relic trees yielded some mottled, bug-bitten apples and pears, would vanish beneath the rush of muddy water. Then the storm would quit, the water would recede and clear, and the orchard would return.

The first warm days in May got the bass jumping in the river, and the fishing could be quite good, but it was the pursuit of steelhead that became my obsession. The steelhead had to make it past a host of threats, from sea lions to drift nets, to reach the valley, and the difficulty of their journey, the long, mysterious miles that echoed the progress of sperm, gave them a sleek, bright, undefeated quality. In the Russian, they were not very big, maybe six or eight pounds on the average, but if you hooked one, you felt the sudden shock of being connected to something wild.

So I would stand by the river, often in a chilling drizzle, and cast my line and hope. Hope was about all I had back then. In my mind, the hope of writing a tolerable sentence and the hope of catching a steelhead were of a piece, joined also to a grower's hopes that his grapes would be blessed as they ripened.

I loved Alexander Valley as well as anywhere I'd ever lived, and when it came time to go, I left it reluctantly, with the same sorrowing heart that marks the conclusion of any romance. More than a decade had gone by since then, and I was eager to see what had happened to the valley, if the sort of changes I'd witnessed elsewhere had touched it in any way.

ALEXANDER VALLEY IS AMONG THE MOST HIGHLY regarded viticultural regions in California, where about three-quarters of the wine made in the United States is produced. It runs roughly parallel to Highway 101 between the towns of Asti and Healdsburg. A strong walker can hike it in a day. Quite narrow at the top, it broadens considerably in its lower third, and on maps it bears an odd resemblance to South America.

The climate in the valley is ideal for almost any type of grape. The Coast Range to the west blocks the heaviest fog and the rawest weather. Winters are wet and sometimes cold, but frosts are rare. The summers are very hot but never humid, thereby keeping *Botrytis cinera,* a destructive mold, from forming on the vines. An unbroken string of dry, fiery days helps to raise the sugar content of the crop— a major advantage. In the wine business, sugar equals alcohol, and alcohol equals money.

Geyserville, where I left the highway, lay toward the middle of the valley. I crossed some old railroad tracks and drove over a bridge on the Russian River, surprised by how shallow and sluggish it looked. A canoer would already be scraping bottom in a few sections. It seemed too early in the season for the water to be so low, but then I realized that I was seeing the river from a new perspective. My journey had showed me where it fit in the great scheme of water distribution in the state.

Now when I thought about the rivers in California, I pictured them all flowing from a single tap that was turned on full force up in the mountains of the Far North, pouring out in a gush that lost some of its power in the foothills. In the Sacramento Valley, the water flattened out, and the Russian was its final trickle. All along the line, people were dipping into it with cups—farmers, ranchers, subdividers—more and more cups every year, taxing the resource beyond its ability to deliver.

In Alexander Valley, happily, the grapevines were still there. June was a quiet month on the vineyard calendar, a month of subtle growth, so the fields were largely absent of workers. The fruit on the vine was just beginning to bud, and when the buds flowered toward the end of the month, every farmer would cross his fingers against a damaging heat wave or a fluke rain.

After a couple of weeks, the crop would be set and not quite so fragile anymore. The main job in summer was to guard against anything that might hamper the grapes from developing—weeds, pests, too much or too little water. The harvest began in late August and continued into October, and it was then that a farmer earned his keep.

I could recall the first harvest that we'd lived through. One morning, with the dawn light, the vineyards around us filled with Mexicans, both men and women, working in teams. It was as if a secret signal had gone out while we were asleep. The workers used sharp knives with curved blades to sever the grape bunches from the vines. Then they put the grapes into plastic buckets and dumped them into the trucks hauling gondolas.

The valley roads were never busy, but during the harvest they bristled with traffic right through until dusk. From the fields came a rich smell of fermentation, slightly acid—a bloody ripeness. At the close of each day, tired fieldhands collected at the Jimtown store to replenish their vital fluids with copious cans of Budweiser, and Budweiser alone. Everywhere you heard the same refrain. "Crush is on," people said in Jimtown and at all the Healdsburg markets and saloons. It was a strangely volatile time, one that alternated between frustration and celebration.

Selling your grapes could be a tricky business, in fact. Naïve growers sometimes chose to deal with small, boutique wineries where the craft of wine making was revered. They wanted their own hard work to be reflected in the bottle, but the boutiques, while well intended, were occasionally slow to pay their bills. It was not unusual for one of them to go belly up, leaving cartons of elegantly designed labels to molder.

Other growers belonged to co-ops that marketed grapes to a variety of sources, but the biggest buyers in Alexander Valley and all of California were the Gallo brothers, Ernesto and Julio, whose headquarters were in Modesto. The Gallos could be counted on to pay promptly, but they played hardball. To get top dollar, a farmer had to bring his grapes to a Gallo winery outlet in Sonoma County when the sugar content was exactly right, up to a high standard. Sugar was measured on a Brix scale, by degrees. It happened that farmers sometimes hit the Brix just right only to have their trucks turned away at the winery because so many other trucks were lined up ahead of them.

We knew such a farmer in Alexander Valley, a cautious, serious-minded man who was proud of his grapes. After being turned away one afternoon, he parked his gondola at home, and the grapes kept ripening through the night and became sweeter and sweeter. At the winery the next day, his crop was downgraded to distilling material, or DM, the inferior stuff that went into cheap brandy and such fortified Gallo wines as Thunderbird and Night Train. It cost him thousands of dollars.

After the crush, farmers could relax a bit and watch the vineyards go through their autumnal show of color, the leaves dying in shades of red and gold. Starlings migrated through the valley in dense flocks and patterned the sky like buckshot. Pruning started around Thanksgiving, with workers shearing away the old canes and burning them in piles. In winter, the vines were dormant, but they leafed out in March, and the dance was on again.

Along Chalk Hill Road, there were a few new wineries whose architects had exceeded the boundaries of good taste, and a few new estates for weekending attorneys and dentists, but the valley had not changed very much in a decade. It was still a rarity in California—

a place where the land was valued for what it might produce and not for what might be built upon it—and so it had retained its integrity.

ON OLD REDWOOD HIGHWAY, where the redwoods are few and far between, I stopped for a hitchhiker, Luis Martinez, who had a small Samsonite suitcase at his feet that was bruised in many spots. A decal was stuck to it, like the old decals from grand hotels that travelers used to glue to their steamer trunks. It showed some palm trees against a blue sky, a picture-perfect image of what you might see while floating on an inflatable raft in a swimming pool in Los Angeles.

Luis, a carefree man in his early twenties, was going to the Greyhound Station in Santa Rosa to catch a bus to San Diego. He had a huge gap between his two front teeth and a little curlicue of a scar beneath his right eye. He couldn't have been much taller than five-foot-three, but he looked tough and durable, reminding me of certain Mexican boxers, bantamweights and flyweights who could always be counted on to last ten rounds.

He spoke some English, and I had a bit of Spanish, so we could communicate after a fashion.

"Do you like *boxeo?*" I asked him. "Julio Cesar Chavez?"

On hearing the great champ's name, Luis lit up and seemed to take a new comfort in his surroundings. He relaxed and told me that he had come north from a village about sixty miles from Tijuana for the grape harvest the previous autumn. He had two cousins in Sonoma County, and they had helped him find a job, but he'd been idle for a few months now and missed his family back home.

Luis liked my car. He liked everything Californian. It was a joke to him, all the wealth around.

"*Muy bonita,*" he said, touching the dashboard and letting a low whistle escape from his lips.

I could see that he was working on his memories, refining the sensations and descriptions of life north of the border that he would retail to his village friends back home. Hesitantly, not wanting to scare him, I asked if he had his legal documents. No, not really, he said—but he had thought about getting them. Mere intention held some valor for Luis.

Anyway, he believed that he would have no trouble sneaking into Mexico. The only hot spot would be the San Diego bus station, he said, where border patrol agents sometimes were on the prowl.

Santa Rosa was the county's big city, although it didn't look like one. Instead, it resembled a gigantic shopping mall with various subdivisions inside it. The population had doubled in the past ten years, leaping from fifty to a hundred thousand or so, and Santa Rosa, once a slow-paced country burg, had become a frenzied spot, with everybody rushing around trying to outwit the circumstance of being among the overpopulated.

The growth in Santa Rosa had been almost entirely unplanned, so the city had traffic problems, water problems, and serious problems with its overburdened sewage system. When the city's treatment plant was pushed beyond its capacity, the untreated sewage had just been pumped into the Russian River—a lackluster solution and one for which the appropriate state agencies had inflicted penalties. Downstream, in late summer, swimmers had risked colliding with tampons, condoms, and scraps of toilet paper.

About half the land in Sonoma County was still in farms and ranches, but they were fading fast, except for the vineyards. There were fewer chickens in Petaluma, fewer dairy cows in Valley Ford, and fewer Gravenstein apples in Sebastopol. Again, subdivisions were the culprit. Commuters who worked in and around San Francisco were buying into them and moving up from the city and from Marin County because they got more house for their money.

Right on Old Redwood Highway, the new houses and condominiums were piled up one upon the other, often so close together that you could literally stick an arm out a window and shake hands with your neighbor next door. They looked hastily built, too, as though the developer had packed up and left in a hurry.

As we went by one tract after another, I remembered a passage from Stendahl's *The Red and the Black* and later looked it up. In speaking of Verrieres, a lovely town in the Franche-Comté, the novel's narrator says that we might imagine that the inhabitants are consistently influenced by, and even enlightened by, the notion of beauty. In fact, though, every decision in Verrieres, down to the trees that were planted, was made according to a single principle, *yielding a return*.

The hastily built houses, the sewage in the river, the frenzy in Santa Rosa—they were *yielding a return*.

I pointed to a new home in an offensive color not yet named and said to Luis, "How'd you like a *casa* like that?"

He surprised me. *"Mas grande,"* he replied. Too big.

At the Greyhound station, he tried to give me three wrinkled dollar bills. I wished him good fortune in San Diego.

"Will you come back for the next harvest?" I asked.

All Luis could do was shrug, as though I'd raised a perplexing matter that could be answered only by the gods.

IN CALISTOGA, a spa town at the northern end of Napa Valley, east of Santa Rosa, I went looking for traces of Robert Louis Stevenson, who had turned up there in May of 1880. He was almost penniless, tubercular, and madly in love with his bride, Fanny Van de Grift Osbourne, a Californian.

They had met at an artists' colony in France, in 1876. Fanny was a married woman, but Stevenson had followed her to the states and pursued her from Monterey to her home in Oakland until she agreed to divorce her husband and wed him. They came to Calistoga for their honeymoon. Stevenson was apprehensive about the place. He felt that he had gone back in time, to an England of a century ago. There were outlaws about, he noticed, highwaymen who robbed the local stagecoaches.

The Mayacamas Range runs through Napa Valley, and Mount

Saint Helena, its towering peak at about 4,400 feet, is visible from almost anywhere in Calistoga. All around it, Stevenson discovered, were geysers and boiling hot springs. Miners had once worked the foothills for silver and cinnabar, but the mines had played out, and now there were many abandoned camps that were slowly capitulating to the usual ruin.

On the advice of a merchant named Kelmar, the newlyweds elected to squat at a camp where the Silverado Mine used to be, about nine miles from town. The altitude would supposedly benefit Stevenson's lungs, but he had an anti-Semitic streak and didn't trust Kelmar, a Russian Jew. He was also doubtful about Rufe Hanson, their escort to the camp. Hanson was a dimwitted hunter given to demon bouts of poker playing that caused him to be undependable.

Rufe Hanson put his charges on a stagecoach that went over the mountain to Lakeport, on Clear Lake. The Stevensons got out at the Silverado Hotel, an establishment on the brink of collapse. They were amused by its grassless croquet pitch made of hard-packed dirt. On foot, they climbed a trail that took them through an enchanting forest to their camp.

As Kelmar had warranted, the camp was deserted, but it was also a shambles. The mineshaft was still there, along with some chutes and platforms, but a film of red dust covered everything.

The Stevensons chose a trembly two-story building as their home. The ground floor had been an assay office and was littered with debris, part natural and part human, sticks, stones, straw, nails, and old bills of lading. This became the squatters' sitting room and kitchen. Upstairs, they found a bunkhouse with eighteen bare-frame beds and transformed it into their bedroom.

In the afternoon, Stevenson applied himself to making the camp habitable. He walked back to the hotel, got some hay, and spread it on two beds for mattresses. There was some fresh water dripping into a hole behind the mineshaft, and he deepened it with a pick and a shovel. He lit a fire in a blacksmith's forge in the evening, and he and Fanny sat by it waiting for Rufe Hanson to deliver their effects, which included a cooking stove.

Poker had apparently detained Hanson. He finally showed up about nine o'clock. He had brought the Stevensons' stove, but he had forgotten its chimney, just as Fanny had forgotten the keys to the locks on the packing cases containing their books and their kitchenware.

No heat, no food, no furniture, no plumbing, only a candle for light, and yet how tenderly Stevenson painted the scene in *The Silverado Squatters,* published in 1883. I read his book while soaking in a warm mineral pool at Roman Spa among some stout Baltic types who were playing chess on a floating board. The pools were fine by day, but they were truly wonderful at night, when steam rose from them in plumes, as though tension were evaporating from all the submerged bodies, dead cells and nagging worries burning away.

Stevenson's health did get better. His life at Silverado was simple, just Fanny and the lapdog Chuchu and an occasional visitor from such civilization as Calistoga could muster. He was the first to wake each day and made the coffee and the porridge, and then spent hours resting and reading, listening to the hum of insects and watching for the rattlesnakes that slithered through the chaparral.

His residence, even after some repairs, was half-house and half-tent. The elements penetrated it at will, with sunshine flowing through a hole in the roof to illuminate the tattered floor. But that was all right with Stevenson—he was with his beloved in a wild canyon of blooming azaleas and calycanthus, high up in the clouds.

Often as I soaked at Roman Spa, I'd close my book to look up at the buttes of Mount Saint Helena through a fringe of ornamental palm trees, thinking about Stevenson and Fanny. At Silverado, they must have experienced the same kind of seduction I'd undergone in Alexander Valley, the palpable splendor of California as a compliment to their romance.

Stevenson had appropriated a broad platform to use as a deck,

and he liked to pace it before going to bed, luxuriating in the near-
total dark and gazing down at the Napa Valley, "to where the new
lands, already weary of producing gold, begin to green with
vineyards."

THE AGRICULTURAL COMMISSIONER OF NAPA COUNTY, Nate George,
drove a car with grape clusters stenciled on its doors. He had an
office in Saint Helena, from where more cases of premium wine are
shipped than anywhere else in the state. He offered me a chair when
I dropped in on him and gave me a copy of his annual crop report
to look through.

The report showed how essential wine grapes were to the county's
economy and listed some new varietals that growers were trying out,
such as Grand Noir, Sangioveto, Flora, and Malvasia Bianca. They
were still experimenting in the vineyards, just as Haraszthy had done.

After that, our talk turned to real estate. There seemed to be no
way to avoid it in California. You could begin by discussing decon-
structionist theory or the San Francisco Giants, but sooner or later,
inevitably, your sentences slid toward property values, and you were
shamelessly throwing around phrases that you never expected to utter
in polite company, such as "curb appeal" and "adjustable-rate mortgage."

George, a Napa boy by birth, had just bought his first house, so
his interest in and depression about real estate was still strong. He
hadn't been able to afford anything in Saint Helena, of course, or in
Yountville or even Napa proper, so he now lived in Angwin, up in
the hills among some Seventh-Day Adventists, who had a college
there.

Saint Helena was the society town in Napa Valley. On the streets,
I saw immaculate hairdos and thin lips and restaurants that prepared
exuberantly priced meals unrecognizable to most Americans. At its
worst, Saint Helena could be as recherché as the old TV series "Falcon
Crest," which had been filmed not far away. I walked for three blocks

downtown and went by seven real estate offices. They all had full-color photos of fetching country homes and vineyards for sale. Here was a plain house on 8.8 acres planted to Pinot Noir that was priced at a mere $1,350,000. Here was a nasty house for only $160,000—not a fixer-upper, the realtor told me, but a knocker-downer on a buildable lot.

Napa Valley below Calistoga was Wine Country writ large, a Bruce Anderson nightmare, more than 250 wineries strung loosely together along Highway 29 and luring almost 2 million tourists a year from all over the world. The highway was bumper-to-bumper on most weekends and on most weekdays in summer. The wineries came in all shapes and sizes, from minuscule family operations where a geriatric crank doled out miserly thimbles of rank rosé, to baronial châteaus modeled on the grand estates of Europe.

In tasting rooms, hearty lads and gals dealt courageously with a diverse stream of visitors who were capable of saying the most absurd things possible about wine. Maybe it was the Cabernet Sauvignon that I was sampling, but at one winery I started hallucinating and heard people conflating their real estate talk with their viticultural inanities.

"Nicely herbaceous. Adjustable rate."

"Wonderful nose. Creative financing."

"Aged in oak yet affordable."

"A thirty-year fixed—buttery!"

Thank goodness for the trailer-park dudes who rolled in off the tour buses in a daze, hitching up their slacks and having at their hair with a plastic comb. Dragged forward by their wives, they were your basic Doubting Thomases and not about to be impressed by the monumental casks at Beringer Brothers, or by the Beniamino Bufano sculptures at Robert Mondavi. They knew what they wanted, and it wasn't wine.

I watched a young wine waif pour some Sauvignon Blanc for such a fellow, who was pining openly for his Barcalounger.

"Oh, I don't much like that," he said, making a face.

"Let me pour you some of our Chardonnay."

"I already tried it down the road."

"Every Chardonnay is different."

"Well, you couldn't prove it by me."

There were moments in Napa Valley when I felt that I was in a budding theme park, where the activity was orchestrated by unseen wizards in far-off places. The crunch of businesses devoted to *yielding a return* was so stultifying that I soon became numb to the humor I might ordinarily have extracted while passing the Vintage Inn or the Chablis Lodge or, worse yet, the John Muir Inn, where the rooms looked out on Marie Callendar's House of Pies.

EARLY IN THE CENTURY, when Europeans began settling in Napa Valley, they were often from countries where the growing of wine grapes was a tradition, such as Italy and Spain, home of the great *riojas*. In 1914, John Piña, whose forebears were Spanish, had bought some valley land and built up a business in vineyard management, tending vines for other people or supplying the labor for a job. Piña had died at the age of seventy, but his four sons had kept the business going and now worked out of a family compound on Shellinger Road, near Saint Helena.

John Piña, Jr., was one of the brothers. He was a bright, informed man, who knew about all the major trends in viticulture and liked the physical pleasure of being in the fields. He had played football in college, and though he carried a few extra pounds now, he still enjoyed hiking into the wilderness to hunt for deer and would pack out a carcass from the mountains even if it took him fourteen hours, as it had done on his last trip to the Nevada backcountry.

"A lot of people would have just cut off the head for a trophy," Piña told me.

We were sitting in his office, a plain room on the home place that nobody had bothered to enliven. It had a phone, a typewriter, and some filing cabinets. Farmers always resisted the idea that they should have an office, no matter how complicated their business was, so they seldom made the space comfortable enough to tempt them to linger.

Piña was a well-connected member of the community in Napa Valley and occupied a seat on the Farm Bureau's board of directors. I had visited him to see if he could help me solve a puzzle. The valley appeared to be booming, but all the trade journals reported that the wine industry might be heading for trouble.

The sales of wine had slumped, said the journals. Formerly hot items like jug wines and wine coolers had faltered. The start-up and production costs for a vineyard had gone off the board, and phylloxera were once again a serious threat. At the same time, the price of cultivated land continued to rise, up to $50,000 an acre in some areas. Grape prices were also rising. The best Chardonnay and Cabernet Sauvignon grapes were bringing about $2,000 a ton, a record for the valley.

We had a paradox before us, but Piña could explain it. The first thing to understand, he said, was that Napa Valley land only *seemed* expensive. By any world criterion for fine vineyards, the acreage was a bargain. In Bordeaux or Burgundy, if you could find any vineyard land for sale, it would cost you $300,000 or $400,000 an acre, and up to nearly $1 million an acre in a famous appellation.

On the other hand, the buy-in to the wine game around Napa was more costly than ever. The days of earning a profit on a five-acre hobby farm were over. The newest ventures in the valley were often funded by wealthy industrialists, corporations, and, naturally, real estate developers.

Foreign money was also making its presence felt, Piña said. The French had bought in and were going to produce sparkling wines by the champagne method, as Louis Roederer was doing in Anderson Valley. The Japanese were becoming important players. Sanraku had recently paid $8 million for the Markham Winery. Otsuka Pharmaceuticals owned Ridge Vineyards ($10 million), Kirin Brewery owned Raymond ($18 million), and Suntory owned Château St. Jean

($40 million). Heublein, the American liquor giant, had just paid about $300 million for two big wineries, Almadén and Mont La Salle.

Piña attributed the escalating price of grapes to better farming techniques and higher standards of quality. The University of California at Davis, south of Sacramento, was a pioneer in viticultural science, and its researchers supplied growers with data on everything from the proper rootstock for a micro-climate to the effect of sunlight on various fruiting vines. Every advance in technology upped the ante for a farmer, however, so a beginner, whether an individual or a corporation, needed deep pockets to survive.

I asked Piña how he felt about the growth in Napa Valley. It had been good for business, he said, and good for him personally. In harvest season, he was employing about eighty people, and his house was worth four times what he'd paid for it, in 1977. But with the boom had come new customers—gentlemen farmers. Some of them were the nicest people you'd want to meet, Piña thought, but some were merely arrogant.

"They think they're above you," he told me.

The new subdivisions that were encroaching on farms had caused him some problems too. If he went out to apply sulfur to some vines at two in the morning, for instance, when there wasn't any wind, he could count on the new neighbors to protest. They understood nothing about the special demands of grape growing, and sometimes they didn't care to learn.

On balance, Piña did not favor stricter controls over growth. He believed that it was always the new people who wanted to shut the gate behind them. Somebody would move from Los Angeles to Saint Helena, say, and immediately start pushing measures to protect the town's "rural" character.

To a native such as Piña, the notion was silly. Napa Valley hadn't been truly rural for decades. He had even written a letter to the editor of the Saint Helena paper expressing his opinion.

"How did the letter go?" I asked.

Piña looked bashful, but he quoted me a line from it.

" 'Apparently, you have to have lived here for less than ten years to know what's right for Saint Helena,' " he recited from memory, clearly pleased with the turn of phrase.

AT BUENA VISTA WINERY, I sat on a bench in the shade and fed three cloying cats who had sidled out of an ivy-covered fieldstone building in which Agoston Haraszthy had once made wine. The cats were cute and spoiled and had the well-fed look of pigeons working a blue-ribbon beat. They ate scraps from my turkey sandwich and begged for more, rubbing against my legs so insistently that I had to stamp a foot to drive them away.

And yet what a perfect moment! A bench in the cool shade, the light-dappled trees along a creek, the violas and the pansies spilling from planters, and a picnic for one consisting of a turkey sandwich on sourdough bread, an apple and . . . a *buttery* glass of Buena Vista Chardonnay.

Maybe you should never look too closely at anything in California, I thought. We had a paradox before us.

Wine grapes on the Russian River, in the Sierra Nevada foothills, in Lake County, in Lodi, Stockton, Modesto, and Merced. Wine grapes down south in Temecula and Santa Barbara and the Santa Ynez Valley. Wine grapes even in Yolo County, where speculators were buying up raw land in unfashionable Esparto, preparing the ground for goat cheese and second homes.

More acreage in the state was already planted to wine grapes than to apples, olives, peaches, pears, plums, and prunes combined. If you added table grapes and raisin grapes to the total, you had a crop worth about $1.5 billion annually.

In California, the gold, too, was subject to transformations and kept changing its shape.

CHAPTER 10

My CAMP on the South Fork of the American River was in a grove of oaks. In the warm evening air, observed by squawking scrub jays, the yentas of the forest, I set up my tent. The river was swift and riffly, but I took two small, hatchery-reared trout in minutes and made them my dinner. With a heel of bread, I mopped up some pan juices from the skillet, buried the trout bones so no birds would choke, and finished the last of the Buena Vista Chardonnay, my back against a log and my thoughts in the big sky above.

It felt good to be out in the country again, real country, after the bustle and the congestion of Wine Country. This piece of Placer County, toward its western edge, was in the Mother Lode, where the Gold Rush had burst forth and changed the course of history in California.

The Mother Lode was the single richest mining region in the days of '49. Many miners believed that it was an unbroken vein of quartz studded with gold that ran from Georgetown to Mariposa, near Yosemite, a distance of about 120 miles, but the vein was actually cracked and splintered and snaked haphazardly through a mineral-strewn band that was 2 miles wide in some spots and 200 miles wide in others. Gold was deposited in placers, too, in the gravel and the sand of riverbeds.

Traces of the earliest road to the gold mines could still be picked up around Folsom, northeast of Sacramento. It was nothing more than a pack trail before James Marshall's discovery, but the Argonauts had rapidly turned it into a superhighway. Men walked it on foot, thousands of them. Stagecoaches carried passengers and mining supplies. Mexicans trod it with flyblown, heavily laden mules, while Oregonians hitched themselves to teams of horses pulling covered wagons.

To get to the South Fork of the American, I had followed the modern roads that skirted the old one, starting near Folsom State Prison, a cell-type institution surrounded by stone walls, where about 6,741 inmates battled for 3,796 beds. I went past Mormon Island to Green Valley Road, and at Rescue I traveled north toward Four Corners. The foothill earth was an orangey-red, and the dry grasses caught and held the sun.

Then the river came into sight, and I pitched my tent, ate my dinner, and rested a bit. Now I was ready to face the dishes, washing them in a plastic bucket while a long-forgotten verse from an old miners' song about a drowned girl bubbled into my head:

In a cavern, in a canyon
Excavating for a mine
Dwelt a miner, forty-niner
And his daughter Clementine
O, my darling! O, my darling!
O, my darling Clementine!
You are lost and gone forever
Dreadful sorry, Clementine.

As I worked, I imagined how the foothills must have looked in 1849, throbbing with the energy of all the wistful souls pursuing the

Vast Unknown, men as avid for experience as they were for gold. The Gold Rush, as in adrenaline rush, was something not to be missed. In the mining camps and in the sudden, new cities that exploded into being like flares, the world's biggest party was going on, and the boldest, baddest, wildest, most free-spirited people around couldn't resist the invitation.

Those who made it to the mines and staked a claim often returned home with nothing to show for the trip but experience, their pockets still empty, but many of them seemed to have accepted their failure with equanimity. Tapped out and rueful, they'd shrug and say, "At least I've seen the elephant!"

The phrase was borrowed from a folk story about a farmer who was carting his vegetables to market and diverted his team to watch a circus parade. His horses were spooked by some circus animals, and they bolted and dumped his produce into the street, where it was trampled, but the farmer refused to cry over his loss. He appeared to be oddly happy, in fact, and whenever anyone asked him why, he shouted, "At least I have seen the elephant!"

So it was, too, with the forty-niners.

THE GOLD IN CALIFORNIA was whispering to dreamers long before 1849. Padres at the Spanish missions knew that it was around, but they discouraged their Indian charges from digging for it. Robert Jameson, a Scot and a mineralogist, published a report in 1817 that described an alluvial plain in the west where gold was scattered, but he gave no clues about the precise location.

In the late 1820s, a trapper named Black supposedly had a huge strike on the San Joaquin River, but some Indians killed him. His partner Smith, the only person in on his secret, vanished into Arkansas without telling anybody anything—shades of The Lost Cabin, all over again.

In Placerita Canyon, in what would become Los Angeles County,

Francisco Lopez pulled up some wild onions in 1842 and noticed flecks of gold clinging to the roots. Within days, miners from Los Angeles, Santa Barbara, and Sonora, Mexico, had descended on the canyon, but the deposits were shallow and scarcely worth the work. They were played out in less than a year.

James Marshall's find was the significant one. A carpenter from New Jersey, Marshall came west on the Oregon Trail, and in 1847, after some reversals as a rancher, he joined forces with Colonel John Sutter, a German who'd been raised in Switzerland. Sutter had constructed an adobe fort on a vast land grant of eleven leagues, or 48,400 acres, on the east side of the Sacramento River, where it debouched into the American. With winter coming on, settlers were thronging to the fort to wait out the snows before trying to make it over any mountain passes.

Marshall agreed to be Sutter's partner in building a sawmill on a separate land grant in Coloma, about forty-five miles away. On January 24, 1848, while workers were digging a tailrace, he caught "a glimpse of something shining in the bottom of the ditch." Years later, he recounted for a correspondent from the *Century Magazine* what it had felt like to touch the nuggets:

> There was about a foot of water running. I reached my hand down and picked it up; it made my heart thump, for I was certain that it was gold. The piece was about half the size and of the shape of a pea. Then I saw another piece in the water. After taking it out I sat down and began to think right hard. I thought it was gold, and yet it did not seem to be of the right color: all the gold coin I had seen was of a reddish tinge; this looked more like brass. . . . Putting one of the pieces on a hard river stone, I took another and commenced hammering it. It was soft, and it didn't break; it therefor must be gold, but largely mixed with some other metal, very likely silver; for pure gold, I thought would certainly have a brighter color.

The camp cook and laundress, Jenny Wimmer, devised a test to determine if the pieces were authentic. She dropped them into a pot of lye that she used to make soap. Real gold nuggets would tolerate the acid and still be intact in the morning—and in the morning, buried in potash, there they were.

Marshall hastened to tell Sutter the news. He brought about an ounce-and-a-half of gold with him. The partners hoped to keep things quiet, but it must have been tough on Sutter, who dealt in broad strokes. Ambitious to a flaw, he had a talent for the grand gesture, and that made him ideally suited to exploit the raw potential of virgin territory.

Sutter had arrived in New York in 1834, running from a painful marriage and some bad debts in Switzerland. He bounced from St. Louis to Santa Fe to Oregon and made voyages to the Sandwich Islands and Alaska before reaching San Francisco in 1839. In order to get a land grant, he became a citizen of Mexico, and Don Juan Bautista Alvarado, the Mexican governor, awarded him the property on the Sacramento. Alvarado had been having trouble with the Indians up north and also wanted an outpost there to keep his uncle, General Vallejo, from gaining any more power.

The local Indians, presumably from the Maidu tribe, were indeed a problem, all of them armed, war-painted, and looking hostile. Sutter believed that he might have been murdered by them if it hadn't been for his cannons and his big bulldog.

"When they came slyly near the house in the Night, he got hold of them and barked most severly," Sutter wrote in his memoirs, still appreciative.

The colonel soon had the Maidu in harness. He put them to work tending cattle, harvesting wheat, and serving as domestics around the fort. Some of them were inducted into his private militia and costumed in a white cotton shirt, blue trousers, and a red bandanna. Although they were sometimes paid a pittance in the unique money that their patron had coined, they were little more than serfs.

In 1847, as U.S. Indian agent for the region, Sutter submitted a tally of his colony, Nueva Helvetia, to the federal government.

Whites,	Male	218	Female	71
Indians, Tame,	Male	306	Female	173
Indians, Wild	Male	11,224	Female	10,649
Half-breed Indian Children	Male	3	Female	7
Sandwich Islanders,	Male	3	Female	7
Negroes,	Male	1	Female	1

The total population of Nueva Helvetia was 22,657, nine-tenths of it so-called wild Indians. The Hawaiians were souvenirs of Sutter's swing through the Sandwich Islands, and the single Negro was a barrelmaker imported to hammer the casks in which the patron's homemade wine and whiskey were stored.

As the only sociable kingdom in the north, Nueva Helvetia hosted any and all prominent visitors—Russian fur traders from Fort Ross on the coast, emissaries from the U.S. Navy, and guests of the French consular service. Edwin Bryant also stopped at the fort and praised Sutter for courteously providing his party, *gratis,* with beef, salt, onions, and tomatoes. He ate well at Sutter's table, as he had at General Vallejo's. He was served soup in china bowls, two meat dishes, and a dessert course of bread, butter, cheese, and melons.

"The day is not distant," Bryant intoned, "when American enterprise and American ingenuity will furnish those adjuncts of civilization of which California is now so destitute, and render a residence in this country one of the most luxurious on the globe."

The viability of Nueva Helvetia ended with Marshall's find. Word of it leaked out, and the fires were fanned. Sam Brannan, a hard-drinking Mormon backslider who was always looking for a score, dashed through the streets of San Francisco, where he published a newspaper, showing off a bottle of gold dust and shouting, "Gold!

Gold! Gold in the American River!" Brannan owned a general store near Nueva Helvetia and became the state's first millionaire.

In no time at all, the foothills were ringed with rough mining camps. There were about six thousand people living in the vicinity of the mines in 1848. Four years later, at the peak of the Gold Rush, there were about one hundred thousand.

The forty-niners spelled doom for John Sutter. Nobody would work for him anymore, not while the gold fever was raging. Squatters commandeered Nueva Helvetia and soon ran it into the ground. By 1852, Sutter was bankrupt. Ten years later, the state legislature presented him with a monthly pension of $250 as a sop for his losses, but he continued petitioning the federal government for the return of his land, even moving to a Moravian community in Lititz, Pennsylvania, to be closer to Washington, D.C. No California was Lititz!

James Marshall, who stayed put, fared no better. His minimal holdings slipped away, and he was transformed over the decades into a ragged, bitter old man, the town crank of Coloma, who supported himself with odd jobs and piecework, the pounding of nails and the raking of leaves.

IN COLOMA, at Marshall Gold Discovery State Historic Park, people were still looking for gold, or for its shadow. At nine the next morning, a lanky man in a bowling-team Windbreaker could be seen rushing from monument to monument and sprinting ahead of his wife, who shouldered a videocam and fell into step with me. Together we examined the replica of a Chinese store, where tinned herbal medicines crowded a shelf, and she was careful to point out to me the stuffed turkey that dangled from the ceiling by a cord.

"It must have been almost Thanksgiving," she said, confusing the celestials with the Puritans.

We paused at a miner's log cabin, and she pressed her nose to a dusty window.

"Look!" she shouted. "There's a little man inside!"

The little man was a dummy miner. He resembled Gabby Hayes stretched out for an autopsy, asleep for the duration beneath a cotton sheet. The woman's husband came along and interrupted us, fidgety because he hadn't yet found what he called "the actual site" of Marshall's discovery.

"Look at the little man, honey," his wife instructed him, filming his response. "How'd you like to live in there?"

"Better than a tent,' he said.

The little man didn't have it so bad, really. He had no mortgage payments and owed nothing to a bank. He had never even heard of curb appeal. Gold mining was much easier for him in Coloma than it would have been in Alaska or South Africa. The snow fell infrequently in the foothills, and there were fruit and nut trees. There were trout in the river and deer for venison steaks. The little man had a can of tobacco on a bench and doubtless some whiskey under his cot. He had his paradise.

Another song leaped into my mind, one that the artists and the bohos used to sing when they could still live cheaply around Monterey, in a time before the coming of the realtors:

Oh! some folks boast of quail on toast
Because they think it's tony
But I'm content to owe my rent
And live on abalone.

The woman's husband had found *the actual site*. "Yo, Judy!" he yelled. "The gold's over here!" They filmed a sequence of him standing by another monument, after which he held up some pebbles from the stream and pretended that they were nuggets. He did some digging with an invisible shovel and mopped his brow with a handkerchief, overacting like a star of the silent cinema. Then they got into their car and left, ready for the Gold Country's next attraction.

•   •   •

I drove highway 49 through the Gold Country for a week or so and made a few notes.

Some towns and mining camps of the Mother Lode: Gold Hill, Fair Play, Shingle Springs, Enterprise, Volcano, Fiddletown, Sutter Creek, San Andreas, Drytown, Felix, Tiger Lily, Calaveras, Pleasant Valley, Jackass Hill, Mokelumne Hill, Frogtown, Indian Diggins, Negro Hill, Coyoteville, Jesus Maria, Angels Camp, Bummerville, and El Dorado.

What you see in Mother Lode towns: retired people; new subdivisions and trailer parks; old frame houses with clapboards and gable roofs; porches where old dogs snore; quilts and rocking chairs; picket fences; taverns with card rooms; museums; gold samples sold in bottles, as jewelry, and in tiny, plush-lined caskets; ruins; mini-malls; renovated hotels with flocked wallpaper and an upright piano; chiropractors and acupuncturists; vineyards; biker girls in oil-stained jeans; and many images of miners on signs and on billboards kneeling, panning, or having a general hoot.

A thing to be avoided in the Mother Lode: the Mark Twain Center, a mini-mall in Angels Camp.

What the miners at Bret Harte's fictional Roaring Camp contributed to Cherokee Sal's infant son, orphaned at birth: a silver tobacco box; a doubloon; a navy revolver, silver-mounted; a gold specimen; a diamond breastpin; a diamond ring about which the donor, a gambler, remarked that he had seen the breastpin "and went two diamonds better"; a slingshot; a Bible (nobody would own up to giving it); a gold spur; a silver teaspoon; a pair of surgeon's shears; a lancet; a five-pound note drawn on the Bank of England; and about two hundred dollars in loose gold and silver coins.

Mark Twain, in Roughing It: "It was in this Sacramento Valley . . . that a great deal of the most lucrative early gold mining was done, and you may still see, in places, its grassy slopes and levels torn and guttered and disfigured by the avaricious spoilers of fifteen and twenty years ago. You may see such disfigurements far and wide over California—and in some such places, where only meadows and forests are visible—not a living creature, not a house, no stick or stone or remnant of a ruin, and not a sound, not even a whisper to disturb the Sabbath stillness—you will find it hard to believe that there stood at one time a fiercely flourishing little city, of two thousand or three thousand souls, with its newspaper, fire company, brass band, volunteer militia, hotels, noisy Fourth of July processions and speeches, gambling halls crammed with tobacco smoke, profanity, and rough-bearded men of all nations and colors, with tables heaped with gold dust sufficient for the revenue of a German principality— streets crowded and rife with business—town lots worth four hundred dollars a front foot—labor, laughter, music, dancing, swearing, fighting, shooting, stabbing—a bloody inquest and a man for breakfast every morning—*everything* that delights and adorns existence—all the appointments and appurtenances of a thriving and prosperous and promising young city—and *now* nothing is left of it all but a lifeless, homeless solitude. The men are gone, the houses have vanished, even the *name* of the place is forgotten. In no other land, in modern times, have towns so absolutely died and disappeared, as in the old mining regions of California."

COPPEROPOLIS, a foothill town in Calaveras County, was trying to revive itself from the dead. It had a population of one hundred and fifty, but that could change at any minute if the mining operation at Royal Mountain King Mine were to strike some serious paydirt.

Royal Mountain King was a high-tech, $62 million attempt to recover all the gold that the forty-niners had missed. The 2,100-acre property included the famous Madame Felix mining district—the Madame had once owned a stagecoach depot at the south end of Salt Spring Valley—and there were three open-pit mines in it that were being scoured and probed with the finest machinery available.

At its peak, Copperopolis had about two thousand residents. Its copper mines were among the most generous in the country. There were four hotels, three schools, two churches, and dozens of stores. Mark Twain had spent a reluctant night in town in 1865, waiting for a stage that would take him to Stockton. He'd been staying at a friend's cabin on Jackass Hill, doing some desultory surface mining, writing in notebooks, and studying French, but he had tired of the rustic scene and was eager to lodge again at the Occidental Hotel in San Francisco, which he called his "heaven on the entire shell."

I had an appointment with John Gruen, the president of Royal Mountain King, and he met me at his office promptly at one-thirty on a scorching afternoon. Punctuality was probably second nature to him. He was a scion of the famous watch family from Ohio. His teen-age son, Jonathan, accompanied him, and they were dressed alike in Izod shirts and khakis.

John Gruen reminded me of those amiable, principled eastern gents in the movies, who come to California unassumingly on a stagecoach and soon get the other half of their education. He was a former stockbroker and investment banker and had the happy buzz of somebody who had thrown off the shackles of the predictable to grab for the brass ring.

Gruen introduced me to Kim Witt, his director of safety and human resources, a title that baffled me. I guessed that Witt must hire miners and then do his best to keep them from being hurt. He was from Utah and had learned his mining around Park City.

Witt had a twenty-minute spiel that he gave to the mine's neighbors and opponents that demystified large-scale gold mining by framing it in homely analogies. The furnace where gold was baked into bars was like a microwave, he explained. He showed me some chalky lumps of cyanide in a Mason jar. The cyanide was used to extract gold from ore, he said, but people were afraid of it. They didn't understand its place in everyday life. Caterpillars gave off cyanide, and so did lima beans as they cooked. Anybody who smoked cigarettes inhaled massive amounts of it.

"I'd rather sleep with this jar than next to a propane tank," Witt revealed, and I pictured the two of them in bed.

After the instructional talk, we piled into a Blazer to look over the mine. The three open pits were very deep and wide, and bulldozers were gnawing at them. In the north pit, there were thousands of numbered blast holes with ash and debris around them. The subsoil had been sent to a lab for analysis. The forty-niners had prospected by eye, Witt said, and they'd been pretty damn good at it. The gold that remained was buried deep.

To get at it, Royal King had to move the earth. That robbed it of all vegetation, and the mildest breeze raised dust clouds. Dust turned up in your pockets and in your shoes. Water trucks circled and sprayed about five hundred gallons of water a day.

A loader and a hauler were working the pit. Gruen let it drop that the machines were not cheap. The loader was made by Hitachi and had cost about $1.3 million. That was a lot of money to sink into a speculative venture, Gruen implied.

It took four scoops of a big, toothy shovel for the loader to fill the hauler with dirt, sand, pebbles, and stones. Some loads were delivered right to the primary crusher at a fully automated gold mill. Although the mill was huge, it could be operated by as few as three men. One of them sat in a dark, cool computer room before TV monitors and a computer screen that informed him about everything that was going on at Royal King, from the blasting schedule to the crushing of ore.

We stood on a catwalk to watch a conveyor belt ferry some ore into the mill, where a series of progressively smaller grinding balls pulverized it. The residue would be sifted through, in one way or another, for gold. A good, rich, mineral smell accompanied the grinding. At times, a pungent, acidy smell of cyanide cut through it, and you could feel a scratchiness in you throat and your nose. Up to four thousand tons of earth cycled through the mill every day.

The doré bars from the furnace were stored in a vault. Each bar was about the size of a large loaf of bread and contained unrefined material—70 percent of it gold, 20 percent silver, and 10 percent other minerals. Behind the vault's many locks, a fortune of untold proportions might be slumbering.

According to John Gruen, miners in the Mother Lode had left about two-thirds of the gold in the ground—scientific studies had determined as much. But since the mill had started grinding and sifting about four months ago, Royal Mountain King had not recovered as much gold as projected. There were layers of copper blanketing the better deposits.

In spite of the chanciness of mining, Gruen seemed to be weathering his gamble well. Sometimes his face had the hopeful energy of somebody working a slot machine that might still pay off with three cherries. As we left his office, we ran into a solid wall of Mother Lode heat, and he offered to treat us to cold sodas. A vending machine nearby foiled him, though, and Jonathan had to take over and align George Washington's head with the secret motors scanning dollar bills.

We walked to our cars, sodas in hand, and Gruen remembered something.

"Hey, Jonathan? Did you get the change?" he asked.

Jonathan stared at his old man as if to say that fifty cents, plus or minus, was a meager sum to worry about when you'd already invested a share of the family's fortune in a gold mine. So Gruen himself went back to the vending machine, dipped two fingers into the coin-return slot, and came up with two quarters.

"Look," he said, smiling and displaying the coins on the palm of a hand. "Silver."

AT PARDEE RESERVOIR OFF HIGHWAY 49, outside Jackson, I thought to extend my camping streak, but the land around the lake was a gritty slice of Oklahoma. The trees were scrubby, sapless things trying to stay alive on the driest earth.

Pardee Dam impounded the Mokelumne River. There were many other rivers in the foothills, not only the Sacramento and the American but also the Mokelumne, the Stanislaus, the Yuba, the Tuolumne, and the Merced, and they were all dammed, too, forming a series of pools on the western fringe of the mountains.

The pools were needed to feed the growing cities of the Central Valley, places such as Lodi, Stockton, Modesto, and Merced. Subdivisions had also cropped up around them. They had names like Jackrabbit Ridge and El Dorado Flat and were pitched to pensioners on cable TV channels late at night and early on Sunday mornings, gold being mined from the Golden Years.

A verse from another song came into my mind, this one by the Gatlin Brothers:

> *All the gold in California*
> *Is in the middle of a vault*
> *In the middle of a bank*
> *In Beverly Hills.*

I decided to go on to Sacramento and splurge on a hotel, like Twain at the Occidental.

SACRAMENTO WAS ANOTHER GOLD RUSH CHILD. Settlers had cobbled it together between 1848 and 1850 from logs, bricks, glass, canvas, and sheet iron. At an embarcadero on the Sacramento River, ships from all over the world disgorged their motley passengers, who were often malnourished, lousy, filthy, sick at heart, and infected with various diseases that would fester and bloom in the opportunistic atmosphere of a California boomtown.

The ships that came up from San Francisco carried a less traumatized human cargo because cabin passage was expensive, about thirty dollars. There was no guarantee of a return trip, however, because gold-smitten crews sometimes made their own way into the Sierra Nevada to see the elephant themselves.

Store owners in town raked in their profits in little sacks of gold dust. Prices changed by the hour, reflecting an economy whose outer limits had yet to be set. A hammer could cost you $10 and a pickax $20. Butter was $3 a pound. A quart of milk and a shot of whiskey were both a dollar—woe to the man who had to choose. A nice hotel might run to $50 a night, but some miners cut deals that let them toss their bedroll on a bench, or on the floor to bunk with the roaches.

Bugs were a bane in unhygienic Sacramento, and remedies were traded freely. One household manual of the period advised that you could get rid of flies by mixing black pepper, brown sugar, and cream, and leaving it out on a plate. So awful, infested, and foul-smelling was the city's first gambling emporium that it became known as the Stinking Tent. Inside it, miners drank, played poker and euchre, and bet on anything that moved. The Stinking Tent's success bred imitators such as The Gem, Mansion, The Empire, and, of course, The El Dorado.

For more genteel entertainment, the miners queued up at The Eagle, California's first theater. A repertory company put on such plays as *The Bandit Chief; or, the Spectre of the Forest* and *Love in the Humble Life*. The men seemed not to care very much about the caliber of the productions. They came to look at the female members of the cast and applauded boisterously at the rare sight of any woman. They were an antic crowd, and when the river flooded the theater in winter, they were apt to shove each other in.

By 1850, the year California was admitted to the Union, Sacramento loyalists were pushing for their city to be the state capital, but that January an exceptional storm washed away many of the buildings on the embarcadero. Citizen volunteers dammed the sloughs and made some levees as the water retreated, but then a fire raged through the city and devoured the structures of canvas and wood.

In the autumn, a boat called the *New World* arrived bearing the seeds of a cholera epidemic that sent most people scurrying into the hills for safety, and the new legislature chose to convene its initial sessions in San Jose, the former Mexican capital of Alta California.

The legislators were not happy with the choice. They couldn't find any decent places to live. They felt that their lackluster adobe capitol was beneath them and sometimes repaired to the parlor of a nearby house for meetings. They dressed in denim and flannel and India rubber coats against the rain, echoing the style of their constituency. At their desks, they chewed tobacco, spat, and whittled. Liquor was dispensed liberally.

Still, the politicians earned high marks from Hubert Bancroft, the historian, who commented, "All were honest—there was nothing to steal."

Don Mariano Vallejo, who was the wealthiest person in the state, asked the legislators to consider moving to a site on San Francisco Bay and promised to put up $370,000 for a new government complex. He hoped to name the town Eureka, but the recipients of his generosity were so overcome that they insisted he name it after himself instead. General Vallejo failed them, though, and did not complete the project to their satisfaction. At their first meeting, in 1852, the men had to sit on nail kegs and console themselves with frequent trips to a saloon and a bowling alley in the basement.

They moved yet again the next year, selecting Benicia as the new site for their deliberations. Benicia was on Carquinez Strait, a channel between San Pablo and Suisun bays. Gossip had it that the legislators picked it because the Young Ladies Seminary was located there, a fact of prime importance in California, where men still outnumbered women by about ten to one.

In 1854, Sacramentans launched a sneaky campaign to wrest away the capital. About two hundred of them rolled into Benicia before the first congressional session and rented all the available rooms in hotels and boardinghouses. The stunt worked, but what really swayed the legislators to vote for still another move was simple bribery. Votes were always for sale, and there was a rumor that fifty thousand dollars had been paid for a vote at least once.

For a time, the legislature met in the courthouse in Sacramento, but in 1856 a bill was passed to fund construction of a new capitol, Corinthian in style. Labor disputes dragged on for years, and the first session was not held in the building until 1869—an event that was graced by the presence of Emperor Joshua Norton of San Francisco, the self-appointed Ruler of the United States and the Protector of Mexico.

Emperor Norton's grasp of reality was slight. He had gone bankrupt trying to corner the rice market and had snapped after that, donning a vaguely military uniform to perform the duties of the offices to which he'd assigned himself. He wore a hat with a plume, and his two dogs, Bummer and Lazarus, always went with him on his rounds.

In Sacramento, the emperor decreed that the new capitol was just fine, but he was angered by the dirty streets and ordered that they be cleaned. There is no record of how he felt about the gilded copper ball that was hoisted into the capitol's dome two years later.

"Our fair state," read an inscription on it, "may its bright name and reputation remain as bright and untarnished as this golden ball."

FROM MY ROOM AT THE MARRIOTT HOTEL, I could see the capitol dome through some leafy trees. Tour groups were milling on the lawn, and after breakfast I shuffled with them through the corridors of power and admired the restored chambers of the treasurer and the secretary of state. The furniture and the fittings in ivory, brass, marble, and mahogany suggested a lost grandeur, even a time when society had been orderly and reasonable instead of unruly and daft.

Sacramento had the steady, sluggish moods of its namesake river. Nothing seemed to move expeditiously through its channels, not legislative bills or traffic. Some of the downtown streets were blocked to form a mall for pedestrians, but at night the mall was empty save for the homeless who camped there, often drugged or drunk. Government clerks and petty bureaucrats used the mall by day to pick up sundries or to grab some lunch. They were people on a budget and sat on benches or on the lawns around the capitol to eat.

Adam was a congressional aide in his late twenties, who'd been working in government since college. He had been a true believer at first, but now he subscribed to the familiar theory that politics was the art of the possible and came to work in cheap suits from Mervyn's and talked about buying a Harley-Davidson and riding around the West.

"Half the time, things get boiled down to their lowest common denominator," he told me on the afternoon that we met, while standing in line at a sandwich shop.

In the evening, over a beer, Adam gave me his view of politics in California. The state was so big, he said, that a politician needed to be a personality in order to survive. Issues counted, but only a handful, like water, were pertinent everywhere. The north and south were really two different countries. At the capitol, you still heard jokes about drawing a dividing line at the Tehachapi Mountains, a plan first concocted during the Civil War.

Adam saw four major constituencies at the nucleus of the political scene—the San Francisco Bay Area, including Oakland and Berkeley; metropolitan Los Angeles; the southern sunbelt that revolved around Orange and San Diego counties; and the Central Valley. Mrs. Albaugh was correct, I saw, in saying that the Far North played a minimal part in the affairs of the state.

The most populous area was the southern sunbelt, where almost half of all Californians lived. They tended to be conservative and middle-class. San Francisco stood for liberalism, activism, and a flakiness that could be totally unpredictable. But in Los Angeles, you had an explosive melange of rich and poor. Voters there were often divided by race and by class. Agriculture and the Central Valley were synonymous, although the new suburbs were altering that pattern a little, pushing it in the direction of sunbelt values.

"What do they think of Jerry Brown in Sacramento?" I asked.

"They try not to think about him," Adam said.

Jerry Brown, our Governor Moonbeam, was the person that most Americans singled out as the symbol of a California politician. He was not very popular on Capitol Hill or among his fellow Democrats. What people disliked about him, Adam felt, was his arrogance. He wanted to play the insider's game while appearing to be above the fray. Yet Brown was contrary enough to be intriguing. He had an honest passion for his causes and a hint of genuine idealism. The same blend of Buddhism and seminary logic that infuriated the veteran pols knocking back bourbons at Frank Fat's held some appeal for the wide-eyed young.

In his days as governor, Brown had wrapped himself in self-denial. He had shunned limos for an old Plymouth and had slept on a mattress in a small apartment rather than in the gubernatorial mansion, cribbing his political style from his earlier life as a seminarian.

His father, Pat Brown, a former governor himself, had once sketched a fascinating psychological portrait of his son for an interviewer. He mentioned three factors that motivated Jerry—failing the bar exam on his first try, being dumped by a college girl friend, and his time in the novitiate. Jerry was essentially a loner, he said, who might never get hitched.

"It would be tough on the dame if he got married," Pat Brown had speculated. "He certainly has no inferiority complex. If the door opens, he'll grasp it and go through it."

With his contradictions, Brown seemed to embody the vicissitudes of the state, but he belonged only to the north. The south had its own symbol in Ronald Reagan. Old Dutch was the Ultimate Californian—tall, tanned, handsome, and sunny, a fine swimmer and a former lifeguard, an accentuator of the positive, somebody who ignored bad news, who was fit, narcissistic, and so unwilling to show his age that he still dyed his hair to mask the snowy white.

Reagan had Golden State charisma. He could take an assassin's bullet, rise from his hospital bed, and soon be back chopping wood at his ranch above Santa Barbara. Like his predecessor, former U.S. senator George Murphy, the first modern California actor-politician, he had used the presidency of the Screen Actors Guild to propel himself to the top. He was a red-baiter and an arch conservative who had learned to moderate his stance in public. As governor, he had railed against wasteful spending and ranted about the lefties in Berkeley. On the environment, he sided with the miners and the lumberjacks.

"If you've seen one redwood," he said once, "you've seen them all."

During my time as a Californian, a ballot initiative and not a politician had affected the most change, however. On June 6, 1978, the state's voters had passed Proposition Thirteen, a measure that amended the constitution to limit severely the amount of property taxes that local governments could collect. If you had bought a house before 1978, your tax bill was fixed at that level and could never be increased.

Cities, counties, and special districts had suffered an immediate loss of about $7 billion annually. Proposition Thirteen was so drastic that such corporate giants as Atlantic-Richfield, Bank of America, and Southern California Edison had opposed it, fearing the effects on the business economy. Some people were convinced the proposition was at the root of the bankruptcy California might be headed toward.

The closed libraries, the shuttered clinics for the mentally ill, the outdated textbooks in the public schools, even the homeless around the capitol—Proposition Thirteen was a contributary cause of them all, at least to some degree.

One afternoon as I stretched out on the capitol lawn talking with Adam, I looked around at the assembled faces of government workers, black, Asian, and Hispanic, and realized how much change was still in store for the state when these new faces began to have an impact on the electorate.

"What's in the political future, Adam?" I asked.

"The future?" He laughed and plucked at a blade of grass. "Arnold Schwarzenegger."

GOING HOME. The Fourth of July weekend lay ahead, and I was returning to San Francisco for my break before heading south to the San Joaquin, Los Angeles, San Diego, and the Mexican border.

I took the scenic route along Highway 160. It followed the Sacramento River through the peach and pear orchards of Freeport, Clarksburg, and Hood. Set back from the floodplain were some handsome old Victorian houses that had a quality of permanence denied to the tracts that were spreading inexorably from Sacramento to Silicon Valley, linking towns and villages together into a new megalopolis whose projected population was expected to top 9 millon by 2010.

Past Courtland I went and past Locke, a Chinese hamlet of the Gold Rush that brought back memories. There, many moons ago, a friend had taught me to catch crawfish by baiting a trap with dog food. The mud bugs foolishly crawled in to dine on MPS chunks and later we dined on them, a bounty unsuspected, soaking the crawfish in milk overnight and boiling them in a big kettle with bay leaves, salt, peppercorns, and lemon slices.

Lunch at Williams's Big Horn in Rio Vista, maybe the most curious restaurant in the state. It was part short-order grill and part Museum of Natural History. Old man Williams, long deceased, was a big-game hunter who had stalked trophy game across Africa, one step ahead of Ernest Hemingway, killing many species of animal now endangered or extinct. Their taxidermied heads and carcasses were mounted on the Big Horn's wall, so that you sometimes locked eyes with a dik-dik or a gazelle while you were chewing on your burger—a disconcerting moment, at best.

To the east of Rio Vista stretched the cornfields of Brannan and Bouldin islands. Here the San Joaquin River merged with the Sacramento and became a single, mighty stream that gradually widened into Grizzly, San Pablo, and San Francisco bays. The open land was disappearing, swallowed by lookalike suburbs, Antioch, Pittsburgh, Concord, and Walnut Creek, and soon there was nothing at all to see but houses—big houses, small houses, crummy houses, and terrific houses, houses fully paid for and houses mortgaged to within an inch of their lives.

Houses everywhere.

My own house in San Francisco, a Craftsman-style bungalow built in 1913, was the first we'd ever owned. It stood on one of the steepest hills in the city. At the hilltop, there was a warning sign that showed a big semitruck going down our street at a frightening angle. Next to the truck was the word *Hill,* beneath which some wit had scribbled "No shit."

It was the house's precarious position that had made it cheap enough for us to buy in 1982—although, in California real estate circles, "cheap" is a relative term.

Waking early that first morning at home, unable to stop the forward motion of the road, I left my wife in bed and went out for coffee. A contingent of elderly regulars was already making the rounds. They were familiar faces to me, old-timers in Noe Valley, our neighborhood. They'd seen it go from a blue-collar district to a gentrifying enclave of younger homeowners and had survived the changeover from American cheese and salami to goat cheese and andouille sausage.

Through a Mediterranean haze, I looked downhill to the shimmery blue of San Francisco Bay. The city could be achingly beautiful on the cusp of summer, its pastel colors ideally wedded to the season.

William Brewer had mistrusted the mild weather on his initial visit to San Francisco in June of 1861. He found the climate "healthy, very healthy, lovely" but also monotonous, a drift of feathery days that undermined the work ethic and induced a soporific laziness.

To Brewer, a Yankee raised on Puritan values, San Francisco seemed to pose a moral threat. He regarded it as a dangerous place where delicious but unconscionable things might occur. From the balmy air, he took a troubling hint that the afterlife might not be any more rewarding than the life he was currently leading.

Had Brewer stayed for another month, he would have felt differently, I believed. By mid-July, winds from the northwest would be pushing the punishing heat of the Central Valley toward the coast, where the warm air would collide with ocean vapors, sucking the cool moisture from them and creating the city's trademark fog. Summer in the city could be a mockery, really. I had once worn a pea coat to a barbecue on the Fourth of July.

The miracle mile in Noe Valley was Twenty-fourth Street, a shopping strip both utilitarian and frivolous. Most stores were not open yet, but some workers were unloading crates of organic produce from a panel truck parked by Real Foods. They were the star actors in a cosmic California vegetable pageant that played daily at trendy groceries in the city, and they had costumed themselves accordingly in earrings, shredded Levis, and pirate bandannas—an outlaw band in revolt against iceberg lettuce.

Some San Franciscans felt so virtuous in the presence of tofu, kelp, and unsprayed guavas that the ambience in Real Foods could be weirdly precious and cultlike. On occasion, I had fantasies about starting a Fake Foods nearby, where the carrots would be irradiated and the cook would spit into the soup, but much more often I quietly joined my fellow effetes in paying top dollar for tomatoes that tasted like tomatoes. In my lifetime, the genuine had become a costly item.

A young Japanese man came dancing down Twenty-fourth Street in the blossoming light. He was crew-cut and had on a bop suit with a little plastic Ornette Coleman saxophone dangling from a cord around his neck. He was ready to break into some spacey jazz licks at any minute, courting inspiration as he passed store windows that displayed such esoterica as Iranian caviar, strings for steel guitars, and ponchos from Argentina.

The sight of him was refreshing after my journey to the hinterlands. He was part of what gave San Francisco its unique character. Whether you liked it or not, anything at all could come at you from around a corner. Many Californians didn't like it and projected their fears onto the city. It posed a moral threat to them, as it had done to Brewer. They rejected its liberal attitude, its tolerance, its chaos, and the wild diversity of its population.

All the wishes and the emotions that were secret, hidden, repressed, or quashed in such places as Termo or Yolo or even Sacramento were freely available, even in Noe Valley. Having been away, I recognized again what an island San Francisco was, adrift in the great sea of California. Just as I had been drawn to it while I was groping toward a dimly glimpsed future, so, too, did others flock to it for refuge and companionship.

The gay teenager from Nubeiber, the Hupa devoted to *film noir,* the woman in Fort Bragg wanting to master Indonesian cookery, they cycled through our hub in a dauntless effort to become themselves. The city was willing to take in every misfit Californian, as well as misfits from elsewhere—the wounded, the defrocked, the intellectually adventurous, and the sexually prurient—and it bound them together into a community that somehow managed to work. That was its genius and its salvation.

On Twenty-fourth Street, I came to an upscale coffee store and stopped for a cappuccino. The owners had put a bench out front, where you could sit in the sunshine and let your mind wander. The bench had never been crowded, but something had happened during my absence—it had been discovered, and every seat was taken. Customers were leaning against cars, too, and colonizing the front steps of an apartment building, propping up an entire coffee-drinking scene.

What had once been singular was now plural. The experience of bench sitting as it *used* to be, before anyone knew about the bench, could not be conveyed to the new arrivals, who probably held a misguided belief that they *were* bench sitting, even though many of them were not technically *anywhere close to the bench!*

As I waited in line behind a turbaned man in Birkenstocks, and smelled the rich coffee aroma, I thought to myself, Here's the dilemma of California in embryo.

SAN FRANCISCO WAS YERBA BUENA FIRST, a village on the bay at Yerba Buena Cove, where wild mint, the "good herb," could be harvested.

The village had fewer than forty residents as late as 1846, but it grew quickly after that into a densely populated city complete with a razzle-dazzle cast of international characters such as the Sydney Ducks, a ready-made criminal class exported from the penal colonies of Australia. Eventually, it would spread itself over forty-three hills and forty-four square miles to become one of the most elegantly situated cities on earth.

From its infancy, San Francisco was prone to disasters and had a tendency to burn. Arsonists weren't capable of resisting the thrill of torching its redwood buildings. Six major fires roared through the business district between 1849 and 1851, culminating in the Great Fire of May third, whose dimensions were spectacular enough to merit a Currier & Ives lithograph that showed landmarks like the Apollo Saloon going up in flames.

Saloons were an integral part of life in the city. It was a brawling town that also offered gambling houses, bordellos, opium dens, and bull-and-bear fights. The streets sometimes had the raucous energy of a polyglot fraternity party gone amok, but you could escape from the riffraff by skipping into a hotel and enjoying a civilized, first-rate meal of French, German, Italian, or Chinese cuisine.

San Francisco after dark was not for the timid. Questionable cats such as Billy Holung prowled the alleys of Chinatown, while the

Sydney Ducks committed mayhem on the main boulevards. A vigilante group, the Hounds, had assigned themselves the task of routing
the Ducks, but they often drank too much, forgot their mission, and
instead beat up poor, shanty-dwelling miners from Peru and Chile.

Throughout the 1850s, Gold Rush fortunes were made in San
Francisco on the sale of mining supplies and general merchandise
and by providing transportation to the foothills. People struck it rich,
too, while practicing the budding art of real estate piracy. On the
western frontier, pioneers had simply laid claim to acreage, but land
was at a premium in a compact city, and the selling of "town lots"
became the local equivalent of three-card monte.

Documents pertaining to title were scarce, so a fast-talker such
as Sam Brannan could grab two hundred lots just by vowing that
John Sutter had deeded them to him—Sutter, lost among the Moravians, had no way to disagree. The most heinous realtors sold lots
on a landfill of garbage, junked furniture, sand, whiskey bottles, and
the timbers of sunken ships. The lots were destined to sink into the
ooze.

Shipping was among the chief industries in early San Francisco.
There was a large fleet of fishing boats, as well, and a prosperous
construction trade. Jobs could also be had at the sugar refineries
where California sugar beets and Hawaiian sugarcane were processed.
The patriarch of sugar, Claus Spreckels, a Hanoverian German,
earned so much money that he formed his own railroad to challenge
the Central and Southern Pacific lines of the so-called Big Four—
Charles Crocker, Mark Hopkins, Collis Huntington, and Leland
Stanford.

These instant fortunes demanded fancy flourishes. Mansions
went up on Nob Hill—*nob* was a contraction of *nabob*. The rich
rode to and from their palatial homes on the newfangled cable cars
that made hilltop living possible. The mansions had gas lights, crystal
chandeliers, and fourteen-foot-high ceilings. Parisian chefs turned
out *vol-au-vents* and elaborate *gâteaux*.

In formal salons, a veneer of social pretension evolved to the unlikely accompaniment of opera music. The bawdy tunes of the mining camps were banished, but Lola Montez, a former mistress of Ludwig of Bavaria, attracted a fashionably mixed crowd whenever she did her Spider Dance, slapping at the make-believe insects whose bites caused her to shed nearly all her clothes.

An earthquake burst the pretty bubble. On April 18, 1906, at 5:13 A.M., a sudden shift in the tectonic plates along the San Andreas Fault almost destroyed San Francisco.

The Costanoan Indians had spoken of earthquakes in their legends, but few San Franciscans understood that they were living on a geological eggshell. Fewer still were ready for the sight of their streets buckling and caving in. Electrical wires tore loose and threw sparks, gas mains shattered, and the city burned for three days. So many looters were out that the U.S. Army had to be summoned. When the smoke cleared, about five hundred people were dead and about 28,000 buildings had crumbled. The estimated damages ran to more than $400 million.

San Francisco did not regain its health until the 1930s. It was a solid union town by then, with a lively port, ample hydroelectric power, and a skilled workforce. A. P. Giannini's Bank of America had the courage to fund such massive construction projects as the two trans-bay bridges, the Oakland-Bay (1936) and the Golden Gate (1937).

The federal government, in the throes of an arms buildup, looked to the city's assets and handed several defense-industry plants to Bay Area concerns, encouraging a new wave of migration to the coast. During World War II, shipyards that had long been dormant started operating around the clock and sometimes turned out a finished ship in less than a week. As a consequence, San Francisco's population boomed to a record high of 827,000 in the 1940s.

The war had a similar effect on other parts of the state. About 2 million people came to California to work in the defense industry

between 1940 and 1945. More than a million soldiers passed through
on their way to the Pacific theater, taking with them indelible memories of sunshine and palm trees.

In many respects, World War II affected San Francisco as profoundly as the Gold Rush. So many Americans set foot in California
for the first time that the state lost its air of mystery and became
connected to the rest of the country in a new and different way.
Growth and change on a previously unknown scale lay ahead, and
there was nothing that San Franciscans, bench-sitters in Eden, could
do to stop it.

How STRANGE IT FELT to be home again in San Francisco, slipping
briefly back into my real life. I wrestled against the fit of it, craving
the freedom and the stimulation of the road. It soon became clear
to me that being away had not helped my marriage—a naïve hope,
at best. There was more distance than ever between us, and no miracle
cure or *deus ex machina* was going to make it disappear.

Evenings were the most difficult time. My wife would return
from her job as a social worker, and we would have a drink or two
and eat a pleasant enough dinner before dispersing to sit by ourselves
in separate rooms. Neither of us could face the gap that was growing
between us—it was something I had no experience of, this odd sense
of a particular kind of love, the one that sustains a marriage, slowly
vanishing while another, more general love remains.

We didn't quarrel much, maybe because we both knew I'd be
leaving again in a few days. When we did argue, our house was
often the focus. However unfairly, it had become the repository for
all my griefs. Originally, it had been built as a summer cottage for
an affluent family who lived in an even foggier neighborhood closer
to the ocean. Its east-facing windows had granted them a fine view
of San Francisco Bay, but now we looked out on a wall of apartments
ten feet away.

The house was lightless, claustrophobic, and noisy, I complained, ignoring the high ceilings and the warm hardwood floors. It lacked privacy and needed repairs that we couldn't afford, I continued, without ever mentioning the fireplace in the living room or the backyard garden and deck. Most of all, I railed about what it cost us every month. The same amount of money could buy us a spacious ranch on a trout stream in Wyoming!

I felt the way that Nate George felt up in Napa, as though I'd been robbed of the choicest sections of my city and exiled to Noe Valley, my own personal Angwin, a prisoner in California.

My wife was not unsympathetic, but she had no intention of giving in to my restlessness or my whim. Quite sensibly, she had put down roots. She had responsibilities at work and a social circle that she treasured. In sum, she had a life of her own, one that seemed to be at odds with my life after so many years together.

In the ideal world, where human beings are wise and good, we would have solved our problems in an instant, but we were mortal and sat instead in our separate rooms, in silence and in pain. The troubles were not as simple as I describe them—they never are— but the house did turn into a metaphor for them, and foolishly I let myself be locked inside it, somebody who'd lost the key to a vital relationship and couldn't make it whole again.

WHERE HAD MY LOST CITY GONE, that old San Francisco of light and magic? I went searching for it, kicking over the traces of the past. On Haight Street now, everybody was twenty-two years old and dressed in black clothes that were torn or slashed as if by a razor blade. Their hair came in many intriguing colors—chartreuse, puce, and shocking pink—and their bodies were often pierced or embellished.

Among the faithful and the posers, I saw gaggles of teenagers from the suburbs who were determined to go precisely where their parents had cautioned them not to go. They were easy prey for the hardcore cases peddling loose joints and more elaborate drugs, mostly ragged men in their thirties and forties who had matted hair and were red-faced and missing teeth. The sight of them brought back memories of Haight-Ashbury's decline in the 1970s, when heroin and general bad vibes dealt a final knockout blow to peace, love, and understanding.

On Cole Street, my first apartment: a boxy building with six units and curb appeal, where I slept on a mattress on the floor. The street was nothing then—a couple of Palestinian grocers, a hardware store, and two bars, one for lesbians and one for gay men. I tried hanging out instead at the Kezar Club nearby, but somebody always wanted to pop me one on account of my abundant hair or my ignorance about football.

Stanyan Street was next: a seven-room railroad flat I shared with a roommate, who was a book salesman from Texas. He wasn't a hippie, exactly. He had a real bed, not just a mattress, and piloted an electric-blue Porsche and seduced more women in his end of the flat than I could count on all my fingers and toes. Secretaries, artists, wandering matrons, they hiked up a tunnel of forty-odd steps and gladly surrendered to his charms, while I sat reading the books that he sold.

On the floor beneath us, lonely men who were drying out or failing to dry out rented single rooms. They were mournful and without prospects. Divorced guys, I'd think. I was young and arrogant, and I knew almost nothing about life.

From the roof of our building, we could watch the forty-niners play at Kezar Stadium. "Tar Beach," we called the roof, dragging up chairs to bask in the sun. Sometimes the roller-derby crowd piled into the adjacent Kezar Pavilion for an evening match, eager for a fix of whiplash violence, and we heard screams and bottles breaking long into the night.

Our true paradise in the Haight was on Belvedere Street. An

associate of the Black Panthers, who was desperate for tenants, leased us his home for a year, so that he, a writer, could go abroad to research a book. What a sweet man he was! He even helped us move in, carting our ratty belongings on his shoulders and probably earning himself a warning from the Landlords' Guild. Then he was off to Germany and Algiers, trusting us with a house that was bigger, better, and grander than any I'd ever occupied before.

There was a single drawback. After midnight, we had a few disturbances. A rapid knocking on the front door, followed by a breathy whispering. "Reggie? Hey, Reggie! Let me in."

We'd open the door a crack to show our faces, disconcertingly white. "Reggie's not here," we'd say.

On Belvedere Street, we could walk into the backyard and pluck a plum or a peach for breakfast. The kitchen was done in butcher block and had Dutch windows looking out at the garden. We threw many neighbor-disturbing parties during which hippie wretches in their atrocious attire danced barefoot on the lawn and slept under the trees.

O man. California.

I got to know my wife-to-be on Belvedere Street. She was dating the book salesman, of course, but while he chatted up his other girl friends on the phone we would sit in the kitchen having heartfelt talks. When he quit selling books to accept a short-lived job in New York, heading the wrong way to make his fortune, my wife-to-be and I were soon together and very much in love.

In 1974, we got married to start a family. The wedding was a lively affair at an Italian social club in North Beach. Our minister held credentials from the Universal Life Church, and a Buddhist priest signed our wedding certificate. My wife quickly became pregnant and almost as quickly miscarried, beginning a string of miscarriages and two ectopic pregnancies that would ultimately be attributed to a Dalkon shield.

Hard times but good ones. Two years after our marriage, we

were off to Alexander Valley. San Francisco, I could see now, would never be the same for me again—so innocent and so lacking in the brute confusion of middle age.

THE AIDS EPIDEMIC had brought the biggest changes to San Francisco in the last twenty years, straining the city's budget and placing an extreme demand on its compassion and its psychological reserves. An epidemiologist friend had first told me about AIDS in 1981, when it was still being called a "gay cancer." So little was known about the modes of transmission at the time that he wasn't sure if he could safely kiss his children good night.

My friend was doing some research on tuberculosis now, but he arranged for me to speak with his colleague, Dr. Mark Jacobson, at San Francisco General Hospital. The hospital was an odd structure for the city, dark and foreboding and built of bricks that were sooty and crumbling. It seemed to belong to a much older epoch in human history, when medicine was in its infancy and plagues were still common.

San Francisco General was a public facility, so its staff had to deal with the city's dispossessed. The signs in the lobby were in English, Spanish, Polish, and a couple of Asian languages. In the elevator I boarded, a man of about thirty was steadying himself with a pair of canes. His skin was a grayish color, and he was tight-lipped and paper-thin. It hurt him just to move.

On the fourth floor, Jacobson was waiting for me in his office cubicle. He was in his early forties, a former hippie who still had a beard. He had come to California from Kansas City, his hometown, as a college student, and had fallen for its natural beauty and had lived on a rural commune in Mendocino for a while. Now Jacobson was a specialist in infectious diseases and clinical pharmacology and held the rank of assistant professor at the UC Med School in San Francisco.

Ward 5A—an AIDS ward—had opened at General in 1983, he

told me. It was the only such ward in the country then. Its beds were
prized because patients were assured that they'd get the best, most
advanced treatment possible.

There were about twenty beds available on the ward at present,
or about one-tenth of the total bed space at the hospital. Patients in
the throes of an acute episode, such as pneumocystis, usually got
them, although a bed sometimes went to a homeless man who couldn't
be placed elsewhere. The patients stayed for about ten days on the
average. It wasn't uncommon for a patient to visit the ward a number
of times as his or her condition deteriorated. After the initial acute
episode, most people lived for about two years in increasingly declining health. They died at home or in a hospice.

San Francisco General dealt with about four thousand HIV-
positives in all. They were divided into two groups, half with full-
blown AIDS and half with AIDS-Related Complex (ARC). They
accounted for about twenty thousand visits annually, most of them
on an outpatient basis. That could only be accomplished, Jacobson
said, through an amazing support effort by the gay community.
Lovers and friends had formed a network that did everything from
fetching prescriptions to delivering meals. Jacobson had never seen
such a high standard of home care.

There was also a solid network of support in the medical profession, a consortium of about a hundred doctors in the Bay Area whose
practices were largely devoted to AIDS. But both networks were
beginning to give out, Jacobson said. They were being worn away
by attrition—another tragedy of the epidemic. A person was capable
of attending to just so many deaths, and in the world of AIDS, death
was the only constant.

The beds on Ward 5A were still full, but other hospitals had
similar wings now. When a gay man was diagnosed, he often requested a bed, but the promise of one in the future wasn't good
enough anymore, and he might go somewhere else. So Ward 5A
harbored more poor gay men these days, said Jacobson, sometimes
street hustlers and injection-drug users.

There were also more hetero- and bisexual injection-drug users. They could be difficult and demanding, acting out their anger while shouting for another shot of morphine. The veteran nurses often had less sympathy for them, and the ward had become more tense and polarized.

Jacobson offered to show me around Ward 5A. On the brink, I had an urge to turn and go, knowing what was in store. Everybody in San Francisco had witnessed the wasting away of a friend or an acquaintance or a brother or a colleague.

AIDS in its final stages cruelly accelerated the aging process. Bodies were leached of their vitality. Eyes grew hugely exaggerated, and hair sometimes fell out in patches. Some new therapies helped patients to live a little longer, but that only added to the devastation that they endured—more AIDS-related dementia, neurological breakdown, and, especially, tuberculosis.

Jacobson wanted me to meet a patient and pulled aside the curtain shielding one bed, but the man in it was weeping so hard, curled into a fetal ball, that the doctor apologized and quickly closed it.

In the next bed was John F., who was preparing to go home. He sat on the edge of his mattress in a pair of pajama bottoms and smoked a cigarette in the desultory way of someone who had nothing more to lose, politely brushing the smoke from our faces. His chest was all ribs and as skinny as a ten-year-old's, and that made the gaudy eagle tattooed on his right shoulder look overly fierce and perched on muscles that were barely able to support it.

John F. had a moustache and big ears. He spoke of himself in a fatalistic, self-deprecating way, with a touch of black humor. In his voice, I heard a battlefield fatigue, the same weary acceptance that comes to a soldier who understands that his wound was an accident, not a singling-out by fate. In that sense, AIDS was a bullet inscribed with no particular name. The epidemic had the fragmentary torque of a hand grenade. Two steps to the left and the shrapnel might have punctured your jugular.

We made some small talk for a while, and then, as we left Ward

5A, I asked Jacobson for a prognosis of the epidemic. He said, "A facile solution seems unlikely at this point."

With a frightening precision, he explained to me how insidious the virus was, sequestering itself inside a benign cell, where it could linger harmlessly for years. No one had managed to figure out why it turned pathogenic, or how it could be extirpated without damaging the entire immune system. Doctors and researchers were thinking less about curing AIDS than about finding new methods for slowing it down. Maybe it could be controlled like diabetes, they thought, or beaten into remission like certain cancers.

The work in Ward 5A had taken a toll on Jacobson and his associates. It was a constant struggle not to surrender to depression. San Francisco General was as strapped financially as every other public hospital in California and needed more money from the government, both state and federal. Its staff was exhausted and in need of relief. Every month, another hundred or so patients died in the city. They were young, in their late thirties on the average.

What Jacobson disliked most about his job was counseling those who had tested HIV-positive and were going to die of AIDS some day. He found it very hard and very painful. Whenever he had to face the task, he advised patients to simplify their lives and do what they most wanted to do, considering his own mortality all the while.

In the land of light, a darkness unfolding.

IN THE MISSION DISTRICT NEAR NOE VALLEY, there were also changes. The Mission was thickly Hispanic, a sanctuary for Mexicans from every part of Mexico, as well as for Guatemalans, Nicaraguans, Salvadorans, Peruvians, Bolivians, Colombians—every Latin country was represented.

The Mission had many Catholic churches for the confessing of sins and many teenage gangsters doing *la vida loco* who had sins to confess. The cars cruising the streets were decorated with bumper-

stickers proclaiming their owners' attachment to a home turf, I Luv
Yucatán or I Luv Managua.

Early one gray and misty morning, I came upon a big gathering
of Hispanic men where Valencia Street dovetails into Mission Street.
About seventy-five of them were grouped on both sides of the street,
shivering in the chill. They stood in front of a Taco Bell flying an
American flag, in the shadow of a billboard for Alaska Airlines that
advertised flights to Guadalajara and Acapulco—two "hot spots"
symbolized by chile peppers.

From a distance, they all looked to be about the same size, maybe
five-foot-six or -seven, and the same age, between eighteen and
twenty-five. Some of them held little plastic grocery sacks that probably contained all that they owned and marked them as illegal immigrants just in from the border.

A few men were always hanging around in the Mission District
and looking for work by the hour, but I had never seen so many of
them before. Supply far outweighed demand, and when a pickup
truck stopped at the Taco Bell, the men descended upon it in earnest.

The driver, a white man, rolled a window halfway down and
was immediately engulfed. Six would-be workers raced toward him
and began shouting. They shoved each other and battled for space.
A head would thrust toward the window, and a competitor would
grab it by the neck and yank it back.

Four men, so desperate that they didn't even ask what the job
might be, grabbed at the rungs of a ladder in the truck bed and
climbed in. Some others, latecomers, rushed the truck and swabbed
at the windshield with handkerchiefs, partly to clean it and partly
as a wan attempt to curry favor.

At last, the driver struck a bargain with two fellows. They fought
off the furies, literally throwing punches, and got into the truck on
the passenger side, ready to dig ditches, carry hods, or strip asbestos
from furnace pipes. The driver stepped on the gas, and the crowd
split in half and peeled away. The desperate crew in the truck bed

got to their feet in a frenzy and jumped to the pavement, like sailors deserting a sinking ship.

The men left behind did not appear to be angry or discouraged. Nobody swore or pounded a fist. Instead, they staked out their positions again and went back to waiting and shivering in the drizzle. Their attitude was fatalistic. They had taken a chance on the great California sweepstakes and no doubt expected such whimsical treatment by fate.

So they would stand by the Taco Bell through the afternoon, watching the cars go by, pitching pennies, peeing as necessary in an alley, and conveying their respects to any pretty woman who might pass, just as they would do at a *zocalo* back in Mexico.

THE FOURTH OF JULY CAME UP ACES, all bright skies and no need for a pea coat. We went to a barbecue at the house of a friend, who had an impressive deck that looked out over the Castro District to the city skyline. The partygoers were an eclectic San Francisco mix of straights and gays, solid professionals and dedicated slackers, and we were treated to ample beer and wine and trays of good food all done to a turn over mesquite.

People talked about real estate, naturally, but they also talked about films, books, and movies. They even talked about California, particularly one guest, who was a reporter for a New York paper stationed by chance in the thankless West. I had met her shortly after she'd arrived, and she had gone on about all the New York things that she would miss—the intelligent conversations, the sophistication, Broadway, the publishing scene. You might have thought that she was toiling in the Outer Hebrides.

But now, six months down the line, here she was discussing her favorite jogging trails in San Francisco, looking tanned, healthy, and not at all forlorn. Oxygen and sunshine had proved to be a decent enough substitute for the Big Apple's sizzle.

People talked about Los Angeles, too. There was a guest who wrote screenplays, and she described her agent in Hollywood and how a conversation with him was like being on TV and having to produce sound bites of information for a talk-show host. You made a remark to him, and sometimes he didn't even respond to it, saying only, "Next!"

Another woman talked about how the old San Francisco was disappearing, but I knew from my travels that the old everything was disappearing in California and no going back. I recalled a line that Will Irwin, a curmudgeonly reporter in the city, had once used when somebody asked him if San Francisco was as good as it used to be. "No, and it never was," he said.

Then it was evening, and we were sitting in our separate rooms at home. How wretched I felt, how stupid and blind and panicked! Everybody knows that failing marriages are a dime a dozen, but the knowledge offers no solace, I had discoveed, when the marriage is your own.

JOSHUA NORTON, Emperor of the United States and Protector of Mexico, lay buried at the public's expense in Woodlawn Memorial Park, in Colma, a cemetery town south of San Francisco. On my last morning at home, feeling slightly crazed myself, I paid him a visit. A Woodlawn attendant in a green blazer gave me a map and marked a route past the Portals of Remembrance, the Sanctuary of the Hills, and the Veterans Section to a grave on a little rise framed by palms, eucalyptuses, and Monterey cypresses.

The emperor's tomb, a tannish rectangle, was scarcely a tribute to his stature. Other visitors had left offerings at its base—some red plastic carnations and a shotglass embossed with the name of a vodka drink I hoped never to try, a Stoli-Kazi. In death, Norton had settled down among such ordinary folks as the Richters, George and Nellie, and Wanda Steinley, who had lived to be one hundred and three.

A photograph I had of Emperor Norton showed him astride one

of those old bicycles with hooped wheels. He rode it with fierce concentration, his brow furrowed and his hands clenching the handlebars. The intensity that had touched so many of his contemporaries was evident. The mad do not often possess such dignity.

I wondered how the emperor would have fared in San Francisco now. The homeless were not treated so gently anymore. They ate at soup kitchens if they ate at all and lodged in doorways on pallets of cardboard. The flophouses that used to take them in were gone, refashioned as apartments for immigrant families from Asia—Laotians, Cambodians, and Vietnamese.

Emperor Norton, old boy, you'd be in for a surprise if you were to come back for a few days. Abundant saloons were still around to tempt you, but the exclusive shops on Union Square, everything from Gucci to Tiffany to Burberry's, might puzzle you. The fancy restaurants might make you swoon. And all the tourists in town riding cable cars, feeding the sea lions by Pier 39, and buying tiny souvenir versions of the Golden Gate Bridge, what would you make of them?

Joshua Norton's city was lost, I thought, just as mine was, but other pilgrims would still find new magic and light, believing that they had reached their destined home at last. San Francisco really was an island in the great sea of California, a place for the rich and the poor, for drifters and immigrants. Most middle-class Californians had as little to do with urban affairs as they did with small towns or cattle ranches. They lived in the suburbs.

CHAPTER 12

If you wanted to see the future of suburban California, Hercules, in Contra Costa County, was as good a place to start as any. It was among the fastest-growing towns in the Bay Area, and its appeal could be simply described. The houses there, mostly new in construction, were deemed affordable, and Californians, like Americans everywhere, were slaves to the long-simmering national dream of owning a single-family home, no matter what the psychological cost.

In Hercules, you paid for your pleasures in accrued freeway time, all the lost minutes squandered on the commuter meatrack. Highway 80, the main arterial to San Francisco and Oakland, backed up by seven o'clock on a weekday morning, and a trip of twenty-five miles or so to work could take up to two hours in a worst-case scenario.

Every single weekday morning, fifty weeks a year, the same old grind. As I drove to Hercules, I was awed by the stalled line of cars trying to move in the other direction, creeping forward by inches in a cloud of spent fossil fuels at 7:14 A.M. The drivers did not look the least bit content. Instead, they looked angry, anxious, bored, or miserable. Some of them were about to return to the Land of Nod in spite of the forty-eight-ounce Big Gulp mugs of coffee or Diet Coke balanced on their dashboards. A face not clenched or twisted in stress was rare.

There were devices in place to mitigate the pressure—radios cranked to the max and earphones plugged into Walkmans dispensing investment tips or visualization exercises or the audio version of a John Bradshaw seminar—but they did not seem to be getting the job done. Sometimes a driver cracked and made an aberrant dash toward a vanishing speck of light between cars, triggering a chain reaction that resulted in a jockeying for position where no position could truly be said to exist.

Being trapped in stalled traffic reminded me of my own childhood in Levittown, where an identical crippling rush had begun in our town at dawn, clogging the highways to Manhattan. My father spent half his energy trying to outmaneuver the other commuters, always searching for a new shortcut or a secret back road, leaving a little earlier or a little later, and coming home on summer evenings exhausted, ornery, and soaked in sweat.

It was hard to credit the fact that Hercules had been rural in character not so long ago. It took its name from the Hercules Powder Company, a manufacturer that had supplied dynamite to the forty-niners. Originally based in San Francisco, the company had moved to the East Bay in 1866 when the city had closed in around its explosive operation. Other noisome industries followed it to Contra Costa over the next few decades and located on Carquinez Strait—a smelting plant, a sugar mill, and some oil refineries.

In the late 1880s, there were four miles of docks and granaries on the strait at the town of Port Costa, a world leader in the export of wheat. Now Port Costa was a quaint village wreathed in chemical fumes from the refineries, and Hercules had seventeen thousand residents and houses sprouting like mushrooms after a rain.

In Pinole, I turned around, doubled back on Highway 80, and left the freeway to have a closer look at Hercules. Immediately, I made a wrong turn on a freshly paved road and got lost in a new industrial park where the streets were called Alfred Nobel, Linus Pauling, and John Muir. Muir was a dead end that stopped at a plain building with bold letters on its façade, BIO-RAD. Not good, I thought.

On the other side of the freeway, I found a signboard with arrows pointing to various subdivisions. As ever, the developers had showed a warped brilliance for nomenclature, rivaling the titans in Detroit who'd christened a fleet of Firenzes, Fiestas, Siroccos, and Tauruses. Hercules consisted of such tracts as Mandalay, Seasons, Caprice, Tiffany Ridge, and the Heights, names that had a fairytale piquancy bordering on the nonsensical. It was not so much a real town as a planned community, that bastard child of market research and unintended irony.

A pristine vision of Utopia burned at the heart of every planned community. Anyone who bought a home in one was choosing to break bread with likeminded Californians in a place that had no history and nothing to offer that couldn't be had in any other suburb.

In Hercules, nothing unexpected would ever happen. Everything was nice. Everything was ordinary and familiar. The neighborhoods were clean and neat, and the parks, gardens, jogging paths, and tennis courts were well tended. The town had the uniform appearance of any late-century subdivision in the state, sunny and bicycle-strewn, its streets oddly empty of people.

Only when you drove out a road past Marsten Ranch did the torture of supreme orderliness drop away. The rows of houses stopped abruptly, and you were back in the fields of Contra Costa again, in the wild oats. Unimaginable as it might seem, Hercules still had plenty of room to grow.

ABOUT HERCULES I learned the following things: The town had been incorporated in 1900 and covered 5.5 square miles; its growth spurt had started in the 1980s, and it was adding about 2,000 new Herculeans a year; the residents were split almost equally between men and women, and they had an average age of thirty-two; there were 7,231 Asians; 6,700 whites; 2,150 blacks; 1,758 Hispanics; and, as at Sutter's Nueva Helvetia, a smattering of Pacific Islanders. (Such densely Asian suburbs were not infrequent in California.)

The median price of a single-family house in Hercules was $224,100, slightly higher than the median price ($219,400) for Contra Costa County. That compared favorably with the median price of a home in San Francisco ($298,900), but an Alturan ($47,200), a Yrekan ($66,600), or a Sacramentan ($115,800) would surely find it outrageous. The town's zip code was 94567. Willie McGee, the Giants' outfielder, lived there. Hercules had seventeen cops, a fire department, and no library.

ROADS LOOPED AROUND SAN PABLO BAY, Highway 80 tying into Highway 37 at the base of Solano County, where the towns were growing even faster than those in Contra Costa. The new subdivisions in Solano didn't come with schools, so the old schools in the district were overflowing with new kids from, say, Canyon Meadow or Terrace Gap. The county needed about one hundred new classrooms each year, but it did not have the $9 million required to build them.

California as a whole faced the same problem. Its educators wanted $11 billion to renovate and run the public schools for the next five years, but they would be lucky to get half of it. So the children in the old schools, those whose parents couldn't afford to educate them privately, used the old textbooks that were missing pages and played in playgrounds where the drop from the monkey-bars was onto concrete or macadam. The good teachers struggled to hang on, but they couldn't afford a home in Canyon Meadow or Terrace Gap without a second income.

In some Solano County districts, the students were stuffed into portable classrooms with waferboard walls and scarcely any windows.

The schools in other districts carried a double load, four hundred children in a space designed for two hundred. In California, only the prisons were as overcrowded as the public schools.

MARIN COUNTY, where I picked up Highway 101 in mid-July, was an older suburb, as well as the wealthiest county in the state. It still had decent public schools that weren't terribly overcrowded. It had a good public hospital and fine libraries that were sometimes as plush as private clubs. Insofar as California had a real paradise, Marin was often rumored to be it. The houses weren't affordable ($354,200 median price), but how could they be? Paradise was supposed to be exclusive.

Although the Bay Area was a bastion of racial diversity, Marin County alone remained almost monolithically white. Its great-looking, ideally fit men and women seemed to have been bred in a secret Aryan laboratory somewhere in the woods. Their children were bright and perfectly proportioned. Even the therapists, hypnotists, personal trainers, and realtors pictured in the ads in the *Pacific Sun,* a freebie paper, had an aura of glamour.

Anybody would recognize Marin County as an integral part of the California myth. It belonged in California the way palm trees and blondes in bikinis did. It was a place where the term "laid back" had acquired new meaning.

Hot tubs and saunas were everywhere, and the Stress Patrol was out in force. You could have your cares massaged away at any number of spas and health clubs. Biofeedback counselors were available to clean up your karma and reroute any chakras or negative vibrations that might be adding to your percentage of body fat, a figure that any true Marinite could recite at a snap of the fingers.

For all its wealth, Marin wasn't intolerably ostentatious. The money was often new, but it could still be as quiet as the money in Greenwich or Hyannisport. In such high-end towns as Belvedere, Tiburon, Ross, and Sausalito (median price, $500,001), you saw matrons in muumuus shopping for kiwi fruit right next to the leggy young girls on their mountain bikes.

The residents of Marin were liberal and voted Democratic, but each town had a supervigilant bunch of cops who loved to write parking tickets and enforce the tiniest laws on the books. They were like an upscale version of the cops in "Mayberry RFD" and tried hard not to be discriminatory, but they didn't always succeed.

Despite its flaws, Marin had a signal advantage over most other California counties. The effects of human habitation had not yet overwhelmed the lavishness of nature.

Who wouldn't want to live in a rambling, brown-shingle house in Mill Valley (median price, $445,300) on the wooded slopes of Mount Tamalpais, a holy mountain to the Miwoks? Surround the house with some oaks, say, and some madronas and fragrant bay laurels, and give it a deck with a view of all creation. You'd be close enough to town to walk to Banana Republic and buy some neat safari-esque clothes and then sit reading and sipping lattes among the great-looking guys and gals at the Book Depot. Disease and despair would never find you.

Although Mill Valley was a commuter town, it had done an excellent job of disguising itself as a resort hamlet for the idle rich. Guards were posted at its borders to drive away the bad news, and the roads going west ran into open land and past beautiful, unspoiled dairy farms and on out to the ocean, to calm harbors and deserted beaches.

Mount Tamalpais watched over Mill Valley and all of Marin, somber and brooding one minute and light-filled and welcoming the next. Wispy clouds and scraps of fog got caught in its tall forests. In spring, there were babbling brooks and waterfalls. Five manmade lakes, the county's water supply, were deployed around its slopes and stocked with rainbow trout. Sometimes you could wander for hours on the mountain and never see another soul. Mount Tam had some walk-in campsites, so I walked into one and pitched my tent for a couple of days.

♦ ♦ ♦

HIKING AND DREAMING ON DEAR, old Mount Tam. Days gone by, in
that long-ago time of shedding a skin, I had dived into the ease and
the sensuality of Marin County with a recklessness that would have
given poor William Brewer the shivers.

Sausalito was the place that tugged at me then. Some evenings
after I'd finished work as a stockboy at a book warehouse in San
Francisco, my first California job, I'd pile into an old car with a few
equally disheveled friends to drop into the inviting contours of that
bayside, Mediterranean town. I'd think of Napoli or Amalfi. I'd think
of romance.

Our first stop was always Sally Stanford's restaurant on the water.
Sally had earned her grubstake by once running San Francisco's finest
whorehouse. Her dining room was done in plush, red Victoriana and
could have doubled as a bordello. She was short and crusty and had
a nose that was not unlike the beak of the bright-green parrot that
sometimes rode on her shoulder. Sally knew what it was like to be
young and let us drink at her bar despite our faded jeans, occasionally
addressing us in the manner of a drill instructor.

"Boys," she'd say, looking us up and down as she marched by,
"I don't care about your clothes or your hair. You can stay here as
long as you behave like gentlemen."

We always behaved like gentlemen.

From Sally Stanford's we would proceed to the No Name Bar,
where serious intellectuals discussed the fate of the planet and actual
published writers played studious chess. The writers fascinated us.
They were the last of the bohemians and lived on houseboats anchored
in the bay. They wore flannel shirts, sweaters from the Orkney
Islands, and stupid Greek fishermen's hats, as though they'd been
casting nets into the surf all day and dragging it for inspiration, but
we loved them anyway.

We drank Anchor Steam Beer at the No Name. It satisfied us
beyond all other beers because it was brewed in San Francisco. It

meant that we were really in California sitting on a back patio of a bar in full winter, gabbing, having brilliant ideas, and watching actual published writers play chess. Someday, we believed, the writers would see how special we were and would want to speak to us. They would want to hear our brilliant ideas.

After the No Name, we browsed at The Tides, a bookstore next door, where the coffee was free. In a buoyant mood, we would ransack the shelves for books that would take us a little farther along the path that we were traveling toward our new, barely conceptualized selves—books of poetry or fiction or esoteric religion. Nobody ever bothered a customer at The Tides. You could read quietly in a corner, undisturbed by any conventional notions of commerce.

Then we were off to The Trident for a nightcap. What a cocoon it was, all creamy wood and brass fittings and green ferns dripping from pots hanging from the ceiling! The food served there was inarguably Californian. The sandwiches came with such strange savories as alfalfa sprouts and lecithin, and we ate them in a vaguely hopeful way, wishing that their organic, healing properties would offset any harmful effects of the beer.

The waitresses at The Trident floated to the tables on clouds. They were dippy, barefoot, lovely, and always a little stoned. They called themselves Sunshine and Ethereal and wore long dresses that you could sometimes see through if the light was right. To gaze through transparent cloth at an illuminated mound of Venus was to experience the divine. They didn't care if they showed us a glimpse of their breasts as they bent to serve us, because mere mortals weren't ever going to touch them, anyhow. And we had no hard feelings, either—it was enough just to be gathered up in their smiles.

Mellow in Marin. Sitting outside on a moonlit deck, we stared at the black water and pitched our alfalfa sprouts overboard. The waitresses flashed their breasts and smiled. The Trident was a great California Ship of Fools, but we had no desire to get off it. If this is La-La Land, we thought, please bring us another helping.

◆   ◆   ◆

MARIN COUNTY HAD ITS DARK SIDE, too, like every other place on earth. San Quentin prison, an ugly cluster of aging buildings in the shadow of the Richmond–San Rafael Bridge, dated from 1853. Every man who was sentenced to die in California had a cell on the prison's Death Row, because it had the only gas chamber in the state—one of the few states that still *had* a death penalty.

There were some rundown subdivisions in Marin that had gone to drugs and Heavy Metal. And in San Rafael, the county seat, you saw Hispanic men hanging around outside a Burger King and a 7-Eleven to look for day work, just as their brothers were doing across the bridge. The men lived in the Canal District nearby, a raunchy backwater, often six or eight to an apartment, and whenever they had a problem or needed advice or got into a scrap, they turned to La Familia.

La Familia was a social-services agency on an ordinary block in an ordinary neighborhood in San Rafael. Alejandro Montenegro, its executive director, was Chilean by birth, although his mother had owned a British passport. Montenegro was a reddish man—reddish hair and beard, a fair complexion. He was gracious and polite and owned a doctorate in psychology from UC Berkeley.

Montenegro had not always been a social worker. He had first used his background in psychology as an image consultant, putting pretty faces on otherwise faceless corporations. He had lived in London for a time, but he had found the English to be passionless and told me a story about a friend of his mother's, Lord B., to prove the point.

Lord B. was the CEO at a prominent head-hunting firm. When Montenegro went to the firm for a job interview, he was dressed in his best suit and tie, every inch of fabric neatly pressed. Lord B. had glanced at him perfunctorily and had jabbed a finger at his feet.

"Those brown shoes won't do, my boy," Lord B. had sniffed.

La Familia was definitely part of the brown-shoe universe. It resembled every other underfunded social agency in California, furnished with the same Salvation Army furniture and equipped with the same motley collection of dime-store coffee mugs.

In his office, Montenegro said that he had no idea how many Hispanic immigrants lived in Marin, even though he'd been on the job for five months now. The estimates ran from eight to twenty thousand. The men who showed up at La Familia were in the United States illegally, almost without exception. They spoke no English and came not from Mexico but from Central America, Cuba, Peru, and Brazil. Often they were the poorest of the poor in their own countries, making them, as Montenegro noted, among the poorest people anywhere.

The men usually crossed the border alone, hoping to save enough money to later import their wives, their kids, and even their parents. There were more opportunities for work than you might think, Montenegro said. Marin was a garden spot with thousands of trees to be pruned and thousands of flowerbeds to be weeded. If a man worked ten days a month, he could make his nut and even put some cash aside by sleeping on his uncle's floor.

Whenever work was plentiful, the men caused no trouble. It was the slow times, the dead-broke Saturday nights in an inhospitable land, that led to the loud music, the drinking, and the knife fights. In the past, agents from the Immigration and Naturalization Service had conducted wholesale sweeps through the Canal District, but they were forced to stop because they had bagged many legal Hispanics with the undocumented ones, leading to charges of racism.

Montenegro was frank about playing the race card. He glanced around at his humble office and said, "It's the only weapon we have."

He believed that the veneer of tolerance in Marin County was very thin. Neighbors around La Familia complained incessantly about the men lounging on the steps or leaning against a fence, but when Montenegro met with them to talk about the problem—if it *was* a problem—they could not elaborate. The very presence of the men, it seemed, was objectionable.

The INS had recently taken a new tack in its campaign. Agents waited for somebody to be hired outside Burger King, followed him to the job site, and arrested him. Those who got caught had almost no recourse. They were proud Latinos and often refused any help, even from La Familia. Montenegro had once suggested to some of the men that they draw up a standard contract to use with their random employers, but they rejected the idea. It would be too cold and too formal, they felt.

I asked him about the future, but he wouldn't venture a guess, except to say that the men would keep coming, regardless of the obstacles. He wished that the people in Marin were easier to deal with—he thought that they took criticism personally, while in San Francisco he had been able to hammer out agreements in the framework of a debate.

Still, he loved living where he did, in Sausalito. It reminded him of Viña del Mar, Chile.

"Same weeds, same plants, same everything," he said, sounding just like the Sikhs in Yuba City.

For Alejandro Montenegro, there were really just two places in the world to live, Sausalito and Viña del Mar.

SAUSALITO MEANT *little willow* in Miwok. Twenty years, twenty years, and now The Tides was gone, Sally Stanford was in her grave, and the actual published writers were nowhere to be found. The Trident was as insubstantial as a figment. The waitresses had changed back into Betty and Joan and were probably living with their stockbroker husbands and their kids in Caprice or Tiffany Ridge.

At Cafe Trieste on Bridgeway, I bought a cup of coffee and walked along the docks past sloops, yachts, and dinghies, high on the morning light. A black cat materialized and courteously refused to cross my path. Instead, she hopped up on a railing and purred for some attention. When I reached out to pet her, she nipped at my hand and bit the flesh between thumb and index finger.

Just so, our California paradise.

FROM SAUSALITO I drove through Marin City, the only black town in Marin. It had grown up around the ruins of Marinship, a Bechtel Corporation shipbuilding plant that had opened in 1942. Bechtel had resisted hiring black workers through the 1930s, and only under pressure from black leaders and the threat of legal action did it agree to take the workers on at the new shop.

The unions then screwed the workers by granting them an auxiliary status and denying them the right to vote. One black welder, Joe James of the Boilermakers' Union, rebelled and led a strike, which resulted in firings. The struggle became a legal battle that didn't end until 1948, when the Boilermakers were upbraided in court and ordered to integrate fully, without discrimination. The ruling made little difference by that time. The war was over, the demand for ships had slackened, and the union's black constituency had dropped from a high of about 3,000 to just 150 members.

Ever since the first slave was dragged from the South into the foothills to dig for gold, blacks in California had been subjected to messages that were alternately hostile and conciliatory. The state had outlawed slavery in 1849, for instance, but a law on the books was only as good as the guns enforcing it, and any man who ran away from his master was likely to be apprehended and returned to him as property.

In a celebrated case of the period, Archy Lee, an eighteen-year-old slave from Mississippi, traveled to Sacramento with his master, Charles Stovall, in 1859 and soon fell under the influence of free California blacks. Lee broke for freedom himself, but he was captured easily and tossed into prison for four months while his fate was deliberated upon by the state supreme court.

Abolitionists took up Lee's cause to no effect. The court acted as if the state's fugitive slave law, which had expired in 1856, was still on the books and sent Lee back to his master, showing leniency toward Stovall because he was "young and inexperienced."

Only a few years after the Lee fiasco, however, blacks were relieved of a burdensome law that had kept them from testifying in court on an equal footing with whites, a privilege still denied to Indians and the Chinese. They seem to have done reasonably well in business, too, and documents from the time suggest that a black middle class was emerging.

Education for blacks remained a muddle. Few schools in and around San Francisco were integrated in the 1860s, and the schools that black children did attend were clearly inferior. A report to the San Francisco School Board in 1862 described one typical black schoolroom as a poorly ventilated basement of a military barracks. Whenever the troops did their exercises, upstairs ceiling plaster and water from ruptured pipes rained down on the kids below.

The city did begin to integrate its public schools in the 1870s, although not primarily for humanitarian purposes. Under a court order to provide separate-but-equal facilities for blacks, educators agreed that it would cost less to incorporate black children into the existing all-white system than it would be to repair and renovate the segregated schools. Black teachers continued to be paid at a lower rate than white teachers, though.

In general, blacks were treated badly in San Francisco in the early 1900s. They were often turned down for jobs, even as unskilled laborers, in favor of the Chinese (who were perceived to be a better value for the dollar) and the Irish. Some fortunate blacks got work with the railroads as porters and sleeping-car attendants, but most men and women had to content themselves with far more menial tasks.

Discrimination and racist union policies created the first black suburbs in the Bay Area. Anybody who got fed up with taking a back seat could ride a ferry to Oakland, where about a thousand blacks were living in relative harmony in 1900. The black population had reached about five thousand by 1917, and boosters were so proud that they published a 140-page "Colored Directory" to their community. It pictured their houses and their churches in the best possible light. Similar suburbs were sprouting at an even quicker pace down south, even though W. E. B. DuBois put forth a caution.

"Los Angeles is not Paradise," he said, "much as the sight of its lilies and roses might lead one at first to believe. The color line is there sharply drawn."

The restrictive covenants that kept a black person from buying in a good San Francisco neighborhood did not exist in Oakland. They did not exist in Richmond, either, another largely black town on the bay that grew up around Henry J. Kaiser's shipbuilding plants, much as Marin City had evolved around Marinship.

When World War II ended, many black families stayed on in Marin City, where the daunting housing projects now floated like an archipelago in a sea of utter whiteness. Richmond was also still a mostly black community that was dispersed over a tangled industrial landscape of refineries, docks, and railroad tracks. There were some fine homes on the water and in the hills, but most people lived in modest stucco and wood homes (median price, $144,300) with patchy little lawns.

I CAME NEXT TO BERKELEY, a nuclear-free zone, where the citizens were worried about things.

They were worried about the rain forests in the Amazon, Sendero Luminoso, South Africa, and the Norwegians who ate whales. They were worried about the depleted ozone layer and about the microwave ovens that were short-circuiting pacemakers and about the radon that might be seeping up from the earth into their homes. They were very worried about the nitrates in their bacon and about the cruel way that little calves were butchered into veal.

In Berkeley, nobody believed that Lee Harvey Oswald had shot John F. Kennedy on his own. Everybody knew that it was a plot cooked up by the Mafia in collusion with J. Edgar Hoover, and they knew that Hoover liked boys and played the ponies and sometimes carried a pink purse. They knew of massive conspiracies that the fascist-dominated media had never divulged, plots to assassinate Mother Teresa and to make Pol Pot the potentate of Guatemala and to put little-known bacterial agents into the water supply to control people's sex drives and make them want to live in Tiffany Ridge.

Some Californians thought that Berkeleyites worried *too* much. It was as if they'd been assigned the job of worrying for the entire state, as if all the brain-burning, soul-troubling issues had befallen them and were their responsibility, freeing every other Californian to have fun.

Berkeley was only a few miles from Richmond, but it orbited in another solar system.

Telegraph Avenue was the city's Broadway. It ran all the way from Oakland to the UC Berkeley campus. It was a street of refractory sounds and images, where anorexic poets mingled with jugheads in flak gear who were dedicated to resuscitating the Symbionese Liberation Army. On Telegraph, the dread Cinque might yet pass muster as a philosopher, and Charles Manson could pawn himself off as a misunderstood victim of a dysfunctional family. Manson had started his own Family in Berkeley, in fact, latching onto a librarian and moving in with her.

The street had its own argot, its own codes. As I walked along it, I sensed that signals of various kinds were being semaphored over a tom-tom skin of pavement. Lying on the sidewalk or crouched by the tables of vendors selling life-giving crystals, there were ravaged speed freaks, messianic hipsters, bad dudes in hooded sweatshirts, and Deadheads in tie-dye, each of them looking for the transformative score that would make it happen for them, the big lift-off into the California ozone.

Among them moved an improbably clean-cut group of young men and women, who were purposeful where the others were lost, untarnished where they were scarred, solidly grounded where they were all fucked up—students at the University blithely skirting the perimeters of a lost world.

A walk on Telegraph was another memory garden for me. The street was linked indelibly to certain events of the 1960s and the 1970s that had given me the sort of instruction that I had never got in school. In those early days of exploring away from San Francisco, I had crossed the bridge not only for the bookstores and the cultural institutions but also to be part of the action, the so-called revolution.

I could remember how the store owners on the strip would nail plywood panels over their windows at the slightest hint of a demonstration, and how the cops and the protestors would collide with the inevitability of two football squads marching toward a disputed fifty-yard line. I remembered, too, the smell of tear gas and the air thick with smoke, and the sight of faces and heads split and bloodied by nightsticks, innocence going down with an angelic swoon.

The revolution never came, of course, but the war in Vietnam had ended. There was that to consider when it seemed that Berkeleyites worried too much. Now those days were being raked over and codified, their fragments laid claim to, the mythic Berkeley of intellectual dissent and fervent opposition and too much hair and baggy clothes rising into the pantheon of mythic California.

Where Telegraph Avenue stopped, UC Berkeley began. Sather Gate was the entrance to a campus that stretched over 1,232 wooded acres. Frederick Law Olmsted, the architect of Manhattan's Central Park, had done the landscaping and had given the campus a parklike atmosphere. There were gnomish grottoes, rippling creeks, and charming fieldstone bridges that carried you to secluded footpaths through the shrubbery, where the odd marijuana joint could be smoked and the odd kiss exchanged.

Berkeley was the finest public university in California, the crown jewel in the UC system. It had twenty-six libraries, scads of Nobel laureates, and about 22,000 students. Established in 1873, it was the oldest of the nine UC campuses, which had an aggregate enrollment of about 163,000. Most students were California residents and paid a very low tuition, so Berkeley was severely strapped for cash, like its fellow institutions and like California itself.

The University of California had its fingers in many pies. Its Board of Regents read like a corporate Who's Who. Its scientists and its researchers still had a strong bond to the military-industrial complex. Other branches of the UC system counseled farmers, ranchers, fishermen, the timber industry, and so on. The Davis branch handled agriculture and viticulture, the San Francisco branch did medicine, and the Scripps Institution in La Jolla did oceanography.

A Berkeley grad was inducted into a worthy and valuable club. Students toiled under that tension, but you'd never guess it by watching them at play in Sproul Plaza. They were strumming banjos and zooming by on Rollerblades, passing Hacky-Sacks from toe to toe and flipping Frisbees in looping spirals, eating tacos and falafel and chow mein from carts, and soaking up the suds at the Bear's Lair, as though the very idea of cracking a book were laughable.

Even the faculty seemed absolutely above any academic concerns. Whenever I saw a bearded, graying professor amble through the plaza trailed by a gaggle of female admirers and beaming in tenured delight, I felt a stab of envy and wished that I'd done all my homework on time and had never cut a class, hewing instead to a straight and narrow path that might have led me to a similar Olympus.

BERKELEY WAS A SMALL CITY, but it held a large sway in matters Californian, being the cradle of a *haute bourgeoisie* style of living that had later spread around the state. The style had its origins in the British Arts and Crafts Movement, which was sponsored by William Morris and John Ruskin in an attempt to provide an antidote to the dehumanizing effects of industry. An Arts and Craftser valued simple, organic things and tried to stay attuned to and in harmony with nature.

A Swedenborgian minister, Joseph Worcester, introduced the

principles of the movement to the East Bay. He built a house for himself in Piedmont, near Berkeley, in 1876, that broke with all the contemporary modes of design. The house was open, airy, and light, and drew its elements from the environment. The interior walls were rough redwood, while redwood shingles covered the exterior walls. It could not have been conjured up anywhere else. The essential physical properties of northern California were imbedded in its bones.

Soon the architects around Berkeley were casting away their traditional pattern books and meeting to discuss the theories of the Arts and Crafts Movement. Bernard Maybeck plunged into the new world with particular abandon and made redwood his building material of choice. He so disliked the look of raw plaster that he started using stucco instead, imitating the straw and adobe walls of missions. Sometimes in a Maybeck house the dividing line between a parlor and a garden appeared not to be there at all.

Another architect in the circle, A. C. Schweinfurth, designed a Unitarian Church in Berkeley in 1898 that was an Arts and Crafts monument. It had two porches beneath its pitched roof that drew their support from unpeeled redwood logs. The church became the locale for meetings of the Ruskin Club. The club had such members as the architects Maybeck, Schweinfurth, Charles Keeler, Louis Christian Mullgardt, and Willis Polk. Keeler's *The Simple Home,* published in 1904, was their handbook.

The Ruskin Clubbers had a women's satellite in the Hillside Club, whose members fought to save the "wilderness" of the north Berkeley Hills. The women were fanatically pure. They slept in the fresh air, showered in cold water, and worked out to keep fit. They wouldn't touch coffee, tea, or meat and believed that any house was merely "landscape gardening with a few rooms to use in case of rain."

Precisely at this historical moment, the cultural elite in California, all centered in the state's great university, began turning its collective back on the beaux arts of Paris to appreciate the natural wonders in front of them—the light, the trees, the air, and the ocean.

The Ruskin Club's knack for transforming the specific attributes of a place into something special, borrowing as necessary, would be recapitulated more than seventy years later when a young woman in love with Provence and the stories of Marcel Pagnol opened a restaurant in a shingled Berkeley house. She grew her own herbs and lettuces in a backyard garden, bought free-range chickens fed on organic grains, and relied on local ingredients that were fresh, aromatic, and pure.

"I am sad," she would write one day, "for those who cannot see a lovely, unblemished apple just picked from the tree as voluptuous, or a beautifully perfect pear as sensuous. . . ."

In Berkeley, she had found an armada of kindred souls. The little shingled house, Chez Panisse, filled with gourmets and gourmands clamoring for a taste of her spit-roasted capon or her rocket salad with goose fat and garlic-rubbed croutons. So it was that Alice Waters paid an accidental homage to the Ruskin Club and struck it rich by launching California cuisine.

OAKLAND, SOUTHEAST OF BERKELEY, was orbiting in still another solar system. It was a tough, drug-wracked city, the fifth-largest in California, anomalous in the suburban landscape and almost out of control.

In the Oakland hills, there were pockets of gentility and many people of a liberal conscience, but down in the infernal flats you came upon decaying old houses and horrid housing projects that had been burned and gutted, where crime was taught in busy tutorials. Gangs of Crips and Bloods plied their trade there and distributed crack cocaine and heroin, with boys sometimes no older than ten hooked into service and outfitted with beepers.

The gangsters and their wanna-bes dressed as if to advertise the fact that they were dealing, hip and nonchalant in Raiders' paraphernalia with its piratical emblem and its buccaneerish colors of silver and black, or in FILA T-shirts, baggy pants, and pump-em-up Air Jordan sneakers. There was something of the clown or the fool in the mix, at once streetwise and heartbroken, but that changed when the gangsters were in their late teens and understood that they were in the life for good, with no chance of escape. Then their eyes grew hard and cold and murderous.

Friends kept vanishing, that was part of it. They got busted and were shipped off to prison, gone to Susanville or Pelican Bay, locales as exotic to an inner-city kid as Bucharest might be. Or they turned up dead, stabbed or shot or overdosed. A young person in the worst sections of Oakland became intimate with death in early childhood, and with sex not much later, as girls just beginning to menstruate gave birth to infants out of wedlock, babies making babies.

I walked around Oakland and saw the young mothers as they waited at bus stops for a ride to a clinic or a hospital or maybe to a relative's house. They put on a brave front while they clutched their children to them, looking proud and loving but also terrified and overwhelmed, barely managing to hang on to their squirmy bundles.

A curious look of annoyance sometimes crossed a mother's face, as if it had just dawned on her that she'd be stuck with her infant now and forever—that she'd been tricked into playing a game without knowing all the rules.

Oakland wasn't unattractive. It had handsome lakes and parks. The architecture had a distinctive 1930s sturdiness, spared from the glass-and-steel skyscrapers that were interchangeable among California cities. It had a good museum, a good zoo, and a fine sports complex for baseball and basketball. Its port continued to grow, earning substantial revenues from two big military tenants on its waterfront, depots for the army and the navy.

Yet Oakland still fought against every attempt at redevelopment. Millions had been sunk into renovating a downtown area around Henry J. Kaiser Convention Center, but the shops and the restaurants couldn't stay in business, because nobody wanted to be on those streets at night, although a project to construct a new Federal Building was supposed to change all that.

Gangs appeared to be the true bosses in Oakland. The city had a murder rate that had blasted right off the scale. Drive-by shootings were an everyday affair. Often the killers—teenagers acting out of a warped sense of honor—were too stoned or dumb or inept to hit their target and instead sprayed bullets from their Uzis, the modern equivalent of the sawed-off shotgun, into homes or apartments where grannies snored before a TV.

The Crips and the Bloods weren't the only ones in business. Tongs ruled the roost in Oakland's thriving Chinatown and banged heads with the gangs of Vietnamese immigrants who were closing in on them. Hell's Angels were also partial to the city. They did their usual trading in weapons and speed and buried their dead at Evergreen Cemetery.

Whenever an Angel was blown away in the line of duty, or got wasted in a crash, or relinquished himself to premature liver failure, his fellow bikers turned out for a slow ride to Evergreen. Such honchos of the club as Charlie "Magoo" Tinsley, Doug "The Thug" Orr, and James "Fu" Griffin were all pushing up daisies there. A heavy-duty Angel like "Irish" Mike O'Farrell, sent to his maker by four gunshot wounds and seven stab wounds outside a bar, had earned a black marble tombstone and a floral arrangement in the shape of a flying skull.

Sometimes it seemed that Oakland was laboring under a curse. Its public schools were a shambles, so bankrupt and mismanaged that they'd been taken from the hands of local educators and put under the auspices of an overseer from the state. In a way, the schools were at the heart of the matter, as they were everywhere in the suburbs, in every DMZ. The old notion that hard work and studious behavior were a path out of the ghetto held little credence among California youths these days.

The kids in Oakland sat in their grungy classrooms and spun their eyes to the heavens when confronted with *A Tale of Two Cities* or some other relic bit of literature, and they drag-assed home after class and saw before them what hard work would bring them—a cramped bungalow on a seedy block. The bungalow and the life that went with it, those were your rewards for thirty years at a Ford plant or thirty years as a domestic. The kids in Oakland saw all that daily, and they rebelled, silently or otherwise.

There was no denying the truth. The adolescents in Oakland's rundown high schools, and in rundown high schools all across the state, knew that they were being monitored and contained, not prepared for advancement. In California, only the prisons were as overcrowded as the public schools.

Harsh realities were the real music of Oakland, its rasp and its resonance, the Oaktown Sound, with rappers and hip-hoppers spelling out in big, bold words what everybody felt in secret. Frustration and anger were the city's juice, the very source of the energy that primed the pump for the graffiti artists who sprayed walls and boarded-up buildings with slogans like the one I saw on a concrete highway abutment as I drove away, the one that said, Oakland *Is* South Africa.

CHAPTER 13

OAKLAND OUT. I crossed the Bay Bridge, some eight-and-a-half miles of steel, the longest such span in the world. There were frenzied gulls winging about in a clear blue sky. Past Army Street, the freeway split in two, with the right fork, Highway 280, branching off to Daly City, where about thirty thousand Filipino–Americans lived close by the shopping paradise of Serramonte Mall.

Daly City was fogged in from May until September, but those who remembered Manila claimed not to care. Around Serramonte, even the streets are air-conditioned, they liked to say.

The left fork, Highway 101, ran down through the suburbs of the San Francisco Peninsula. Near Candlestick Park on the bay, home of our amazing Giants and forty-niners, the same wind that made outfielders pine for thermal underwear was whipping up a froth and propelling sailboarders forward at breakneck speeds. I had a vision of Willie McGee commuting to work, Hercules to the baseball stadium, Hercules to the baseball stadium, *ad infinitum,* calculating his batting average while listening to his Bradshaw tapes.

Farther on came Redwood City. People didn't usually connect it to Silicon Valley, whose epicenter, Sunnyvale, was about forty miles away, but in a nondescript building there, Jaron Lanier of VPL Research, Inc., was refining his contribution to Virtual Reality, which had the potential, its disciples believed, to be bigger than Nintendo by the millennium.

Lanier had all the hallmarks of a techno whiz kid. He was under thirty, eccentric, and brilliant in the way of certain mathematicians and divines. When I called on him at his office, he gave me a doughy handshake that seemed to be a metaphor for his entire being. He did not walk so much as pad softly, a person born to go barefoot. His eyes were cool and translucent, and his hair was coiled and braided into massive dreadlocks.

Lanier's pale white skin spoke of countless nights spent wandering in the stratosphere of computer syntax, where the oxygen gets thin. He conversed with a dizzying cerebral energy, selling both the sizzle and the steak.

"I couldn't exist anywhere but in California," he said in a quiet voice. "Except maybe around Boston."

The route Lanier had followed to the Coast was composed of many eventful twists and turns. His parents were nomadic, possession-free sixties people, he told me, and they had moved from New York to the deserts of southern New Mexico shortly after his birth. Young Jaron went to grammar school in Juarez, across the border, the lone white kid in a Mexican classroom. He described himself as a "very, very strange child," sensitive, bored with his teachers, and already leading a rich fantasy life.

His father, a science writer, set up a tent in the desert and began building a house around it with Jaron's help. The house was enormous and eclectic, assembled from found materials. It had four geodesic domes, and through them you could see crystal shapes beaming and flashing.

At the age of fifteen, Lanier prematurely advanced himself by forging a high school diploma and matriculating at New Mexico State University. Music was his first love then, the hum of synthesizers

and the allure of keyboards, and he went on "an artist trip" and
played his music at coffeehouses in New York, often destroying his
instrument as part of a performance.

That got old after a while, so Lanier, not yet twenty, cycled back
to the university and discovered the compelling power of computers.
He liked the made-up quality of computer imagery, all the little
worlds you could generate, so many of them vastly more interesting
than the real world. The tragic thing about *actual* physical reality,
he had learned, was that it was mandatory.

Silicon Valley summoned him to the Coast. To transport himself,
he rescued a car that someone had abandoned in the desert after a
drug arrest. Bullet holes poked through its hull in large numbers
but, against the odds, the car made it to California and Lanier was
launched on his career in the chipland of instant millionaires.

He designed a computer game, Moondust, which incorporated
music and imagery, and won some awards and earned some money.
For a time, he designed games for Atari and later, on his own, devised
a visual programming language, Mandala, whose merits were touted
in *Scientific American* as a major advance in software. When an editor
phoned in 1984 to ask about Lanier's corporate affiliation, he invented
VPL Research, Inc., on the spot.

That was the essence of the computer business—to produce
something out of nothing. Investors and would-be partners were soon
knocking at his door, and he chose to establish his workshop in
Redwood City because, he said, Silicon Valley was "too sterile." Now
Virtual Reality was Lanier's main interest. He defined *virtual* to mean
anything that existed only as an electronic representation.

Virtual Reality created an artificial environment, but that was
nothing new. In the 1940s, NASA had used such environments for
flight simulation. There were patents on record for whole techno-
worlds. An engineer at MIT had built a prototype of a head-mounted
unit in 1968, and an inventor had once come up with a Sensorama
Stimulator that tickled the central nervous system with 3-D images,
a binaural soundtrack, and smells from an odor cannister.

VPL's most valuable wrinkle so far was a DataGlove (list price, $8,800) that NASA used. The glove was a sleek, form-fitting sci-fi item laced with flexible fiber-optic cables. When you put it on, it reproduced the motions of your fingers and hands in a computer-generated landscape. You pointed to something, and your virtual hand pointed.

The worlds to be explored were as diverse as the individuals drawing them, Lanier believed. All you needed was a good graphics program for your computer. You drew the world in full color—a jungle, a baseball diamond, the set of a porno flick—donned your gloves and your EyePhone (a head-mounted display unit with stereo sound), and entered your own brain, courtesy of the VPL RB2 Virtual Environment package—work station, tranceivers, software, and so on, at a list price of $45,275.

Those who had taken the journey often invoked the name of Walt Disney. The virtual worlds seemed real in the way of a cartoon. The psychedelic aspects of the trip were obviously enticing. For Lanier, though, the big payoff might still be somewhere down the line, with the Home Reality Engine.

As he imagined it, the Home Reality Engine would plug into a phone outlet. The owner would have display goggles with little stereo speakers to catch the noises of a virtual world. The goggles might also have sensors to relay facial contortions to a virtual face.

Lanier gave me an example. Suppose that you decided to be a cat prowling in some garbage cans. If you rolled your eyes, the cat's eyes would roll. Or you might like to become a mountain range, a galaxy, or a pebble. The Home Reality Engine would have access to arbitrary physics, too, so that a saxophone could play not only notes but words or cities or comets.

In a virtual world, anything was possible. Lanier, who accepted the seer's mantle with a minimum of protest, felt that Virtual Reality might be used someday in biomedicine and communications. It was, he said, the ultimate gadget, and its skin had barely been peeled. At moments, he thought that VR would breed a successor to the telephone—he'd been having enthusiastic talks about this with Pactel, in fact.

Lanier was not without concerns about his brainchild. He knew how an innocent technology could be corrupted. The best Virtual Reality units in the country belonged to the military. Then there was the problem of information replacing experience. He also fretted that Virtual Reality might mutate into a kind of mega-television in the wrong hands. The idea was thoroughly repugnant to him. TV watching, he said, was a clinical form of death.

SOUTH, SOUTH, down the peninsula. Say it's the year 2008, and the average commuter has sailed home to Palo Alto from his San Francisco office in just under three hours, not bad for a Thursday in July. He unlocks the door of a two-bedroom bungalow that he and his wife, Judy, have paid a million dollars for, financing the mortgage through Osaka Securities. She's still on the road, working her way back from Contra Costopolis (elapsed time, ninety minutes), so the average commuter—let's call him Ed Hastings—pops open a cold brewskie and thinks about some dinner.

Ed's up for a barbecue, but it isn't his allotted monthly burn day. Besides, barbecuing hasn't been much fun since the sky turned that funny color, and the water department outlawed lawns. Ed lifts a Venetian blind, stares at the weeds out there, and ponders whether or not he should haul in a truckload of crushed rocks from Yardbirds, like the Farquarsons did next door.

In the fridge, Ed finds some nice tomatoes, beautifully irradiated. It's incredible how long the damn things last. He slices one, sprinkles on some virgin olive oil from Napa, and eats it al fresco, the way old Alice Waters suggests. That Alice is something—she must be nearly a hundred. The tomato has an off-flavor, but Ed grins and bears it. He's not about to shell out thirty bucks a pound for those vine-ripened beefsteaks over at Real Foods.

The clock ticks, but there's still no Judy. Ed pops open another brewskie and falls into a reverie about his impending vacation, three days at Yosemite. Don Farquarson said that they were lucky to get in, but, hell, they'd tried the lottery for nine straight years without even scoring a campsite.

Ed shuts his eyes and dreams about fishing the Merced River. It'll be turned on that Monday and Wednesday. He imagines a romantic dinner at the new John Muir Hotel and Spa, and his heart skips a beat at the prospect of all the neat nature that they'll see, great birds long gone from the Bay Area, bluejays, robins, and even crows.

Eight o'clock and no Judy. Ed pops yet another brewskie, lifts a Venetian blind, and hears a familiar buzz all down the block, the sound of Home Reality Engines being switched on. He's been hoping to cut back on the time he spends at his workstation, but with Judy stuck on the freeway—and why do they call them *free*ways, anyhow, when you have to pay a toll?—there's no point in being a martyr.

So he toddles to the entertainment center and gets into his virtual suit. Darn, but the fiber-optic cables are giving him a skin rash again! He flips on the Apple Mac XXXXIV, fits it with a graphics package, and starts sketching.

He doesn't recognize what he's drawing at first. It's got a little dog, a lawn, some willow trees—hey, it's his boyhood home in Levittown! Those were the days, all right, way before he met Judy and before he knew anything about California, back when there were no burn schedules and you could fire up the Weber whenever you wanted to, when tomatoes actually grew in suburban gardens.

Gee, Ed thinks, it was a regular paradise out there on Long Island.

SURELY ED AND JUDY HASTINGS would be subscribers to *Sunset,* "the magazine of western living," which had its offices in Menlo Park, not far from Redwood City. Any doubts I might have had about *Sunset*'s success at spreading an image of California as a place from

which controversy, black moods, impetigo, ugly people, and plain
old trouble had been banished was put to rest by the grandeur of its
corporate headquarters.

Lane Publishing Company sprawled in hacienda-style over seven-
and-a-half acres. It was lunchtime when I arrived, and everywhere
employees were hurrying to get in some exercise before their break
was over. They could attend a company-sponsored aerobics class, join
in a basketball game, Nautilize themselves at the fitness center, or
simply go for a jog. The hardcore jocks headed for Stanford, where
they ran up and down the steps of the football stadium.

Never before had I seen so much Lycra and spandex in a business
environment. The workers made me uneasy. They were doing too
much oxygen.

At *Sunset,* the myth of human perfectability still seemed to be
in ascendance. If only you ran fast enough, ate healthily enough,
thought chastely enough, and so on, maybe you could occupy a special
plane in time and space that would be like Michael Jackson's hy-
perbaric chamber and keep the aging process at bay.

For eons, the magazine itself had been selling a similarly unblemished vision. Once a month, the editors served up an ideal blend
of perfect gardens, perfect meals, perfect vacation trips, and perfect
antidotes to dry rot. The formula could drive a person over the edge.
You looked at the food on your plate, and it did not look like the
food on the plates in the photograph, *even though you'd followed the
recipe perfectly!*

Lane Publishing had a library where visitors could peruse back
issues. The earliest ones dated from 1898 and bore the imprimatur
of the Southern Pacific Railroad, whose promotional geniuses had
founded the magazine to encourage tourist travel on such trains as
its *Sunset Limited.* Even as an embryonic venture, *Sunset* had a creed.
Its editors hoped to supply "publicity for the attractions and advantages of the Western Empire."

Yosemite Valley was the first attraction it pushed. In a featured article illustrated with the photos of Joseph Le Conte, a Berkeley geology professor and a "member of the Sierra Club," the merits of the park were touted in heroically banal prose that relied heavily on certain adjectives that would cling to Yosemite forever—majestic, inspiring, sublime. The old warhorse, Ralph Waldo Emerson, was even trotted out for a testimonial.

"It is the only spot I have ever found," Emerson said, "that came up to the brag."

A roundtrip train ticket from San Francisco cost thirty-eight dollars, and the final leg of the journey involved a "picturesque" stagecoach ride through the Sierra Nevada foothills.

In 1914, Southern Pacific sold *Sunset* to its staff, who turned it into a literary journal and thereby insured its unprofitability. It limped along until L. W. Lane, an advertising man, bought it fourteen years later for sixty thousand dollars.

Lane was an innovative thinker. He saw the West as a nation apart from the rest of the country, with its own special climate, mores, history, and family arrangements. The West had a tradition of independence, he thought—a pioneering spirit and a how-to attitude. He insisted that articles should be practical as well as charming. His editors were also instructed to concentrate on areas of expertise that were crucial to an understanding of life on the Pacific Coast, such as gardening, cooking, travel, and home building and remodeling.

Above all, *Sunset* was intended to be useful, targeted at an audience that was laboring hard in its spare time to turn their little patch of backyard into the New Eden. The magazine lost money for a while, but it was in the black by the mid-1930s, with subscribers avidly awaiting such helpful stories as "Weekend Homes for Woods-Loving Westerners" and the best recipes for chipped beef pudding.

In a brilliant editorial stroke, Lane eventually split *Sunset* into four separate editions, each catering to the needs of a distinct bioregion. The fuchsia grower in Crescent City, say, faced different challenges than the one in San Diego. The magazine's circulation soon topped a million a month and hundreds of books were spun off from it, addressing in glossy fashion such questions as the building of decks and the pruning of fruit trees.

Sunset held family values dear. Written by an in-house staff, it developed a bouncy, insular optimism. In all the volumes on the shelves in Menlo Park, there was never a hint of darkness. Instead, flipping pages, I stood face to face with the perfect fern, the perfect hot tub, and the perfect avocado.

EDWIN BRYANT HAD NEVER VISITED Menlo Park and Lane Publishing, of course, but a tall tale that he had related in his book came into my mind. As an example of the rumors about California that were flying around Kentucky, he offered the story of a poor Californian who had lived to be two hundred and fifty but had not yet died.

The old man was beside himself. He'd had quite enough of being alive, but the "youth-preserving" climate on the Coast had kept him in perfect health. He became so unnerved that he thought about suicide, but the holy padres at the nearest mission advised him that he would fry in hell. At last, deeply upset about continuing to exist, he had accepted some advice from a relative—possibly an heir, Bryant remarked—and moved away into the Nevada territory, where he promptly expired.

But the old man had made an awful mistake! In his will, he'd expressed a foolish wish to be brought back home for his burial, and once his body was interred in California, the "health-giving zephyrs" went to work on him, and he leaped back to life with a renewed vigor and an otherworldly physical prowess.

PALO ALTO (median house price, $457,800) used to be strictly a satellite of Stanford University, but during the boom years in Silicon Valley, roughly from 1970 to 1980, some big spenders from the chip factories had drifted into the area and had started buying up some prime real estate. In the hills around town, in Woodside, Mountain View, and Los Altos, brave new homes had blossomed on a scale previously associated only with the excesses of Hollywood.

The houses seemed to be engaged in a mute competition, each trying to outdo the other in terms of size and expense and most of them having little or no architectural relevance to the land upon which they'd been built. There were mock villas in the Tuscan or Provençal mode, turreted fortresses flying pennants, horse ranches off the Montana plain, and great boxes of glass and redwood so divorced from any aesthetic concerns that their sole effect was to scream, "My owner's rich!"

Not for nothing did the name of Walt Disney keep cropping up around Silicon Valley. Nolan Bushnell, Atari's founder, the progenitor of Pong, Pac-Man, and Miss Pac-Man, those first-generation video games that already seemed as whimsically primitive as cave paintings—Bushnell had roared out of Utah's Mormon wastes after college hoping that his experience as a worker in an amusement park would earn him a niche in the Disney empire. He was turned down cold, but he had the last laugh, parlaying his company into a mansion in Woodside.

During the same go-go epoch, Stephen Jobs, a driving force behind Apple computers, whose net worth had been assessed at $200 million at the time, had acquired a massive Tudor estate in nearby Los Gatos. Another Los Gatan, Philip Hwang (net worth, $610 million), who had started TeleVideo Systems, resided in a faux Welsh castle that had a dining room comfortably seating four hundred guests.

In California real estate circles, such residences were sometimes known as "I-made-it" houses. An "I-made-it" house marked the exact historical moment when a Californian rose above the masses and was liberated from the confines of a melting-pot suburb like Hercules, where the detective powers of a Sherlock Holmes were required to tell one home from another.

"We're building a house in Wildcat Canyon," you heard people say, or "We're building a house in Blackhawk," and the words appeared to give them a potent lift. A custom-built house was assertive and implied a certain control over your destiny.

In the past decade, the average "I-made-it" house was getting bigger, with the floor space doubling from 2,400 to 4,800 square feet. The houses had gyms, screening rooms, Nintendo midways, and subterranean quarters for au pairs from foreign lands. Children slept in their own wing, miles from their slumbering parents.

SILICON VALLEY, USA. I watched the morning sun bounce off mirrored buildings, while cars ripped and swirled through hastily planned intersections, performing the daily push-and-shove of the money dance.

In the dicey maneuvering from stoplight to stoplight, there was a weird mimickery of computer-board circuitry, wires and switches in bright, Mondrian colors processing information at the quickest possible speed. The drivers had the look of overextended debtors, in hock up to their ears just to keep the Jag or the Lexus free from the clutches of the repo man.

Sunnyvale was often cited as the key town for computer wizards, but Silicon Valley's boundaries were really indistinct. It didn't draw its coordinates so much from any fixed points on earth as it did from the overheated force field that sparked and crackled between the lobes of its central players' brains. The computer game inspired a consummate amount of gossip, and you absolutely couldn't function if you weren't in the loop.

A venture capitalist once said that the greatest *legal* creation of wealth in world history had taken place in Silicon Valley—yet another California Gold Rush, then.

So rich, complex, data-dense, and militarily important was the valley that the old Soviet nuclear team had selected the San Francisco Peninsula as one of its top-ten targets in the country. I drove to Ground Zero at Walsh Road and San Thomas Expressway in Santa

Clara and pictured it as a nuked-out crater, where mongrel humans from beyond the mushroom cloud were wandering in oblivion.

Electronics and high-tech businesses had always found a home on the peninsula. The intellectual climate was conducive to innovation, to the swapping of new ideas and the jerry-rigging of new firms. The list of inventions born here was long—two-way radio telephones, shortwave radios, the klystron tube (essential in radar and in microwaves), transistors, and transmitters.

In San Francisco proper, Philo T. Farnsworth had done his first experiments with the Frankenstein that became television, but Palo Alto was a more significant place for brainstorming on account of Stanford Industrial Park, more than eight thousand acres of university land committed to R&D by Frederick Turman, Stanford's dean of engineering, in the 1930s. Hewlett-Packard, Ampex, and Fairchild Semiconductor were all initially situated in the park, a start-up heaven.

The peninsula was well prepared to receive the new breed of high-tech entrepreneurs who began to collect there in the late 1960s. They were the maverick geniuses from the American fringe, readers of *Mad* and *Dune,* gizmo lovers since the second grade, pale and unathletic, owners of chemistry sets and remote-control cars, devotees of Dungeons and Dragons, diligent masturbators, adolescent in their ardor and their enthusiasm, serious consumers of junk food, celebrants of Dr Pepper and Diet Coke, envoys of the late night— fantasists, savants, and dreamers.

The new entrepreneurs were courageous. Having been out of step all their lives, they were not thrown by the rapid advances in technology that flustered the less flexible. Computers were their catnip. Give them access to a mainframe, and they'd gather around it in a red-eyed knot, hacking away at all hours, breaking into phone-lines or databanks and pondering the "what-ifs" of the future. The military knew of their escapades, and its procurers sometimes used the big Crays at Lawrence Livermore Lab to seduce them into defense work.

The hackers put out underground papers and dealt in *samizdat*. They held beer busts where everyone got drunk and exchanged techno-secrets. To support themselves, they often took lower-echelon jobs at electronics firms on the peninsula and distinguished themselves by not following orders and asking too many questions.

Stanford was the hot spot. At the Home Brew Computer Club, Steven Jobs and his high-school chum, Steve Wozniak, started selling personal computers to their pals in the mid-1970s. They relied on scavenged hardware and put together their prototype, Apple I, in a garage, using a twenty-dollar microprocessor. They pitched the personal-computer idea to their respective employers at Atari and Hewlett-Packard, but there was little interest, so they branched out and sold the machines at a byte shop in Mountain View.

Jobs, a bearded, long-haired vegetarian, was the business person, while Wozniak handled the science. In 1976, they came up with Apple II, a significant technological advance. The PC weighed just twelve pounds and was so simple to operate that IBM and other corporations became convinced of the market appeal of such computers and embarked on a crash program to manufacture them.

When Apple went public in 1980, Jobs and Wozniak made millions, as did their investors. Arthur Rock, a venture capitalist, earned about $14 million on stock he'd bought for nine cents a share two years earlier. In the boom years, with the mingling of investors, MBAs, and entrepreneurs, there were many similar scores. In 1983, for instance, toward the end of a huge growth cycle, nine men and women hit the big time by going public with their stock. The smallest payoff to any of them was $31 million.

By 1984, Apple was profitable enough to slip into the Fortune 500, the first company ever to do so after only five years in business. The stakes were high now, and a new seriousness set in. The halcyon age of hacking and goofing was over. Computer Shack was transformed into Computer Land and Kentucky Fried Computers turned into North Star. As the entrepreneurs got more sophisticated, their hobbies did, too—private airplanes, superluxury automobiles, and such esoteric pursuits as Transcendental Meditation, est, and Scientology, as though everyone had simultaneously perceived a spiritual void blipping across their monitors.

The early 1980s were a watershed moment in Silicon Valley. The valley had a past now, a history—it had fallen from grace. The same year that Apple joined the Fortune 500, Atari laid off a thousand workers, while founder Bushnell veered wildly in the direction of Pizza Time Restaurants and Chuck E. Cheese. A grand shakeout was under way.

In the bars were hopeful programmers and MBAs met for exploratory discussions, the talk had a wistful flavor of nostalgia at the passing of a golden age. It was the same nostalgia you heard in San Francisco when gay men talked about a time before AIDS, the same sad acceptance that came into the voices of loggers and fishermen when they spoke of the lost abundance of the forests and the seas— the same high-pitched note of regret that hung in the air everywhere in California when the party was over at last.

Silicon Valley was not dead, though, not by a long shot. In such hangouts as the Lion & Compass in Sunnyvale, youths with bad haircuts and too many pens and pencils in their breast pockets still hunkered over pints of beer to whisper about matters pending.

The single constant in Silicon Valley was its intellectual fecundity. Only in this sliver of the state—in this sliver of America—could you rent an office, install a phone, and begin a round of blind calling to the very best minds in the high-tech universe, each genius listening closely to see if you were a clue to the next thing coming.

ON MAPS, Santa Clara Valley is a welter of urban and suburban density, red lines that crisscross and cancel one another out. The density breaks only on the southwestern flank of the valley, where the Santa Cruz Mountains form a barrier between progress and the ocean.

Native Californians of my generation, people who grew up

around Campbell or Cupertino or San Jose, sometimes become emotional when they tell about what happened to Santa Clara Valley
during their childhoods. They have sweet memories of being born
into a pastoral landscape where peach, pear, prune, and apple trees
put out a plethora of blossoms every spring, but they remember, too,
how by the time they turned eighteen and left for college, the orchards
were all gone, replaced by houses, strip malls, shopping centers, and
industrial parks.

Among planners in California, Santa Clara Valley, congested and
overbuilt, its greenbelt reduced to scattered blades of grass, is often
held up as a model of what not to do. And yet the lesson of my tour
of Bay Area suburbs was that the model was being repeated ceaselessly
and consciously, with no hope for a let-up in sight.

The San Francisco Bay Area had a population of about 7.5
million, fully a quarter of the state's residents. There were still 2
million acres of agricultural land—row crops, farms, orchards, vineyards, and pastures—but about 30,000 acres of it fell to development
each year.

A farmer in Brentwood, in Contra Costa County, might have
paid about $6,000 an acre for farmland in the mid-1980s, but he
could get about $15,000 an acre for it now by selling it as ranchettes
in five-acre parcels. If the local planning commission rezoned the
area to allow for subdividing, the price would shoot up to about
$85,000 an acre.

Happiness, for a moment.

IN SAN JOSE, I walked through the old downtown past Mexican
restaurants that smelled of peppers and cooking oil and ate my dinner
at a Vietnamese hole-in-the-wall, the only white man in the joint.
Families sat quietly at tables spooning in *pho,* a nourishing beef broth
of lean meat and tendons sprinkled with bean sprouts and cilantro.

San Jose was a bigger city than San Francisco now. Asians from
all over were moving in, dispossessed Cambodians, Laotians, and

Thais. They were not worried about the vanishing open space in California and the ongoing slaughter of the greenbelt. They were the newest bench-sitters, glad for an indoor toilet and a window with a view.

I ordered Vietnamese coffee at the end of my meal. The shy, teenage girl who brought it, reedlike in a silk dress, was the very stuff of haiku. And what a lovely smile! I felt a blackness in my heart for ever worrying about anything.

Watch it, brother, I counseled myself. You'll wind up living in Berkeley.

Tomorrow, the twentieth of July, I would hit the road again, hellbent to reach the border before autumn, so I meditated for a time on simple, direct things—on the high, cool cirques of Yosemite and the dusty farming reaches of the San Joaquin.

PART FOUR

SAN JOAQUIN

By the roadside the dust lay thick and grey, and, on either hand, stretching on toward the horizon, losing itself in a mere smudge in the distance, ran the illimitable parallels of the wire fence.
—*Frank Norris,*
The Octopus

Lines of people moving across the fields.
—*John Steinbeck,*
The Grapes of Wrath

CHAPTER 14

PROFESSOR JOSEPH LE CONTE of Berkeley, Georgia-born, holder of a doctorate in medicine from New York State University and a post-graduate student of the great Louis Agassiz at Harvard, took leave of his family in Oakland in the following way on July 21, 1870:

Amid many kind and cheering words, mingled with tender regrets; many encouragements, mingled with earnest entreaties to take care of myself, and to keep out of *drafts* and *damp* while sleeping on the *bare ground* in the *open air;* many half-supressed tears, concealed beneath bright smiles, I left my home and dear ones this morning. Surely I must have a heroic and dangerous air about me, for my little baby boy shrinks from my rough flannel shirt and broad-brim hat. . . .

Le Conte and nine other men, the "university excursion party," were embarking on a horseback trip to Yosemite Valley, which had been designated as a state park six years earlier. Although he made light of the journey, assigning all fears to sentimental women and innocent babes, there was some genuine concern beneath the jaunty surface of his prose.

Yosemite Valley had come to symbolize everything wild in California, every untamed natural force that could not be controlled. Its name was derived from an Awani Indian word that was presumed to mean "grizzly bear." Even before the Southern Pacific began promoting tourism, J. M. Hutchings, an English writer, was carrying on in his *California Magazine* about the awesome dimensions of the valley, where he happened to own a hotel. Seven miles long, its rocky walls rose to a height of 4,800 feet in some spots.

In salons on Montgomery Street in San Francisco, passersby were moved to gasp at the mammoth-plate portraits of Half Dome and Bridalveil Falls, the work of such expeditionary photographers as Carleton Watkins and Eadweard Muybridge. Yosemite Valley was both compelling and disturbing. It outstripped the power of the brain to imagine it.

In Le Conte's departure, too, you could see the origins of wilderness adventuring as a leisure activity, nascent backpacking and mountaineering, with Everyman and Everywoman cast as Natty Bumppo. The idea of risking pneumonia by sleeping in a bedroll on the ground held an increasing appeal to the stout of heart. If you survived, you'd be a better person, a more fully fleshed Californian.

Professor Le Conte had just turned forty-seven and hadn't mounted a horse for ten years, but he was determined "not to be an encumbrance to the merry party," whose goal was to cover about thirty miles on their first day, riding over Contra Costa Ridge and through Hayward Pass. The men got so excited, though, that they pressed on for an extra five miles to Laddsville before striking camp. That proved to be a miscalculation. Le Conte estimated that Laddsville had a mammalian population of about two hundred, one hundred and fifty of which were dogs that barked all night and kept the campers awake.

Laddsville was Livermore now, a town still on a main route to Yosemite National Park, in which the valley reposed. Livermore had a weapons lab, many replicating subdivisions, and some land planted to vineyards. It had a Mobil station where I stopped to fill my tank on the way to the park. The owner-dealer was Pyung Jung.

It was a lovely, breezy morning, and the hills around Livermore had gone to their summer gold-brown. I thought of the country in Le Conte's time, of the ranches, cattle, and rippling wheatfields. I saw the saddle-sore, dog-persecuted university crew waking up, the men coughing, farting, and peeing on the campfire embers after a breakfast of bacon, cheese, bread, and good tea, feeling refreshed and comforted.

Ahead of them lay the unknown mountains and their mysteries. The only mystery confronting me was whether or not I'd get a campsite without a reservation from Ticketron.

From Livermore, I climbed over Altamont Pass on Highway 580, where turbines spun with the ecstatic energy of pinwheels to harvest electricity from the wind, and then I crossed the California Aqueduct, a conduit that brought water from the Sacramento Delta to the San Joaquin.

Turning southeast, I took Highway 99 into Modesto under a sky that was gray with dust, smoke, and chemical fumes. A Rotary Club sign pumped the virtues of Water, Wealth, Contentment, and Health. The town's founder, William Ralston, a railroader, had refused to let it be named after him, but he hadn't quite succeeded. *"Muy modesto,"* said his Spanish constituents, commenting on his humility and bestowing a backhanded tribute.

Turlock, Atwater, Merced. The plains of the San Joaquin, and the noon heat ablaze. There were no dams or aqueducts when Le Conte had galloped through. The land was still as arid and very nearly as treeless as the Sahara.

The university crew suffered from parched throats, baked lips, and bloody noses. They saw mirages and had fantasies about water. Their thighs ached and their butts hurt—"an exquisite tenderness of the sitting bones." One rider, Everett Pomroy, known to the company as "Our Poet," tried to ease his haunches by sitting side-saddle, but his mount threw him. Pomroy, infuriated, set the beast right by punching it.

The men rode on across the plains and came in the late afternoon to the San Joaquin River, a real stream then but now a churlish, brown murk in July, and they took a swim and ate some peaches. The wind kept blowing, a wind from a blast furnace tearing at their faces and peeling away their skin. In the village of Grayson, Le Conte paused briefly to mail a letter to his wife, assuring her that he was still alive.

Highway 140 broke off to the east of Highway 99, a ribbon unfurling to a gate of Yosemite at El Portal. There were big, broad, western-looking valleys until the road started its ascent.

Le Conte, the geologist: "Country beginning to be quite hilly; first, only denudation hills of drift, finely and horizontally stratified; then, round hills with sharp toothlike jags of perpendicularly cleaved slates, standing out thickly on their sides."

The men reached Mariposa on the seventh day of their journey, riding smoothly through town in double file, in a military procession. They did not have to contend with overheated cars stalled and tangled in knots or have to listen to shouting matches between irate parents and overwrought kids. They rode on into the forest, higher and higher, and it brought them a welcome relief. They basked in the cooling shade of the yellow pines, the sugar pines, and the Douglas firs.

"No moon," Le Conte wrote that night. "Only starlight."

The university crew was close to their destination and teased themselves by taking a rest. They turned out their horses and napped in a meadow and smoked tobacco and sang songs as the spirit moved them. They washed their filthy clothes in the Merced River, squatting like squaws on the rocks, soaping and scrubbing and wringing, a moment of unconscious baptism, of cleansing, before entering the valley.

Then they rode on through Big Trees, a redwood grove, in the morning and later met another touring party among whose members

was a rather pretty (though stout) young woman in a very short
bloomer costume that showed "a considerable portion of her two fat
legs." To the men, she became Miss Bloomer.

"The captain, I think, is struck," said Le Conte, "but he worships,
as yet, at a distance."

Then, in the afternoon, a first glimpse of Yosemite Valley from
Ostrander's Rocks. The men on horseback, the horses pawing and
whinnying—"magnificent." They rode on until early evening, dismounted, and hiked up Sentinel Dome to a point some 8,500 feet
above sea level for a twilight look at the valley.

Le Conte: "To the left stands El Capitan's massive perpendicular
wall; directly in front, and distant about one mile, Yosemite Falls,
like a gauzy veil . . . to the right the mighty granite mass of Half
Dome lifts itself in solitary grandeur . . . in the distance, innumerable
peaks of the High Sierra . . . such a sunset, combined with such view,
I had never imagined."

Two days later, the men rode into the valley proper. Le Conte
exclaimed to his journal, *Yosemite today!"*

AT THE ARCH ROCK GATE, just beyond El Portal, I paid a ranger five
dollars for a weekly pass, thinking that Yosemite National Park must
be the bargain of the century. The road in traced the course of the
Merced River, still high and slightly discolored from the spring runoff.
Whenever the dark shadows cast by the pines, firs, and broadleaf
maples broke apart, I looked up at a keenly blue sky piled with
clouds in puffy columns, a sight common in the Sierra Nevada
through all seasons.

Though I had been to the park many times, the crowding around
the Visitor Center in Yosemite Valley never failed to astound me.
As if in some crackpot corollary to the fact of nature being raised to
its highest power, the sheer thronging of people and machines sur-
passed any version of the ordinary.

The minute you got near the center, you had to start circling for a parking spot, on your guard not to run down any children or stray pets or crash into any of the tour buses whose drivers seemed to be in training for the Indy 500. Vehicles from the Corporation Yard cut across the grain of traffic at odd angles, like free radicals tossed into the pot to test your already overburdened reflexes.

I had to remind myself that things were not that bad, not yet— in August, the valley succumbed to absolute gridlock.

Yosemite Valley had been ceded to the automobile long ago. There was a picture in one of the books in my traveling library that showed a big-bellied man in a white shirt and a bow tie motoring along a dirt path in his locomobile exactly thirty years after Le Conte's trip on horseback. Cars were not officially permitted into the park until 1913, when the U.S. secretary of the interior, under the urging of such groups as the Motor Car Dealers Association and, implausibly, the Sierra Club, lifted a ban against them.

James Bryce, the British ambassador to the United States, was a sage dissenter in the debate and invoked the specter of Old Nick for the sake of comparison.

"If Adam had known what harm the serpent was going to work," Bryce advised, "he would have tried to prevent him from finding lodging in Eden."

Smog, traffic, and noise. The Visitor Center was obviously best avoided, but it had a way of getting to you in the end. You'd have to buy the coffee that you had forgot, or a postcard for Aunt Emily, or a Yosemite sweatshirt for a sniffling, bee-stung child. Or you had to drop in, as I did, to see what sort of accommodations were available, if any.

Everything in the park was booked. Everything.

"You should have used Ticketron," said a lad whose nametag identified him as Dwayne from Pocatello, Idaho.

How to explain to Dwayne that I was in foolhardy rebellion against such procedures, trying to strike a balance between the modern world and a precomputer, Le Contian ideal of wilderness adventuring? No matter—I would go back and arrange something in

El Portal, the court of last resort, but again I got bad news. Every motel was sold out and all the decent campgrounds were filled. With the light beginning to fade, I had to settle for Indian Flat Campground right off the highway. It won't be so bad, I thought. At least the river is close by.

As I pitched my tent, kicking myself for not getting to the park early enough to hike into the backcountry, a superbly tanned, gorgeously built woman in a red mini-dress came sashaying down a path. She held the hand of a brutish surfer, who was slugging at a Mickey's Big Mouth and booting away the twigs and the empty cans that might endanger her bare feet. They were Indian Camp campers, too, three tents down.

I smacked at the metal tent pegs with a rock and asked myself, What is this about? I mean, what is this about?

And the Merced River answered, *I have no idea.*

The aboutness of things—there was an earnest theme for a sleepless night. Waking fifty times to nocturnal ramblings, raccoons in the underbrush, sweeping headlights, radios and tapedecks and Aretha Franklin singing "Respect"—waking, I say, fifty times to a single pebble, pointed, that refused to be dislodged from under my sleeping bag, and to the haunting image of the babe in red, imagining her in dishabille, in opera hose, in a top hat patting the pinecones with a walking stick, I nodded off at last only to wake again in minutes to the revving of a motorcycle.

Five in the morning. I fetched the leaves from my hair, drank a lukewarm soda, and lay in my straggly kip for a while reading a biography of John Muir by flashlight.

At six-thirty, I broke camp and drove into the park, stopping to count the incoming cars. They entered at the rate of about four a minute. Almost 3.5 million tourists visited Yosemite every year, and I saw what a job it must be just to keep the restrooms clean.

Running the whole Yosemite show amounted to a triage situation, with environmental concerns sometimes secondary. You could count on the tourists to trample the meadow grasses and give rise to giardia in streams. They didn't do it on purpose. The ecosystem didn't look fragile, not when the park was so vast and sturdy and beyond apparent injury. Yosemite Valley projected a weary benignity. It seemed kind, tolerant of human foibles, and that brought a sort of peace, although at the park's expense.

I felt this peace as the morning went on. Cars kept pouring through Arch Rock, but everywhere people were having their private Yosemite experience, and so were the creatures of the valley, blacktail deer searching for berries and gray squirrels jumping from branch to branch.

Near El Capitan, an artist on holiday had put up her easel to paint the great hunk of granite, and as she applied colors to her canvas in vulvic shades, three coyotes loped right past her, but she never looked up. The coyotes resembled German shepherds, although they were leaner and stringier and had a proud and cagey aspect, ignoring the Sunday painter just as she had ignored them.

I walked toward Ribbon Meadow and soon was alone, my lack of sleep no longer of consequence and the sun beginning to make its presence known to the knotted muscles of my back. On the Merced I found a glassy stretch of water that the light had not yet struck, and I fished it for a while, falling into a hypnotic state that momentarily relieved me of any burdens.

Then I had some company. Three little girls had snuck up behind me. They were towing a freckled boy in a red sweatsuit, who immediately started throwing pebbles into the stream, unable to stand the calm. He was made of sticks and stones and so on, and I wanted to reinstitute the now-forbidden practice of spanking.

The girls were cousins. They lived in Chino, California, and in Las Vegas, Nevada. The boldest of them, Laura, who at nine or ten had the disconcertingly adult face of a chorine, told me that they'd been coming to Yosemite since they were two for family reunions. They were camped by a waterfall.

"How is it?"

"Beautiful," they all sighed at once.

"Is Nevada different from California?" I asked.

"Nevada is desert," Laura said, with certainty. She'd just got her first fishing rod, but fishing perplexed her. "One thing I want to know?"

"Yes?" said I, the aged angler-muse.

"How come only boys can catch a fish?"

THE PATRON SAINT OF Yosemite National Park, John Muir, had set sail for San Francisco from New York in 1868. On the docks in Manhattan, he bought a dozen large maps from a dealer who convinced him that they could be sold for twice the price in California, where everything was scarce.

Muir was a Scot from Glasgow. His father had brought him to the United States when he was eleven and had raised him on a Wisconsin farm. At the university in Madison, he studied chemistry, botany, and geology, and became in his youth a tireless hiker and explorer, once walking from Indiana to the Gulf of Mexico and keeping a journal that was inscribed with his name and address *John Muir, Earth-Planet, Universe.*

His fascination with Yosemite Valley began while he was recuperating from an accident in an Indianapolis hospital. He'd been employed at a factory where carriage wheels were made and had nearly blinded himself with a file. Machines were his nemesis from early on. An illustrated brochure about the valley caught his fancy, and he started for it as soon as his ship had landed, trekking into the Sierra Nevada on foot.

Muir was as captivated by Yosemite Valley in reality as he had been by images of it. He took up residence on its fringes and supported himself with short-term jobs. He broke horses, harvested grain, ran a ferry from Mariposa to Stockton, and sheared sheep. Throughout the fall and the winter, he tended a flock for Smoky Jack Connel and hired on as a shepherd for Pat Delany in the spring. Come summer, he took Delany's sheep into the High Sierra to graze.

"We are in the mountains and they are in us," he wrote of his journey, "kindling enthusiasm, making every nerve quiver, filling every pore and cell of us."

In the Sierra, Muir hiked and kept notebooks and listened to the sounds around him. He lay in green meadows and slept on a rock in the middle of a creek and knew in those moments out of ordinary time the true character of his calling, simply to exist and to pay attention to existence, close attention, although he did not quite know how he could make it happen.

In the crispness of September, first leaf fall, Muir returned with the sheep to the San Joaquin, but he was back in the valley a few months later and signed on as a jack-of-all-trades to J. M. Hutchings, who, faced with abundant customers, was upgrading his hotel and actually putting wood partitions between the rooms instead of just dividing them with a blanket.

Muir cared for the livestock, pounded nails, led guided tours, and ran a sawmill where, on August 5, 1870, Professor Joseph Le Conte stopped by accident to ask directions to Yosemite Falls.

Le Conte: "Here found a man in rough miller's garb, whose intelligent face and earnest, clear blue eyes excited my interest."

He had heard about Muir from his fellow academics, but he was still impressed with Muir's scientific knowledge, particularly of botany.

Le Conte: "A man of such intelligence tending a sawmill!—not for himself, but for Mr. Hutchings. This in California!"

Muir agreed to hike to Mono Lake with the university crew later in the week. He had his reasons. He believed that Le Conte, as a pupil of Agassiz, the world's foremost expert in glaciation, might be open to his theory that glaciers had helped to form Yosemite Valley. The theory went against the conventional wisdom. Professor Josiah Whitney, for instance, considered it to be claptrap, in spite of some evidence that his survey team had dredged up.

William Brewer: "We have found so much of interest here [in Yosemite], among the rest finding enormous *glaciers* here in earlier times, first found on the Pacific slope, that we have been detained much longer than we expected."

Whitney still held that the work of glaciers was incidental. The primary cause, he said, was violent faulting, the earth uplifted and tilted. Le Conte, in five days of wandering with Muir, accepted the importance of glaciers, though with some reservations, citing in *his* journal the equal importance of preglacial forces.

Not until Muir located an actual glacier at Red Mountain did he receive his satisfaction. He sent an article about it to the *New York Tribune,* and it was published in 1871 and rocketed him into the public arena. The author got two hundred dollars, no mean sum for a man who lived on beans and bread.

Ralph Waldo Emerson came to call that year, seeing in Muir the same independent spirit as he had in Henry Thoreau. Though Emerson declined an invitation to camp out—his minders were afraid that he might catch cold—the two men became friends and corresponded with each other. Muir always included, not surprisingly, "Self Reliance" among his favorite essays. His favorite books were the poems of Robert Burns, the New Testament, and *Paradise Lost.*

Muir spent the winter of 1873 in Oakland writing stories for the *Overland Monthly,* but he wasn't happy. Cities tore at him. He hated the concrete, the poverty, the filth, and the absence of plant life. What city dwellers missed were the seeds of freedom sewn in nature, he thought, but he was troubled by what people did to the wilderness once they'd discovered it. Sheep and cattle were decimating the meadows in Yosemite, and timbermen were topping its virgin stands of trees.

Muir began traveling widely to pursue his botanical studies. He went to Mount Shasta, to Utah and Alaska. In 1880, during a thunderstorm that thrilled him, he was wed to Louie Wanda Strentzel. He was forty-two, and she was thirty-one. Her father, a dentist, had a home in Martinez, in Contra Costa County, where he grew pears and table grapes, and his new son-in-law gradually assumed the management of the farm.

Evidently, Muir felt he had to prove himself to Dr. Strentzel, putting the lie to any notion that he was merely a dreamy mountaineer. The archetypal loner strapped himself into the harness of the Good Provider and threw himself so vehemently into marketing his crops, hassling with brokers and other middlemen, that his health deteriorated. He looked drawn and sickly as he delivered his profits to the bank in laundry sacks. One of his sole pleasures was taking his two little daughters on nature walks.

Muir was ultimately forced by his conscience to rejoin the fray. In 1889, Robert Underwood Johnson, the editor of *Century Magazine,* visited California to solicit some writing and went to Yosemite Valley with Muir, who was appalled at the continued devastation there— corrals and pigsties, more meadows gone, more trees felled, the landscape altered and looking artificial.

Enraged, Muir did one article for Johnson about the destruction of wilderness areas and another about the need to create a new national park that would include Yosemite Valley and afford it more security. His stance earned him some enemies. Preservation was not a concept that most westerners clasped to their bosom. It belied every notion of land use in the West, but Muir had his way, and the U.S. Congress passed the requisite bill in 1890. The boundaries of the new national park were expanded again in 1905 to encompass a total of 1,189 square miles of acreage.

Muir's defense of the valley would prove to be his last big victory, and out of it would come the Sierra Club, formed in 1892 with Muir as its first president. By then, too, he had knitted a final version of himself as a bearded, lanky, roughhewn proponent of the wilderness, who was cordial and garrulous and affected a Scot's burr when he had to lay something on thickly.

Although Muir had strong ties to the wealthy and the powerful, such as Teddy Roosevelt, he couldn't stop San Francisco politicians from flooding and damming Hetch Hetchy Valley, the park's other jewel. It was located some twenty miles northwest of Yosemite Valley, between Lake Eleanor and the Grand Canyon of the Tuolumne

River. The deal was so firmly in place when a public outcry occurred that it couldn't be derailed. Along with many others, Muir argued that there were alternative sources of water available, but the press portrayed him as an irascible old coot out of step with the times.

O'Shaughnessy Dam was built in 1923, impounding the river behind a curvilinear concrete arc. Hikers still go to the valley for picnics or to fish, sometimes on the same trails that the Awani and the Pauites used when they gathered acorns to grind in mortars for *atch atchie,* an edible mixture of grains, grasses, and seeds.

Muir did not live long enough to see the dam. He died of pneumonia at his daughter Helen's house in the Mojave Desert, in 1914, passing from the earth into the universe with his memories of an unspoiled Hetch Hetchy Valley still intact.

EVERY SUMMER IN HIGH SEASON, John Muir's worst predictions for Yosemite National Park came true. About fourteen thousand men, women, and children were in the park on an average day, and they transformed it into a place unlike any other in California, afflicted with a host of difficulties and subject to its own peculiar dynamic.

Hikers, for example, got lost in the wilds and had to be rescued. Novice rock climbers had to be rescued, too, and so did the kids who fell from trees and broke their arms and their legs. Swimmers drowned in the Merced River. Campers neglected to stash their food at night, and hungry bears roared down out of the mountains to scavenge and growl and bang on cars.

Raccoons in the park ate garbage and grew as fat as sows. Squirrels learned to beg for corn chips and popcorn and lost their ability to forage. The human bacteria in streams could cause the fish to go belly up. Accidents and arrests for drunk driving abounded on the two-lane roads. Thieves worked the campgrounds, while pickpockets worked the valley. Occasionally, a tourist was murdered.

There was little that anybody could do to control Yosemite. The budget for operating the park had been slashed to the bone over the past few years, and a dispirited skeleton crew was in charge of things. Rangers who had joined the Forest Service because they loved the great outdoors wound up playing Smokey-the-Cops and having to do the job of an urban police force.

At the park headquarters, I talked one afternoon with Lisa Dapprich, a public affairs officer. She was from Marin and had moved to Yosemite when her husband took over a school for environmental education that was located there.

Lisa told me that about 70 percent of the visitors to Yosemite were Californians, 20 percent were from overseas, and the other 10 percent were Americans from elsewhere. The average stay in the park, whether at a campsite, a tent-cabin, or a hotel, was one-and-a-half days, or just enough time to take some photos and a guided tour and buy a Yosemite coffee mug or a Yosemite T-shirt.

About 89 percent of the land in the park was designated as backcountry, Lisa said, but hardly anyone used it. Permits to camp there had topped out in 1979 and had been declining ever since. People felt safe in the valley, in a California suburb.

I SPENT THREE MORE DAYS IN YOSEMITE NATIONAL PARK, and they were good days, unexpectedly good.

For two days I camped by myself in the backcountry off the Pacific Crest Trail. The long, rugged hike in tired me in a wonderful way, and I fell asleep like an old dog in the afternoon, waking at twilight to a flurry of butterflies around my head.

On the second day, I hiked to a little alpine lake and passed two young women setting up camp not far from me. Yvette and Marie were from a town near Paris and wore smashing outfits in cotton and khaki. They were touring California for a month or so from their base at Marie's uncle's house in the Napa Valley.

"What do you think of Yosemite?" I asked them.

"Magnificent, no?" Marie looked to Yvette, and Yvette nodded in agreement. "We have camped in the Pyrenees, but that is not this."

"I like your outfits," I said.

They giggled. "Ba-na-na Ree-pu-blique!"

They invited me to supper that evening. They had a bandanna spread on a rock, and on it were some bread and some cheese and a bottle of red wine. We became terrific friends in our isolation, and when I returned to my own camp a bit giddy from the wine and the altitude I decided that I wanted to marry them both and run away with them forever.

On the third day, I reserved a campsite in the valley, just to see what it would be like. The cars went round and round, and I moped and fiddled with my gear until the guy next door came out to light his barbecue grill and started chatting. He was from Modesto and recently divorced, and he had his three daughters with him for a week's vacation. His tent was as commodious as a tract house. He was happy, carefree, briefly released from his job and his worries, enjoying the mountain air—I don't know, it touched me.

All around the campground, people were lighting their barbecues. Families were joking, playing Monopoly, listening to music, and even watching battery-powered TVs. Yosemite Valley was growing ever more weary, I thought. The wilderness ideal and all that it represented in California was vanishing from our hearts.

CHAPTER 15

DROPPING DOWN FROM THE SIERRA NEVADA through scrubby brown foothills and stray little mountain towns, Oakhurst and Coarsegold, I made for the San Joaquin. There were barns, farmhouses, and railroad tracks, hawks perched on telephone wires, some cattle and some horses, the earth no longer tilted upward in granite blocks but flattened to a gentle plain—acre upon acre of dry grasses and wild oats, the fabled sun of the valley burning low on the horizon, evening, and all I could think of when I passed Twenty-two Mile Roadhouse, a solitary shack at the edge of Highway 41, was an ice-cold beer.

Twenty-two Mile Roadhouse was a marker on the road to Fresno, maybe left over from stagecoach days. Inside, it was smoky and cramped and only a few degrees cooler than the sweltering air outside.

Two bikers in soiled motorcycle leathers sat at a small bar staring into fourteen-ounce draft Budweisers as a form of meditation. One man had tattoos running up both his arms, flames and pitchforks and horned devils, the Book of Revelations dancing on his skin. The other was younger and cleaner and appeared to be less doomed. He was about six-foot-four and had a moustache and long, wavy hair, Buffalo Bill returned from the dead to sit astride a Harley.

For a moment, I considered leaving, but the beer looked awfully tempting, so I fell to a stool between the bikers and ordered a Bud from the bartender, who was bald and wrinkled like a sun-dried apricot and spoke in a twangy voice that was as flat and dry as the surrounding plain.

The silence in the roadhouse was immense. Tiny things stood out—flies buzzing, a spider climbing a wall, a big beetle crawling across the floor. It seemed to be a place where nothing had ever happened, where nothing ever *would* happen, but then, out of the men's room, a third customer emerged and changed all that.

He stepped to the bar and ordered a glass of rosé wine, a wimp's brew to any biker. The bartender tapped a spigot on a cardboard box to release a stream of pinkish liquid.

"Here you go, Baker," I heard him say.

Baker, if that was truly his name, had a beard and wore a white painter's cap. His bare feet poked out of sandals. A white T-shirt, faded jeans—Baker was more hipster than biker. Wine in hand, he shuffled to an upright piano that was pushed against a wall, seated himself without ceremony, and commenced to play.

From the very first notes, we were transported. It was as though the soul of Arthur Rubinstein had been planted in Baker and miraculously instructed in the entire canon of stride and boogie-woogie. He was a virtuoso, a stone genius. In seconds, he was putting out so much energy, physical and mental, that the joint was literally rocking. When he stamped his sandals, I could feel tremors coursing up the metal legs of my stool.

Baker, Baker. His body swayed from side to side as he snatched melodies from the ozone. You could hear familiar things here and there, a bit of Jerry Lee Lewis or a riff from an old Fats Waller tune, but Baker was quick to embroider whatever popped into his mind and make it his own. He hammered at the keys, hammered at them, hammered. Incredible sounds gushed from the battered piano, arpeggios followed by guttural rumbles evocative of a fat man ascending a flight of stairs, then instances of lyric grace, a slowing of the tempo to embrace possibilities far beyond the scope of a rough-and-tumble barroom.

The only clue to Baker's roots was that glass of rosé wine. It suggested ties to a city somewhere, to civilization and an educated past. Maybe our boy was a lost prodigy, an angel with dirty wings, the black sheep of a prominent family who'd veered from the demanding path to Juilliard to pound the ivories in the dust and torpor of the San Joaquin.

We were in awe of the flaming music. It came as a great gift and bound us together as friends.

"Go, Baker!" cried the tattooed man. It was too preposterous, really, to be treated to an epic concert, and all for free. Call the newspapers, I thought. Somebody in California is actually giving it away!

The mood in the Twenty-two Mile Roadhouse was so mellow that Buffalo Bill leaned across to introduce himself. He was Wade from Bakersfield.

"Where're you from?" Wade asked.

"San Francisco."

"Are you gay?"

"No."

Such were the assumptions in certain parts of the San Joaquin Valley, agribusiness's cradle, a raw-boned land of oil fields and cotton fields, of profitable farms and ranches and the poor migrants who worked them. It had lots in common with Texas, Oklahoma, and Arkansas—the heat and the dirt, the pickers in the fields, the honky-tonks and the banjo pluckers, a gumbo of influences from the American South and Southwest. The San Joaquin was huge, as big as all of Denmark. It stretched from Lodi near the Sacramento River Delta to the Tejon Pass north of Los Angeles.

I heard a phone ring in a room behind the bar. The bartender picked it up and shouted over the music, "It's for you, Baker."

Baker quit playing. He grabbed his wine, went into the room, and closed the door behind him. We never saw him again. O, mysterious prodigy! We could hear his muffled conversation, knew him to be present still, but the spell that he'd cast was broken. It was as if a giddy, collective hit of nitrous oxide had worn off, and we were turning back into mere mortals.

Wade challenged me to a game of eight ball, and I felt compelled to accept but also to throw the game, assuming that he would stomp me if I beat him. Bent over the table and ready to miscue, I was interrupted by a skinny, ragged, feral man who bumped into me as he entered. He was a Dust Bowl vision incarnate and carried a dented can of Pennzoil, grinning in the fatuous way of a person who has been forced to make a fool of himself in order to get his wish.

To the bartender, he said, "I'd like to make a trade with you, sir. I'll give you this oil plus sixty cents for a pack of cigarettes."

"I'm not in the automotive business," the bartender cautioned him, although we could tell that he was amused. "What I sell here is beer and wine."

"Listen, I'm not trying to joke you." The penitent's grin got broader and dopier. "They say this is real good oil."

"All right. All right. What kind of cigarettes is it that you want, anyway?"

"Camels. Luckies. Any old kind." There was a time-warp quality to his choices, as though he had been spared the last forty years of medical research and had no notion that a filter tip might lower his chances of lung cancer. He was chasing after a strong hit of tobacco, pure and simple.

"Is Marlboros all right?"

"Marlboros is just fine."

The deal was done. Out the door he blew, a dust devil spinning, and Wade racked up another set of balls. The bartender held aloft the Pennzoil, narrowed his eyes to inspect it, laughed, and said, "You know this here can's bound to contain water."

Welcome to the San Joaquin.

♦   ♦   ♦

BEFORE THE GOLD RUSH, the San Joaquin Valley was untouched by farmers and ranchers. Indian tribes of the Yokuts family had lived there in wigwams made from tule reeds and arranged in neat rows. According to Stephen Powers, they had a political solidarity that was unusual among California Indians. They crafted their sandals from elk hide, tanning them in water infused with powdered deer brains. They had no cedar, so they bought their bows from mountaineers.

They took trout, chubs, and suckers from streams, and snared rabbits and quail with milkweed cords. The women were fierce gamblers. Powers approved of their manzanita cider, which was better than "the wretched stuff seen among the Wintun."

Rattlesnakes were sacred to the Yokuts, but the white men who began settling the valley in the 1850s shot them with impunity. Many of the men were failed miners. Some of them had purchased their small plots of land with the scrip that they'd earned by enlisting in the army.

Settlers without any money or scrip worked on the wheat farms that were taking over the San Joaquin. Wealthy businessmen, often absentee owners, availed themselves of the water in rivers and lakes. They didn't need much because wheat wasn't thirsty. It was easy to grow. New machinery—massive plows and harvesters, along with tractors—multiplied the yield.

In 1852, just over a hundred thousand bushels of wheat came out of San Joaquin and Tuolumne counties, but by the 1870s California was the principal wheat-growing region in the United States, exporting its crop to Europe and Russia.

The settlers also signed on as ranchhands at the enormous cattle spreads of the Miller and Lux empire. Henry Miller, a German émigré, had worked as a butcher after his arrival in California in 1850—he'd adopted his name from a nontransferable ship ticket that he had finagled—and later had superb success as a wholesaler of beef. He teamed with Charles Lux, another German, to acquire land, concentrating on the San Joaquin.

Miller was a slick operator, who played the angles and was not above an occasional bribe. He and Lux manipulated state and federal laws to buy swamps, deserts, and mountains for a pittance. They convinced army vets to sell them their scrip for land options, sometimes paying as little as a dollar an acre. They also picked up parched and unpromising ranchos that had been deeded to their owners by the Mexican government in the days before statehood.

Ultimately, Miller and Lux amassed about 1.4 million acres. They owned a hundred miles of riverfront along the San Joaquin and fifty miles along the Kern. They had property in Oregon, Arizona, and Nevada, and held a million head of cattle and a hundred thousand sheep. Their enterprise, along with the vast wheat farms, marked the origins of corporate agriculture in California, the first "factories in the field."

The Southern Pacific Railroad was also gobbling up the valley. Essentially a monopoly, the railroad was the largest landowner in the state. It had received a congressional grant in 1865 that awarded it ten square miles of land for every mile of track its workers laid. The railroad's engineers had hoped to extend service south to Los Angeles by laying tracks along the coast, but so much of the coastal property was in private hands that the focus had shifted to the San Joaquin.

To keep down the tax bill on the real estate that it was acquiring, Southern Pacific offered parcels to settlers to farm or to ranch, guaranteeing them a chance to buy the land at a later date for not more than $2.50 an acre, or—the catch word—"upwards."

Texans were among the first to respond. They were used to a hardscrabble life and collected at Mussel Slough, now Lucerne Valley, for its access to the Kings River. In 1876, as the rails drove south, Southern Pacific took possession of Mussel Slough and made good on its promise, but the asking price for the land was indeed "upwards," between $17.00 and $40.00 an acre.

The Texans refused to pay. They waged a losing battle in court and subsequently turned into vigilantes, costuming themselves as Indians and going on a barn-burning rampage to intimidate anybody who had cooperated with the railroad.

In May of 1880, two Southern Pacific hirelings, Mills Hart and Walter Crow, were sent to the Henry Brewer ranch in Mussel Slough to pose as its new owners. Twenty armed settlers were waiting for them. Six of them died in a gun battle, and so did Mills Hart. Walter Crow disappeared into a wheat field, but the settlers found him and killed him, too.

The incident became the central episode in the first great California novel, Frank Norris's *The Octopus*. Norris had moved from Chicago to San Francisco as a teenager and had fallen under the spell of Émile Zola while studying at Berkeley. He wanted to be a naturalistic novelist and in 1899 hit on an idea for a trilogy about wheat. For two months, he lived on a ranch in Hollister to gather material and actually worked the harvest as a sacker on a combine.

His description of spring in the San Joaquin:

The ploughing, now in full swing, enveloped him in a vague, slow-moving whirl of things. Underneath him was the jarring, jolting, trembling machine; not a clod was turned, not an obstacle encountered, that he did not receive the swift impression of it all through his body, the very friction of the damp soil, sliding incessantly from the shiny surface of the shears, seemed to reproduce itself in his finger-tips and along the back of his head. He heard the horse-hoofs by the myriads crushing down easily, deeply, into the loam, the prolonged clinking of trace-chains, the working of the smooth brown flanks in the harness, the clatter of wooden hames, the champing of bits, the click of iron shoes against pebbles, the brittle stubble of the surface ground crackling and snapping as the furrows turned, the sonorous, steady breaths wrenched from deep, labouring chests, strap-bound, shining with sweat, and all along the line the voices of men talking to horses.

Four hundred horses pulling plows, 40 million bushels of wheat harvested from the fields in 1889, and yet such farming would soon be relegated to a minor activity, done in not by the Southern Pacific but by a water war.

Miller and Lux were big users of the valley's water. They had always maintained that the streams in California ought to be subject to the riparian laws of England. Water was strictly for a landowner and shouldn't be diverted. It was a form of property.

The Kern River Land and Cattle Company, a competitor, tested them in 1875 by claiming a large section of the stream near Bakersfield and digging a canal to irrigate some of its ranches. Miller and Lux filed suit to stop the canal, asserting that their water was being stolen. They were victorious, but the Kern River group kept lobbying, and Congress appeased them at last by passing the Wright Act in a special session in 1887.

The Wright Act permitted fifty or more neighboring farmers and ranchers to come together as an irrigation district and divert water for such purposes as conservation and flood control. The new availability of irrigated water meant that growers could diversify into crops that were both thirstier and worth more than wheat, and soon the delicate rustling of a wheat field was a sound rarely heard in the San Joaquin.

AFTER ESCAPING FROM TWENTY-TWO MILE ROADHOUSE, I reached Fresno at last, where the tallest building around is the Security National Bank. That was how the town felt to me, secure somehow—deeply rooted, self-aware, and quietly prosperous. It seemed to be perfectly balanced on its fulcrum, far enough from San Francisco and Los Angeles to be impervious to their lures. It was a thing unto itself, with no sense of longing in the air, no big-time aspirations. Fresno was honest. What you saw was what you got.

To William Brewer's eye, the "city" had consisted in 1863 of "one large house, very dilapidated, one small ditto, one barn, one small dilapidated and empty warehouse, and a corral." Brewer had visited before the Southern Pacific spur went through, however, and before well-to-do Armenians from Boston, Worcester, and Providence, merchants and sellers of rugs, moved into Fresno and bought the best vineyard land to cultivate Thompson seedless grapes for raisins.

The first to come were Hagop Seropian and his brother, Garabed, who arrived in 1881. In their letters home, the Seropians likened Fresno to the Armenian heartland, with the San Joaquin and the Kings rivers cast as the Tigris and the Euphrates. There were also Japanese farmers around Fresno, and Danes, Germans, and Russians, and by the 1890s they were producing more raisins than all of Spain. Chinese immigrants did the stoop labor, bent in the blistering sun.

Only about half the land in Fresno County was planted to farms now, I found, but the taste and scent of farms were everywhere. The life of the town was farm life. It dawdled along at an unhurried clip, minding its own affairs. Although the population topped three hundred thousand, most streets were rolled up after dark. There were lots of churches. Religion was in the city's blood. Newsboys rode by on bicycles delivering papers, as bells tolled at dusk. On porches and verandas, old people sat in chairs drinking iced tea and fanning themselves against the evening heat.

There was no denying that Fresno was a regular inferno. In May, the daily maximum temperature was 82.5. It hit 91.2 in June and 98.7 in July. August brought scant relief with its daily maximum of 96.7.

Here was a city of short-sleeved shirts, of shorts and sandals and long-billed caps, a city where everything seemed to be in a constant process of ripening, where the splash of swimmers in pools and in lakes could be heard from early spring until the late fall.

Fresno still harbored many races. It was about 25 percent Hispanic and 10 percent black. Its Asian community was rapidly expanding. One lunch hour, I saw two Nigerians turned out in regal, tribal robes and little embroidered hats. They were standing by a Mexican restaurant, getting into an orange Pinto.

"And did you enjoy your burrito, my friend?" asked the first Nigerian.

"Ewo!" the other one exclaimed, snapping his fingers. "It was wonderful."

I liked the early morning in Fresno, that hazy cocoon of warmth before the heat got really intense. I came awake in stages, gingerly, taking my time—nothing to push against, no obstacles, nowhere to rush to or from. Outside my motel, there was always a smell of lawns being mowed, a chore best done while the sun was still gathering its energy. Teenage kids scooted past on skateboards, doing spins and pirouettes, tap dancing, screeching up the sidewalk ramps for the handicapped and celebrating their summer vacation.

Almost everybody in Fresno owned a house. The motel clerk, the fireman, the mailman—almost everybody. I stopped at Trend Homes one morning, a three-year-old subdivision that was nearly sold out. There were six Trend models available, all for under a hundred thousand dollars. The models were called Boca Raton, Charleston, Providence, Santa Fe, Coronado, Crestwood, and Manhattan.

Tracts such as Trend were a prominent reason why so many businesses were relocating from urban areas to the San Joaquin. An employee could shoehorn his way into a house for just five thousand dollars, plus closing costs, and Trend would handle the financing. A realtor told me that as he polished the fender of his new Mercedes with a rag, luxuriating in the glow.

In Fresno, I ate well. At George's Shishkabob, an Armenian place where the chef was "fully credentialed," the local lamb was excellent. I found a Chinese place with "authentic Chinese Chefs" that served a good chow mein. Sometimes I got take-out food at a Von's supermarket that had a tortilla factory inside. The aisles were laden with the flavors of Mexico, sacks of masa harina, big sacks of pinto beans, sacks of chicharrones, and ovals of jalapeño peppers curing in a ceramic bowl.

I ate Basque food at the Iturri Hotel, where some shepherds in transit still lived upstairs, and after a meal, feeling sleepy, I rested for a while by the lovely old Sante Fe train station, reclining like a hobo in the shade of its two carob trees.

THE ROADS OUT OF FRESNO ran swiftly into farmland. There were tiny towns like Biola, Rolinda, Raisin, and Tranquillity that had a gas pump or a country store. Roosters pecked at the dirt, hens squawked and scattered, and goats were tethered to sheds. Somebody was always operating a roadside stand of one kind or another, selling produce or nuts from a front yard or the back of a pickup truck.

In Kerwin one hot afternoon, I saw a handwritten sign that said, Oranges Sweet and Juicy, and it conjured such a powerful image of fragrant, refrigerated oranges being squeezed that I had to buy some.

On the porch of an old, wood-frame store stood the orange salesman, Gerry Karabian, who had the fidgetiness of somebody needing to talk. He was lean and hard-muscled and had a thick shock of black hair going gray and glasses resting on the bridge of a strong nose. In his face, there was an intense, hawklike aspect.

Karabian was agitated because his father, at the age of ninety-one, was dying. He told me that right away, before I could even ask about the oranges. His father was among the last surviving Fresno-born Armenians of the first generation, he said. The old man was comatose and had been moved from a hospital to a hospice to pass his final hours.

The store in Kerwin had been a family business for a long time, Karabian said, but it was almost empty now, except for a few archaic items on shelves and a black-and-white TV that was playing to an audience of flies. Karabian's mother, who was eighty, lived in a house behind it on a twenty-acre farm. She was in good health, but he worried about her being alone and was anxious about what might come next.

The Armenian era in the San Joaquin—the one that had started a century ago with the Seropian brothers—was drawing to a close. Raisin grapes had been the cornerstone of the Armenians' wealth, but they had also worked in shoe repair and as barbers and tailors. They had opened grocery stores. Their rugs were in demand, riding the crest of a vogue for anything Moorish or Byzantine.

In William Saroyan, the Armenians had found their laureate. His autobiographical novel, *My Name Is Aram,* published in 1940, was a sentimental but accurate account of growing up among Armenian families. Fresno had always been their city, but now they were established, and new immigrants were beginning to repeat their experience.

Gerry Karabian was familiar with the new immigrants. He worked as a teamster and drove through their neighborhoods delivering cases of beer and soda. He had heard that there were 38,000 Southeast Asians in Fresno County, many of them Hmongs. They were moving into subdivisions that used to be Hispanic. Karabian had a home in the Blackstone area and sometimes considered selling it and trading up, but he didn't want to go into debt.

"Those new houses with the fancy cabinets and all that," he said, shaking his head. "No way are they built as well as mine is."

Almost every type of crop had grown on the Karabians' twenty acres, even alfalfa. In the fields across the road, there were some zucchini squash and some Thompson seedless grapes. Farther down the road, there were some almond trees, but citrus trees were unusual around Kerwin, Karabian told me. Most citrus orchards were planted on the east side of Fresno, toward Visalia and Tulare, where the climate was more accommodating.

After a while, Karabian took me over to his orange grove. He wanted to check on the pickers that he'd hired. The trees in the grove were thick-trunked and very leafy and gave off a wonderful citrus perfume.

A flatbed parked nearby was filled with crated Valencia oranges that were good for juicing. Karabian got about fifty boxes from five or six trees, a yield that pleased him. His problem was that the trees were too tall and needed to be topped. The machine that sprayed for scales, an ugly but harmless blotch on the fruit, couldn't reach to a height of fifteen feet.

As he was explaining this to me, a young Mexican picker came down a ladder from the halo of a tree and smiled amiably. He had a burlap sack slung around his neck. It practically covered his entire chest, and in it were many oranges. The picker would be paid ten cents a pound.

Back at the store, there were still no customers. Karabian sighed and said, "People prefer navels."

I felt for him there on his old wooden porch, nervous, grief-stricken, and alone. He was doing his best to hold himself together through another of the furious passages that we all must endure on earth. He had sold sixteen sacks of oranges the day before, he said, and he believed that he would sell that many again on another day. Things were just slow right now. He'd had fifty-sack days in the past.

Like most people who work at a solitary task, Karabian seemed to be keeping private records. A day would come when he'd sell every sack on hand, I thought, maybe a hundred sacks in all, and then he would rejoice.

IN THE FRESNO BEE, I read an article about Derrel Ridenour, Jr., who yearned to be the king of mini-storage facilities in California. He wanted his name, Derrel, to become synonymous with "mini-storage," so that customers would say, for instance, "After the wife threw me out, I stored my stuff at a Derrel's" instead of just saying, "After the wife threw me out, I put my stuff in storage."

Derrel Ridenour, Jr., had a question of his own for the *Bee* reporter.

"If I go into a small town, am I going to eat at Joe's or at a McDonald's?" he asked. "I'm going to McDonald's because I know what to expect."

It made me feel foolish. I always ate at Joe's.

Already Derrel Ridenour, Jr., had fifteen Derrel's in the San Joaquin and planned on having more. He was looking at small towns where the land costs and the development fees were low, and the permit process was fast. By his photo in the *Bee,* he appeared to be a tall, genial, intelligent fellow, and I thought that he might understand things about California that I didn't, so I phoned him and asked if we could meet.

"There wouldn't be any use in it," he said, and though he was probably right from his standpoint, I kept the clipping in my glove compartment and referred to it on many occasions.

IN THE *FRESNO BEE,* I read that some Hmong Buddhists wanted to build a fifty-seven-foot-tall pagoda at their compound on North Valentine Avenue. They were scheduled to go before the County Planning Commission for a hearing at the Hall of Records, an Art Deco marvel in the city center.

On the morning of the hearing, I found about sixty Hmongs waiting in a second-floor hallway to be called before the commission. Only two women were among them, a toothless crone and a very young wife, maybe fifteen, with her little son. The Hmong men were a nut-brown color and rather small and compact. They didn't seem to be put out by the wait. It was as if they'd had considerable training, as if waiting were a skill that they had mastered over the centuries and then had inbred.

They were perfect at it, really. Some men stood patiently without moving a muscle, while others slid down to a squatting position, elbows resting on their knees and the small of their backs pressed against a wall. When they tired of squatting, they sat on the floor and crossed their legs. They were comfortable touching one other.

They grinned and grabbed at each other's arms and tapped each other on the shoulders. There was even a little friendly Hmong goosing going on. They might not have behaved any differently in the fields at home.

I watched the Hmongs and realized that some of them were watching me, staring directly and intently, making no bones about it. I knew what they must be thinking: He's about the right age; he could have been there.

From doorways and office windows, the clerks and typists of Fresno were watching the Hmongs, too. In the diversity of faces, I saw again the new face of California being formed.

Although the Hmong people were usually from either Laos, Thailand, Vietnam, or China, this group claimed to be from Cambodia. Of the eighty different ethnic groups in Fresno County, they were the latest to arrive and the lowest on the totem pole. Some farmers resented them for working so hard and relying solely on their families and relatives for labor. Already they'd cornered the cherry-tomato market in the San Joaquin and were moving in on other crops.

Some people in Fresno complained about how the Hmongs lived, with as many as five families sharing a single tract house. They complained that the Hmongs grew backyard poppies for personal-use opium and dealt in child brides. They complained about how the Hmongs drove. Every Hmong neighborhood had a designated driver who'd managed to get a car and a license, and these drivers were supposed to be a menace. I had seen some evidence of this— a Hmong behind the wheel in white-knuckled terror over the horsepower at his command.

A story was going around about a Hmong who got a speeding ticket and killed himself, both from shame and because he was afraid of the punishment. The Hmongs were frequently accused of eating dogs, a bogus charge that had been levied at every Asian immigrant group in California since the Chinese.

When the doors to a hearing room opened, the Hmongs rose as

a body to go inside. For the first time, I noticed their clothes. It looked as though they'd been set free on a shopping spree at K mart. As newcomers to the state, they had no mastery over the language of apparel, so they had gone wild and crazy, mixing and matching whatever clothes appealed to them. A curious element of Hmong cool was on display. One flashy dude was got up in a wrinkled trench coat and a pair of expensive cowboy boots, like a private eye who worked part time on a ranch.

Once the Hmongs were seated, the Planning Commission members came in. They were all white and middle-aged or older. A couple of them appeared to be perplexed, not out of any negative feelings toward the Hmongs but from a general disbelief at what was happening, Buddhists from maybe Cambodia wanting to build a pagoda on ag-land in Fresno County. It just didn't compute.

The hearing went smoothly. The Hmongs' attorney, a white Fresno man, presented an impressive array of documents and architectural drawings. He lectured the panel about Angkor Wat and explained that the height of the pagoda was an homage to Buddha. In response to an obvious question, he said, "We would appreciate the nonrepeating of things over and over again."

The opposition to the pagoda was minimal—two calls, one letter, and one petition. Only one person showed up to protest in the flesh. He was mean-faced and uncompromising and seemed to see himself as the last sane man in the San Joaquin fighting for the flag, God, and country.

The Hmongs made noise during their celebrations, he said, and they used loudspeakers. Their drivers might run down children. The pagoda would have an adverse effect on property values. And what about the impact of the Hmongs' "lifestyle"? He wondered why they couldn't scale down the project.

"They should Americanize their ideas a little bit," he suggested.

He was no match for the Hmong, who responded through an interpreter.

"When the government of Cambodia fell down to Communist

regimes," the Hmong speaker began, "thousands were killed or tortured. We lost lives, children, family, everything. The Communists took over and banned all religions. Nobody can have a religion except for Communism. All pagodas, even Christian churches, were demolished.

"*This* country give us freedom. Our temple will be both for worship and education. We want our children born in Fresno to be Americans—but to preserve our own culture, too. We want to live in peace in this community.

"All kind of volunteers will work on the pagoda," he continued, his voice rising. "Thank you to government of U.S.A. for letting us have this freedom! We want to help you, to share all kind of responsibility and lifestyle with you. We want to calm and educate our people. Many thank you!"

Wherever these Hmongs were really from, they knew their way around. We listened to some further discussion about such fine points as sewage disposal and the groundwater situation on North Valentine, but everybody in the hearing room knew that Fresno would soon have the only Buddhist temple between Stockton and Bakersfield.

ALTHOUGH FRESNO STILL FELT LIKE A FARMING COMMUNITY, its rural character was in jeopardy. Among California cities with a population of more than one hundred thousand, it was the fastest-growing, and that had caused some problems.

For one thing, there wasn't enough water around to fuel the growth. For another, the water that *was* around had often been contaminated by industrial chemicals or pesticide residues. Four city wells were shut down during the week of my visit. Three were polluted with ethylene dibromide, a soil fumigant, and the fourth was polluted with a degreasing solvent used in dry cleaning.

In all, Fresno had 234 domestic wells. Thirty-three of them were currently shut down on account of being polluted.

The air in Fresno County had also created some concern. The

farm machinery, the heat and the dust, the merciless traffic on I-5 and on Highway 99 all contributed to the leaden skies. Even the distant oil refineries near Hercules played a role. The prevailing winds swept down from the upper Central Valley and were tugged south by a sort of whirlpool effect. Fresno hadn't met the goals that the Air Quality Board had set for it. The city was a "nonattainer" and had the wherewithal to become the worst air-quality region in the United States.

The unemployment rate around Fresno was high, shooting to 13 or 14 percent at times. Farm laborers worked through a growing season and then collected unemployment. The crime rate was very high, too, especially for burglary, auto theft, murder, and rape. Gang-related crimes were mounting. I asked an officer at the Police Department about the crime, and he blamed it on "poor procedures." I thought he meant that the cops weren't performing, but he went on to list some of the poor procedures—it was a poor procedure to buy dope at two in the morning, a poor procedure to drive your car while you were drunk. . . .

People kept coming to Fresno, anyway, despite the problems. The young people weren't leaving, either, as they were in so many other places in the state. Construction projects in the county were proceeding at a record pace, and so were requests for building permits and zoning changes. Downtown Fresno made no pretense that it was anything other than a center for banks and government offices. To shop and have fun, everybody went to two big malls.

Preservationist issues were seldom addressed at planning sessions in Fresno. Any hearing to discuss them, I was told, would be so lightly attended that you could fire a shotgun blast into the chambers and not hit a single soul.

IN THE *FRESNO BEE,* I read that Nisshinbo Corporation was going to open a $59 million textile plant in Fresno. *Japan M&A Reporter,* a trade journal, had recorded 187 Japanese-American business deals in the previous year, and 59 of them were closed within California.

The Japanese liked to invest in electronics, computers and telecommunications, and banks and services, but they also dabbled in chemicals and food. Kyotaru, a sushi chain, had just bought eighteen Arby's roast-beef outlets, for example. It was said that the corporate concerns in Japan responded to California's mild climate, its unique blend of farming and high-tech, and its air of promise. The only state that got anywhere near as much money from them was Texas.

The economic ties between Japan and California were strong. Of all the commodities exported from the state, $8.3 billion worth had gone to Japan in 1989, more than twice as much as went to Canada, our second-largest customer. California cities ran vigorous campaigns to market themselves to investors on the Pacific Rim. Fresno had an Economic Development Corporation that did the prospecting, making cold calls to firms and pitching them on what the city had to offer.

One of Fresno's major incentives was its Enterprise Zone, a concept that had originated in England. In an Enterprise Zone, the rules could be bent slightly, the red tape could be cut, and the entire process of permits and hearings could be streamlined. The land could be sold at rock-bottom prices. A company located in the zone got tax breaks and preferential treatment.

A California trade office in Tokyo had channeled the Nisshinbo deal to Fresno. After the initial contact, a protracted period of negotiation had followed. Executives with the EDC had come to expect this.

"An American firm plans for one year and takes five years to implement the plan," one official told me. "The reverse is true of the Japanese."

Nisshinbo was buying thirty-six of the two thousand acres in the Enterprise Zone and being subsidized by the Japanese government. In its first phase, it would build on only eighteen acres. To induce Nisshinbo to build on the other eighteen, Fresno had agreed to pay the development fees. At the Fresno EDC, the Japanese were regarded as very clever businessmen, capable of winging it as they went along, applying innovative tools to each new venture, public or private.

So clever were the Japanese, in fact, that they had acquired such California jewels as the golf course at Pebble Beach and the Beverly-Wilshire Hotel, not to mention the wineries up north and Columbia Pictures in Hollywood. The transactions had not gone unnoticed. There was a nasty streak of anti-Japanese sentiment fermenting in the state, and it found expression among TV commentators and other media pundits, and in the Letters-to-the-Editor columns in news-papers.

"Twenty years from now most of us will work for Japanese-owned companies," wrote a San Jose man to the *San Francisco Chronicle*. "We will need to learn Japanese in order to talk to our supervisors. Few of us will be able to afford houses so we will rent tiny apartments from Japanese landlords. Automobiles will be too expensive to buy, but when we need one for a special occasion we will rent a Japanese car from a Japanese rental agency."

The blame, said our distraught scribe, fell to Ronald Reagan, the Ultimate Californian.

THE FIRST THING KAZ FUJISAKI DID when I visited the Nisshinbo plant was to hand me his business card. After that, he led me to a conference room, paused on the brink, and changed the little sign outside from Vacant to In Use. This seemed to satisfy him.

Fujisaki, a Nisshinbo director of marketing, wore a dark-blue tie, a white short-sleeved shirt, and polyester slacks. I believed that he would never voluntarily waste a second. Up front, he informed me that Nisshinbo was not buying any real estate or golf courses in Fresno. He would mention golf and golfing often during our chat, always dismissively, as if he'd rather run naked down Tulare Street than swing a sand wedge.

Fujisaki was precise in answering questions. He gave multipart responses—Reasons One, Two, and Three. He had lived in California since 1983, most recently in Los Angeles, so I asked him how Fresno compared.

"It might be a little boring if you were a bachelor," he said. "Nothing much to do on Saturday night."

For a family, though, Fresno had lots of advantages, Fujisaki thought. His two sons had made plenty of friends and really enjoyed the town. Mrs. Fujisaki wasn't adapting quite as easily. In L.A., where there was a big Japanese community, she didn't need to speak English well, but in Fresno that had put her at a loss. Other Nisshinbo employees were around, but they had dispersed themselves deliberately to a variety of neighborhoods, so that they couldn't be accused of clumping up.

The Nisshinbo plant was almost completed. Technicians were installing the textile machinery as we spoke. Fujisaki apologized for using only Japanese-made machines. The technology, he said, was too advanced for American parts to be interfaced. Soon thirteen young women from Japan would fly to Fresno and start training California workers. He allowed himself a smile at that, as though the training would meet an unexpressed, unconscious need.

Two other cities, Bakersfield and Riverside, were finalists in Nisshinbo's search for a plant site, and I wondered how Fresno had won. There were five reasons, Fujisaki told me.

One, the word *Fresno* stood for superior cotton in Japan, although the very best cotton was *Pima* from Arizona. Two, there was easy access to the cotton in the fields of the San Joaquin. Three, the city was a strategic location midway between San Francisco and Los Angeles, good for exporting to the Pacific Rim. Four, there were the incentives of the Fresno EDC. And five, there was a readily available work force.

Fujisaki explained further about the work force. If you looked at the unemployment rate in the U.S.A. over the past ten years, he said, you saw that it averaged about 6 percent in most of the country. In Fresno, however, it rarely dipped below 12 percent because of the seasonal workers on farms. Textile manufacturing relied on unskilled labor, so Nisshinbo was gambling that it could find a core of about two hundred people who wanted to work year-round and could be taught the Japanese way of doing things.

The workers, in all probability, would be Hispanic. That was another clever stroke, it seemed. By virtue of the work that they did cheaply on farms, Hispanics could be seen as the Koreans or the Taiwanese of the San Joaquin, a great source of economic potential.

The only criticism Kaz Fujisaki had about Fresno was that it took forever to push papers through city hall. Nisshinbo staffers were required to grab a number from a rack and wait in line behind guys in Can't Bust 'Ems who were after a permit to build a chicken coop. That didn't happen in Louisiana or in Texas, where the authorities greased the wheels.

"Well, something is better than nothing," Fujisaki said, in the way of someone who has long since given up on the idea that a paradise existed anywhere on earth.

He invited me to come back and visit again when the plant was in operation. We got up and left the conference room, and Fujisaki paused to change the little sign outside from In Use to Vacant.

HEAT AND DUST, DUST AND HEAT. A sign along a dirt road: Chile Pickers Wanted, 14 Cents a Pound. Cotton fields dry and brown, the tender green of baby crops. Thick clusters of pink and white oleanders on highway islands, where Mexican illegals sometimes slept. Billowy turkey feathers blowing about on a turkey farm.

Bill's Bait and Tackle near Mendota. Minnows, crickets, and two cases of handguns. The big stink of sun-warmed cow manure. A man in an onion field, hoeing down the rows. A grocery store advertising peda bread. A variant of pita?

Said the clerk, "I don't know. I'm not Greek. I'm not even Armenian."

Deep pockets of shade, full summer coming on.

Somebody on North Valentine Avenue was marketing pit bulls

for twenty-five dollars a pup. Tracts, apartments, a trailer park. A yard sale offering hubcaps, wheel bearings, car seats, chains, and bike pedals, the sum of it swimming in oil.

At the Hmongs' compound, home of Fresno Cambodian Buddhist Society, a monk in a saffron robe padded out barefoot to get the mail. He had a look of bemusement on his face—the mail! The compound was neatly fenced. Photos of monks and parishioners were tacked to a bulletin board. Yellow-flowering squash grew in a little garden by the monks' white house.

Two competing signs: PEACHES; PEACHES.

I stopped at a warehouse where the farmers were Japanese-Americans. An older man in a Panasonic cap fiddled with his hearing aid and said, "They had an earthquake in Los Angeles this morning."

Cardboard flats of fruit with that rosy, peachy glow and a marvelous smell. One box was marked RIPE FOR ICE CREAM. I bought a half-dozen plump freestones from a shy young woman for $1.50. They'd have peaches through August, she said, five different varieties, including Elbertas.

"You don't find many Elbertas in San Francisco," I told her, and she lowered her eyes and blushed.

CHAPTER 16

FRESNO TO KERMAN, then south to Helm and Five Points and across the California Aqueduct again to Coalinga in the desiccated wastes below the Diablo Range, where the grandest fete of the year was the annual Horned Toad Derby. During Derby week, the citizens hung a banner downtown that was so frayed and sun-bleached it inspired no confidence that the event would actually occur. That was in keeping with the spirit of things, really. Horned toads were scarce, veering toward extinction.

Coalinga knew plenty about loss. Some of the world's richest asbestos deposits surrounded it, but asbestos miners were hard to come by anymore. The oil in the famous Coalinga field didn't flow as freely as it once did. You had to feel for a town whose chief claim to fame was that a monster earthquake had almost leveled it on May 2, 1983.

I was in a new part of the San Joaquin now, a tougher part. The land was drier, whiter, harder, more trashed and scorched, and even less forgiving, although it didn't seem possible. Trees that had found a purchase in the crusty alkaline soil shimmered greenly in the heat, while buzzards and red-tailed hawks hunted for carrion by riding the thermals that bounced off the mountains. The parched air made my throat scratchy, and my eyes began to burn.

In places like Coalinga, there were pockets of substantial wealth, fortunes earned in oil or in cotton, but borderline poverty was the norm. The streets in town were flat and dull, and the faces passing often appeared to be without prospect, robbed of hope, heavily lined, and singular in their avoidance of any upbeat emotion.

Coalinga was a corruption of Coaling Station A, a stop on the Southern Pacific spur that was added in 1888 to permit access to some lignite mines, but a petroleum boom had put the town on the map. Oil had first disclosed itself by bubbling up in diatomaceous seepages in the foothills, and enterprising men had scooped it up in cans and sold it from corner to corner.

By 1897, Blue Goose Well, 1,400 feet deep, was producing as much as a thousand barrels of oil a day. Other fertile pools were discovered on the west side in 1900, and Coalinga had its own version of the Gold Rush, that old California story retold, fueled this time by another mineral and giving rise to a Whiskey Row with gambling, prostitutes, and thirteen saloons.

People used to say that Coalinga wasn't known for its farms. All it raised were jackrabbits and hell.

The oil fields nearby were not so munificent now, but they were reliable. Everywhere rigs pecked at the earth like big, mechanical birds, dipping their beaks up and down. Chevron had outfits working, and so did Shell, but whatever profit they made did not readily spill over into town.

At the local museum, all alone among the exhibits, I looked at some chunks of asbestos with their terrible fibers and at some materials pertaining to the Horned Toad Derby. I looked at photos of the earthquake aftermath, too: houses unmortared and reduced to piles of bricks, streets splintered with foot-long cracks, and the contents of shelves dumped and broken. When I stepped outside, I saw waves of heat ripple off the pavement, one hundred degrees and counting, and listened to a withered old fellow prescribing a cure for Coalinga to his equally bent companion.

"What Coalinga needs," he said, "is a damn prison."

THE SAN JOAQUIN VALLEY HAD A NEW NICKNAME, Prison Valley. There were prisons in Madera, Corcoran, Delano, Avenal, and Wasco. In other sections of the Central Valley, in Chino, Folsom, Ione, Soledad, Stockton, Tracy, and Vacaville, there were also prisons. More prisons were being built in California than anywhere in the world. Frequently, they were built on farmland stripped of its value, gone to pebbles and hardpan. Corporate farmers, the titans of agribusiness, often sold the dead land to the state for a handsome score.

If you thought of prisoners as a new sort of crop, drought-resistant and growing incrementally, the future in California seemed bright. In the early 1970s, fourteen out of a hundred convicted felons were sentenced to a prison term. The current ratio was thirty-five out of a hundred. Drugs were an excellent fertilizer, and the crop tended to reseed itself. A high rate of recidivism was guaranteed. No wonder, then, that prisons were known as "gray gold."

Avenal was just down the road from Coalinga, so I drove over to take a look at it. Along the way tumbleweeds blew across Highway 41 and caught in fences. A single black cow stood in a huge field that was so dry and rock-strewn that my eye couldn't pick out a hint of green. The temperature kept rising.

Avenal made Coalinga look like a cultural mecca. How poor, small, and isolated the town was—as isolated as some towns in the backwaters of the Far North. The distance from Avenal to a supermarket or a movie theater was about thirty miles. Nobody wanted to live there. Correctional officers earned $2,400 a year in hardship pay just for working at the prison. The warden got as far away as he judiciously could and had a house in Hanford, near Fresno.

Asking around town, I learned that the prison had come to

Avenal through the efforts of a local pharmacist, Nick Ivans. He had read an article in the paper about how the state had $495 million to spend on prison construction, so he and some other town leaders began their successful lobbying.

Avenal State Prison, built in 1988, was a Level Two facility for lower- to medium-security inmates. It had 3,034 beds, but 3,289 cons had to jostle for space two months after the cells were opened for business. There were about 4,200 inmates now.

Around Pelican Bay State Prison, I had witnessed a weird euphoria and had seen the impact a prison could have on real estate speculation, but only in the San Joaquin did I hear about the most significant wrinkle in the scheme—prisoners could be counted as residents of the town or city where the institution was located. By kiting its population with bad guys, Avenal had set itself up for an annual bonus of several hundred thousand dollars from various state agencies, earning funds that it would not have been eligible for otherwise.

No other bonus seemed to be accruing to Avenal, though. The vaunted boom was sounding no more loudly than the tap of a spoon against a washtub. A new motel, its parking lot empty, had rooms by the month, the week, and quite probably by the minute. A new apartment complex let the public know that it was "Now Renting," as if the privilege had not been available yesterday.

Hillside Vistas, a proposed subdivision, amounted to an arrow pointing to open fields. Foxborough had fared a little better. A few three- and four-bedroom houses had gone up, but the carpenters had put down their hammers halfway through some others, leaving behind framed walls and two-by-fours in stacks. Tagged stakes marked the borders of many lots where no houses stood. Instead of lawns, weeds sprouted copiously from the annealed and useless earth.

Through Foxborough more tumbleweeds were rolling, great, thatched spheres bowled across the plain by unseen hands. The smattering of luckless owners who'd closed escrow before the demise had a view of migrant shacks, laundry hanging on clotheslines, and scrawny children with even scrawnier dogs.

A Mexican man moved along the semipaved streets of Foxborough, pushing a white cart and crying, *"¡Helados! ¡Helados!"* His ice-cream bars found no takers.

For a long time, I studied the tumbleweeds and heard the vendor's plaintive cry, thinking with a warped brilliance brought on by incipient sunstroke that the California Department of Corrections ought to cut a deal to buy the unsold Foxborough units at a discount and transform them into prison adjuncts for the bedless cons of Avenal. The houses could then be allotted by crime, with the rapists here and the molesters there, all the bug-eyed killers and the narco-creeps thrown together on the same block to create an entire suburb dedicated to casual mayhem and first-rate violence.

The plan had a simple elegance. It would please everybody from developers to reprobates to penologists to homeowners who were concerned about drugs and crime in *their* suburbs. They all came out ahead. Any way you looked at it, from any angle, the plan was a winner.

CORCORAN STATE PRISON, where Charlie Manson was taking a long vacation from the streets, was not far from Avenal, so I made an appointment to talk with Warden Bernie Aispuro there. Aispuro had put in forty years of service at California's penal institutions and was the ranking warden in the state. He had worked at Soledad, Tracy, Susanville, and San Quentin before coming to the San Joaquin, and Corcoran was his last stop before retiring.

A sharp, chemical stink infected the air in Corcoran. It came from a plant that processed cotton and alfalfa seeds. The plant belonged to J. G. Boswell Company, an agribusiness titan in the West. Named after a retired colonel from Georgia who'd established the company in 1924, Boswell held more than 140,000 acres of farmland in California alone, the Miller and Lux of its time. Its fortunes had been built on irrigation and on loans made to other farming concerns in the San Joaquin, and its global operations were directed from some high-tech offices in a Los Angeles skyscraper.

In effect, Boswell owned and managed Corcoran, another dry, desolate, unredeemable place. Prison families, black and Hispanic, strolled the streets and cashed their checks at a check-cashing outlet painted a shocking pink. They had a new, pork-barrel YMCA and a theater that alternated Hollywood films with movies in Spanish. There was a boarded-up, rust-colored Santa Fe Station where the trains didn't stop anymore.

When the Department of Corrections had chosen Corcoran for a prison site, they had bought a parcel of land from J. G. Boswell—land that was maybe not quite so useful for farming anymore. It was a few miles from town in a belt of cotton fields furrowed with irrigation ditches. In the standing water, in mosquito-dense clouds, avocets were wading and feeding. The soil was grayish and dotted with cotton bales.

In the distance, behind a chain-link fence topped with concertina wire, loomed the prison complex. It bore a strange resemblance to a power-generating facility. The prison building proper was a concrete block with slits for eyes, and what the eyes looked out on was so much nothing. Even sounds were in limited supply, rationed like every other tactile sensation—cars coming and going, the clank of a flag against a metal pole, birds chirping obliviously under a gnawing sun.

How remote the prison seemed from anything having to do with California, I thought. Few Californians would ever see it, much less know that it existed, and yet, increasingly, our prisons and all that they represented were becoming more and more integral to life in the Golden State.

At a guard station, I identified myself and the purpose of my visit. After that, I sat for a while in a sterile waiting room in the prison's reception area. The room had a hospital feel, an antisepsis

meant to disguise all the festering illnesses within. A sickness of the
soul was the chief complaint at Corcoran, and those who suffered
from it were supposed to be just as invisible as AIDS patients or the
victims of terminal cancer. We had given up on trying to heal the
soul's complaint.

Correctional officers marched through the waiting room at intervals, going at a military clip. Their combat boots rapped against
the clean, unscuffed surface of the glossily waxed floors. They were
dressed like commandos in green camouflage uniforms. They looked
rugged, solid, and devoid of all sympathy, particularly the younger
ones, who seemed years away from making a compassionate gesture.
Not a few of them had grown symbolic moustaches, as boys do when
they're sent to war.

The guards didn't appear to be the sort of men who'd have much
in common with the prisoners. Instead, they projected a soldierly
apartness. You could have dropped them into any foreign jungle and
put them to work killing guerrillas. Doing time at Corcoran, out in
the vast reaches of nowhere, would not be easy.

MOVIES HAD CONDITIONED ALL MY NOTIONS ABOUT PRISON WARDENS, SO
I expected to find Bernie Aispuro closeted in a dark little bunker
smoking a cigar and barking orders over a loudspeaker to armed
guards on a catwalk, but he was in a modern, efficiency-oriented
office that could as easily have housed a tax accountant.

Aispuro was a gregarious, outspoken man. His suit was an in-
offensive bureaucrat's suit, but he also wore a Navajo bracelet and
a turquoise-and-silver belt buckle. When I inquired about his ancestry, thinking he might have had an Indian father or mother, he
chose not to respond. He did this slyly, in a spirit of fun. He seemed
to like his secrets. There was a flare about him that he kept under
wraps.

For Aispuro, the challenge of a warden's job was in trying to
maintain his dignity in the face of overwhelming odds. He wanted

to be seen as fair, as a decent guy, as someone who took no more bullshit from his bosses than necessary, while at the same time refusing to be manipulated by any of the prisoners and their whining.

He shared a common background with many of his inmates, being a poor kid. He had grown up in Gonzales, a farming town near Soledad, and had known hard work from an early age. As a teenager, he had stooped in the fields to pick vegetables under the grueling valley sun and had learned that the price of the labor was to wake in the morning with hands so stiff and sore that he almost needed a crowbar to pry apart the fingers.

It did not take long for Aispuro to decide that the fields were best avoided. He signed on at a milk plant when he was a few years older, but the work was almost as bad. He froze his butt through the winter in an unheated brick building. Then, at twenty-two, he took a job as a correctional officer at Soledad State Prison, not for the badge or the gun but because it was the best-paying job that he could find.

Conditions at the prison were abominable at the time, Aispuro told me. The inmates slept in bunkbeds squeezed into cramped and fetid rows, and he had to listen through the night to their weeping, their farting, and the grinding of their teeth, consoled only by the size of his salary, more money than he had ever thought he would make.

It was okay with him if the job was rough, he said. He had never anticipated an easy life or dreamed of getting something for nothing. His mother had always kept him in line. Every year, at the start of school, she would go to his teacher and give permission for her son to be smacked if he fooled around in class, which, in consequence, Aispuro seldom did.

The prison world had changed substantially since January 3, 1949, the day that Aispuro had first punched in at Soledad. Prison technology was much more sophisticated, and guards had to graduate from a rigorous academy.

Corcoran was a state-of-the-art institution, the warden said. It consisted of six interracial mini-prisons. Designed to house 2,900 men, it currently housed 4,200. In its cells were some of the most malign convicts around, Level Fours so dangerous and volatile that they were under perpetual lockdown and were granted just ten hours outdoors each week.

Aispuro considered himself a realist. Over the years, he had accepted the hard truth that many convicts really were bad guys. They were bad right to the core, and they were their own worst enemies, as well. A prison sentence in California was not that horrible compared to one in, say, Alabama, he thought, but still the cons complained. The state gave its wards clean bedding, three square meals a day, and some peace and quiet, and yet they were always on one another's case, fighting, bullying, scamming, and raping each other.

No matter how decently you treated the men, Aispuro believed, somebody would always file a grievance. Somebody would always claim to be abused or not fed properly—this in a prison that occasionally served a half-chicken per plate!—and however outrageous the claim might be, some liberal bleeding heart on the outside would swallow it whole and offer to help.

"Not every prisoner can be saved," Aispuro instructed me firmly. "That's one lesson that the public needs to learn."

Some men at Corcoran, he continued, were so callous that it seemed to be their very nature to commit heinous crimes. They had no idea what else to do, having been thrown into the slam as juveniles and having come to maturity behind bars. In prison, they understood the order of things and could rise to a position of authority. They could join a prison gang such as the Mexican Mafia or the Aryan Brotherhood, or they could gain protection by playing the punk to a strong-armed lover. Out on the streets, the same men were walking ciphers, while in the joint they had a measure of cool.

Aispuro was astounded by how indolent his prisoners were. If they hadn't done something wrong, they'd probably be on welfare. 'They're too dadgum lazy to look for work," he said in disgust. The

prison offered them counseling, education, and job-training programs, but they diligently avoided all help. It upset him that the state
spent an average of twenty thousand dollars a year to clothe, feed,
support, and confine each prisoner. "Why not just send them to
Stanford for a couple of semesters instead?" the warden suggested.
"It would be cheaper."

Corcoran was filled with criminals going nowhere, big fish in a
little pond. Charles Manson was a prime example. Aispuro had talked
with his most famous inmate a few times, but he hadn't been impressed. Yet some prisoners were still afraid of Manson because of
his juju reputation. He was a con's con, a real pro, sucking in the
other inmates with his Rasputin stare and his scrambled philosophy.

To the warden, though, Manson was merely another product of
the system, somebody who had spent thirteen of his first twenty-five
years in cells before lighting out for California and his own peculiar
transformation.

Once a young man got caught in the revolving-door syndrome,
bouncing from one institution to the next, you had no chance with
him, Aispuro felt. The cycle had to be broken very early, but that
was getting harder to do. The population in Youth Authority camps,
schools, and pens had doubled in the last decade. Under the auspices
of the state, a boy was tossed in among the already ruined and was
taught such esoterica as how to eat a meal in seven minutes, how to
conceal and use a shank, and how to sodomize.

Aispuro was concerned about the growing lack of parental supervision for children.

"Mothers are out there working now," he said, a touch of irate-
ness in his voice. "What's going to happen to all the latchkey kids?
Parents ignore their children. The way it is, kids have every opportunity to get into trouble."

Prison, I saw, was the last step in a process that began much
earlier. I went back in my mind over other parents I'd met who'd
expressed a similar concern, Emma Black in Herlong and Bruce

Anderson in Anderson Valley, and thought how simple it was for a child to take a fall in our California paradise.

At the end of our meeting, Aispuro showed me to the door and gave me a hearty good-bye. He was a man at peace with himself, about to be finished with prisons and gone, for all I knew, to a fishing hole or a casino somewhere.

As I was leaving Corcoran, the wives of inmates were lining up for visiting hours. Their children were bathed, combed, powdered, and beribboned. Sometimes the women were in pairs or in threes, and they seemed almost frolicsome as they approached the prison door, giggling as if they were headed for a party. Surely it was just nervous tension, a final surrender of effervescent humors before they passed through a security check and entered a universe of pain.

AT THE SHILOH INN IN CORCORAN, I stayed up late reading about Charles Manson. He was the wrong kind of Californian, somebody whose leap toward self-invention had taken a strange left turn and had led him down byways that nobody ought to travel.

Manson had made his first stab at reaching the Coast in 1951 by running away from an Indiana School for Boys and pinching a series of cars to speed him on his way. He and a couple of merry pals pulled juvie stickups at gas stations across the West until they had the misfortune to hit a roadblock near Beaver, Utah, where the cops were looking for somebody else, and they were busted at last.

Charlie was sixteen. He was gnomelike, musically gifted, and of average intelligence. Psychiatrists described him as intensely anti-social.

He was sent to Washington, D.C., and bounced from institution to institution, losing a chance at parole by raping a fellow inmate while holding a razor blade to his throat. That got him classified as a violent homosexual in need of close supervision, and he was not set free again until 1954, when the court released him to an aunt and uncle in McMechen, West Virginia.

Manson's mother lived in Wheeling. She had robbed gas stations, too, and had once done some time in a state penitentiary for knocking over a till and banging a poor fuel jockey on the head with a Coke bottle. They were peas in a pod, Charlie and his mom. He went to see her often in Wheeling, and there he met a waitress, Rosalie Jean Willis, and married her.

Shortly after the wedding, he started boosting cars with a renewed vigor, including a 1951 Mercury that became his magic carpet to the Coast. He drove the Mercury to Los Angeles, where he was arrested for car theft and ordered into his first California state prison, Terminal Island in San Pedro. He languished cellbound while Rosalie gave birth to a son. She divorced him before his parole in 1958, disappeared, and never contacted him again.

Manson, now twenty-three, began to diversify his operations. His skills as a con had sharpened. He moved to Malibu, roomed with a bartender, and took to pimping, working a stable that consisted of two girls—a sixteen-year-old off the streets and another girl from Pasadena, who was overweight, rich, and dependent.

Charlie controlled them. He had learned to locate the soft spot in people and to play on their fears. In his little ménage, he must have seen great promise, a vision of his future Family, but he was uncomfortable and barely functional in society and soon committed a simpleminded offense, presumably to get back inside.

In 1959, he tried to cash a forged check for $37.50 at a Ralph's Supermarket in L.A. After his arrest, he must have had second thoughts about returning to prison because during an interrogation, he grabbed the evidence when the cops turned their backs, tore it up, and ate it. He had a genius for such things.

By the time the court hearing rolled around, Manson had recruited a hooker friend to lie on his behalf. She claimed to be pregnant, virginal, and deeply in love with him. Her performance aided and abetted Manson's earnest and yet wildly disingenuous vow to go straight, and a judge who may still suffer from nightmares set him free and kept him in circulation.

The sixties were about to happen, and Manson was ready for them. His dreams had inflated and he had acquired a Dolby soundtrack. Bit by the Hollywood bug, he created a phony entertainment company, 3-Star-Enterprises, and printed up some business cards naming him as president. There were always pretty young things around Los Angeles who could be foxed with the usual promises, and Manson sold them on his "Nite Club, Radio, and TV Productions." He knew that almost everybody in California ached to be discovered, to be in the limelight just once. Foolish girls invested their savings with him. One of them he drugged and raped. Another he blessed with an ectopic pregnancy.

In supreme violation of his parole, he transported prostitutes across state lines. The feds indicted him under the Mann Act and nabbed him in Laredo, Texas, after which he went into McNeill Island, a U.S. penitentiary in Washington, for a serious ten-year term.

To McNeill Island, Manson brought all the trappings of his new incarnation as a Californian. He told the other cons that he was a religious person, a Scientologist. His auditor, he said, had registered him as a theta clear, someone whose plate of karma was absolutely clean. From Scientology and L. Ron Hubbard, Charlie had borrowed abstruse ideas wholesale and had built his own demented vocabulary of apocalypse. The Bible, especially Revelations 9, was another of his favorite sources.

In the privacy of his cell, he spent hours strumming his guitar and imagining the masterly career as a singer that was in store for him when he was released. He had gotten a whiff of the music business and had realized that it was just another con. Everything was a con in the end.

Manson listened unstintingly to the Beatles and grew obsessed with their music. Would he ever be as famous as they were? Were they sending him coded messages in their songs? Alvin Karpis, a triggerman from the old Ma Barker gang and a longtime McNeill resident, taught Charlie to play the steel guitar.

In the summer of 1966, Manson was transferred to Terminal

Island prior to his release. He was so frightened by the prospect, believing that he could only function in prison, that he begged the authorities to keep him inside, but they turned him loose the following spring. From Los Angeles, he went immediately to the San Francisco Bay Area and rented a place in Berkeley, supporting himself by plying the spare-change circuit around Sather Gate and the university.

The new world of hippie flower children was an ideal match for Manson's talents as a necromancer. His years behind bars had hardened him, making him more cynical and giving him a chance to perfect his rap. In Berkeley, there were thousands of innocent, gullible young people who were searching for their own personal guru, and Charlie, sensing an opportunity, was happy to oblige.

One afternoon, while out panhandling with his guitar, he chatted up a chubby, homely librarian who was taking her poodle for a walk. He met with such success that before long he was living with her. She objected when he brought home another young woman to stay with them, but Manson wore her down, and soon there were many lost souls in residence, both girls and boys.

Charlie became the great orchestrator of lost souls. He relied on a potent combination of hallucinogens and hokum to induce them into orgies, where the goal was for them all to peak at the same time—to "come together," as John Lennon had sung, "right now." The mega-orgasm never happened, but juices were spilled, and the seed of the Family was smeared and spread in a fleshy binding. Manson had them where he wanted them, he was *in control.*

In 1967, the Summer of Love, the loveless one felt bad vibrations in the Haight-Ashbury. His intuition told him that the entire scene was crumbling under the attentions of the police, the FBI, and other sinister forces. Somehow he got his hands on an old school bus and ferried his children away from the city, down through the San Joaquin and into the desert west of Bakersfield.

◆   ◆   ◆

ALONG HIGHWAY 99 BOXCARS ROLLED, Union Pacific, Western Fruit Express, Pacific Fruit Express, Burlington Northern. *Hydra-Cushion for Fragile Freight, Cos Petroleum Transport.* A train against the western sky looked blameless. It suggested continuity, links made and retained over time, life as a purposeful journey from cradle to grave.

I was glad to be leaving Corcoran and Avenal, that stunned stretch of backcountry smack in the middle of the state. I passed Elk Bayou Ditch and Railroad Ditch and Tulare Canal, where egrets stood white and contemplative, the most patient of fishers. Outside Tipton, there was a Sunkist plant with two brimming, green gondolas parked nearby, *oranges sweet and juicy.*

Then came Pixley, a town named for Frank Pixley, who had founded the *Argonaut,* a barbed literary quarterly of the late nineteenth century. For a while, the wicked Ambrose Bierce was a columnist, but he and Pixley didn't get along, so Bierce switched to the *San Francisco Examiner* and wrote a column called "Prattle" for William Randolph Hearst. On Pixley's death, he supplied an epitaph. "Here lies Frank Pixley—as usual," he wrote.

Maybe it was the sight of those gondolas by the Sunkist plant, but I had a sudden desire for an Orange Crush—nothing else would do. Pixley didn't have much in the way of stores, though. It was a prairie town with a one-room school, where farmworkers lived. Poverty of the severest kind hung over it like a layer of grit.

At midday, many unemployed men were on the streets. They had the look of prisoners from Corcoran or elsewhere who'd been paroled or who had finished their term and hadn't yet summoned the energy to imagine where to go next, or who knew deep down that there wasn't a next place to go, not ever.

Noon, and the temperature was fixed at 103 degrees. The only industrious person around, a stout fellow pouring sweat by the bucket, scraped thanklessly at the weeds growing between sidewalk cracks, his shovel clanking.

"We have good hunting around here, anyway," he told me. Doves, grouse, and lots of quail.

At the General Store, I had to reconcile myself to a 7-Up and sipped it while I leaned against the storefront. A Greyhound stopped, and a driver in bright blue trousers opened the bus's door and shouted, "Any passengers?" There were none.

When the 'Hound left, a little hatchback rattled up to the store. The car was very old and as smashed as a cast-off aluminum can. A Hispanic man was at the wheel. His lover glared at him from the seat opposite as though he had never earned a nickel in his life and was never going to. She was a rail-thin white woman, her body worn to the bone before she'd turned forty.

Her daughter was stuffed into the backseat with two small children not yet ready for school. She was a child, too, really, no older than seventeen and already twice a mother. She had a lovely, open face that was as unmarked as a new pane of glass. I thought of all the difficulty that lay ahead of her, and how the deck was stacked for fair whether she chose to stay or to go. Hers was a face that might have showed up among the Manson Family, at once beaming and lost.

In 1908, COLONEL ALLEN ALLENSWORTH, a former slave and an army chaplain to the 24th Infantry Buffalo Soldiers during the Spanish-American War, claimed some land southwest of Pixley with the intent of starting a rural community for black pioneers. The site was a state historical park now, home to animals and birds.

At Allensworth, I saw hundreds of ground squirrels skittering around. Yellow-headed blackbirds were trilling in the sagebrush, while four tiny burrowing owls hopped around their nests in the earth. At the borders of the park were cotton fields and tar-paper shacks—migrants, itinerants, and tenant farmers collecting any tossed-away object, no matter how rusted or defunct.

Colonel Allensworth had charisma. By 1910, more than three hundred black families had joined him on the land. One of the pioneer houses still stood. Its wood frame was partially concealed by paper meant to simulate brick, and the fake bricks were bleached to gray now, spotted brown from the sun and rippled with cracks. As I walked toward the house, the soil turned to powder beneath my feet. There were no streams or creeks anywhere close, nothing wet to damp the dust.

The pioneers had access to four artesian wells, but the wells had slowly given out. The crops had slowly failed. The community had no tie to a railroad and no link to the outside world.

Progressive blacks in Los Angeles took issue with Allensworth, charging him with promoting segregation. In less than a decade, his settlement was dead, but it had lived on in memory for a long time. The land in Allensworth had been touched by something special, a spirit that lingered.

In the twilight, I watched the cranky owls do their hip-hop dance and knew how a day such as this one, an ordinary day, must have ended for the pioneers, their hoes and plows put to rest, the animals fed and sheltered, the cooking fires lit, and the air alight with swirling sparks. Families would be regrouping, the weight of their harsh labor briefly lifted, hands blistered and calloused, their feet tired and their backs aching.

I could hear the braying of mules, the scratch of silverware against tin plates, and the slosh of precious water as the dishes were carefully washed. I could see the great western sky darkening toward night, a half-moon rising, and stars in their untold millions.

Said Percy Williams, a boy from Allensworth:

In the evening during the summer months, the nights were very warm and balmy, and the children played. We didn't have cars.

One or two had bicycles. There were no sidewalks, so there was
no rollerskating. But we played yard games, hide-and-seek, things
like that. We didn't have radios or television, but we had phono-
graphs and played records. Had to crank them by hand then. And
then the old people would tell stories. . . .

Heat, dust, tumbleweeds.

CHAPTER 17

ALONG THE BUMPY BACKROADS of the San Joaquin I bounced, listening to country music on the radio and slaking my thirst with soda and beer. Pond, Wasco, Shafter, here was the brittle country that John Steinbeck had traveled in an old bakery truck in 1936 while reporting on the sorry state of farmworkers for a San Francisco paper and gathering the raw material that would become, in time, *The Grapes of Wrath*.

Everything had changed since then, of course, but also nothing had. At the North Shafter Farm Labor Center, I saw a man in coveralls spraying chemicals up under the eaves of some shacks that housed migrants and their children, poisoning whatever lingered there.

Cotton was the king crop in the lower valley. It loved the land and thrived on the weather. After grapes, it was the most valuable agricultural commodity in California, worth more than $1 billion a year. Its importance was global as well as local. No other crop earned our farmers as many dollars in export.

Dick Bassett knew all there was to know about cotton, having worked in the San Joaquin for more than thirty years. I met him at the U.S. Department of Agriculture's Cotton Research Station outside Shafter one afternoon. The scientists at the station had the job of tending to growers as growers tended to their fields, advising them on new farming methods and sharing the data that they collected on their rounds.

Bassett was a Wyoming native and had a degree in soil sciences from Rutgers University. There was a western spareness to him, all gristle and no fat. His eyes were alive with good humor, and he liked to be active and out in the sun and was looking forward to a vacation trip to his home state, where he planned to go trout fishing with his son.

Although the Spanish padres had grown a little cotton at their missions, relying on seeds imported from Mexico, Bassett told me that its true emissary in the San Joaquin was W. B. Camp, an employee of the federal government. During World War I, a shortage of a special type of cotton—extra-long staple—had developed, and Camp was sent to California to try and cultivate some. The cotton, which was also known as American Egyptian (and, later on, as pima), had a number of war-related uses, most especially in the canvas wings of biplanes.

Camp arrived in the valley in 1918 with seeds from USDA labs around the country. He did a big test planting in Arvin, southeast of Bakersfield, at the foot of the Tehachapi Mountains, and followed it with others. The crop did moderately well, but the bottom fell out of the cotton market after the war, and the price per pound plummeted from a dollar to a dime. Camp's experiments continued, anyway, and he opened the Shafter Cotton Research Station in 1922, on forty acres that the Kern County Land and Cattle Company had donated.

After the failure of American Egyptian, most San Joaquin farmers went back to the standard cottons that they'd been growing before—such upland varieties as Durango that were old familiars in the United States. Camp and his associates at the USDA believed that the farmers would be wiser to concentrate on just one variety, the better to master its subtleties. Why not find the type of cotton that was most ideally suited to the specifics of the region?

Alcala proved to be the choice variety. Its discovery was something of an accident. In the early 1900s, when boll weevils were decimating the cotton fields of the South, USDA researchers scoured Mexico and Central America, where most cotton seeds had come from, to search for a weevil-resistant variety. In Mexico, they located a strain that satisfied them and called it Alcala after the town where it grew. When the cotton was tested more thoroughly at home, it flunked—the weevils did not resist it—but some Alcala seeds made it to the San Joaquin and flourished.

The match was very nearly perfect. Alcala loved the arid climate and the alkaline soil of the valley. It yielded fairly large bolls with fibers that were unusually strong and quite long, cotton of the finest kind. By 1925, Alcala had so outpaced the upland cottons in terms of production that farmers were petitioning the legislature to designate the San Joaquin as a one-variety community, thereby preventing low-grade, bastard strains from "mongrelizing" it.

Alcala still grew in the valley and still yielded abundantly. It was relatively common for a farmer to get three bales, or 1,500 pounds, of cotton per acre. In spite of that, the region had dropped its one-variety status in the late 1970s, when the USDA had canceled its breeding program. Private breeders filled the gap and offered several new possibilities, and now there were about six varieties growing, all of a uniformly high quality.

About a million acres in the San Joaquin were planted to cotton at present, largely because the price supports in the United States were so favorable. The supports allowed American growers to compete against growers abroad who got government subsidies, and also helped the beleaguered farmers in such southern states as Texas, Oklahoma, and Mississippi. Those farmers had to contend with pests, floods, freezes, and hurricanes just to harvest an inferior cotton whose weak fibers were consigned to the cheapest denims instead of the finest yarns.

In California, the price supports were pure gravy, and every farmer grew as much cotton as he could.

"The farmers down South are envious, all right," Bassett said, with a chuckle. "They think this state is a big greenhouse, but that's a misconception."

True, he went on, the climate was mild and the irrigated water was inexpensive—there wasn't much irrigation in the South—but California cotton growers did have to deal with a few pests. In the past, the farmers were inclined to solve their problems by applying liberal doses of pesticides, but that strategy had killed off the beneficial bugs along with the evil ones, and the USDA was encouraging a more efficient approach known as integrated pest management, or IPM.

The sterile moth program was a good example of IPM in action, Bassett claimed. It had been evolved in Arizona in the mid-1960s to combat a scourge of pink bollworms. The female bollworms laid their eggs on the leaves of cotton plants, and their progeny later devastated the bolls, but the USDA scientists had hit on a scheme to fool them. They bred sterile moths in the lab and air-dropped them by the billions, overwhelming the females with males who could go through the mating dance but couldn't reproduce—bugs who got the fun but not the responsibility, as Bassett put it.

The growing of cotton, I learned, had a basic rhythm. The planting occurred in late April or early May. A month or so later, most farmers began irrigating. In September, the preparations for the harvest started. Toward the end of the month, a defoliant such as sodium chlorate was applied in low concentrations to rid the plants of leaves and facilitate the picking. Machines did all the picking now, depositing the cotton in a module at the end of each row.

The harvest was over by mid-November, but ginning continued into January. About three-quarters of the processed cotton from the San Joaquin wound up in overseas markets, with Japan being a major consumer.

I had enjoyed my botany lesson. Cotton farming in California, at least in Dick Bassett's version, had an attractive ease and romance. Even the imagery was beguiling—the sterile moths like confetti in the sky, the fields in autumn crowned with whitish bolls. That the federal government would guarantee a profit only increased the charm. Without too much trouble, I could picture myself astride a tractor toting up my annual earnings, while a Merle Haggard tune played through my Walkman.

Bassett must have taken note of my dreaminess because he asked if I wanted to visit a farm where he had some test plots.

"When?" I said.

"How about now?"

THE CRETTOLS were a modern California farming family. They had a spread of about 2,500 acres in and around Wasco and Shafter, neither big nor small for the San Joaquin.

"It's only a little ways from here," Bassett said, but he was a westerner applying a western yardstick to a trip of fifteen miles.

Bassett had a beat-up Toyota. He climbed in and instructed me to follow him. The road was a two-lane blacktop, straight and dead flat, and he drove it like a bat out of hell. Pity the poor crow caught dining on roadkill, I thought, for the bird shall be no more. We passed some nurseries where rootstock for roses was cultivated in an ideal microclimate and some potato fields that were a memory from the time when Shafter was the spud center of the world, with two hundred carloads a day departing from town on the rails.

In a while, Bassett turned onto a dirt road that led to some cleared ground in the midst of cotton fields. Two Mexicans were inside a barn-sized aluminum shed filled with tools and farm machinery. I saw a hydraulic hoist and some welding equipment. The men jumped at our approach, trying to cope with the unexpected fact of our arrival while simultaneously wishing that we'd disappear.

Louie Crettol was talking on a phone in a corner of the shed. He didn't fit the farmer stereotype. His graying hair was stylishly

barbered, a Bakersfield trim, and he wore a little gold chain around
his neck. You could tell that he cared about the figure that he cut.
He was comfortable with himself and had a puckish grace.

Bassett introduced us. "You getting any?" Louie asked, with a
stagy leer.

Jim Crettol pulled up in his truck a few minutes later. At forty,
he was the older brother by a year, as handsome as Louie but not
yet graying. Where Louie could be funny and even a little biting
sometimes, Jim tended to be earnest and a touch high-minded. He
handled the farm's business details, while Louie supervised the fieldwork. Both brothers had enormous energy and were devoted to
having fun. They had another partner in Crettol Farms, their father,
Art, who was sixty-seven.

It was Art's father, Victor, who had come to the San Joaquin
from Switzerland in 1916 and had started a farming dynasty. Victor
Crettol fought in World War I, gained his citizenship, and worked
as a custodian at Wasco High School, saving his money to buy land
in small parcels. He would later sell much of the land to Wasco as
the city expanded, earning a handsome profit. He died when he was
eighty-three, but his wife, Marie, the boy's grandmother, still lived
in the adobe house that her husband had helped to build. Marie was
ninety-nine.

All the Crettols were going to Switzerland that winter for a
family reunion. They were from Saint Luc, a village not far from
the Matterhorn.

"Good wine over there," Louie said.

"Good wine and good food," Jim agreed.

The Crettols alternated their crops from year to year, depending
on the circumstances. Sometimes they grew sugar beets, "dehydrater"
onions, garlic, and alfalfa, but they always grew almonds—California's second-largest export crop—and cotton. They had about 1,200
acres planted to cotton now, the maximum that they could grow and
still receive their price supports. Almost every farmer in the San
Joaquin followed the same rule of thumb.

They led me out to look at some crops in a field nearby—the "desert place," by family tradition. The soil did seem miserably dry, like something from the Mojave, but Jim toed it with a boot and showed me how, a few inches down, the dirt was dark and moist. In the valley, the sun dried up any surface water in seconds.

"Last year was a bad one for cotton," Louie grumbled, with a farmer's hurt at being let down by the earth.

The plants, he said, were slow to grow, and then three-and-a-half inches of rain fell from April to May, much more than usual. The rain knocked off the young leaves and trashed the crop.

This year's crop was different, however, among the best that Louie could remember. He yanked up a young plant to demonstrate. It was about twenty inches tall and had a long taproot that resembled a parsnip. The geraniumlike leaves were full and green. They had blotches caused by thrips, a sucking insect, and by such manmade pollutants as smog, car exhausts, and smoke from oil rigs. Thrips was normal, though, and no cause for worry.

Louie separated the leaves to reveal the fragile beginning of a boll. By harvest time, it would be about the size of a large golf ball. He drew my attention to the ground, where the weeds were scarce. The year before, he said, weeds had dominated the field, and the cost of weeding, the only cotton-related task still done by hand in California fields, had leaped from forty to fifty-five dollars an acre.

The brothers sold their cotton through CALCOT, a grower-owned co-op that represented thousands of farmers in California and Arizona. CALCOT moved about 3 million bales annually. That kept Jim and Louie satisfied. They were more interested in the actual farming than they were in the sales angle, anyway. They didn't agree with Bassett that growing cotton was mysterious or complicated.

"We've been riding tractors around here since we were about eight," Jim said, nodding toward the fields. "You just know how to grow things."

"You're born with it," Louie added.

We moved to the shade of the aluminum shed. It was their

machine shop. On a farm, something always needed fixing. I asked them if they were the only children in the family, and they burst out laughing.

"Hell, no!" cried Jim. "But we're the only *boys!*"

Louie looked at Jim, and Jim burst out laughing again. Louie was getting ready to enumerate, and he clearly relished the task.

"We have five sisters, see," he said. "There's Mickey in Santa Barbara. She's on her fourth husband. I like to say that she's given us more brother-in-laws than all our other sisters combined."

He paused to glance at Jim. This routine had been playing for a long time. "Jeanne's next in line. She's married and lives with an oil driller in Bakersfield. Shirley's in Texas, where her husband— he's Jim's wife's brother—leases geothermal rights for a Kuwaiti company. Carolyn lives around here and runs the farm office. She does our accounting. Claudette's the baby. She lives in Bakersfield, too. Our mom is in Wasco. She and Art are divorced."

Things had changed among farmers since the days of "Little House on the Prairie," I thought. I couldn't imagine Michael Landon getting a divorce, even if his crops failed and his wife put on eighty pounds and began savaging the dog.

"Hey, would you like some garlic to take with you?" Jim asked, so I said good-bye to Dick Bassett and got into Jim's truck, which was outfitted with a lot of high-tech gear—a thermometer for tracking soil temperatures, a company radio, a calculator, and a cellular telephone.

We drove by an alfalfa field and stopped at a field where dehydrator onions were being grown as a contract crop. They were a hybrid and had much less water in them than normal onions did. Spice manufacturers bought dehydrators to use in onion salt and flakes, chipping and shredding them.

Jim grabbed an onion stalk and jerked it up. He brushed off the dirt, peeled away the crinkly outer skin, cut the onion into rough halves with a jackknife, and sliced a thin piece for me to sample.

"That'll put a heat on your tongue," he warned with a smile, and it did—a raw, dense, superoniony taste as sharp as a chile pepper.

Across from the onions were sugar beets, their cabbagey leaves wilted and yellowing. Jim repeated the tasting procedure, serving me a beet sliver on the tip of his knife.

"It'll be sweet, then bitter," he cautioned me again, proceeding to a garlic field and bending to harvest several bulbs. Fresh out of the ground, the bulbs had an odd look of surprise, as though they'd been disturbed at sleep. You could smell them fifty feet away.

Jim handed over the garlic. He told me to cure it for a couple of weeks in the basement of my house. He knew San Francisco a little from his trips there to lobby for lower water rates before the Public Utility Commission. The city was nice, he said, but he was always happy to get back to Wasco. The farm, his family, some dirt beneath his fingernails—that was California to Jim Crettol.

THE CRETTOLS HAD ABOUT TEN STEADY HANDS, and Sam Cravens was among the most valued. He'd been with the family since 1952. He was a product of the Dust Bowl. An uncle of his had blown into Arvin during the 1930s, and when Cravens turned sixteen he had migrated to his uncle's place and had picked squash for six months before deciding to retrace his steps. It wasn't the hard work that had put him off. It was the girls.

"Damn California girls just didn't suit me," he explained to me one afternoon, while I was hanging around the machine shop. "So I had to go on home and get me an Oklahoma one."

Cravens returned with his bride, settled in Wasco, and worked for several farmers in the area before hiring on with Art Crettol. He was an expert at holding a grudge, and he liked to point to the other outfits where he'd been and say, "I used to work for that son-of-a-bitch over there, and the son-of-a-bitch next to him, and the son-of-a-bitch over yonder. . . .

Sam Cravens did look like a farmer. What hair he had he kept hidden beneath a tractor cap. He wore overalls and workboots and blew his nose in a bandanna. He served the Crettol boys as a general factotum and would-be majordomo. They had known him since they were little kids and sometimes deferred to him even when they thought he was wrong, out of respect and because of his temper.

Although Cravens couldn't read or write with any proficiency, he had learned to sign his name over the years and was proud of the fact. His lack of a formal education had not affected his command of cuss words, though. He swore with brilliance and ingenuity. I listened in awe one day as he spent half an hour berating the Texas rod weeders attached to his cultivator. Made of spring steel, the rods were gentle enough to brush against mature cotton plants and yet tough enough to tear up the weeds between rows.

Cravens fiddled and fiddled with the rods, studying them from various angles, but they still refused to adjust to the proper height. He stomped around, kicked at the dust, and stooped a last time for a microscopic inspection of the problem, which continued to resist all solutions. Then he rose to his feet and let those goldarn, son-of-a-bitching, good-for-nothing Texas rod weeders have it.

You could usually find a few other people hanging around the machine shop with Cravens when there wasn't much else to do—Jim and Louie and often Tommy Dunlap, a big man who handled the welding chores and cared for the various motors and engines, his T-shirts oil-spotted and seldom quite reaching to his jeans. Tommy's brother, Jimmy, liked to hang around, too, and he was just as big and showed more flesh between the garments meant to clothe him. The Dunlaps had been with the Crettols for more than thirty years.

Then there was Preston McCurdy, a lanky, red-skinned fellow who did odd jobs and tended to some irrigation. He kept to the fringe while I was at the shop and seemed bashful and quiet. He spoke so seldom that I couldn't understand exactly what he was up to, so I asked Louie about it once.

Louie shouted over the roar of Tommy Dunlap fixing something, "Hey, Preston! What is it you do for us?"

"Little as possible," was Preston's droll reply.

One morning, Randy Priest stopped by the shop. He had the solid build of a bronc rider, somebody you'd mess with only if your life depended on it. Randy was younger than the others, a valley bon vivant. He had a neat beard and lustrous cowboy boots. He worked as a salesman for Pioneer Equipment, but he was new to the job and seemed exasperated by its demands.

"Where's your territory?" I asked him.

"Oh, hell!" he exclaimed, as though he were overwhelmed by the notion of such scale. "It's every damn where. Yesterday, I was in Pixley. Today, I had to go all the way down to Buttonwillow."

Priest and some of his pals were about to go across the border for a two-week vacation. They'd rented a motor home and had chipped in a hundred dollars apiece to stock it to the gills with Tecate beer.

"That's the Budweiser of Mexico," he informed us.

"You heard any good jokes lately, Randy?" Louie asked.

Priest looked sheepish and pawed at the ground with a boot. "Well, I have, but I don't think I ought to tell them while B.J.'s around."

B.J. was Jim's boy, Brian. He had just finished seventh grade in Wasco and hadn't figured out what to do with his summer yet, so he came to the machine shop to hang around, too. He was a wholesome, bright-eyed kid who ached to be more grown up and able to take a bigger bite out of the world.

Louie and Jim had four children between them, two each, but B.J. was the only male. He was aware of certain pressures, however indirect. He would inherit a farm someday, and a son's place at the center of it, but did he have farming in his blood? He didn't know. He couldn't even test things by riding around on a tractor as his father and his uncle had done in their youth, because of safety issues and liability insurance. California farmers were drowning in paperwork and government regulations, Jim complained to me once.

B.J. was a bit car-crazy. Cars were potent symbols for him of everywhere he wanted to go. His father used to own and drive a pair of speedballs, but they were stored in the machine shop now. One was a yellow 1970 Mustang Mach 1 made for burning up the roads. B.J. showed it to me one day, lifting aside a tarp as if to reveal a treasure.

"All right!" he said, whistling in admiration. "It's *sooo* bad."

The doors of the Mustang opened onto a scene of devastation. The bucket seats were eaten through and covered with mouse turds. There was a stink of rot and decay.

"Phew, rat piss!" B.J. fanned a hand in front of his nose as he slid into the driver's seat. "This would still be a pretty good first car, though, wouldn't it?"

The other car was a dragster that Jim and Louie had built from scrap. They had called themselves the Alpine Okies, playing on their Swiss ancestry, and had competed at drag races in Bakersfield and Hemet and at the sand drags in Salt Lake City, at tracks all across the West.

The dragster rested in neglect on a catwalk under the eaves of the shop. Again, B.J. had to lift away a tarp and broach a swirl of dust and odors. He touched a finger to the script, *Alpine Okies,* stenciled on a door.

"Well?" he asked eagerly, traveling in his mind at great speeds. "What do you think?"

THE UNITED FARM WORKERS OF AMERICA were in their sixth year of a boycott against nonunion table grapes, so I decided to go to Delano, where the UFW had an office, for a look around. When Jim Crettol heard about this, he phoned a farmer friend there and arranged for me to attend a special banquet that was held twice a month at the Slavonian Hall.

"You're a Yugoslav, you'll enjoy it," Jim said, patting me on the back.

I appreciated the gesture, but my feelings about the banquet were mixed because Yugoslav grape growers in Delano and elsewhere in the San Joaquin had been the archenemies of Cesar Chavez, the UFW's president during the great farm-labor strikes of the late 1960s and early 1970s. As the Armenians had done in Fresno, the Slavs had pooled their capital to buy land cheaply in the valley, often for as little as $125 an acre, starting right after the Depression. They were industrious and ambitous, plowing their money back into the ground and creating an iron-fisted fiefdom.

Delano was about fifteen miles north of Wasco on the Southern Pacific line. It had vineyards on its east side and cotton fields on the west.

The streets in town were crowded with retired farmworkers going about their daily chores. Some of them walked with the help of canes, while others had a peculiar, stiff-legged gait that came from eons of bending over crops. Their skin looked burnished and leathery. In their ranks, I could see each successive wave of immigrant labor that had washed over California to tend the farms.

A young Hispanic woman at the Delano Chamber of Commerce was puzzled when I inquired about the UFW and its office, asking after Cesar Chavez, who was still alive then, and his associate, Dolores Huerta.

"Cesar? Cesar?" she wondered aloud, trying to place him.

Had so much time gone by? I spoke of the grape boycott next, and that seemed to stir her. From a phonebook, she pulled an address for the UFW on Garces Highway and also gave me a statistical abstract of Delano that had been printed for visitors. There was a handwritten addendum on the last page: "250 new homes," it said. "More being constructed, 2 large shopping centers."

I drove out on Garces Highway through vineyard land, where the earth was again caked and powdery and created a misleading impression of being inimical to growing things. The grapes dozed on the vines. They were becoming sweeter and fleshier and taking on a hint of color now that August was almost here. Soon they would weigh heavily on the trellises and droop in ripening bunches in the heavy air of the San Joaquin, that familiar moil of dust and chemical fumes.

Pesticides and their application, their impact on the health of farmworkers—those were major issues in the current UFW boycott. Cesar Chavez contended that workers and their families were regularly exposed to herbicides and fungicides without adequate supervision or advice about how to handle them. The union claimed to have found a cancer cluster among children in Earlimart, between Delano and Pixley. There were five afflicted boys and girls under the age of fifteen.

A specialist in occupational medicine had been hired by the UFW to examine the evidence. Afterward, she told reporters, "These people live in a soup of chemicals. It's in the air, it's in the soil, it's in the water. It's everywhere."

The parents of the children, all Hispanic, did not speak. They had no English.

Grape growers in the valley felt that they were being unfairly singled out. They were no better or worse than other farmers, they said. The California Table Grape Commission, a trade group, was threatening to sue the UFW over what it believed to be false statements about the safety of eating grapes treated with pesticides. They accused Chavez of fomenting the boycott to prop up a union whose influence had dwindled.

As an outsider, I found it impossible to untangle the arguments, but I knew for sure that the price for wanton use of agricultural chemicals in California had yet to be extracted. The poisoned wells in Fresno, the tainted wells in Shafter, the wildlife refuge at Kesterson swimming in selenium, the deformed embryos of birds, and the teratogenic effect all through the chain of life—we were only beginning to admit to the damage. On farms, toxins were clinging to each bud and leaf.

The UFW office on Garces Highway was across from a Voice of America transmitter that broadcast propaganda to the assumedly benighted of other countries. I realized that I was at Cuarenta Acres, a forty-acre plot that had once been crucial to the union's mythology. Chavez had talked of his dreams for it—a cooperative farm for cattle and vegetables, inexpensive housing for seniors—but Cuarenta Acres had not flowered. There were weeds, beer cans, bottles, and pariah dogs.

Inside the office, the receptionist smiled brightly and said, "Cesar and Dolores are at our headquarters in Keene, out Tehachapi way." She gave me the phone number.

I saw a single-story building that looked like an abandoned motel. It turned out to be Agbayani Retirement Community, another broken dream from more hopeful days.

At the time of the first big grape boycott, Filipino activists had demanded a concession from the UFW. They wanted Agbayani as a pilot project, one that could be duplicated elsewhere to accommodate the rapidly aging Filipino workers in the San Joaquin, maybe as many as thirty thousand unmarried men over sixty whose adult lives had been spent in the fields.

The Agbayani project had never been properly funded, though, and now there was just this one sorry, tile-roofed building, where a handful of old men were sitting out front. They were sitting very still and didn't speak to each other or to visitors. I tried to talk to one of them, but he didn't respond, and I looked more closely and saw that he was blind.

The men lacked energy. They were old and tired and sick. They had done their laundry somewhere that morning and had draped their worn cotton shirts and their threadbare jeans over some bushes to dry.

THE HISTORY OF FARM LABOR in California was a history of abuse. The Chinese were the first to suffer. When the Exclusions Acts of 1882, 1892, and 1902 banned immigration from China, their numbers were reduced significantly, and the Japanese, who had been forbidden by law from leaving their country until 1866, took their place, working for even less money, raising their own crops in the poorest soil, and demonstrating an acumen for business. They were despised for all those qualities.

The United States government rewarded them with a fate similar to the Chinese by forging a "Gentlemen's Agreement" with Japan in 1907 to prevent such workers from entering the country. The Alien Land Law of 1913 barred the Japanese from owning any real estate, including farms, although they were sometimes able to circumvent the law. Antagonism against them peaked after Pearl Harbor was bombed, and they were rounded up and incarcerated in "relocation centers" for the duration of World War II.

The Filipinos followed the Japanese. They were primarily young men from Hawaii, single and indentured, who were sent to the state en masse in the 1920s to harvest grapes, lettuce, and asparagus. They were belittled and called homosexuals because of the absence of women among them. Their willingness to work for rock-bottom wages caused them to be vilified in the same way as their predecessors. Attacks on them were common. They were set upon and randomly beaten in Exeter, Salinas, and Watsonville, often by unemployed white laborers. In 1935, state legislators passed a bill guaranteeing any Filipino a free trip home if he promised not to return. Many Filipino workers took advantage of the deal.

Mexicans by the thousands filled their slots. They began sneaking across the border after the Mexican Revolution uprooted them. They had no legal standing, so they had no recourse or defense when farmers exploited them.

Okies and Arkies rode in on the last wave of farm labor, men and women already so bedraggled and sucked dry that they got the shabbiest treatment of all and rarely had the strength to protest.

Other migrants came in smaller numbers—some Europeans, some Sikhs, some Armenians, and a few blacks from the South to pick cotton. They endured lives of great difficulty, as John Steinbeck, a native of Salinas, would document in his newspaper articles. In one report, Steinbeck described what a migrant could expect at a camp in the San Joaquin:

> The houses, one-room shacks usually about 10 by 12 feet, have no rug, no water, no bed. In one corner there is a little iron wood stove. Water must be carried from a faucet at the end of the street. Also at the head of the street there will be either a dug toilet or a toilet with a septic tank to serve 100 to 150 people. A fairly typical ranch in Kern County had one bathhouse with a single shower and no heated water for the use of the whole block of houses, which had a capacity of 400 people. . . .
>
> The attitude of the employer on the large ranch is one of hatred and suspicion, his method is the threat of deputies' guns. The workers are herded about like animals. Every possible method is used to make them feel inferior and insecure. At the slightest suspicion that the men are organizing they are run from the ranch at points of guns. The large ranch owners know that if organization is ever effected [sic] there will be the expense of toilets, showers, decent living conditions and a raise in wages.

Union organizers had been soliciting farmworkers for some time. The Wobblies (a nickname for Industrial Workers of the World) were active in Fresno as early as 1910. Their main organizer, Frank Little, whose life would end in Montana when vigilantes hung him from a bridge, held meetings on streetcorners to promote free speech. The tactic was designed to enhance the self-image of uneducated laborers and to teach them that they really could have a voice in things.

Blackie Ford, another Wobbly, was involved in a riot in Wheatland, in the Sacramento Valley, in 1913. Ralph Durst, who grew hops, had advertised harvest jobs far and wide to draw a crowd of pickers, pit them against one another, and lower his costs. The scheme backfired when about three thousand migrants came to his farm and went into rebellion.

Ford called for a public protest, and when the authorities tried to arrest him during it, a brawl broke out and resulted in the deaths of a deputy sheriff and the district attorney of Yolo County. Subsequently, Ford was caught and convicted of second-degree murder, although he'd never pulled the trigger of a gun.

Between 1930 and 1933, there were almost fifty agricultural strikes in the state. One of the biggest, an attempt to shut down the cotton harvest, occurred around Corcoran and Pixley. More than eighteen thousand workers participated. Ranchers killed three of them, but they did no prison time. The strike was a bust in spite of its size, limping along for twenty-four days before ending in a worthless settlement. Scabs from Mexico were already picking the cotton, and no union members were ever hired to join them.

In another ploy to discourage organizers, growers banded together as the Associated Farmers of California. They accused the unions of being Communist-inspired, a serious charge in the heartland. Thugs from the American Legion served as their hired guns, cracking skulls with ax handles and lobbing canisters of tear gas into rallies.

Cesar Chavez was the first organizer to make any headway against the growers. He was born in Yuma, Arizona, on the Colorado River, in 1926. His father lost a little farm when Cesar was ten, and the family became migrants. Chavez would attend more than thirty different schools before his parents settled in San Jose.

In his early twenties, he went to work for Community Service Organization, a social-work agency, remaining for twelve years until CSO refused to back him in an effort to unionize farmworkers. His ties to the field were still strong. With his eight children, he moved to Delano, where his wife's family was from, and ran his fledgling operation from a rented house.

He chose an opportune moment to begin. Public Law 78, a keystone of the *bracero* program, was about to be rescinded. The law had permitted a grower to import fieldhands—*bracero* means "strong-armed one"—from Mexico if he claimed to be unable to find American workers to pick his crops, but it no longer obtained after 1964.

Chavez had trained well for his crusade. He knew his Saul Alinsky and had read Gandhi and Thoreau. He believed that he could not prevail without the total support of the community. Wisely, he assembled a diverse coalition that had such partners as Robert Kennedy, Jerry Brown, Filipino leaders, liberal journalists, youthful idealists on the left, and the Catholic church. He was smart enough to cloak the struggle in saintliness and cast it as a simple battle of good against evil.

The grape growers never had a chance. You had only to glance at a single newspaper photo of their private security guards threatening UFW pickets with German shepherds to be convinced that they were in the wrong. While the dogs' were baring their teeth, Chavez was fasting on water and looking holier with each tick of the clock. *¡Huelga!* The grape boycott had succeeded—the first strike-related boycott ever to do so in California.

SLAVONIAN HALL IN DELANO, a plain, auditorium-sized building, had no sign to identify it. A fence topped with concertina wire kept uninvited visitors from dropping in, while a rent-a-cop checked off the names of guests at the door.

The host for the day's banquet was Kenny Kovacevich, a tall, graying, imperturbable man born in Reedley of immigrant parents from Yugoslavia. He was friendly and slow-moving and happy to do a favor for Jim Crettol, favors being a kind of currency in the valley as they are anywhere else. He walked me about the hall and escorted me to an open bar. The company that bought his grapes had donated the liquor, and local farmers had donated the peaches, cherries, and plums in bowls on the folding banquet tables.

"You might get a few cracked pits," Kovacevich said jovially. "But it still eats good!"

The banquet had a different host every time. Its purpose was fraternal. Those in attendance were having a laugh and a couple of drinks while getting a little business done. More than a hundred men, many of them grape growers, were in the hall. Maybe two-thirds of them were Slavs.

Six burly fellows were cooking steaks over charcoal on an outdoor grill, turning the meat with forks and tongs. There was something primitive but vital about the scene, a rich carnality. The cooks reminded me of my own relatives, the balding uncles in T-shirts and khakis, stocky and broad-shouldered and quick to indulge a passion. Their faces were rosy from the fire.

The steaks came from National Market in Delano and not from Von's, where the management supported the grape boycott. Kovacevich made that point. I saw no Hispanics anywhere in the room.

Our meal was served family-style and fell to the tables unceremoniously, a salad first, then pasta with a thick meat sauce, and then the steaks on a platter. Circling volunteers threw down some supermarket bread still in its cellophane sack. Jugs of Gallo Chablis and Burgundy were evenly distributed. The sounds of hearty appetites took hold, knives and forks set to clattering.

The man sitting next to me, George Ezikian, was an Armenian-American product of the valley, who'd bolted from Visalia, his hometown. He sold the growers "agricultural employee benefits," which translated into medical insurance for farmworkers. In the Delano area, nine out of ten big farms bought it.

Ezikian was of the opinion that such programs had cost Cesar Chavez quite a few members. He stated this flatly as a fact, taking no cheer from it. He was a sophisticated person. The UFW tended to represent the seasonal migrants now, he said, and not the workers who had put down roots.

Ezikian lived in Irvine in Orange County and loved it there—the golf, the tennis, the jogging, and the mild summers that were

nothing like the infernal Julys and Augusts in Visalia. His house had
doubled in value over the past two years, and he played with the
idea of selling it and buying something better. He had just got married
for a second time, and he and his new wife were wondering whether
or not to have kids. Ezikian had two children from his first marriage,
both preparing for college. His worries were the worries of the age
in California.

Ice-cream bars landed on the table, thrown from cardboard boxes.
One of the bartenders took the floor and rapped on a glass with a
spoon. After thanking Kovacevich for the feed, he cleared his throat
and told a joke.

"What's the difference between herpes and AIDS?" he asked.
He paused for a minute to let us ruminate. "Herpes is a love story,
but AIDS is a fairy tale!"

The laughter was uproarious. At our table, only Ezikian seemed
to be cringing a bit.

Another man stepped up to tell some jokes. He was a semipro, the sort of lounge act that you might find yourself confronted
with in Sparks, Nevada, after you'd lost all your money in Reno,
had drunk too much, and had locked yourself out of your motel
room.

"Hey, how about the size of those steaks?" he said with a wink.
"Even in my fantasies, the meat isn't *that* big!"

He hitched up his slacks and told another joke in the form of
an exchange on "Jeopardy," the TV quiz show, that cast Batman
and Robin as a homosexual couple.

I felt myself awash in casual cruelty, recalling the sickly sensation
of being in a high-school locker room and joining in on some mindless
macho posing. With a sinking heart, I understood that the distance
between the Slavonian Hall and Ward 5A at San Francisco General
was so imponderable at the moment that only a stoop laborer might
know how to calculate it.

◆   ◆   ◆

On my last morning in wasco, Jim Crettol materialized at the machine shop looking as if he'd passed the early hours rolling in a field and trying to harvest dehydrator onions with his teeth, but he'd just been crawling in the dirt for a tightly focused tour of two test-plot plantings of sugar beets.

With a pest-control adviser from a chemical company, he had examined the effects of a new treatment that was supposed to increase the amount of sugar in a beet by a half percent. That didn't sound like much, but if you had a hundred acres in beets, as the Crettols did, the gain could amount to two or three thousand dollars a year.

Around Wasco, farmers referred to pest-control advisers as snake-oil men. The PCAs walked a fine line between science and selling, but Jim felt that the reliable ones afforded him some useful information at times. Besides, a test didn't cost him anything.

He took me with him on the rest of his morning rounds, driving first to Nikkel Ironworks in Shafter to see about a new cotton planter that he and Louie were buying. Lloyd Prather, the manager at Nikkel, was a lean stick of hickory. He was stewing about a shortage of bearings from Japan.

"No bearings, and you're in a big world of hurt," Prather said, putting it succinctly.

Farmers are loath to discuss money, but I gathered that the cotton planter would cost about $25,000. Nikkel would build it from scratch and paint it International Red.

Jim and Louie didn't mind the price, but Art Crettol was up in arms about it—a customary response among the Crettol elders, Jim said, when the younger generation usurped the power. Art's father, Victor, had howled in pain when Art had insisted on shelling out seven thousand dollars for a new cotton picker in 1949.

In Wasco, Jim bought a tri-tip roast and asked me to a barbecue at his house that night.

On the drive back to the farm, he was acting hyper and said that he'd always been like that, loaded with more energy than he knew what to do with. It had kept him from staying in college, down in Bakersfield. The pace of education had seemed so slow to him that he literally couldn't sit still and had to drop out. The army had drafted him right away and sent him to helicopter school at Fort Rucker, Alabama, in 1968.

Rural Alabama was no dreamland, even for a farmer. Jim was certain that he'd soon be flying over the jungles of Vietnam, but he got lucky and was assigned to a base in Korea instead, where the army put him in charge of the motor pool, which was like tossing Brer Rabbit into the briar patch.

Korea made Jim grateful for what he had at home. The resourcefulness of Korean peasants astonished him. They scavenged the military dumps and made use of almost everything that the army threw away. They built houses from cardboard and aluminum cans, lashing the cans together three-deep with wire and stuffing the cracks with insulation against freezing winter temperatures. To amuse himself, Jim became a test-drive ace. He tested every vehicle in the motor pool, whether or not it needed testing, pushing the pedals to the floor.

After his discharge, he had started working on the farm full time, gradually assuming his father's duties. It was really all he wanted to do.

"Farmers like to farm," he said cheerfully.

I could hear the satisfaction in his voice, a peace that comes from doing what you want to do. Jim didn't feel that he was missing anything—no sirens were whistling in his ear. When he had some free time, he played golf or listened to music or took in a Dodger game in L.A. He had a brand-new IBM computer and a subscription to *InfoWorld*.

Behold the modern California farmer, I thought, not without envy. There was a satisfaction in making things grow. There was a sweetness to the mockingbird's song. For all its contrariness, I liked this heat-seared, light-blinded country of the San Joaquin. It didn't need to go searching for a narrative. It still knew what it was about.

Even a farmer who was phasing himself out, such as Art Crettol, seemed reasonably content with his lot. We stopped at Art's house to bring him some groceries. Tall palm trees lined his block, and he had a cool blue swimming pool in the backyard.

Art had recently remarried and wore a gold chain around his neck, just like Louie did. He knew his local history well and could remember when you had to carry a sidearm at the desert place to nail all the rattlesnakes in the sagebrush.

Art irrigated a couple of almond orchards for the boys and growled at them if he caught them doing something wrong, but that was the scope of his involvement. They still consulted him before making a major decision, but the torch had been passed. Why slave in the fields when you could take your new bride on a cruise to Panama?

In the end, Art said, farming was no picnic. He guessed that about half the farmers around Wasco and Shafter ran good, clean operations and were solvent. Others were getting by on a wing-and-a-prayer, while still others were failing because they were overextended or bad gamblers or just plain stupid.

JIM CRETTOL LIVED IN A RANCH HOUSE on a lightly traveled road, with no neighbors nearby. Dogs poured out the front door, six or seven of them, licking and sniffing at me in greeting.

Barbara Crettol was in the kitchen preparing Rock Cornish game hens from a recipe in the *Los Angeles Times*. She was a pretty, cultured woman, who had been teaching ballet since she was fourteen and still taught a class in Wasco. She and Jim had married young. That was still the way in California farm country.

Their daughter, Suzanne, had finished her first year at Shafter High. She was a volleyball star and let me thumb through her yearbook and look at the pictures. I read the semisecret scribblings and the vaguely articulated dreams until B.J. dragged me down the hall to his room and showed me the pellet rifle that he used for plugging crows.

"They're *sooo* tough," he said. "The BBs bounce off 'em."

He had rock tapes scattered around a boombox—Metallica, Guns N' Roses, and Run D.M.C. There was a photo of the Alpine Okies' dragster on his wall and also a poster of a hard-nippled Budweiser girl in a state of perpetual arousal. A big desk took up most of the floor space, though, as if to remind him that he'd never be entirely free from his studies.

Louie came at dusk with his wife and two kids. The brothers socialized often. They were different as men and yet remained closely knit in the blood. We ate at a table on the patio—two tables, actually, one for the adults and one for the children. Like an early marriage or the unbroken link among generations, this, too, seemed like another country thing preserved.

The Crettols served fine food and vintage wines. For dessert, we had vanilla ice cream and homemade apricot cobbler. Crickets chirruped under the gathering stars, and the night was huge and sweeping. I was aware of how softly everybody was talking and took comfort and solace from the mesh of voices. At that moment, it seemed that there was nothing more to life—nothing to be pursued, all cruelty erased.

When it was time to go, I walked down a driveway where candles were glowing inside paper sacks. The kids had insisted on putting them out, and their parents had indulged them. The candles gave my leave-taking a festive edge.

In the dark, I imagined the sleeping cotton fields and heard the sound of water trickling in irrigation ditches. I wondered how long the farm landscape would last in this part of California and how long it would offer such nourishment to those who tended it. In Suzanne's yearbook, a question had been put to the graduating seniors, and their answer had surprised me.

"Are you afraid of the future?" they were asked, and almost half the students had answered, "Yes."

CHAPTER 18

On HIGHWAY 99 the next morning, Dwight Yoakam came over my car radio singing his country hit, "Streets of Bakersfield," an old Buck Owens tune that told of a well-meaning youth who stumbles into town, gets into a fight for which he's not to blame, and lands himself in jail. Yoakam might be a slinky-hipped Hollywood cowboy in dry-cleaned jeans, but he'd still put his finger on a pulse. The song's refrain was an echo and a reminder: *"You don't know me, but you don't like me."*

Buck Owens was a Bakersfield boy by birth and knew what he was talking about. He and Merle Haggard, who grew up in nearby Oildale, an even raunchier place, had both been married to the same woman, although at different times. They were all divorced now, but the woman kept a job playing backup in Merle's band. She was a survivor.

That was a Bakersfield story, all right. The city was legendary for its toughness, and you had to be able to swallow your disappointment if you hoped to stay afloat. The central metaphors were all stolen from the oil business, where you set your sights on a target, took one good shot at drilling, and learned not to piss and moan if the bit just swirled in sand and water.

Bakersfield had no tolerance for crybabies. It ate nails for breakfast and might even have hung a few kittens from trees. I'd heard a rumor once that whenever a new franchise opened in town, the home office dispatched its top supervisors to oversee the operation, because you only got one chance to please your customers. Feed them an off-color french fry or a warm soft drink, and you were finished. They'd never forgive you, and they'd never come back.

The Baker in Bakersfield was Colonel Thomas Baker. He brought his family from Visalia to an abandoned cabin of logs and thatched tule reeds in the swampy sloughs around Kern River in 1863. The colonel reclaimed some land and planted ten acres to alfalfa—Baker's field. In that time before dams and irrigation, the river could be wild and ferocious, and it still recaptured some of its former glory each spring as it dropped steeply out of the Sierra Nevada.

Merle Haggard had paid it a wary tribute in his beautiful ballad, "Kern River":

I'll never swim Kern River again
It was there that I lost her
There that I lost my best friend.
Now I live in the mountains
I drifted up here with the wind
I may drown in still water
But I'll never swim Kern River again.

I grew up in an oil town
But my gusher never came in
And the river was a boundary
Where my darling and I used to swim.
One night in the moonlight
The swiftness swept her life away
And now I live on Lake Shasta
And Lake Shasta is where I will stay.

The Sierra Nevada lay to the east of Bakersfield, but I couldn't even see the foothills. The entire range was camouflaged in a dense, stinging smog. The southern tip of the San Joaquin was unimaginably hot and dry, the bottom of a cauldron I'd been sinking into inch by inch. Foul air from all over the state got trapped in the tail end of the valley and sat there growing more and more fetid, like dirty socks left under a bed.

At my motel, the air conditioners droned incessantly and dripped machine sweat down the stucco walls. They seemed to be the only forces working against inertia, little athletes of the ozone pushing the envelope of their Freon and their coils.

Slow-stepping maids trudged across a courtyard to feed their wages into a soda machine, trying to quench an unquenchable thirst. The man in the next room was a horrible white from avoiding the sun and could be glimpsed seated in his skivvies before a TV, not a sight for the faint of heart. He resembled a grub rousted from under a rock.

You don't know me, but you don't like me—maybe it was the nearness of Los Angeles, 109 miles away, or the talk of twisted relationships, but I felt that I was moving toward an archetype of California that any American would recognize.

Bakersfield was smaller than Fresno, but it felt larger. Crude desires were afoot. The city had a cadre of spiral-permed blondes and Yuppie wanna-bes trembling on the brink, wishing that they could be in Hollywood or in Malibu but afraid to take the leap. Those who had taken the leap and had failed were home again, smarter and wiser, big shots of the San Joaquin who demanded the best tables in restaurants and liked to tell about an exciting movie party they'd once attended, where Danny DeVito had been present.

The cotton money in the valley might be quiet, but the oil money was loud, screaming like a banshee. There were monster I-made-it houses in Bakersfield, scores of BMWs, Mercedes, and slick little Porsches. The many banks downtown were tall, glassy, and imperious. Registered Republicans ran neck and neck with registered Democrats, a retrograde quirk of politics that became more pronounced as you moved farther south in the state, as though you were sliding into Mississippi.

For all the city's wealth, its black ghetto was as torn and as shabby as any place I'd seen in California. It looked every bit as bad as the photographs of Dust Bowl migrant camps, precisely that ravaged and inhuman sixty years down the line.

You don't know me, but you don't like me. . . .

One afternoon in Bakersfield, a redneck cop on a motorcycle roared from behind a billboard to write me a ticket for going thirty-seven in a thirty-mile-an-hour zone. I fled to the countryside, where the farms were a triumph of agribusiness. The average holding in Kern County was a whopping 1,347 acres compared to 260 acres in Fresno County. Kern County had more than 300 million acres in farmland, almost double its closest rival in the state, but it was the paraphernalia of oil recovery that dominated the sagebrushy desert.

Out toward McKittrick, Buttonwillow, and Taft, the big petroleum companies had their compounds. Trucks motored about in a maze of pipes, steam generators, derricks, gas lines, capped wells, and storage tanks. Here, the San Joaquin was as brightly hallucinatory as Saudi Arabia. Any minute, I thought, Bedouins on camels will come riding over a ridge.

OIL WAS GOLD, too, our black gold. The substratum of southern California was layered with deposits that began around Coalinga and continued through the San Joaquin, oozing over to the coast at Santa Barbara and Long Beach and coalescing into rich pockets in the Los Angeles lowlands.

Indians of the region had depended on a tarry substance to caulk their boats. Mexicans and Spaniards had used the oil that they found in seeps as a roofing material for their adobes, but there was little commercial drilling for petroleum until the 1860s, largely because whales were still being slaughtered in great enough numbers to keep the oil lamps burning.

Geologists had also thrown people off the scent. They had investigated the asphalt, a sort of coal tar, in the state in the early 1860s and had judged it to be wanting as a source for providing illumination. It was inferior and clogged with carbon—so Josiah Whitney reported, relying on some tests that William Brewer had done for him.

Brewer was more enthusiastic, though less scientific, than his boss. In March of 1861, he rode west from Santa Barbara along the ocean, past cattle and sheep ranches, to view the asphalt bubbling out of rocks and solidifying in the sun.

"It occurs in immense quantities and will eventually be the source of considerable wealth," he predicted, but the first big gusher to spout in California seemed to support Whitney's conclusions. It blew in Ojai Valley in 1867. An exploratory drilling team trumpeted its merits, but the oil, which quit flowing in short order, was too crude to be processed at the primitive refineries then in operation.

Drillers working in the San Joaquin had better luck. They brought in significant wells around Maricopa and McKittrick, and there were similarly rewarding finds elsewhere in the area. Oil production throughout the state jumped from 40,000 barrels in 1880 to more than 1.2 million barrels in 1895. By 1900, a thousand or more wells dotted the land northwest of Los Angeles. Near Taft, not far from Bakersfield, the Midway and the Sunset oil fields were among the richest around, but the Lakeview Gusher, which blew in 1914, put all the other fields to shame.

There had never been anything like the Lakeview Gusher—not anywhere, not ever. It yielded 18,000 barrels during its first twenty-four hours, a record still unsurpassed. Photos of the period show a wood derrick coughing up a giant plume of smoke while awash in oil. The oil rolls out into the desert in slicks, like a body of water. Workers had to navigate it in skiffs. It kept overflowing and washing into camp, and families were evacuated. Everyone prayed that an idle smoker wouldn't set it on fire with a match. For eighteen months the gusher pumped, yielding about 9 million barrels before it ran dry.

The Lakeview and the Midway-Sunset made the fields on the west side of Bakersfield famous around the world. In the early 1900s, the Midway was still producing 72,760 barrels a day, while all the wells in Texas combined were producing 28,800 barrels a day. One out of every three barrels of oil in the United States came from California. Visitors from abroad arrived to look into the situation, among them two gentlemen from the Nippon Oil Company of Japan.

In 1913, Fatty Arbuckle came to Taft to star in an oil-based romance, *Opportunity*. Fatty played a poor but exemplary youth who captained the Standard Oil baseball team and earned so much respect for his virtuous behavior that he rose to the station of mayor. Arbuckle reveled in the high life and enjoyed being on location in Taft, where the beer, sometimes trucked in from Saint Louis by Anheuser-Busch, flowed as freely as the oil.

As the supply of petroleum increased, so did its uses. In its crudest form, it was burned in boilers on ships and in factories, and it fueled the refineries in the valley where beets were turned into sugar. In the form of kerosene, it replaced coal as a source for heating homes and buildings, being cheaper and cleaner. The railroads ran on coal, too, but they switched after the Santa Fe tested a locomotive engine retooled to burn oil and saw that its operating costs had dropped by a quarter.

The most significant single demand for oil came from the burgeoning ranks of automobile owners. By 1910, there were already twenty thousand cars in Los Angeles County devouring gasoline. Ford City, north of Taft, was so named on account of all the Model T's in town. Scarcely in need of any encouragement, the oil companies kept drilling, and the economic epicenter of California began to shift slowly from north to south, sucking the juice from San Francisco and delivering it to L.A.

♦   ♦   ♦

IN BAKERSFIELD, oil was news that had stayed news. Along with a
Gideon Bible, my motel room was stocked with a California Oil &
Gas Telephone Directory that had been published in Forth Worth,
Texas. It listed hundreds of geologists, petroleum engineers, and oil
operators and producers, and ended with a listing for "Xmas Tree,"
conjuring an image of roustabouts singing carols as they strung their
derricks with blinking lights.

The *Bakersfield Californian,* a daily, carried a column about oil-
field happenings that was so technical it made my eyes spin in their
sockets.

"The low at DOE's No. 934-29R is from three perforate intervals
totaling 130 feet in the overall interval from 17,000 to 17,365 feet,"
Bill Rintoul, the columnist, would write, and I would groan and feel
stupid and stare at Rintoul's mug shot—a kindly faced man, no
shadow of the recondite—and think that maybe I could understand
something about the oil-and-gas game if he'd be willing to decipher
it for me, which he graciously agreed to do.

Rintoul lived on a quiet, tree-lined block in town, where dogs
were sleeping and insects hatched in heat-driven swoon. He was a
Berkeley graduate and had met his wife, Frankie Jo, while working
in the oil fields as a youth. In the flesh, he was a wiry, rugged man
in his late sixties, who looked as though he could still put in a full
shift on a drilling crew without bellyaching.

Rintoul wore a wide-brimmed straw hat to shield him from the
sun. He told me how he had gone to Egypt once to do a story for
a trade journal and how his hosts had apologized to him for the
sweltering temperature.

"Well, it's cooler than Bakersfield," he'd said to them, and for
the first time I heard the *bake* in Bakersfield and saw a red-hot cookie
sheet fresh from the oven.

We got into Rintoul's car and automatically committed the first
maneuver in any Bakersfield journey undertaken in August by turn-

ing on the air conditioning and carefully adjusting the little vents and plastic blades. There was probably a special technique to the vectoring that I had yet to master, but soon a miniature breeze was blowing, and we were off.

We drove up Panoramic Drive to a spot above the city, so that Rintoul could point out three historic oil fields through the haze—Kern River, Elk Hills, and Midway-Sunset. They had all yielded a billion or more barrels of oil. Another field in the vicinity, South Belridge, was hidden by hills, and it, too, was capable of yielding a billion barrels. Only twelve other oil fields in the entire United States had ever matched that feat, Rintoul said. A note of civic pride crept into his voice, but he was dismayed by the miasmic air we were breathing.

"What good is it going to do if everybody gets rich, and we all die gasping?" he asked, with a laugh.

The Kern River Discovery Well was nearby, hand-dug to a depth of forty-three feet—very shallow for such an important find. Rintoul had me imagine what the field was like in 1899 when dozens of bare-chested men were hammering together derricks from wood. He was a boxing fan and told me that Jim Jeffries, the future heavyweight champ, had labored there as a boilermaker, building tanks for the oil. The derricks were gone now, turned to sawdust and splinters by termites and windstorms, or simply torn down because they were outmoded.

People did earn lots of money in oil and gas, of course, and Rintoul took me to meet a pair of them. Rod Nahama and Frank Weigant were petroleum geologists who'd left their jobs with big firms to work as consultants. After a few years on their own, they'd quit consulting and had formed Nahama & Weigant Energy Company. They had done handsomely enough over the next decade to take the company public in 1971, a feat that many independents aspire to but don't always achieve.

Nahama and Weigant were unpretentious fellows. Over coffee, they explained to me how they had got started. They were short of ready cash in the beginning, so they had to search for investors to buy into their projects and share the risk in exchange for a share of the profits. John Hancock had underwritten many of their efforts, but they were also funded by much smaller concerns.

Once the funding was in place, Nahama and Weigant would target some likely land that showed good potential for oil or natural gas recovery and lease it. Sometimes they went after land that other firms had already picked over, aiming for deposits that had been missed. Farmers were more than glad to be paid twice for the same parcel.

In the early days, Nahama and Weigant often concentrated on the Sacramento Valley, where natural gas was plentiful and the mineral rights were not generally tied up by the oil conglomerates, as they were in the San Joaquin. They had their first major strike at Conway Ranch in the Putah Sink, near Sacramento, where they located sixteen gas wells. Now they had fifteen employees and kept busy whether the market was bull or bear, surviving even in the most difficult periods.

They were an unusual company, Weigant said, in that they netted more money from gas than from oil—although other companies were regrouping in a similar way due to the lowered profitability of the petroleum industry. Natural gas was cleaner and cheaper to produce, preferable from an environmental standpoint, and the price didn't fluctuate as much, so they had no trouble selling every molecule that they found.

Nobody had done much oil exploration recently, Nahama added, but the ground still held lots of oil. Of the 6 million barrels extracted in the state every day, 600,000 of them came out of Kern County.

Petroleum was easier to find than investors, both partners agreed. These days investors shied away from the chanciness of exploring and the high attrition rate of independent companies. Nahama and Weigant had been talking lately to some Japanese investors about potential joint ventures, but they weren't satisfied that they had made much progress. "The Japanese want to invest and earn a return on

their investment," Weigant said, shrugging. "They just don't want
to take any risks."

ELK HILLS and the U.S. Naval Petroleum Reserve were in the Saudi
Arabia west of Bakersfield. The hills were bare and ugly, but thousands of tule elk, pale-skinned little creatures, used to roam them.
The last of the elks had a preserve on the East Side Canal, sharing
it with egrets and great blue herons.

The U.S. Naval Petroleum Reserve dated from World War I,
when the federal government had set aside some 46,000 acres of oil-
drenched land to guard against any wartime shortages. Edward Doheny, who'd made a fortune on oil in Los Angeles, did the initial
drilling in 1923 after cutting a suspicious deal with an old pal of his,
Albert B. Fall, the secretary of the interior.

Doheny agreed to pump the oil and store it in tanks. The land
was leased to him for free, and he got to keep a share of any profits.
In return for such favors, Doheny enlisted his son to serve as a bagman
and bring Fall $100,000 in cash to help him buy a cattle ranch—just
a loan, Doheny claimed later, but he and Fall were swept up in the
Teapot Dome scandal of 1924, and Fall was sent to prison.

Doheny beat a bribery rap and suffered less damage than his
attorney, William Gibbs McAdoo, who was presumed to be guilty
by association. When McAdoo ran for the Democratic presidential
nomination in 1924, he heard shouts of, "Oil! Oil! Oil!" every time
his name was put forth.

Bill Rintoul had a friend at Elk Hills, Ken Schultz, an employee
of the navy, who was in charge of the drilling program. He was
crew-cut and had the spine of a military man. Rintoul bragged about
him and let me know that he had drilled about 1,200 wells on the
reserve, among them the deepest well in California at 24,426 feet.
Schultz seemed in awe of his own feat. After all, he had worked his
way through college by toiling in a muffler shop.

"If you'd've told me I was going to do that when I was a young man graduating from USC in 1947," he said, in wonder, "I'd have asked you what you were smoking."

Schultz wanted to show us a well that he was currently drilling, one that was targeted for 17,000 feet. It was hard to think about such a hole. Wouldn't it lead you straight to China? We were given hard hats to protect our innocent heads. Objects sometimes fell from an oil rig, hurtling toward bystanders from on high. A wrench, a lugnut, a lunchpail—brainbusters were everywhere just waiting to happen.

There were about two thousand wells at Elk Hills, and about half of them were active. The Department of Energy had Chevron as a partner now instead of Doheny and granted the oil giant 20 percent of the take.

Schultz's rig was visible from a long way off. It was a towering assemblage of girders, cables, ladders, and steps. Tiered platforms rose in a pyramidal shape some seventy or eighty feet into the sky. The rig was centered over the well, and the drill pipe had some small, industrial-grade diamonds imbedded in a hard matrix.

"It took more than twenty trucks to bring that rig in," Schultz said appreciatively.

A subcontractor, Parker Drilling Company from Tulsa, Oklahoma, owned the rig. Mr. Parker was supposed to be so patriotic that he wore red, white, and blue underwear. An American flag was flying by the rig near a sign that said, 77 days without an accident— not long enough for me. The rig operated on a three thousand horsepower motor, cost about $250 an hour to run, and would remain up for about a month.

I liked the look of the rig. It had a structural integrity from all the tensed and braided metal. A wily artist might have pawned it off as a sculpture. The derrick stamped it inalterably as an oil rig, but at the same time the platforms, the busy workers, and the billowy flag suggested a ship that had somehow gotten stranded in the desert.

A drilling crew of five men was scurrying about—three rough-necks as all-purpose floorhands, a derrick man, and a driller to push the buttons. The driller was the top dog, followed by the derrick man. The roughnecks did dirty, dangerous, back-breaking work for a pittance. They made about nine dollars an hour, while the lowly roustabouts who laid pipe, set pumping units, and handled the mopping up earned just six bucks an hour.

Still, a job at Elk Hills was considered a good one, Rintoul said. The men were guaranteed steady work and had a certain degree of security. They could live at home or rent a trailer in a trailer court. Other crews were much more mobile. If you happened to be out drilling shallow development wells, for instance, you had to move with the rig every three or four days. Sometimes you ended up sleeping in your car or pickup and subsisting on burgers and grease for weeks at a time.

In some ways, Rintoul observed, the oil business had gotten worse, not better, over the years. The technology had improved, but the profits had dropped, and the big oil companies had suffered losses and were constantly cutting corners. They were laying off more and more workers, and the men still working were pushed harder. When a rig was up and running, it ran around the clock in twelve-hour shifts. A man would work a forty-hour day shift and then rotate to a forty-hour night shift. Going from shift to shift screwed up the workers' body chemistry and their internal clocks. Sometimes they drank to come down, an oil-field tradition.

It used to be that a man might show up a little drunk of a morning, Rintoul told me, but now, in spite of screening tests for drugs, a few workers relied on cocaine and speed to propel them through. That upped the ante, in terms of accidents.

"At least you can tell when a person's been drinking," he said.

If I wanted to see how perilous oil-field work really was, Rintoul went on, I could go to Oildale, where many workers lived, and count the missing fingers and the missing limbs.

Loggers, millworkers, fishermen, and roustabouts. If you're a working stiff, I thought, California is not the Promised Land.

These days, the big oil companies continued their policy of cutting costs, occasionally at their own expense. As an example, Rintoul cited the Exxon *Valdez*, which had foundered, he believed, because Exxon had stopped paying for a pilot ship to guide it through the narrow channels up in Alaska.

"Penny-wise and pound-foolish," he said.

PETROLEUM CLUB ROAD, Shale Road, Midoil Road, and Gas Company Road were all byways in Taft, a desert town almost naked of vegetation. If shade could be bottled and sold, you could make your million there. Taft was renowned for its hard-nosed attitude and its redneck bent, going Bakersfield and Oildale one better. The town had not even considered integrating its schools, Rintoul told me, until its football team had started losing games to schools that had admitted blacks.

He remembered a time in his youth when Cab Calloway had been invited to appear at a charity event in Taft. There was plenty of consternation among the citizens, and a bargain had to be struck. Calloway and his band would be allowed to play, but they had to agree to stay somewhere else and be gone before dark.

Rintoul remembered sweeter things, too. He remembered being in kneepants and riding his bike ten or twelve miles to a gas station built all of wood. At a "little-bitty" counter, he bought wonderful chili beans for a dime a cup. Along the road, he passed the local bootlegger's house, which seemed like a palace to him with its hardwood floors and the two grand columns that marked the driveway.

He remembered old friends and acquaintances and took me to the cemetery in Taft and walked me around it. A Lufkin pump on a timer began dipping on a hill behind us, the sound of it metallic and clanking. The country around Taft was not as harsh as it looked in high summer, Rintoul said. In spring, it could be spectacular.

"You ought to visit then," he advised me. "There're wildflowers all over everywhere."

◆   ◆   ◆

THE PREMIER COUNTRY-MUSIC radio station in Bakersfield, KUZZ-AM and FM, didn't play very many Buck Owens records, even though Buck owned the station and was the boss. He didn't test well with the listeners, and neither did Merle Haggard. They preferred the sanitized songs of Garth Brooks and Clint Black to the gritty twang born during the diaspora of Okies and Arkies to California.

The real Bakersfield Sound cooked. It had some Woody Guthrie in it, and some Bob Wills, too, some rumbly washboard stuff along with the creak of a front-porch rocker and the sizzle of fatback bacon in a pan. It went in for mother-of-pearl buttons, biscuits with gravy, grits, and whiskey straight from the bottle. It tore you up with its melancholy, but it still made you want to dance. It was what you heard on the air twenty years ago, when Buck Owens had bought the station.

Evan Bridwell, KUZZ's program director, was also perplexed about the listeners' preferences. He felt that Bakersfield had the potential to become a Nashville West, but he had learned that the fans of country music were sometimes an enigma wrapped in a question.

"This is one tough town to impress," Bridwell said, stating the obvious. In the new Bakersfield, he thought, all that mattered was selling real estate.

Buck Owens was not anywhere around KUZZ. Thanks to Dwight Yoakam, he had been liberated from an enforced retirement and was out touring again. His nephew, Mel, really ran the station, but Buck had an office suite there that was done up with the obligatory gold records. Its centerpiece was a piano upon which penciled songs-in-progress were spread, their penultimate notes still trapped in Buck's head.

There were photos of Buck playing golf with Presidents Nixon and Ford in his "Hee Haw" days. There was a very conspicuous photo of Buck and Dwight Yoakam. Buck's gap-toothed grin was sizable.

In Buck's private bathroom, above the sunken tub and the Ja-

cuzzi, some tiles in the storied red, white, and blue of Mr. Parker's
underwear spelled out BUCK OWENS. But the sign that said it all
was the one over his desk, a link to Dust Bowl memories and the
long haul to California: Poverty Sucks.

IN OILDALE, the blue-collar poor were making their last stand. Here,
Merle Haggard, the holy infant of country heartbreak, had been raised
in a converted railroad boxcar, but there wasn't any monument to
him. Folks in Oildale were too busy trying to pay their bills.

    Oildale had no suburban frills, just trailers and bungalows. Res-
idents parked their old cars in claustrophobic alleys between them,
sometimes never to be moved again. Some alleys were death rows
for automobiles. There were constant disputes about who had the
right to which alley space, and men had been shot with handguns
for violating a code known only to the killer.

    In Oildale, there was a hapless store, Life Is a Beach, that sold
bikinis and other swimwear appropriate to a seaside that was as
distant as a fantasy.

    The public life of the town revolved around two saloons, Bob's
and Trout's. Oil-field workers still in their oily clothes drank at them
with their tidy brethren who were about to depart for a shift. The
armless and the fingerless were indeed propping up stools, just as
Bill Rintoul had predicted.

    Hard-faced young women in tight jeans stuck out their butts
while bending over the pool table, having left the kids with a neighbor. The older women of Oildale watched in disgust from the bar.
They were consigned now to the droopy men sitting next to them,
earnest losers whose eyes brimmed with self-pity—the prey of skip-
tracers, fellows who would as soon disappear into Mexico as come
up with the monthly rent or alimony. So devoted to failure were
these men that if you confronted them with a door marked "New
Life," all fervent opportunity on the other side, they would not be

able to open it and instead would set to kicking it until they broke a toe or somebody called the police.

In the afternoon glare outside Trout's, I saw a California vision. Down the main drag swooped a biker in mirrored shades. He had a sweaty red bandanna wrapped pirate-style around his head. Riding behind him, arms circling his waist, was a little boy in a baseball uniform wearing a crash helmet. They sped down North Chester Street to Bakersfield Junior League ball park, where Pop dismounted and replaced his son's helmet with a baseball cap.

THU LE OWNED L'EAU VIVE, a Vietnamese restaurant, that was in a Bakersfield shopping center. She was among the second generation of immigrants to come to California from Vietnam, part of a much more substantial and heterogeneous Southeast Asian wave that continued to wash over the state.

The Le family had tried living in San Francisco first, but the city had stretched their pocketbook, so when Thu Le's husband got a job in the oil industry, she was glad to relocate in the San Joaquin. She had been in Bakersfield for thirteen years now and seemed to be liking it less and less. The town was losing its semirural character, she thought, and becoming more like a suburb of Los Angeles.

Although business wasn't terrible, L'Eau Vive was for sale. Thu Le had two teenage daughters, and she wanted to quit working and spend more time with them before they left home.

"Once they marry, you never see them again," she told me, fluttering her hands in the air.

When I walked in, the restaurant had been jumping with loud rock music. Thu Le changed over to a classical tape and came to my table to apologize for the disturbance. It was her children's doing, she said. She had granted them a kind of holiday and had let them dress in their street clothes instead of the more formal Vietnamese attire that they usually wore while they were at work.

Thu Le performed some mental reckoning and guessed that her daughters were about 55 percent Californian. They loved California, in fact. To keep them in touch with their roots, she and her husband took them regularly to Little Saigon in Orange County and immersed them in the culture of the old country.

"We feel lucky to be here, but we love Vietnam," she said, pressing a hand to her sternum. "Would we go back if we could? Yes, we would."

One of the Le girls brought me a menu. I did my own reckoning and judged her to be at least three-quarters Californian. In the new California, I reflected, things would be measured by the yardstick of Saigon, Phnom Penh, Rawalpindi, or Guadalajara, not by the European standards of my forebears.

As I was paying my bill, Thu Le gave me a business card certifying her as a color analyst and image consultant. I must have looked puzzled, because she began to elaborate, gesturing toward some shelves behind the cash register that were stocked with cosmetics in jars and bottles. Beauti Control Cosmetic Boutique had manufactured them all, and Thu Le had attended a BCCB school to master the subtleties of their application.

Beauty had interested her even in Vietnam, she said—she was a striking woman, after all. The accent at home, however, was on a natural look. A woman attained beauty by eating well, caring about her health, and working hard. No woman would ever dream of putting on any makeup until she was married, and then she would wear only what her husband desired.

Thu Le felt that her BCCB clients in California might rebel against such a beauty regimen, especially the hard work. They had come of age in a different tradition, she told me, and had been taught to rely on cosmetics to do the job of nature.

SOMETIMES DURING MY FINAL DAYS around Bakersfield it seemed to me that the entire San Joaquin Valley ran on beer. As each sizzling afternoon limped toward its conclusion, I could sense a buildup of dust on my teeth, like a strange, agricultural form of tartar, and I began to look upon the usual remedies of iced tea, ice water, and Diet Coke with disdain.

Only a daily ration of Bud or Coors or Rolling Rock would do the trick, so by five or six o'clock I'd visit a deli or a grocery store for a refill. I had learned to rank the stores according to the relative frigidity of their stock, *cold beer* being words that were much bandied about in the valley and often used with impunity.

In the San Joaquin, I drank beer at low-rent taverns and high-class bars, in Taft and in McKittrick and in Ford City, and at last I drank some beer in Buttonwillow, a prosperous town of about two thousand, where I stopped after a ride out to the Temblor Range by the San Andreas Fault. The fault had ruptured in 1952 and had dealt Bakersfield some significant abuse, but there wasn't much to see other than dry creekbeds, salt lakes, and abandoned mines.

A solitary buttonwillow tree stood at the north end of Main Street in Buttonwillow. At that spot, in 1895, the great cattleman Henry Miller had built his headquarters, naming the post office and the railroad station after the landmark tree. Pumps and derricks had taken over from the cows, and now cotton grew thickly in the fields around town, often watched over by quietly affluent farmers of Italian descent who were capable of hiding a few thousand dollars in cash beneath a mattress.

Buttonwillow, then, on a Friday afternoon toward quitting time, with the air stinking of oil and gasoline. Ahead, I saw four or five cars parked by a storefront from which all manner of merry noises were issuing, and after a brief second of foreboding that recalled the standard hitch in consciousness preceding any cowboy's plunge through the swinging doors, I slipped into the BS Saloon.

The BS was storming. Friday was payday, and checks were being cashed. Oily galoots drank in boisterous knots, their faces raw and beaming. At a pool table, a gigantic machinist was bashing at balls and saying that he still owed the damn IRS five grand, but who cared, really? His daughter was his opponent. She was big, too, and she didn't care, either. It was good not to care in Buttonwillow on a Friday afternoon.

The bartender, Betty Stiers, resembled Tuesday Weld. She was the eponymous BS and owned half the bar. There were three bars in Buttonwillow, she said, but hers was the only one that might qualify as a joint. Buttonwillow was her hometown. She had come back to it lately after a long time away working as a legal secretary in Tracy, in the Bay Area. Tracy, once a country town, was too hectic for her now. She was a country girl at heart.

"I like to look out the door at those cotton fields," Betty said dreamily, and you knew she meant it.

In her year or so as a co-owner, she and her partner had brightened up the BS. They'd stripped the walls and had painted them. They had papered over the men's room with a spritely print of horses galloping, but when I went in I saw that some dim-witted prankster had already marred the print by drawing an arrow to one nag and writing beneath it, "Sea-fucking-biscuit." The future of the bar's new finery could be predicted.

The afternoon wore on. I talked with a man who contracted to supply work crews to the oil companies. Things were tough in the fields, he said. The companies were more demanding than ever. They were outlawing beards, ordering the workers to show up in reasonably clean clothes, and forcing them to keep pace with a clock whose hands spun faster and faster. They were after soldiers, not employees.

The crews were angry and depressed, the man said. A few workers in any crew were on drugs, he guessed, regardless of any testing procedures.

Maybe we were speaking too loudly, or maybe I was asking too many questions. From a dark corner of the BS, a fellow stepped forward to confront me. Jet-black hair fell slackly to his shoulders, and he had the disagreeable odor of somebody sweating out booze from the night before. He wanted to know what the hell I was doing in Buttonwillow. What about a business card? Didn't I even have a business card? A real writer would have a business card.

Intimidated, I fished around in a pocket, found Thu Le's card, and decided against trying to pass myself off as a certified color analyst from Vietnam.

"Why, you're just a fly-by-nighter!" my accuser wailed. He pointed a finger at me, like some grand inquisitor, and wailed again. "He's just a fly-by-nighter!"

It would be unwise, I realized, to overstay my welcome. After a round of hasty good-byes, I made for the door, half-expecting to be hit from behind with a barstool leg. But I got to the car all right, took a deep breath, and saw that the BS was a perfect bookend to Twenty-two Mile Roadhouse, one a greeting and the other a farewell. In my head, I heard dear old Baker pounding the ivories and collected myself for a trip over the mountains and into the Mojave Desert, leaving behind the farms, the heat, and the light—the *summa* of the San Joaquin.

You don't know me, but you don't like me. . . .

CHAPTER 19

THE MOJAVE DESERT in August. I had done better planning in my time.

From Bakersfield, I drove east to where the San Joaquin Valley ended around Lamont and Arvin and continued on into the Tehachapis, a fault-block range that marked the southern terminus of the Sierra Nevada. Some people believed that the mountains were the true dividing line between northern and southern California. They were not as grand or as intimidating as the mountains of the Far North and were forested mainly with scrubby oaks rather than tall pines, firs, or redwoods. The hillside grasses were tinder-dry and smelled of fires waiting to burn.

At Tehachapi Pass, at an elevation of 4,604 feet, Refugio Rangel was selling some miniature windmills from his pickup truck on Highway 58. He had a broad Hispanic face and a watch cap pulled down over the tips of his ears. His windmills were arrayed on a shoulder of the road and ballasted with rocks. The blades spun madly. Tehachapi Pass was among the windiest spots in the state and gave him an ideal showcase for his wares.

"I'm here most every weekend," Rangel told me as he hammered together a new windmill. "I come up from Arvin."

Rangel knew the Tehachapi country well, having studied it on his hands and knees. Before retiring, he had worked for many years as a laborer laying water pipes in Tehachapi Valley, all the way to the local prison. He pointed out the prison for me, a malign shape in the middle of some apple orchards.

"I don't expect to get rich on these," said Rangel, grinning at the very thought. "I just do it to keep busy."

While he kept hammering, I sat on his tailgate and took in the view. The canyons were littered with clothing that the wind had robbed from unwary tourists—hats, sweaters, scarves, and T-shirts. Big winds were common in the Tehachapis, often gusting to fifty or sixty miles an hour on the most ordinary days.

William Brewer had gone on about the winds in 1863, calling them "unruly" and saying that they blew "most fearfully." At the same time, he was charmed by Tehachapi Valley, "a pretty basin five or six miles long, entirely surrounded by high mountains." The pasturage was so fine that a half-dozen Methodist families from Missouri had settled there. The Piker men raised cattle. The Piker women were devout and liked to dip some snuff after their church services.

There were still some cattle in the valley, and the settlers were still arriving, too, forsaking the congested suburbs around metropolitan Los Angeles for the budding subdivisions of Tehachapi. I could see hundreds of new houses below me, their red-tile roofs often packed in so closely that they looked like the heads of matches in a matchbook. The settlers were said to be pursuing that phantom, *a simpler life.*

Tehachapi Pass had always been a major gateway to the state. Route 66 ran through it out of Arkansas and Oklahoma and had emancipated the Dust Bowl hordes—Sam Cravens off to pick zucchini with his uncle, and Woody Guthrie plucking his banjo and singing, *"If you ain't got the do-re-mi, boy, then you can't get into California, boy."* Charlie Manson might have traveled the same route on the lam from West Virginia.

In 1876, the Southern Pacific had opened the Tehachapis to rail travel by completing the staggering task of looping some tracks over the mountains. It was on an SP train from Des Moines, Iowa, that a young sportscaster at radio station WHO had made his first trip to California, ostensibly to cover the Chicago Cubs' spring-training camp on Santa Catalina Island, off Santa Barbara.

February of 1937, the farms of Iowa gripped in a chilling freeze, and there was Ronald "Dutch" Reagan boarding a railroad car at the depot, readying himself in secret to test the waters in Hollywood and beginning the process that would transform him into the Ultimate Californian.

IN TEHACHAPI, some teenage girls were talking about a recent Junior Miss Pageant that had taken place at their high-school gym. They were sitting behind me in a booth at T. Juanito's at lunch, and over nachos and sodas they were recalling the epic moments from the pageant and also relaying previously unreleased gossip about which contestants had thrown up or had gotten the giggles before the main event. They seemed to find a seed of cosmic justice in the trials of the chosen.

Beauty mattered everywhere in the world, of course, but it mattered most in southern California, building to its peak in Los Angeles and falling off by degrees from that epicenter. Every big town in the South and many big towns in the North could be counted on to select an annual Rose Bowl Queen (Pasadena) or a Garlic Queen (Gilroy). Such contests were often assumed, however naïvely, to be the first tentative step in the impossibly long march to movie stardom.

I was able to dig up a leftover program from the Junior Miss Pageant and learned that there had been eight finalists: Becky, Amy, Penny, Kristy, Laura, Helen, Joanna, and MaEllen. Only four of them were California blondes, but almost all of them had affected the spiral perm I'd seen so much of in Bakersfield.

The overall sponsor of the event was the Tehachapi Lions Club, but the finalists had an individual sponsor, as well—Farmer's In-surance, Benz Propane, Cee-Cee's Boutique, and so on. On the back page of the program, there was a message from last year's Tehachapi Junior Miss, Stefani Stark. She thanked God for her good luck and quoted Phil. 4:13, "I can do all things through Christ who strengthens me."

While I flipped through the program, I couldn't help remem-bering my own adolescence and how for a time in my early teens nothing was as vital or as potentially defeating as the image con-fronting me in the bathroom mirror. I felt that I'd be judged by it (and I wasn't far wrong), so each blemish or pimple struck me as a betrayal of the flesh. How I longed to look like an actor—any actor would do! Hollywood, the home of all transcendent beauty, was more than three thousand miles away, but I knew boys and girls in high school who secretly believed that they were destined to be discovered and transported to the Coast.

Similar dreams of glory must have prompted Ronald Reagan to board that train to Los Angeles under false pretenses. Dutch had seen his twenty-sixth birthday come and go, and he was craving more from life. In his suitcase, he was carrying a brand-new suit of white linen. He put it on after checking into his hotel at Hollywood and Vine, hailed a taxi, and rode uncomfortably through a stifling winter heat wave to Republic Studios, where he dropped in on some ac-quaintances, the Oklahoma Outlaws.

Reagan had met the Outlaws at WHO during his broadcasting sojourn. They were filming a cheapie western with Gene Autry, but Dutch, who'd been thinking about breaking into the movies, didn't like the look of things at Republic, or the way that he was treated. He got a better reception at Paramount and an even better one at Warner's, where a friend even arranged for him to have a screen test before he went back to Iowa.

This friend was a singer with a big band, and she did Reagan another favor, too. He still wore glasses, but she urged him to remove them and never be seen with them in public again. He did his test without them, and the Paramount executives received it so enthusiastically that he was awarded a seven-year contract at two hundred dollars a week, a fortune in those days. Dutch was on a roll.

No doubt Ronald Reagan would have understood the fantasies dogging those potential Junior Misses. The pageant was not supposed to be about beauty, its sponsors claimed—there were no bathing suits or cheesecake posing—and yet beauty was still the subtext. A Junior Miss could not escape from being conflated with Barbie dolls and fairy princesses and giving into a fantasy that she would one day light up the silver screen.

Our eight Junior Misses were lovely, sweet, vicious, churlish, and wholly human, a compendium of teenage desires in conflict, and after the pageant was over and the winner had been crowned, seven of them had started a slow retreat into the dimensions of an ordinary life in California, having seen the elephant.

TEHACHAPI WASN'T A COUNTRY town anymore, but it still had twenty-three varieties of apples, including Red and Golden Delicious, MacIntosh, Rome, Jonathan, and Tydeman Red. It had turbines to harness the big winds and the fifth-largest prison in the state, where 4,802 inmates fought for 2,757 beds and made flags and office furniture.

Tehachapi was expanding so rapidly that Bob Carl, a recent refugee from overcrowded Huntington Beach, would say dispiritedly to the *Tehachapi News,* "Tehachapi's probably grown twice as fast as we had anticipated." It had traffic problems and land-use problems and irate natives such as Manney Cowan, a laborer and a pig breeder, who blamed all the problems on the newcomers.

"There's a bale of losers in town now," Cowan would tell the *News.* He had a hog pictured on his cap and looked like Haystacks Calhoun, the old wrestler. "Rather than thirty losers, now there are three hundred."

There was a new golf course in Tehachapi, Horse Thief Country

Club at Stallion Springs. The Southern California Golf Association had given it a rating of 72.1. Newcomers played it, and so did daytrippers from Bakersfield and personnel from Edwards Air Force Base. I played it once with rented clubs, hooking, slicing, shanking, and lurching my way to a 102 as I fulfilled a hitherto unexplored aspect of what it mean to be a Californian.

I was ready for the desert.

THE MOJAVE DESERT IN AUGUST. To contemplate it was akin to contemplating blank space or negative capability. You couldn't rightly think about it. It could only be experienced.

Mojave was a word with many romantic associations. It felt good in your mouth, like a stone worn smooth in a stream, and conjured images of blazing sands, tired cafés, motels harboring loutish gunmen, and old pack mules trekking the last few miles to the boneyard.

The desert was a strict master, slow to reveal its secrets. It put a dose of pure anxiety into any fearful soul. Out on the backroads that led from one nowhere to the next, travelers were ripe for worry. Were there enough soft drinks in the cooler? Enough gas in the tank? What if you got lost? A person lost on a backroad might never be found. The Mojave had no use for a concept such as "enough." It was a meat-eater.

In all, the Mojave covered about fifteen thousand square miles, fully a sixth of the California landmass. It was contained entirely within the state. The temperatures in summer were severe and lived up to their billing, but winters could be mild and pleasant, with brilliantly starry nights and occasional frosts. Between four and fifteen inches of rain fell each year, mostly in winter, although summer cloudbursts sometimes invigorated the desert, flooding dry washes and summoning a smattering of wildflowers.

Spring was a gorgeous season in the Mojave. The yucca sent out their white spikes, and you could smell the red blossoms of the ocotillo and the yellow blossoms of the paloverde. Creosote, not sagebrush, was the dominant plant. It grew sometimes to a height of seven feet, its gray-brown clusters masking the more tender vegetation beneath it, sea blite and pickleweed, salt grass, desert trumpet, and Mormon tea.

Wherever the soil was moist, there were clumps of mesquite and cottonwood. Bulrushes sprouted in puddles. Higher up, on the slopes, grew Joshua trees, all members of the lily family, their trunks twisted into crippled shapes. Above them were the junipers and the piñons. In a few isolated spots in the mountains, you came on relict white firs from a time when the desert had ample water to support such species.

During the Pleistocene, the Mojave had glacial streams running through its meadows. Great herds of animals grazed on the grasses, but the glaciers had subsided, the air warmed, the clouds thinned, and a dry, treacherous climate established itself. The herds died off, a mass extinction, and now when you walked about, you saw playas everywhere, the salty, desiccated beds of dead lakes.

Three Indian tribes had made the Mojave their home. The Che-mehuevi were hunter-gatherers of the middle desert. They were poor and primitive and subsisted on rats, reptiles, jackrabbits, and mesquite seeds. The Serrano also had a trying existence, but the Mohave—the largest tribe—flourished along the Colorado River on the Arizona border. They were farmers and practiced the typical flood-basin agriculture of the Southwest, raising pumpkins, beans, corn, and melons. They seined for fish, or coaxed them into sloughs and speared them.

Although the Mohave were known to be warlike, they could also be kind and enlightened.

"No indians I have seen pay so much deference to the women as these," confided Jed Smith to his journal, while crossing the desert in 1826. "Among indians in general they [women] have not the privilege of speaking on a subject of any moment but here they harangue the Multitude the same as me."

A chief known as Red Shirt impressed Smith. He was a favorite among the women and slept with any of them that he chose.

The Mohave were fond of travel and passionate about dreaming. It was an art to them, something to be worked at, and when they let their dreams drift into speech and become myths, the dreams so transformed acquired a purity and symbolic order as keen-edged as poetry.

Drifting was integral to any notion of the desert. The wind, the wind—things kept scattering through. Vultures drifted in the sky, thoughts drifted, the sands drifted, all in slow motion.

Human drifters were hugely present, people who collected Depression-era milk bottles and paintings of Haile Selassie, people hiding out, people with grave mental disorders, survivalists and shotgun buffs, charter subscribers to *Soldier of Fortune,* toothless hombres in touch with UFOs, dune-buggy freaks and dirt-bike commandos, men in love with dogs, people devoted to solitude, prayerful people, religious zealots and Christs incarnate, heavy users of crank and LSD, imbibers of Sterno, borax miners, bad dudes about to commit a crime or relaxing in the aftermath of one, Scientologists, blowers-off of small arms, illegal aliens, people who needed people, people who didn't need people, and people who just didn't fit with other people at all.

Praise the Lord, then, that the U.S. military-industrial complex controlled the Mojave. More than thirty thousand American military personnel were installed in the desert, with every branch of the service represented. The marines had a training base at Twentynine Palms and a marine supply depot in Barstow. The navy maintained an ordnance test station at China Lake. At Fort Irwin, where G.I.s had once geared up for the North American campaign, army boys did their basic. Edwards Air Force Base had the most advanced air-test range in the country, while the boys at George Air Force Base near Victorville handled jet-flight training and were assigned the job of defending Los Angeles against air attacks.

Nowhere but in the Mojave could you see such convincing evidence of the importance of the military to the economy of California. All day, almost every day, the whoosh of jets on the wing hovered over the desert, and the evening sky was streaked with contrails.

IN THE LITTLE DESERT TOWNS of the Mojave, life did not appear to be all that much fun. It wasn't the sort of life that anybody imagined when they toyed with moving to California. The hot sun on an aluminum trailer roof, a bored dealer in a card room, easy access to chiropractic care—you might not even give up Akron, Ohio, for it. The desert people were frequently scraping by on fixed incomes, welfare, or disability insurance. There wasn't any gainful employment unless you were in the service.

In a certain sense, the Mojave was still the Wild West, effectively lawless and too big to police, although malefactors were so numerous that a few of them did get caught and were arraigned at Ridgecrest Court, as reported in the *Mojave Desert News*. They were not, by and large, the kind of folks that you would pick as neighbors.

Timothy Marshall Bachman—Spousal abuse, being under the influence of a controlled substance, possession of a controlled substance.

Jeffery Paul Osburn—Being under the influence of a controlled substance, possession of marijuana, carrying a concealed weapon, carrying a destructive device without a permit.

Maxine Case—Charged in 175 counts of improper care of dogs, estimated in the hundreds.

John Patrick Slaughter—Felony shooting at an inhabited building or vehicle.

Mariano Asenas—Possession of a deadly weapon while serving time at Tehachapi State Prison with a prior prison offense.

The destructive device was a cause for concern. I thought about stolen warheads, about somebody riding around stoned and furious and equipped with nuclear capability.

In spite of the debilitating living conditions in the desert, the little Mojave towns were growing. In Rosamond, the subdivisions were going up fast, even though high levels of dioxin, a carcinogen particularly lethal to children, had been found in some local eggs, a pig's liver, and the soil not far from residential areas. The state was still investigating the cause of a Rosamond cancer cluster that had purportedly killed nine children some years earlier.

The new homes in Rosamond were deeply affordable. For seventy thousand dollars, you could buy a three-bedroom house. The buyers were senior citizens, commuters priced out of Bakersfield, and soldiers, sailors, marines, and flyboys. Here, in Rosamond, on the dioxin flats, was their treasured piece of California. If Rosamond failed to capture them, they could always buy in nearby California City, another subdivision in the sand, where the billboards advertised a lifestyle "worth living."

Beyond California City lay the Desert Tortoise Natural Area preserve, a subdivision for tortoises. A familiar wind, hot and dry, swept across the Mojave while I slowly negotiated five miles of dirt road to an empty parking lot in a creosote jungle. Signs directed me to an Interpretative Center, an open-air structure with concrete-block walls and a roof balanced on two-by-fours. It would not have been out of place in Malawi.

On a bench behind a wall, all alone, sat a thin young man, Jeff Holland, whose eyeglasses were coated with dust. Holland had longish hair, and the skin on his face was peeling from exposure. He looked terribly forlorn. In defiance of the wind, he was trying to fix a tuna sandwich for lunch, studiously applying mayo to one slice of bread while holding down the other slice with a tube of Pringles. The sight of him was curiously monkish and devotional.

Holland, a graduate student at UCLA, was doing a four-month

stint at the preserve. He specialized in lizards and desert ecology, but he knew a lot about tortoises, too. They were an endangered species that had tolerated every sort of abuse, he said, dead beneath the wheels of off-road vehicles, plinked at by rifles, trampled by cattle, and carted away as pets and souvenirs.

The tortoises were worse off than ever this year, Holland continued, because the greenery and the wildflowers that kept them alive were in short supply. It had rained in the Mojave but not on the tortoises' preserve. He told me how frustrating it had been to look out over the desert and watch clouds break apart less than a mile away.

The preserve enclosed thirty-eight acres. A wire fence protected it from off-roaders and grazing cattle and sheep. Off-roaders and ranchers felt that such precautions were unwarranted. They assumed that the tortoise in its tanklike armor was a hardy creature. It had sampled the lakes and the meadows of the Pleistocene, and it was still around.

Actually, though, the ongoing destruction of tortoise habitat showed how the entire Mojave ecosystem was being destroyed. For the past few years, legislators in California had gnawed at the fringes of a Desert Protection Act without turning it into a law. The act would designate 7.5 million acres of the Mojave and the adjacent Colorado Desert as a wilderness area, thereby curtailing ranching, vehicular assault on the land, and the building of houses.

The Mojave Desert had already been appointed a protector in the Bureau of Land Management, in fact, but a recent report from the Government Accounting Office had criticized the BLM for not doing its job. The GAO accused the bureau of failing to spend enough time or money on the desert—a serious error, because the desert, once wounded, was very slow to heal.

Some of the BLM's attempts at protecting the Mojave were downright zany. Its agents had recently embarked on a misguided program to improve the habitat for tortoises by killing ravens, who preyed on tortoise eggs. They had set out poisoned, hard-boiled chicken eggs on platforms. The agents were selectively shooting rav-

ens, as well, presumably believing that they could separate a good
bird from a bad one, but the Humane Society had slapped them with
a restraining order.

I told Holland that I was going to scout the preserve.

"If you really want to see a tortoise," he recommended, "you'd
do better to knock on doors in California City."

Out in the creosote, the glare of the sun burned my eyes. It was
tough to see anything in the desert. So many of the plants and animals
had a protective coloration, and so much of the activity occurred at
night. To understand how complex the Mojave was, you had to be
patient and quiet and do some crawling. There were 120 plant varieties on the preserve, and quite a few of them were inconspicuous
enough to escape all but the most inquiring eyes.

On my walk, I counted two lizards, one cricket, no ravens, and
no desert tortoises.

IN BORON, not far away, U.S. Borax operated the biggest open-pit
borax mine anywhere. The sky had a whitish cast, and dusty miners
were driving through town in the late afternoon on their way home
from the pit. Every working day, they hauled ten thousand pounds
of borax out of the earth. They must have had bad dreams about
borax, must have seen it drifting over them in powdery clouds.

Some uniformed lads from Edwards Air Force Base were handing out free coffee in Boron, informing the public about F-16s and
B-52 Stealths. The letters they wrote home would all be like the
letters we Peace Corps trainees had written so long ago, each beginning the same way but conveying a sharply different sentiment. "Dear
Folks," they'd say, "California isn't like I expected it to be . . ."

Borax dust, cement dust, dust from the rock quarries and the
gravel pits: I was starting to feel a little overwhelmed in the desert,
not unlike a biblical wanderer paying in spades for an indescribable
sin. My atlas showed acres of white space sparsely veined with thin
red lines, Hill Truck Trail, Mirage Lake, and even a Doberman

Street. Which direction to go? I took Highway 58 to Barstow past sewage ponds, junked cars, and tire tread ripped from eighteen-wheelers, but Barstow brought no relief. It used to be a railroad town, but now traffic clogged its center. The old Santa Fe switching yard had the aura of a faded photograph.

Ahead lay Daggett and Yermo and then nothing for 286 miles. Then Needles on the Arizona border, a town that was the hottest spot in California on any TV weatherman's map, nine times out of ten.

So I went south instead, toward Victorville. The peaks of the Calico Mountains stood out above the embattled air, which was becoming darker and thicker, more diseased. In Victorville, giant American flags were flapping. The town seemed to be eagerly awaiting the next war, any war at all. It was home to the Roy Rogers–Dale Evans Museum, where Trigger's hide was stretched over a fiber-glass body and postured in an eternal gallop. Critics had once accused Rogers of having the horse stuffed.

"Would you rather I put him in the ground and let the worms eat him?" the old cowpoke had responded.

Adelanto saved me. Every sinner in that godforsaken corner of the Mojave had convened there to frolic in the light of a crimson sunset. Adelanto had honky-tonks and watering holes. Under a special dispensation from the state, it had a casino, the Hi-Desert, where plungers could play poker, pan, and pai gow, a Chinese game of chance. It had a new massage parlor where the needs of the boys from George AFB could be answered. At the Hi-Desert Motel, guests had to leave a two-dollar key deposit and contend with a woman desk sergeant who'd seen it all and then some.

After the bliss of a long shower, I joined the gamblers at a poker table, Doc and Ace and Red and Shorty. They were people who were too old or too lazy to drive to Las Vegas, or people who'd driven to Las Vegas and were trying to divest themselves of the last of the money burning a hole in their pockets before returning to their homes in subdivisions elsewhere.

Twenty minutes into my stay, Ace looked at me funny and said, "You sure are getting the cards tonight." I sure was.

An Armenian couple, John and Jasmine Mgrdichian, owned the Hi-Desert. The Mgrdichians published a bi-monthly newsletter listing their poker tournaments and praising their employees. They were considerate toward their customers. Several tapped-out gents were asleep on couches and in chairs when I walked into the casino the next morning, but nobody was pounding on their feet with nightsticks.

A man came over and sat at the table where I was sipping coffee and savoring my windfall profit of eighty-four dollars—not Ace or Doc but Carl, a retired bus driver. Carl smoked Merit filters and wore a bolo tie. He had observed my hot streak and complimented me on it.

"Don't you wish it could always be like that?" he asked, with a twinkle in his eye.

I pondered the metaphysics. "Yes," I answered truthfully.

Carl was seventy-eight, but he still got around and even knew The Oaks card room in Emeryville, near Oakland. His wife enjoyed gambling, too, but she only played Bingo, he said. They were staying in Adelanto a while longer to take advantage of the special fifteen-day gambler's rate ($345) at the motel before they went home.

And where might home be? Lathrop Wells, Nevada, up Death Valley way.

THE CONCEPT OF DEATH VALLEY had fascinated me as a child. I had imagined it as a great, sandy hellhole where the bodies piled up in stacks. In the valley, I believed, death came in forty-eight flavors. You could be bit by a rattlesnake, slaughtered by Indians, or fried in your skin by the sun. Worst (or best) of all, you could die of thirst, your throat contracting as you limped in total isolation across the desert floor.

Death Valley had indeed made its name by claiming lives. William Manly, a New Englander, had left a record of its power. He was a '49er who had departed for California from the Wisconsin lead mines, traversed the Oregon Trail, and then went by boat to Arizona, where he elected to take a shortcut to Eldorado by crossing the valley. Several families joined him, as did the Jayhawkers, all single young men from Galesburg, Illinois.

The two parties entered the desert at Furnace Creek around Christmas and split up. Manly's group went south and the Jayhawkers went northwest. Thirteen of the Jayhawkers would die of exposure and dehydration. The Manly party found a spring and fared better, although they struggled through enough hardship that Manly, a survivor, was able to publish a popular memoir of their ordeal in his old age.

In *Death Valley in '49*, he recalled the moment when the remaining members of his party were liberated from their tribulations.

> We took off our hats, and then overlooking the scene of so much trial, suffering, and death spoke the thought uppermost in our minds, saying, "Goodbye, Death Valley!" ... Many accounts have been given to the world as the origin of the name, but ours were the first visible footsteps, and we the party which gave it the saddest and most dreadful name that came to us first from our memories.

Inyo County, where Death Valley was located, had more than ten thousand miles of land, but the prevailing measure of density was about one person per square mile. The only incorporated town in the county, Bishop, had less than four thousand occupants. It was simple to vanish into the landscape, into the pinks and roses of the Panamint Range, on the valley's west side.

Charlie Manson had brought his Family to live in Death Valley and had camped with them at the abandoned Barker Ranch in the Panamints, up Goler Wash, where the ground was so rocky it could scarcely be negotiated in a Jeep. No towns were around, but sometimes the Manson girls traveled to far-off Shoshone to panhandle, shoplift, and sell marijuana. The boys made forays out to steal guns and cars.

Somehow Manson had managed to get his school bus into the Panamints. The floor of the bus was a foot deep with oddments of clothing, and the Family members plucked their wardrobes from it. Here in the mind-blowing heat and the unearthly desolation, they read about Hitler and about Rommel's desert campaigns and did lots of dope and sex. Around the campfire, they listened to Charlie play his guitar and sing his songs.

At the Barker Ranch, the Family dreamed of melding with the Beatles and forming an elite corps of dune-buggy marauders to patrol the desert. In the aftermath of their creepy-crawling, they would be arrested by surprise in the Panamints—some of them naked, some of them stoned, and Charlie all in buckskin pulled like a nasty little Hobbit from his hideout in a tiny bathroom cabinet.

Death Valley had also figured in Dutch Reagan's life. His career as a successful movie actor had ended in the early 1950s, and he had sunk so low that he was working as a sideman with The Continentals, a barbershop quartet, in the lounges of Las Vegas, when General Electric tapped him as the host of its new dramatic series on television.

GE wanted a clean-living, moral, all-American type, and Dutch fit the bill. He liked the job and even liked to tour GE plants and chat with the employees. His bosses marveled at his ability to charm both men and women. Because he was frugal, he always dressed in dated suits, but he had an unusual recall of names and birthdays and seemed humble for a former Hollywood star. In essence, Reagan was honing the political skills that had made him a six-term president of the Screen Actors Guild through the 1950s—a position he used to celebrate Republicans and bash Commies.

By 1962, "General Electric Theater" had run its course, and Reagan was looking for work again. His brother, Moon, an adman and a bon vivant, had U.S. Borax as a client. Like GE, U.S. Borax sponsored a TV show, "Death Valley Days," but its host, the Old Ranger, had become a problem. He delivered his lines so slowly that it took almost as long to shoot his two introductory minutes as it did the rest of the episode.

At first, Reagan didn't want to replace the Old Ranger, but after his brother and his agent sandbagged him at a lunch at the Brown Derby in Hollywood, he sank under the weight of the dollars being offered to him and hitched himself to the 20 Mule Team. The teleplays dealt with subjects that he enjoyed, themes both western and archetypal, and also kept Dutch's face before the American public— no small thing for the Ultimate Californian, who was already quietly running for the presidency of the United States.

IN THE SWEET AIR OF EARLY MORNING, before the sun was high, I left the Hi-Desert Casino and drove away from the Mojave Desert on Route 18, a road lined with yuccas and palm trees. It led me through Llano and Pearblossom, where roadside stands were stocked with baskets of fruit and sacks of almonds and pistachios. Truck farmers from Antelope Valley, in north-central Los Angeles County, were unloading their last crates of produce, stripping off the flannel shirts they'd put on at dawn and using them to mop their sweaty faces.

In Littlerock, some men were sitting in folding chairs by the California Aqueduct, improbably fishing in the manmade stream coursing through a wide, concrete chute. This was desert-style angling, fiendish and illusory.

"We catch bass and catfish, mostly," one old boy told me, reaching into a cooler to refresh himself.

Near Three Point, northwest of Littlerock, the Los Angeles Aqueduct fed into the aqueduct system, diverting the Owens River in Owens Valley. It represented the first big water grab in the history of southern California, a coup pulled off by Fred Eaton, who was then the mayor of Los Angeles, and his associate, William Mulholland.

Eaton's city had a burgeoning population of more than 200,000 in 1904. There was plenty of land left to develop, but the Los Angeles

River had almost run dry. Eaton saw the Owens River, some 250 miles away, as a resource that might be able to supply a city ten times as big as the current one and asked Mulholland to design a gravity canal on a scale not attempted since the days of the Romans. He guessed that the canal would cost about $23.5 million. The money had to be raised through an immense bond issue.

The project proceeded in secrecy. With the secrecy came skulduggery, chicanery, and rapacity. In Owens Valley, Eaton conned ranchers into selling their ranches, making no mention of the water plan. The U.S. Reclamation Service had an eye to building a reservoir for irrigation in the valley, and Eaton had to journey to Washington and lobby Teddy Roosevelt to kill the idea.

The aqueduct took about five years to build. Mulholland brought it in on time and under budget. The system went into operation on November 5, 1913. Thousands of Angelenos motored out to San Fernando to witness the miracle.

"There it is," said a proud Mulholland, as the water began to flow. "Take it."

IN PALMDALE, red roofing tiles and plastic gutters were stacked in the desert. Like Lancaster, its immediate neighbor in Antelope Valley, Palmdale was growing swiftly. Nothing was shrinking in California, I thought, except for California itself.

Palmdale wasn't as close to Edwards Air Force Base as Rosamond, but the houses were fancier, and some military families were moving in. There were also many buyers who commuted to jobs in central Los Angeles, a trip that could take two hours each way and made the Hercules-to-San Francisco run seem tranquil.

In other sections of Antelope Valley, you still came upon windswept plains alive with poppies, and to alfalfa fields and some orchards. The fields, the crops, and the poppies were all about to go. They were to become another new town, California Springs, a suburb of Los Angeles built out of nothing, a Levittown.

I drove along an ordinary block in Palmdale and watched the neighborhood waking on a Sunday morning. The light was a soft and hazy gold. It made the big houses in their unscarred newness look artificial, as if a movie company had put them up and would tear them down again at the end of filming. On a lawn where the blades of grass were a vigilant green, as yet untouched by sneakers or bikes, a man in his bathrobe was standing with his arms crossed and staring blankly at his street, intent on a private matter.

The man appeared to be doing an internal calculation, maybe adding up some things—his cars, his children, his commute time, and his mortgage payments—and then dividing his insurance premiums by the sum of his property tax to try and arrive at a formula that might explain how he had come to be where he was: at the edge of the Mojave Desert, rootless, a Californian.

STILL WANDERING TWO DAYS LATER, not yet ready for a descent into L.A., I was headed along Highway 58 toward San Luis Obispo on the coast when I passed seven pronghorn antelope grazing on the tall grasses of a fenced preserve on the Carrizo Plain. They blended so perfectly into the tans, golds, and whites of the plain that I almost missed seeing them. They were yet another museum piece, the last of their species in California.

The Carrizo Plain was west of Bakersfield between two mountain ranges, the La Panzas and the Temblors. It was among the most remote regions in the state and suggested a remant section of the Great Plains. It had the aridity of a middle-latitude desert, but the soil was good for growing winter wheat and providing seasonal pasturage for sheep and cattle.

The area had a timeless feel. Prehistoric peoples had left some paintings on a singular sandstone butte, birds and suns and undecipherable symbols. Soda Lake, a playa, was a shallow bowl at the center of the plain. Ranchers had once gathered salt from the lake to use as a preservative.

I wanted to press on before dark, but hunger got the best of me, and I stopped at a café that sat all by itself near the ruins of a motel. Ranch families took up most of the tables. A boy of six was sprawled on the floor by me, coloring with crayons. He had silky hair and blue eyes and had just finished first grade at the local one-room school. He would go there until he was ready for high school, he said, and after that he would board in San Luis Obispo, sixty miles away, as most ranchers' children did.

When I reached the coast later that night, I understood how it would be for the boy and how wide his blue eyes would grow. San Luis Obispo was a lovely, civilized city. After the ceaseless torpor of the desert, the fog blowing in felt wonderful—wonderful and romantic—and I took deep breaths of the bracing sea air. Streetlights shone on boulevards, revealing store windows filled with books and CDs and smashing clothes, all missing from the Carrizo Plain and the Mojave.

Students from Cal Poly sipped cappuccinos and lattes in cafés, falling in love with ideas and with each other. I became uncommonly aware of words and the many voices around me, an agreeable contrast to the desert's silence. Freed from the demanding geography of solitude, I began to feel less tired and resolved to spend a couple of days recuperating by the water before finally starting for Los Angeles and the belly of the beast.

PART FIVE

BELLY OF THE BEAST

I couldn't wait to be old enough to move to California. I wanted to be where the movies are made, in that land of sunshine and Gidget and surfboards and convertibles and green lawns and beautiful houses.

—*David Geffen,*
in Rolling Stone

A GURU WAS ON THE AIR, pitching a new foundation for human potential. I tuned him in by chance while inching slowly south on the San Diego Freeway, my car windows rolled up against a sky that was the color of a cotton swab dipped in iodine. His voice was bitter and chastising, intended to sell the old-fashioned apocalyptic vision of a swinish Los Angeles consumed by flames.

"Man is a fallen being," he said with relish, as if the vileness of people were a constant source of delight to him. "You're degraded beings! You're all sinking into the slime!"

The problem, in the guru's opinion, was that little demon in our underpants. The demon was responsible for every social ill, every terrible disease.

"If they cure AIDS, you'll wish you were dead from it!" he cried. "Because there's something worse in the future!"

Flip the dial.

A news report about the health of Elizabeth Taylor, who's had nineteen major operations in her life, a record of some kind.

Flip the dial.

Some Flaco Jimenez chicken-skin music, followed by a public-service announcement in what sounded like Urdu.

Flip the dial.

The Dodgers game. Dodgers leading the Braves, four to two in the sixth.

Flip the dial.

Retro rock with Mott The Hoople. A call-in cooking show, where a woman was pleading in distress, "I must get some help with my meatloaf."

Flip the dial.

A traffic bulletin, the commuter report. An overturned tractor-trailer on Interstate 5. A pickup with an exploded engine on the Santa Monica Freeway. Hollywood Freeway bumper to bumper. Some air-conditioner filters spilled on the Pomona Freeway, and on 405, the San Diego Freeway, a jackknifed big rig clogging the flow.

The traffic guy laughed and said, "That vehicle's going to have to file for a homestead permit soon!"

I shut off the radio and looked into the cars around me, all those private universes on wheels. The man to my right was reading a *Racing Form* while driving a mint-green '72 Chevy. The man on my left had a tiny Geo and held a bashed-in door closed with one of his hands. Whenever we took an unanticipated spurt forward, the door flew open, and he grabbed at it like someone chasing a balloon on a string.

The Geo had a bumper sticker, I Luv Mozart.

An antique VW Bug in front of the Geo began to sputter and die. The teenage girl at the wheel banged the dashboard with her fists and wept. Smoke issued from her tailpipe, and the Bug ground to a halt, destined for the graveyard shoulder of the road where other ditched and wounded automobiles were arrayed in darkling failure.

In the midst of the morass, a joyously coked-out pilot in a splendid, reconditioned 1956 Corvette was trying to weave his way to his dealer's for a drug refueling, racing against the tightly wound clock in his head, a lover of chaos darting from one lane to another and squeezing into spaces where he had less than a micrometer to spare.

Welcome to Los Angeles. The guru had got it all wrong, of course.

The apocalypse had been and gone, and those of us who were sweltering on the San Diego Freeway or the Pomona Freeway or the Hollywood Freeway or the Santa Monica Freeway were trapped in the world's first postapocalyptic, postmodern, postliterate city, a place without absolute boundaries that floated freely beyond the grasp of history, parody, and any concerns other than the momentary.

Los Angeles had always told its stories with a limited handful of variables, among them power, fame, money, speed, beauty, and sex. It played itself out in a highly evolved surface kinetics that offered premium amusement to the masses. It was a brutal and ghettoized arena in which self-dramatization was not only tolerated but encouraged. A moral life, a life of commitment, they could be lived elsewhere, in Wichita or in New Paltz.

Los Angeles had always been the source of all enduring California imagery, a foundry where the component parts of the Edenic dream had first been pounded out and manufactured for export, and in the American mind, as well as the global mind—even the Urdu mind, for that matter—it continued to be the preeminent signifier of all that was holy and rotten about the Golden State.

The city was inescapable, an unavoidable condition. Its highs were the highest and its lows were the lowest. It invited you to a party, threw an arm around your shoulder, drew you into a lavish bathroom, gave you a hit of cocaine, stuffed some dollars into your pocket, and asked if it were really true that you had no strange desires or perverse cravings. It pressed your nose to the candystore window and coaxed you into admitting that you wanted things.

Los Angeles laughed in the face of virtue. It did not go in for unalloyed feelings. It stared you down and forced you to both love it and hate it. It was about fire and being consumed by the fire and living and dying in the fire.

I joined the single-lane queue of drivers skirting the jackknifed big rig and realized by the sudden nearness of the ocean that I was on the threshold of a definitive Los Angeles experience, the one in which the grossness of a desecrated landscape does an instantaneous flip-flop, turns breathtaking, and makes you believe that nothing is as bad as you thought it was a moment ago.

In Santa Monica, where I left the freeway, the weight of the turgid air seemed to lift. I could see the Pacific and a line of gentle breakers foaming across a beach. There were billowy palm trees like those I used to covet as a child in New York. Flowering bougainvillea vines trailed over balconies, and seagulls of an unsullied whiteness winged about them.

On the green palisades, some joggers were running their afternoon laps through an obstacle course of shopping carts and rag bundles that constituted a large encampment of the homeless. Here by the sea, in an environment of unwithered promise, the homeless did not look quite as desperate or as destroyed. Instead, they had a weird sort of vigor, as if they had come to terms with their burden and had decided that if they were going to be poor and hungry, Santa Monica was the paradise in which to do it.

O, California! Two blocks up from the beach, in a quiet neighborhood of stucco houses, was the Sovereign Hotel, soon to be my home away from home.

Built in 1928 and designed by Julia Morgan, the architect of William Randolph Hearst's Castle, the Sovereign had a casual elegance. It was part Mediterranean villa and part Spanish mission, all white stucco, arched windows, and red-and-white striped awnings. It had once been a fashionable place to lodge, but now it catered to Asian and European tourists on a budget, and to screenwriters performing patch jobs on slasher pictures or waiting in limbo for a meeting with a studio executive that kept being postponed.

At some point in time, the Sovereign had rented out its rooms as apartments, so for a bargain price you could have a suite with a sitting room and a kitchen. Sometimes the suite even had a view of the ocean. A continental breakfast was provided, too, and served in a nook off the Art Deco lobby, where guests from abroad seemed always to be grappling in vain with a broken toaster.

Every morning at the Sovereign, I came downstairs to the smell of burnt toast and the sound of invectives in foreign languages, but in compensation there was always some classical music playing from a small radio hidden behind a larger, nonfunctional radio of the 1930s. In some respects, the hotel was a doppelgänger for Los Angeles, never quite what it appeared to be and forever staying one step ahead of interpretation.

I had to settle for a third-floor suite that lacked an ocean view. The door had a peephole for checking out visitors, and the furniture was overstuffed and redolent of powder and perfume. It summoned to mind an era of Gatsby-esque cocktail parties, where the men wore white linen trousers, knocked around croquet balls, and answered to the name of Hal.

A suite at the Sovereign would have been ideal for Philip Marlowe, the definitive southern California private detective, I thought. His creator, Raymond Chandler, had based his corrupt Bay City on Santa Monica. Chandler was raised in England and remained a devoted Anglophile to the end. He claimed that Los Angeles gave him an eerie sense of unreality.

"I've lived half my life in California and made what use I could of it," he once said, "but I could leave it forever without a pang."

He never did leave it forever, though, in spite of having enough money to move wherever he pleased. In his old age, he tried to escape back to England, only to return to the Coast. Chandler became a victim of the unavoidable condition, carping and griping and carrying on about how he wished to be among a better class of people than the Californians he met, whose pride expressed itself "in their kitchen gadgets and their automobiles."

On and on went Raymond Chandler, raving about corruption and blight and deceit and yet never budging from where he was.

"The whole of California is very much what someone said of Switzerland," he wrote in a letter to a friend, *"un beau pays mal habite."*

•   •   •

SAILING ALONG THE PACIFIC COAST in their four-masted caravels, Juan
Cabrillo and his crew came in October of 1542 to the present site of
San Pedro Harbor and saw a sky blackened by smoke from the fires
at Indian villages. They called the place *Bahia de los Fumos,* "a good
port, and a good land of many valleys, plains, and groves." They
were met by some Indians who were dressed in skins and lived on
fish and agave, a plant in the Amaryllis family, and they were told
about a big inland river where maize and other crops grew.

The Indians were from the Shoshonean family and would later
be known as Gabrielinos after their domicile at Mission San Gabriel.
Gabrielinos had a visionary bent and used jimsonweed in their cult
of *toloache,* instructing young boys in spiritual matters while the boys
were hallucinating.

Junípero Serra founded Mission San Gabriel in 1770. His superiors had ordered him to build a compound by *Río de los Temblores,*
the River of Earthquakes, now the San Gabriel River. Serra and his
party of soldiers, mules, and muleteers encountered opposition from
the Indians there, and church legend has it that they would have
been killed if they hadn't unfurled a painting on canvas of Our Lady
of Sorrows, who intimidated the Indians with her grief-stricken face
and caused them to put down their bows.

The River of Earthquakes, though excellent for irrigation,
flooded frequently. The padres had to rebuild their mission compound at a new site five years later. There the Franciscans flourished,
but the Gabrielinos did not, plagued instead with the usual miseries
of mission chattle and dying off from smallpox, measles, and syphilis.
Mission San Gabriel became one of the church's richest holdings,
accounting for the most bountiful wheat harvest in the region. Jed
Smith, no brilliant speller, stopped over in 1826, and sang its glories
to his journal:

"Two thousand acres of land ... An extensive vineyard and orchards of Apples Peach Pear and Olive trees som figs and a Beautiful

grove of about 400 Orange trees . . . a scene on which the eye cannot
fail to rest with pleasure."

The Gold Rush left Los Angeles largely unaffected, although a
few of its merchants made a bundle by supplying beef and wine to
miners. Into the mid-nineteenth century, it remained a sleepy settlement whose attributes William Brewer outlined in 1852, while he
was camped on a hill in a cold December rain.

> Los Angeles is a city of some 3,500 or 4,000 inhabitants, nearly a
> century old, a regular old Spanish-Mexican town, built by the old
> *padres,* Catholic Spanish missionaries, before the American inde-
> pendence. The houses are but one story, mostly built of *adobe* or
> sunburnt brick, with very thick walls and flat roofs. They are so
> low because of earthquakes, and the style is Mexican. The inhab-
> itants are a mixture of old Spanish, Indian, American, and German
> Jews; the last two have come in lately. The language of the natives
> is Spanish. . . .
>
> Here is a great plain, or rather a gentle slope, from the Pacific
> to the mountains. We are on this plain about twenty miles from
> the sea and fifteen from the mountains, a most lovely locality; all
> that is wanted naturally to make it a paradise is *water,* more *water.*
> Apples, pears, plums, figs, olives, lemons, oranges, and "the finest
> grapes in the world," so the books say, pears of two and a half
> pounds each, and such things in proportion. The weather is soft
> and balmy—no winter, but perpetual spring and summer. Such is
> Los Angeles, a place where "every prospect pleases and only man
> is vile."

The shortage of water did not inhibit the first Los Angeles boom
during the 1880s—at the time, water was still an afterthought. The
railroads helped to ignite the growth, as they'd done elsewhere in
the state. With the Southern Pacific and the Santa Fe in competition,
there were constant fare wars, and a roundtrip ticket from Chicago,
say, might drop from a high of $125 to $25.

Midwestern farmers traveled west on holiday and were quickly charmed by the chief agriculture benefit of Los Angeles County—as Brewer had put it, no winter. The low price of acreage convinced many of them to move and take up the cultivation of citrus groves, never again to sniffle and sneeze through another January. Along with their farming instincts, the new pioneers brought with them a heartland fundamentalism, Christian and Republican, that was in marked contrast to the freewheeling liberalism that had always obtained in San Francisco, the capital city of the north.

Ordinary tourists also availed themselves of the cut-rate fares, drawn by the prospect of shirt-sleeve weather at Christmas, and by the glowing endorsements of the Los Angeles Chamber of Commerce, established in 1888, the first such organization in the United States.

The chamber was packed with boosters and go-getters out to sell off Los Angeles as fast as they could. Special trains labeled "California on Wheels" toured the snowy interior and teased the ice fishermen, the bobsledders, and the frigid Scandinavians with photos of beaches, palm trees, and bathing beauties, and with crates of oranges, lemons, olives, almonds, and avocados that showcased L.A. as the primal cornucopia.

There were lulls in the Los Angeles growth curve, moments when it appeared that the city would stretch no more, but something always came along to jump-start the action again—Doheny's oil strike, for instance, or the enticements of a budding motion-picture industry.

Subdividers of every stripe and ethical persuasion were going gangbusters by the 1920s and constructing the first expansive tracts around the city. They lured customers with such incentives as cruises to Hawaii or a chance to kiss the prettiest starlet on the MGM lot. If you checked into a hotel, a realtor was liable to give you a blind call. Bellhops were bribed to slip flyers about tantalizing, affordable property under doors. Midgets and hirelings in sandwich boards walked the streets handing out brochures. Sometimes a hundred ships stacked with lumber were docked in the harbor waiting to be unloaded.

A new booster group, the All-Year Club of Southern California, supplanted the Chamber of Commerce and began promoting Los Angeles as something more than a mere winter retreat. Its prime mover was Harry Chandler of the *Times,* who owned plenty of land that he was willing to surrender if the price was right. To extoll the city's assets, the club advertised in dozens of U.S. papers and sent out its absolutely unbiased speakers to deliver countless lectures to interested groups.

Sloganeering was the club's forte: "A new man in two weeks! You've earned, you deserve, a real vacation!" At its most excessive, the club implied that the ultraviolet rays shining down on Angelenos were so good for humanity that medical researchers were hoping to duplicate them in the lab.

As an adjunct to the All-Year Club, a newly chartered Automobile Club, also the first ever, promoted Los Angeles in its publications. There were almost 200,000 cars in the city at the end of the 1920s, and they had taken over the downtown and had thrown the trolley system out of whack, slaughtering mass transit in the bargain.

Angelenos loved to drive, and they did it with impunity and an alarming sense of entitlement. With the greatest possible goodwill, they harkened to the notion that a Sunday afternoon could profitably be spent motoring the family's Model T to a proposed subdivision in the San Fernando Valley, where they could inspect an architect's rendering of the nearly identical houses to be built rapid-fire by carpenters whose labors echoed the assembly-line techniques of Henry Ford.

The automobile gave developers more freedom. They could stray farther afield and acquire land for even less money because tracts didn't need to be anchored to the traditional modes of transportation anymore. The doomed trolleys were turned into dinosaurs overnight. One entrepreneur even bought some trolley cars for a pittance, put them up on blocks, and sold them off as homes.

World War II had the same stimulating effect on Los Angeles as it did on the San Francisco Bay Area. Employees of such ship-building and aircraft firms as Northrop, Lockheed, and McDonnell Douglas joined returning G.I.s to settle the new towns being constructed where the oranges and the lemons used to grow. The towns shared a number of standard features—most notably, a shopping center or a mall—but schools, then as now, were seldom among them.

The craft of putting together a subdivision was soon refined into a quasi-science, and a crew could complete a house in a few days, although it might take months for an owner to have a phone installed. Sewer systems weren't always dependable, and flooding was common during the winter rains. The philosophy of the period was strictly grab-and-run.

The tracts with their interchangeable parts gave Los Angeles its characteristic look of many diverse little suburbs that didn't quite add up to a recognizable city. When the flatlands were covered, the developers moved on to the canyons and to the ridges. The freeways followed in their path, ever-multiplying ribbons of concrete and asphalt braided together in such intricate configurations that if you looked at an aerial photo of L.A., it seemed to be crisscrossed by ganglia reverberating in an odd neural structure.

In Silver Lake, in Glendale, in Culver City, and in Pomona, houses reposed in neat rows beneath skies that were blackened by smog, not Indian campfires.

THOSE FIRST FEW DAYS IN SANTA MONICA, I felt as if I were on vacation. After so many weeks of sleeping on the ground or in the same generic motel room, I wallowed in the peacefulness of the Raymond Chandler Suite. There were no car doors slamming at dawn, no flustered husbands shouting at their wives to hurry up. The essence of motel living is flight, but a good hotel makes you want to linger.

In bed, while starlings sang in the crowns of the palms, I would drink coffee, open the *Los Angeles Times,* and read about the Dodgers, the random shootings, the intentional killings, the box-office grosses, and especially the real estate deals of the movie stars and the moguls. They were all crucial things to know if you aspired to be an Angeleno.

You were definitely out in the cold if you were unaware, say, that John Landis, the director, had ripped down Rock Hudson's old 1950s hacienda in Beverly Hills to put up a new house of more than 7,000 square feet, or that Mel Gibson was getting $45,000 a month for leasing his 2.3-acre Malibu Colony compound. Such gossip allowed you to calibrate your own worth by the decimeters that separated you from the aura cast by Hollywood.

Along with the baseball scores, the real estate scores, and the murder bulletins, I sometimes read the air-quality report in the *Times.* In fact, I was relatively sure that I was the only person in the city who *did* read it. It measured the levels of ozone, nitrogen dioxide, and carbon monoxide in the air and rated them on the Pollutant Standard Index.

Almost every day, some inland area was in the grip of a first-stage episode (unhealthy) or a second-stage episode (very unhealthy). Third-stage episodes didn't exist. Once the pollutants had reached a certain density, coagulating and mutating, the air was simply described as "hazardous."

In Santa Monica, near the beach, I seldom had to worry about the air. The ocean breezes took care of the excess ozone, nitrogen dioxide, and carbon monoxide on all but the stillest, hottest days. The weather was always balmy when I left the hotel for my morning stroll, and I would experience the same sort of privilege that I had felt so long ago in Westwood, glad to be where I was, in California, drawn irresistibly toward a bright patch of light.

Santa Monica wasn't truly part of Los Angeles, but it *was* the Los Angeles that Americans slavered over in their fantasies. It had its origins as a real-estate development along the ocean, on Santa

Monica Bay, and had been incorporated as an independent town in 1886. Guidebooks often mentioned that Shirley Temple, a confectionary California child, had been born there.

After I'd walked for a block or two, I found it hard to remember any of the information that I had just digested at the hotel. The debilitating news stories seemed not to matter anymore. They were obviously fictions that some despairing editors had dreamed up to sell a few papers. Human misery belonged on the map of elsewhere, a place that you could drive to, like any other.

In Palisades Park, the perennially fit were always doing their exercises, outrunning calories and yesterday, while the facially challenged were nowhere to be seen. Old Eastern Europeans in absurdly heavy clothes, their shawls and their tweed suits like the trappings of the past, sat on benches to converse or to play a hand of cards.

The homeless, too, were always out, regrouping their tenuous community. The cops didn't roust them, but the lawn where they slept had sprinklers that switched on in the middle of the night, so they'd wake and cough and shiver in their rags until the rising of the sun. Sometimes they got a free ration of food in the afternoon, and at dusk they collected again around bonfires, positively upbeat if they had a joint or a poorboy of wine to pass around, all memory of the sprinklers apparently banished from their heads.

Santa Monica had the effervescent mood of a seaside resort. A long pier functioned as a boardwalk, and there you could ride a carousel, toss a softball at weighted milk bottles, or eat homemade potato chips from a greasy bag. After dark, a stroll on the pier was like a journey back to an age of uncomplicated pleasures, when soldiers kissed girls against the trees, and victory was eternal.

The fancy waterfront hotels and restaurants on Ocean Avenue had big glass windows that looked out at the surf and reflected the rippling breakers. The Pacific was the ultimate symbol of sanity for Angelenos, a final refuge for their overheated brains. Everybody longed to be close to it, to merge with it and possess a tiny piece of it as a good-luck charm. It worked against the terrors of the land—

against the hazardous air and the random shootings—cleansing, invigorating, and assisting in the process of forgetting.

A swim in the Pacific took on aspects of the ceremonial. Swimmers turned their backs on the ghost ships of the Puritans and instead looked west toward the mysteries of Asia, toward the future. We dipped into a timeless flow and made a spiritual connection. Yes, the ocean was our benefactor. Even the pedestrians on the boulevard had a strange buoyancy to their steps, as if friendly underground waves were massaging the subsoil to provide a cushion for their tired feet.

AROUND THE CORNER FROM THE SOVEREIGN, Pat Gigliotti, an old friend of mine, was enjoying the sort of big life that everybody hoped to have when they took a chance on California. He and his wife, Judy, and their six children lived not far from the ocean in a fine, three-story house that had a swimming pool in the backyard, and also a paddle tennis court and a wood-burning brick oven where pizzas as authentic as any in Naples were cooked of a summer evening.

The Gigliottis were well within the Hollywood aura. Judy had two half sisters, Daryl and Page Hannah, who were actresses, and some of the children had worked as extras in their aunts' films. Other movie and TV stars owned houses on their block, but the neighborhood was not so much flashy as substantial and family-oriented. Its glamorous elements were held in a rough balance with its mundane ones.

Pat Gigliotti had grown up in a blue-collar Italian family in Kansas City. When we had met twenty years ago, he was managing Cody's Books in Berkeley and wore a beard and longish hair and liked to foment the impending leftist revolution and discuss radical politics with his customers while chainsmoking cigarettes. He had a nervous intensity and the romantic good looks of a doomed Sicilian anarchist.

Now Pat did something called land assembly for Jupiter Realty and put together tracts to be developed in Los Angeles. The company

was huge, based in Chicago, and operated by Judy's father. Instead
of blue jeans, Pat dressed in Ralph Lauren suits and drove to his
downtown office in a white BMW convertible. He had not touched
a cigarette in years, ran six miles on the beach every day, and sometimes spoke favorably of the Republicans.

Like the rest of us in California, he had been transformed. What
he really wanted to do was to write or produce movies.

I had never been to the house in Santa Monica before, so on the
first night I came over for dinner, Pat gave me a tour. The place
was a fixer-upper when they'd bought it, he said. The previous owners
were foreigners with an extended family, and they'd done some
cooking over the fireplace and had stored meat and vegetables in the
closets and, in general, had left the house in a shambles. The Gigliottis
were able to steal it for just under a million dollars.

When I heard those words, *a million dollars,* I felt a shock run
through me, but then I remembered where I was, and I imagined
how much John Landis must have spent on his seven-thousand-
square-foot home and realized that a million dollars was not a mean-
ingful figure in postapocalyptic L.A. Money was everywhere in the
city, miles of money, money dropping from the clouds.

I enjoyed the sensation of being in a real home for a change.
The Gigliottis' place was comfortable, roomy, and unostentatious,
and a guest didn't have to worry about spilling some wine on the
furniture or knocking over a Ming vase. They couldn't have had a
Ming vase even if they'd wanted one, really, not with so many children
dashing around.

The energy of the kids throbbed through the house. The oldest
child, Aaron, was a senior at Santa Monica High, a public school,
and occupied a teenage province of his own, but there were two
preteen boys, Noah and Gabriel, and a pair of twin girls, Katie and
Annie, who put out enough electricity to keep everybody on their
toes. The kids were interested in normal pursuits. The boys liked
sports and rock music, while the girls were fond of horses and dolls.

They all pitched in to help look after their youngest sibling, Michael, who was three and had temper tantrums, his clenched face streaming tears beneath a frame of cherubic blond curls out of a Renaissance painting.

Aaron stopped by the kitchen that evening on his way to an ill-defined somewhere. He was a sweet-natured youth, a little baffled about his future and acting out his confusion in not-so-subtle ways that gave his father indigestion. Pat was busy concocting a pizza from cheese and sun-dried tomatoes, and he asked Aaron to name for me some of the stars who had children at Crossroads School, where Noah went.

"Cher," Aaron said dutifully, weary of having a dad and of having to carry him around on his back like a forty-pound homunculus. "Gary Busey, Harvey Korman. Mel Brooks."

Pat was not starstruck or shallow, but he had the same tireless appetite for Hollywood gossip as everybody in town. He saw it as the true currency of Los Angeles and was both fascinated and repelled by it. The very best gossip combined sex and real estate, but a story about sex or real estate alone still counted, and Pat got to talking about a house—the mother of all houses—that Aaron Spelling, the TV impresario, was building, a behemoth of approximately 56,500 square feet in Holmby Hills.

John Landis must feel virtuous, I figured. Here before us was the crutch that supported the shamelessness of L.A. Somebody would always be more outrageous and recklessly spendthrift than you, would seduce more women or marry more men, would surpass you in terms of wretched excess and relieve you of the burden of thinking that things could ever have been otherwise.

There was another Aaron Spelling story in Pat's repertoire. It had to do with a visit that Pat had made to a friend in Malibu, where Spelling had a beach house. While out for a walk, he had come across some exotic shells in the sand, delicate and multihued like the shells from a tropical isle, and he had picked up a few to show to his friend.

"Those are Aaron Spelling's," the friend had said. "Somebody buys them for him at a specialty shop. He has a daughter who's into shells, so they hide them for her to find."

The entire Gigliotti brood were summoned to the table for dinner. We ate our pizza and a salad of exotic lettuces, and I saw how very far from Levittown I was, as far as Pat was from a tough Italian block in Kansas City.

Both Pat and Judy were brought up by caring parents, and they were caring parents in turn and had put together that unusual thing, a reasonably happy family. They had problems, naturally, but they were not at the mercy of them. They seemed forever fixed at a perfect point in time—fit, dark-haired, slender, attractive—and were supple enough in the bargain to handle the arduous demands of raising their children. Such lives did not exist when I was a boy on Long Island, I thought, California lives that were as charmed and golden and yet as fragile and transitory as any other human creation.

BARRY YOURGRAU, ANOTHER FRIEND OF MINE, turned up in Santa Monica, staying at a motel on Ocean Park to do some work for an L.A. magazine. Yourgrau wrote surreal, funny, wonderfully cadenced stories, sometimes only a page or two long, and had started performing them in cafés and in theaters. That had led him into acting, real acting, and he had just completed his first part in a major Hollywood movie, *Fat Man and Little Boy,* and was waiting out the weeks before its release to see if he'd be transformed.

Yourgrau was South African by birth. He had gone to high school in Denver, where his father, a theoretical physicist, had worked. It was a quirk of fate that he had played the part of Edward Teller in his first featured role.

He lived mostly in New York now and came to California only to read and perform. He mistrusted California—Los Angeles, that is—as many New Yorkers did, but he still swooned over the surf, the weather, and the physical beauty. California was too good to be true, he felt, so he would always return to his apartment in Manhattan, a city of stone and broken glass whose tactility was never in doubt.

Yet California was slowly getting to him, undermining his resolve. He'd made friends on the Coast and had done a scene with Paul Newman. He had even fallen in love with a young painter, but the romance had bottomed out, and its aftermath and the tension over his movie debut had left him in a jittery, self-reflective state.

We arranged to take an evening walk on the beach. When I arrived, Yourgrau was in the motel office agitatedly complaining to a swarthy man behind the desk, who seemed to have just awakened from a glacial sleep and dressed himself in a hurry.

"No, I did not bring them in with me," Yourgrau was saying in a dramatic way. "Somebody must have had a dog in that room."

"We don't have fleas here," the swarthy man said, in defense.

Yourgrau plucked a tiny something from his forearm and put it on the desk.

"Do you see that?" he asked, pointing. "It's a flea. Let's have no more of this. I want another room."

I helped him transfer his bags, and then we took our walk. Evening was slowly bleeding into night. Stars shone above the black Pacific, and along the tide line there were phosphorescent glimmers, luminescent charges in the foam. A half-moon was suspended above the palms. You couldn't have wanted a more romantic setting, but it only accentuated Yourgrau's heartache.

He was obsessed about breaking up with the young painter, heaping all the blame on himself. If only he'd listened to her, if only he hadn't been so arrogant—I knew the litany well, being a world-class denier and having recited it myself.

We talked about love and writing and acting. We talked about Paul Newman. I was as venal as the rest when it came to gossip about the stars. I kept hoping that Aunt Daryl Hannah would show up at the Gigliottis someday while I was there and decide that she'd had quite enough of John Kennedy, Jr., and was really interested in a road-weary, middle-aged writer six inches shorter than she.

Yourgrau scratched at his flea bites now and then. He stopped by a shuttered concessions stand to use a phone and check his messages. Maybe the painter had called, maybe there would be some word from his agent.

"I am nothing without my answering machine," he said, with full ironic intent.

Something was shuffling about in the dark by the stand, making strange noises, so I backed away. An animal, I thought, maybe a dog, but no—it was a homeless man camped in a niche. He was bundled in a blanket, but he shed it to reveal a T-shirt from UCLA Medical Center. His face was tanned to an umber color, and his eyes were squinty little beads. An amulet of some sort hung around his neck, but I didn't like to think what might be in it.

"If you give me a dollar," he challenged me, "I'll recite you a poem."

I gave him a dollar. It seemed the wise thing to do. He recited a poem for me about man's first landing on the moon, one that he'd written himself. The gist of it was that human beings had no business in outer space when they had already fucked up so badly on earth.

"That was good," I complimented him. There we were, three poets under a half-moon.

He shrugged it off. "I'm a second-generation poet and a third-generation artist," he said. "Give me another dollar, and I'll recite the story of my life."

I gave him another dollar.

"My name is Olivero," he began. "When I was in my teens, my father put me out in the desert with a buck knife and sixteen ounces of water. Thank God for that knife, because the water"—he gestured at an empty Evian bottle in his hovel—"well, it didn't last long. I survived on cactus and cactus moisture. And once God saw that I could make it, He took care of me."

Olivero wiped his mouth on his forearm and skipped ahead in time without a segue.

"Well, I was walking around Santa Monica one night not looking for trouble or anything, and a guy was passing by, and I said to him this perfectly innocent remark, like 'How's it going, pal?,' and he reached out and stuck a knife in my neck. And wouldn't you know it? With my luck, he hit an artery. I was bleeding like a faucet. I must have lost seventy-five percent of the blood in my body. But the doctors did a good job."

He stepped closer to show me a jagged scar that ran from below his chin almost to his clavicle.

"They sewed me up, and I can hear everything fine."

"You can hear everything fine?"

"Yes. Give me a dollar, and I'll recite a poem for you."

I was out of dollars, though, and Yourgrau had finished with the phone. No important messages.

"Okay!" Olivero yelled as we walked away. "I forgive you! You can come back tomorrow for the poem!"

A California of the brokenhearted, a California of the deranged. . . .

AN IMMENSE SUPPORT STAFF OF WORKERS descended on the wealthy districts of Santa Monica every day but Sunday to prop up lifestyles and do the menial chores. The workers were unobtrusive and skilled at the art of being invisible. Pool boys skimmed leaves from pools, au pairs delivered children to summer camps, maids did the laundry and the housecleaning, and gardeners did the gardening. You heard the hiss of sprinklers and the clack of pruning shears.

Sometimes the gardeners were Japanese, but more often they were Mexican. They answered questions with a smile. The maids were Mexican, too, or Central American. Their English was better because they studied while they worked, learning from TV. Many maids were devoted to cartoons because the characters used simple sentences and were easy to understand. It was another curious aspect of life in Los Angeles that so many domestics had been instructed in their new language by Bugs Bunny or the Smurfs.

There were moments around Los Angeles when it seemed that Hispanics must be doing every scrap of labor, legally or illegally. The city might collapse in a heap without them. They were like the turtles and the elephants who held up the world in Indian mythology. They never lived where they worked but commuted instead from downtown apartments, far-flung suburbs, or the *barrio* of East Los Angeles.

Their jobs were not always onerous or underpaid. The Gigliottis' Salvadorena housekeeper drove to work in a new Bronco and had saved enough money for a house in Pacoima, but other domestics had to rely on public transport and were probably not much better off than the men who stood on traffic islands selling bags of oranges.

I rode a bus from Santa Monica to the *barrio* one afternoon with some maids who were going home. It took about an hour, but the trip felt much longer because of the heat, the crowding, and the diesel fumes. As the ocean disappeared from view, the sky lost its idyllic marine blue and grew dingy and impervious to light. When the bus crossed the old bed of the Los Angeles River, now a concrete flood-control channel, toward Boyle Heights, the look of the city turned industrial. The landscape offered no comfort. It made you rest your head against the seatback like the maids did, and close your eyes and try to sleep.

In East Los Angeles, the main streets were dense with businesses packed into storefronts. Many things were going on at once—an overwhelming rush of the energy that was restrained or repressed in the white world came bursting forth in torrents. Colors burned. Spanish was the *lingua franca,* a melodious burble, a stream.

My Anglo face stood out on the streets. It was as if I'd journeyed to another country rather than just taking a bus ride across town. Elderly women in lace mantillas, vendors of melon slices, roadside taco trucks, warm tamales, stores dealing in botanicos and votive candles, an impressive Catholic church in the midst of poverty—East

L.A. was Mexico picked up and transplanted, as vibrant and alive, driven by the same forces.

I walked down residential blocks. The playgrounds and corners swarmed with activity, with flirting boys and girls, teenagers courting, and with older guys in their twenties and thirties, the gang veterans who were the true keepers of the flame. Graffiti swirled across walls in declarations of turf and swells of boastful poetry, and music blared from powerful stereos in low-riding Nissan trucks, a pulsing, all-encompassing beat.

Everywhere I could feel the weight of the neighborhood, the press of its history. It offered sustenance, surely, but it could also be a noose. How to escape, to break the cycle? The dropout rate among high-school students in Los Angeles County was 39 percent, but among Hispanic children it ran much higher, almost to 50 percent.

So in the morning the buses would roll, off to Santa Monica, Brentwood, Bel-Air, and Beverly Hills.

CHAPTER 21

FROM HIS PERCH in a fiber-glass lifeguard tower, Captain Don Rohrer had an unobstructed view of Santa Monica Beach, the most popular and crowded beach in Greater Los Angeles. He could see the kids buried in sand and the babes basting in coconut oil, the muscle boys and the bearded swamis and the teenage gangsters smoking reefer, each a potential victim of the swirling tide.

Here, at the beach, an abiding part of archetypal California was reinvented faithfully every day in ritual applications of tanning butters and unspoken acts of communion. On such a beach, Gidget (short for "girl-midget") had romped, countless ingenues had posed in bikinis, and many a tourist had gone totally brainless in the seductive undertow, adrift in a vision of salt, sex, and sunshine.

You could almost hear Brian Wilson singing:

Well, East Coast girls are hip
I really dig the clothes they wear
And the Southern girls with the way they talk
They knock me out when I'm down there.
The Midwest farmers' daughters really make you feel all right
And the Northern girls with the way they kiss

They keep their boyfriends warm at night.
I wish they all could be California
I wish they all could be California
I wish they all could be California girls.

Captain Rohrer was a mid-life lifeguard of fifty-seven. "You have to grow older," he liked to say, "but you don't have to grow up." He had a cheerful, boyish air and the broad shoulders and chest of a dedicated swimmer. His hair was thinning, and his forehead was speckled with the benign skin cancers that were an occupational hazard, flaws to be scraped away by the dermatologist's scalpel.

The beach and Captain Rohrer were wed. His father had worked as a lifeguard in the 1920s, and now he'd been one, too, for forty-one years. He had come of age in Venice and Playa Del Ray in the generous days when surfers were still polite to each other, and you could count on bringing home all the abalone you wanted for dinner.

Implements of the captain's trade were spread around the tower. He had a rescue can that he tossed to victims, so that they'd hold onto it rather than grab at his arms and maybe drown him. He had a bullhorn, sunglasses, a bottle of sunscreen, and a first-aid kit. He had a good pair of binoculars, and he used them to scan the beach and give me an instant readout on the surf.

"It's an average day for August," he said. "We've got a riptide and two- to three-foot waves."

He did a rough tally of the crowd and of the swimmers in the water. A lifeguard had to be aware of such things because the three miles or so of beach were much more dangerous than they appeared to be. The Santa Monica station alone had made about two thousand rescues the previous year. The total for the twenty-three beaches in Los Angeles County was about eleven thousand rescues. The old image of a lifeguard as a handsome, unambitious stud with zinc oxide on his nose used to be valid, Captain Rohrer confirmed, but it wasn't anymore. The job involved real work.

Candidates had to graduate from a six-day rookie school in Los

Angeles, for instance. To be admitted to it, they had to pass an
entrance exam designed to test their swimming skills. At the school,
they were rated on their speed in the water, their mastery of Red
Cross procedures, and their character. If they were accepted as a
lifeguard, they had to keep in training. The ten permanent men and
women on the Santa Monica crew—there were a hundred or so part-
timers—had to exercise for at least a half-hour per day and undergo
periodic cardiovascular testing.

Anybody who rose to the rank of captain could earn between
fifty and sixty thousand dollars a year.

The modern lifeguard had to be a pro, said Captain Rohrer.
Budgetary constraints meant that the crews were often shorthanded.
Six out of ten bathers who were pulled from the ocean were drunk
or stoned or both, and that made them slippery, pumped up, and
tough to handle. The temptation to let them sink must be ever near,
I thought.

Drunks liked to leap off the pier, as well, and rescuing them
could be gnarly because of the sharp-edged barnacles and mussels
clinging to the pier's stanchions. Often a lifeguard was reduced to
being a beach cop, as a ranger was a wilderness cop, breaking up
fights and clamping on the handcuffs when the real police did not
arrive in time.

Captain Rohrer was also a clearinghouse for information. Certain
familiar questions swarmed as commonly as jellyfish in the heads of
visitors, such as:

"Is it legal to take the kelp from the ocean?"

"Have you seen my little boy?"

"Do you have something for sunburn?"

"When do the grunion run?"

"Are there really any grunion?"

Then there was the business about sharks. It was true that sharks
infested the waters off Santa Monica, but nobody had produced any
evidence to confirm a shark attack in the past fifty years. Still, the
tales of mayhem persisted. Every summer, without fail, a swimmer

claimed to have been almost torn apart by a blue shark or a basking shark that only he or she had seen. As proof of a shark's existence, people surrendered teeth and jaws that they'd bought in Mexico. While patrolling in helicopters, officers of the LAPD had mistaken dolphins for sharks once or twice, contributing to the mania.

"A copter guy wouldn't know a shark if it bit him in the ass," Captain Rohrer said, kidding around.

We took a drive on the beach in the captain's four-wheel Nissan Pathfinder. Santa Monica Bay looked so enticing that you'd never guess that it was polluted. Sewage and chemical waste poured into it from storm drains after harsh winter storms, and some locals avoided the water completely. In the wake of a serious rain, lifeguards posted warning signs along the beach, and they were not supposed to go into the ocean, except to make a rescue, until two days had passed.

Most Angelenos remained unintimidated, though. On a holiday weekend like the Fourth of July, as many as a half-million sunseekers would stake out their own little paradises in Santa Monica. On an ordinary August weekday, the county beaches would attract about 1.5 million visitors in all. The beach numbers in Los Angeles County could be staggering—$19 million in annual operating costs, about 2,000 pounds of trash hauled from Santa Monica each year, and 6,493 seagulls counted between Santa Monica and Playa Del Rey in a recent survey.

Captain Rohrer observed an intrepid lad paddling into the water on a surfboard. The scene reminded him of his own youth, back when a surfer never had to fight for a wave, when there were always enough waves to go around. If you heard that Palos Verdes Cove or Point Dume or Malibu was busy, he said, that meant fifteen guys, maximum. To beat the crush, all you had to do was put your board in your woody and head farther up or down the coast, into uncharted territory. In the old days, you could still catch breakers as monstrous as those in Waikiki, waves fourteen or fifteen feet high.

I thought, *Gold, trees, fish, land, even waves!*

It was clear that the captain was tied to the ocean in a special way. For him, the coastline was a living, breathing entity. He knew its specifics as a lover knows the beloved, every dimple and mole. He told me that the sand we were driving on was not simply beach sand but rather a mixture that included dredging material and also dune sand that had drifted to Santa Monica from elsewhere. Such subtle alterations affected the quality of the surfing. Dune sand was coarser than beach sand, for example, and it caused a tighter break.

The beach at Santa Monica was relatively stable now, and the waves tended to be long, rolling, and fairly gentle. In parts of the adjacent beach in Venice, by contrast, the berm was much steeper, and the surf still crashed and ripped. In the suck of the cycle, novice riders could break their necks and their backs. Real surfing was not for amateurs, the captain said.

IN THE ANNALS OF SURFING, the name of Captain James Cook came up frequently. He had sketched one of the earliest reports of Polynesians riding their boards at Oahu Beach in Hawaii, in 1778. The boards were probably made from koa wood, the same material that was used for royal canoes. *Koa* meant brave or fearless.

To prepare a board, craftsmen would select a koa tree and put a fish by it as an offering. Once the tree was uprooted, the fish was dropped into the resulting hole. Next, the tree was chipped and shaped with an adze before being carried to a canoe house, where it was worked over with coral, polished with stones, stained, and sealed with the oil of kikui nuts.

Every board had an elegance, the warm and rosy glow of patient enterprise. Their design was supremely efficient. The boards were of two basic types, *alaia* and *olo*. *Alaias* were functional and intended for day-to-day surfing. They were from three to twelve feet long— the smaller lengths were for children and for bodysurfing—and between eleven and twenty inches wide. *Olos* were what surfers now call "guns," or "Rhino Chasers," very big boards for the biggest waves. Only chiefs got to ride them.

Duke Kahanamoku, a surfing pioneer from Hawaii, once recounted for *Surfer* magazine what it had felt like to catch a killer wave twenty-five or thirty feet high, at Waikiki in the 1920s. Hawaiians seldom used boards then, preferring to bodysurf, but Kahanamoku couldn't resist paddling a sixteen-foot-long gun to a spot known as Castles due to the shape of its breakers.

"I looked at those doggone waves, and said, 'Boy, these are really top waves,' " Duke explained. "Then I said, 'I'm going to take one whether I like it or not.' I had to go."

He caught a wave and stayed with it giddily for a couple of hundred yards before his board hit the wave edge and dumped him into the suds. "That was the end of my run," he continued. "Otherwise ... I would have gone right into Happy Steiner's Waikiki Tavern!"

Kahanamoku became an acclaimed Olympic swimmer at Stockholm in 1912 and later gave some surfing demonstrations in Atlantic City. On the West Coast, George Freeth, a Hawaiian-American in the hire of Henry Huntington, brought his board to Redondo Beach in 1907 to dazzle the public while promoting Huntington's real estate ventures.

Yet surfing's appeal remained limited. The sport looked dangerous, and the gear was cumbersome. Most boards were homemade, fashioned from redwood or balsa blanks, or a blank combining both materials. A redwood gun in the 1930s could be four inches thick and might weigh sixty-five pounds.

Surfing only took off in southern California in the postwar era. Techno-surfers began turning out lighter, cheaper boards in fiber glass and foam, and manufacturers adapted their methods. The new boards lost the sheen of wood lovingly worked and acquired instead a plastic neon brilliance that echoed the newness of L.A., its Day-Glo reds and its canary yellows, the colors of its strip malls and its custom cars.

The stereotype of the surfer as a meditative loner or outsider fated to pursue eternally the perfect wave also changed as the sport was suburbanized. Its styles and its attitudes were studied, packaged, and marketed to the youth of America in the form of movies, records, and clothing.

Gidget, the first surfing picture, was based on a doting bestseller that Frederick Kohner had written about his daughter. Columbia released it in 1959. Sandra Dee came across as Doris Day reformulated for teens, precisely as blond and virginal and equally incapable of anything more sexual than a chaste kiss. To deflower Gidget would be akin to dumping crude oil into the Pacific. Sealed in her bubble of purity, she went Hawaiian and dabbled in hot rods.

The real star of all beach movies was southern California, anyway. Frankie Avalon in a bathing suit only made a viewer aware of what a troubled place Philadelphia must be, but the Kodachrome surf behind him served as a five-star advertisement for L.A.

The Beach Boys were also responsible for selling surfing and beach culture to their peers nationwide. Brian, Carl, and Dennis Wilson, the teens at the group's core, were second-generation Californians. Their grandfather Bud, a plumber and a semipro baseball player, had brought the family to the tracts of Los Angeles in the 1920s and had gone to work in the Mojave Desert, where he laid pipe for the California Aqueduct. His son, Murry, was a hot-tempered, abusive man who instilled a keen interest in music in his kids.

Brian was the Wilsons' pride, a prodigy who could hum "The Marines' Hymn" as an infant and carry a tune when he was three. He sang in school pageants and at church and composed melodies on the family piano. He had an ear for harmony and an undying affection for the way the Four Freshmen employed it. For his sixteenth birthday, he received a tape recorder that enabled him to construct the multilayered, multivoice songs that would become his trademark.

There were as many as thirty thousand surfers plying the seventy-six miles of coastline in the county on a summer weekend in the 1960s. Every town had its own variant of a grungy surfer band like the Wilsons, who called themselves The Pendletones at first and recorded "Surfin'" in 1961.

Brian Wilson had never been surfing—he would never *go* surfing—so it was left to Dennis, who owned a board, to interpret the concept to the guys at Candix Records, an independent label. The company's distributor balked at the group's name, though, and suggested such alternatives to The Pendletones as The Lifeguards or the Beach Bums before hitting on the Beach Boys.

That December, "Surfin'" (backed with "Luau") came out on X Records, a Candix subsidiary, and sold fifty thousand copies while climbing to the number seventy-five slot on the *Billboard* chart, paving the way for "Surfer Girl," "Surfin' Safari," and the amazing "Surfin' USA," a song that tied together teens across the country in a Pacific Coast fantasy.

Brian Wilson sang, *"If everybody had an ocean . . ."*

Surfing spawned a style to go with the movies and the records. The baggy shorts and the cut-off jeans of the Ur-surfers were gradually replaced by designer togs—swimsuits in the same neon colors as the boards, and casual, off-the-water wear that ran to wrinkled Bermudas in outrageous plaids, T-shirts with the logo of a bar or a surfing manufacturer, and drawstring cotton trousers as loose-fitting as somebody else's pajamas.

Surfing, finally, was awesome. When you surfed, truly *surfed,* you were one with all creation. In the ocean, all God's creatures were equal, the starfish, the crabs, the eels, the manta rays, the grunions—especially the grunions, man—the kelp, the anemones, those little things that you could see but not identify, all equal. Astride your board you were transformed into a Surfrider, an environmentalist out to save the planet, right here in California.

•　　•　　•

BEACH-BUM DAYS. I gave it a whirl, trading in my jeans for some old khakis, donning a short-sleeved cotton shirt patterned with bogus tropical flowers, and going around sockless in a scuffed pair of loafers. Shaving became a nuisance, so I let a graying stubble grow on my chin—that badge of indolence that B actors cultivate between roles—remembering Jim Hutton and other deceased stars of infrequent romantic comedies. I felt purposeless, and it did not feel bad.

The Pacific Coast Highway ran along the ocean's tracery beneath a sky pulsing with cormorants and pelicans, my road to everywhere and nowhere that caused me to take up the standard cry, "I love L.A.!"

At Surfrider Beach in Malibu, the waves were flat of an afternoon, but many surfers were trying to catch one anyhow to win the favor of some nonchalant, gum-popping sweeties in Jimmy Z suits. The coastal stretch of Malibu, some twenty-two miles, had been Chumash land until it was deeded to a soldier serving with the expeditionary force of Juan Bautista de Anza in the 1770s. In the twentieth century, the land was worked as a ranch and then sold to subdividers in 1941, who offered it in parcels to members of the movie colony.

Malibu Colony was still a special preserve, home to famous entertainers who were beyond such mortal concerns as money or ambition, the Johnny Carsons and the Larry Hagmans now cooling it on the golf links or on the tennis courts. Here, too, the dealmakers had houses, those whose power was so unlimited that an agent would actually leave the purview of Century City to take a meeting with them on the sand.

Malibu also had a stratum of demi-stars and stars on the wane, actors perilously close to devolving to the rank of mere celebrities, the Ali MacGraws and the Martin Sheens who'd been smart enough or lucky enough to parlay their brief moment in the limelight into a prime chunk of beach real estate.

Celebrities did not live in the Colony or anywhere in Malibu. They lived elsewhere—in San Fernando Valley, say. Their TV series were gone from syndication, and the only work that they could find was as guests on witless game shows or as accomplices to such events as the opening of a new car wash in Encino.

In Malibu, I sensed a world-weariness edging toward absolute repose. Any show of energy, except in sports or in sex, might be regarded as bad form. The town was as inbred and status-conscious as any society town in Connecticut. The beautiful people were highly visible, but I also saw the ones whose beauty was fading, sad-eyed men and women aging awkwardly and beginning to agonize over the possible gains and pitfalls of cosmetic surgery.

Special rites were obeyed in town. The owner of the only theater, a second-run house, had to be careful never to play one resident's movie longer than another's.

After a good dinner at a local restaurant, I thanked the waitress, who said, "This is Ali MacGraw's place," as if the participation of a demi-star guaranteed every customer superior food.

And in the weekly *Malibu Times* there were always items to puzzle over:

Angie Best, 34, former wife of internationally famous British ex-soccer star George Best, the personal trainer of Cher, was married this weekend in Malibu to Terry Amoud of San Jose, owner of a gym and a training facility.

Other days I lounged around in Venice, where my brother had once lived. Often I had flown down from San Francisco to stay at his apartment near the beach in the early 1970s. His upstairs neighbors were a chiropractor who adored Clint Eastwood films and a woman who kept a mastiff as a pet. Sometimes she'd put on a bikini and take the mastiff for a walk, delivering the ultimate in mixed messages.

In little cottages down the block, women who resembled the post-Hitchcock Kim Novak grew roses and reminisced about lovers past. One afternoon, we tossed some horseshoes with a grizzled old bugger who claimed to be Tom Mix's nephew. Were we in California yet, or what?

Venice was a quaint dream that Abbot Kinney, heir to a tobacco fortune, had indulged. Kinney, an insomniac, had left the Midwest for his health. He was a freethinker, who founded two public libraries, published a book about sex (*Tasks by Twilight,* 1893), and planted some of the first eucalyptus trees in the state. In July of 1905, he opened his new real estate development, Venice-by-the-Sea, on 160 acres of tidal flats. It had canals, gondolas imported from Italy, and villas in the grand manner. Sarah Bernhardt did *Camille* on the pier, but the crowds turned out for the Ship Cafe, a replica of one of Cabrillo's caravels that stood on pilings.

As a planned community, Venice never caught on. The canals got swampy and stank. The pier burned down and had to be rebuilt. When oil was discovered on the flats in the 1920s, the last glimpses of faux European splendor were lost to rigs and derricks.

A stroll on Ocean Front Walk in Venice was like being spliced into the world's longest dolly shot. So many films, TV shows, and commercials had employed the boardwalk for color that at least half of the people were there to perform.

One morning, I saw an Academy Award performance on the basketball courts. A pint-size white woman in a leopard-skin bikini, the only female in the game, ran around with terrific intensity, shouting to her teammates for the ball, even though they ignored her.

Defense was her strong suit. She hounded the black man she was guarding, pressing close and brushing him with her fingers and sometimes with her breasts. He didn't know what to do. He looked furious, as if he wanted to drive to the hoop and smash her, but propriety held him back—or maybe it was the thought that he might bump into her again somewhere, in another lifetime, and she'd recall his knuckly biceps and his ridged abdominals and take from the memory another meaning.

A black teenage girl who sat next to me in the bleachers said to her friend, "I'd put my foot in her face and teach her a lesson."

Her friend scowled. "Who does that girl think she is, anyhow? A Detroit Piston?"

IN SANTA MONICA, I became obsessed with Fred Sands, a realtor whose signs were fixed to skyscrapers and exclusive condominiums, and outside mansions and estates in all the choiciest districts of the city. Wherever I drove the signs seemed to be waiting for me, and I fell into a habit of playing a game with myself and seeing how long I could go before I came upon another one, but it was never very long. Fred Sands had always been there first to nail down the turf.

Beach sand, shifting sands, the sands of time. In my freeway reveries, Fred Sands appeared to me as the Realtor King who controlled the dynamo churning in the gut of Los Angeles, somebody who possessed esoteric knowledge about California on a par with Derrel Ridenour, Jr., the Mini-Storage King of the San Joaquin.

But unlike Derrel Ridenour, Jr., Fred Sands agreed through his publicist to meet with me in a few days. Sands was no shrinking violet. The publicist sent me a packet of materials about him, and I discovered that he was extremely successful, among the top five residential realtors in the country. His company was the largest one-owner real estate firm in the state.

In photographs, Fred Sands seemed deceptively bland. He cultivated the mild-mannered look of a harmless accountant, dressing in dark, conservatively cut suits and ties of no special flare. One photo in the packet showed him posed next to George Bush, both of them smiling broadly over some Republican intimacy or other.

When it came to selling real estate, Fred Sands had a philosophy, of course: *Use creativity.* He believed that there was no such thing as an ordinary house—every house was extraordinary to the right buyer. As an example, he liked to cite a tiny, one-bedroom dwelling without a garage. Most realtors would blink at the prospect of listing it, but the place was really perfect for a midget who rode a motor scooter!

Fred Sands thought that creativity in sales was rooted in the ability to listen to a customer. He must be a good listener, I thought, because he'd built his company from the ground up, and now he had a grand beach house in Malibu. He owned a radio station and had been a real estate consultant to the syndicated TV show "Lifestyles of the Rich and Famous."

As I read on, I felt that we were fated to meet, and that from the meeting would emerge the special understanding about Los Angeles that I'd been seeking.

SUMMER WAS IN FULL SWING at the Gigliottis' extraordinary house. The twins were going to a day camp in Malibu, where they rode horses and go-carts. Noah and Gabriel had attended a baseball camp at Pepperdine University and were about to start at a basketball camp under the tutelage of John Wooden, the former coach at UCLA. Aaron had a job as a camp counselor and seemed almost to be liking it, getting out of bed for work with a minimum of fuss.

Little Michael didn't go to any camp at all. Instead, he palled around with his mother or with his Aunt Page, who was sweet on him and sometimes brought him along when she was out with her boyfriend, Lou Adler. They were out together on the Saturday afternoon I came by to watch a boxing match on TV with Pat.

Pat was still logging in his hours at Jupiter Realty and putting in his miles on the beach, but he'd have a break soon when the family went to Italy for their annual vacation at the end of the month.

It occurred to me while we were watching a couple of featherweights duke it out that Pat might know Fred Sands, but he didn't. His interest in real estate was minimal. It was just a place where he'd alighted for a time and from which he would eventually move on. Often he wished that he could be back behind a counter in a bookstore reading Henry Miller or talking to the customers.

He told me that he'd just gone through a bad scene trying to acquire a downtown parcel to include in a development scheme. The owner had liked the deal. Then he hadn't liked the deal. Then he got paranoid, began to queer the deal, and sold the parcel to a satellite company in Sylvester Stallone's empire.

"Stallone's people play hardball," Pat said reflectively. "You know who's good to do business with? Tom Selleck. He and his brother put together shopping malls."

So, I thought, in Los Angeles the stars command the earth even as they manipulate the heavens.

Although Pat was a realtor by default, he kept up with the action. Everybody in town might be railing about the Japanese, he said, but that was misguided. The Germans and the Canadians controlled more of the city. The Japanese were just better at offending people. They could be as arrogant as Americans. Sometimes when they took over a building, they lost tenants through their high-handedness.

Pat believed that the Japanese were buying up all the Adidas's Rod Laver-model tennis shoes in town, because they hated Koreans and Lavers were made in Europe, not in Korea. Some Japanese businessmen didn't like talking to Pat's secretary, who was black. Symbols of status were extremely important to them, he said—so American! They, too, were excited by flash and movie stars.

Once, Pat had led a party of Japanese executives through a building that he wanted to rent to them. He had listed its advantages to no avail. Then, absently, he mentioned that John Wayne had died in the famous cancer hospital across the street.

The executives had exclaimed, "Ah! John Wayne!" and had closed the deal on the spot.

Gabriel dashed into the room as brashly as his namesake herald and interrupted our conversation. "Dad!" he shouted, in the most imperative voice that he could muster. *"You have got to see Lou's car!"*

In the driveway outside was a car such as none I'd ever seen before, black and sleek and low to the ground, mysterious, elegant, and doubtlessly speedy. It looked like a prototype for a twenty-first-century Batmobile, something with capabilities suited to a superhero. The kids were running around it and whooping.

Pat whispered to me, "It's an Aston-Martin Lagonda."

He figured that it had cost about $200,000. Aston-Martin only manufactured a few of them each year, so the demand far outweighed the supply. There was no guarantee that you could buy one even if you could afford it. As a status symbol, the Lagonda put other automobiles to shame. The other luxury cars around Los Angeles now seemed as common to me as weeds.

The driver, Lou Adler, wore the slyly satisfied look of the proverbial cat who'd swallowed the proverbial canary. He was an L.A. legend, tight in all the right circles. In the great California strike-it-rich sweepstakes, he had rolled the dice and come out a big winner.

Adler had earned his millions doing the record thing and the music thing, managing or producing such groups as Jan and Dean and the Mamas and the Papas. Brian Wilson of the Beach Boys was an old pal. They were so close to each other in the Surfin' Sixties that when Wilson decided to get married, Adler booked a suite for him at The Sands in Las Vegas and piled it to the ceiling with flowers. Brian had even named a dog after Adler, Louie.

There were quips of Adler's that still made the rounds. Somebody had once complained to him, for instance, that Los Angeles lacked seasons.

"Nah, that's not true, man, we have seasons," Adler was rumored to have said. "We've got basketball season and the rest of the year."

The children kept whooping. The sly look on Adler's face never budged an inch. He had a cool beyond cool, an absolute mastery of the offhand stance toward being alive that marked the L.A. elite and could only be gained after decades of grooving and being grooved upon.

When Pat introduced us, I sensed that Adler could answer any question I might ask him, however surreal. I could ask him how things were on Planet Venus, and he'd reply, "They're fine, man. Just fine."

"Hi, Lou," I said, shaking his hand. He had on a slouchy hat covered with dancing musical notes.

"Hi," Lou Adler said.

In a minute or two, Page released Michael with a good-bye kiss, and the happy couple drove off. Pat said to his son, "Where'd you go today, Mikey?"

"To Kareem's," Michael said.

Michael was tired from the outing and on the verge of a tantrum. He fell on the floor inside the house and commenced to wail and bang his fists. Everybody was used to the tantrums and inclined to let them run their course, but I was a first-timer and tried to talk the boy down, thinking what a strange California life he had ahead of him, not quite four years old and already passing the afternoon hanging out with Kareem Abdul-Jabbar.

His tears stopped flowing after a bit, his clenched face relaxed, and he asked to see a video. There were a number of them on a shelf in the den, *Bambi* and *Dumbo* and lots of cartoons. Michael studied each box judiciously before rejecting it. He also rejected *Nightmare on Elm Street*—too scary, even though Aunt Page was in it.

At last, I came to a box with Aunt Daryl's picture on it, all blond serenity, and Michael nodded in approval and settled in for a soothing viewing of the old Cyrano de Bergerac drama that Hollywood had retold as *Roxanne*.

CHAPTER 22

In 1887, Horace Henderson Wilcox, a real estate tyro from Kansas, parceled off a ranch outside Los Angeles, in Cahuenga Valley, to forge a new subdivision that he called Hollywood after a friend's country estate back home. It was to be a saintly, abstemious place where alcohol was forbidden and emigrants from the rural Midwest would not risk the bite of temptation. Any religious group could build a church in Hollywood, Wilcox said, without having to pay for the land.

Cahuenga Valley lay in a frost-free belt of orange groves and barley fields. Truck farmers grew tomatoes, green peppers, and watermelons and sold them at produce markets in the city. A photo taken in 1905 shows Hollywood as a tranquil agricultural village, where a few farmhouses were set well apart from one another in a grid of dirt roads and citrus orchards.

Wilcox apparently did not have an abiding belief in temperance. He'd made a sneaky deal with a French family, the Blondeaus, by selling them a roadhouse in his subdivision on the condition that they not open the doors until after he had died. As soon as the good gray gentleman was in his grave, they set the bottles on the bar and enjoyed a profitable run until their neighbors shut them down with a new prohibition ordinance.

The Blondeaus were forced to lease the premises. They found an eager tenant in the Centaur Film Company of Bayonne, New Jersey. Like most small studios in the East, where the fledgling film industry was located, Centaur wished to be as far as possible from the law—in this case, the operatives of the Edison Company, which held the only legal right to manufacture movies. Under the guise of protecting a patent, the Edison cops were trying to put the competition out of business.

In 1911, Nestor, a Centaur satellite, became the first Hollywood-based studio, but movies were already being shot in other parts of California. Since 1908, the Essenay Company had been pounding out Broncho Billy one-reelers in Niles, not far from Oakland, and would eventually complete 375 episodes. The Bison Company had a movie ranch in Santa Monica, while Biograph rented some property in downtown Los Angeles so that its great director, D. W. Griffith, could winter in the sun.

Sunshine was the key ingredient in enticing most movie people to the West Coast. The Chamber of Commerce in L.A. promised them 350 days of it a year. There were so many cloudless mornings and afternoons that most pictures could be filmed outdoors on the cheap. The sagebrush, the canyons, and the desert lent a new authenticity to the oaters that had previously been shot in the wilds of New Jersey. Industry moguls also took advantage of the immigrant labor around and employed Mexican and Chinese workers to construct sets and sew costumes. The moguls were glad to be close to the border, too, ready to disappear across it at the first whiff of an arrest.

A trip to the Coast in those early years was a pastoral vacation for a movie company. The streets in Cahuenga Valley were often unpaved and stopped dead at the foothills. Coyotes howled at night, and deer ranged freely. Signs on the trolleys in town advised against taking any potshots at rabbits from the rear platform. The only cop in town seldom moved from the intersection of Hollywood and Vine.

As the studios grew, they began to restructure and rearrange the valley to their liking. Their unplanned clutter of office buildings and sound stages went up without regard for either the landscape or their neighbors. They cut down the graceful, old pepper trees on Vine Street because the berries left stains on the hoods of automobiles. Non-native species were imported to replace the trees, eucalyptus from Australia and palms from Hawaii.

The arrogance of the studios knew no bounds. Their pictures kept bursting unapologetically out of the frame, with celluloid cowboys galloping across lawns, jungle beasts wandering by schools, and the debris from car crashes blocking traffic. Movie people themselves were seen as a class apart—theatrical, unsavory, and probably guilty of moral turpitude. On occasion, children from established Hollywood families were warned to stay away from movie children.

The homespun settlers that Wilcox had attracted, farmers and senior citizens devoted to religion, were a literal-minded bunch. They had a basic mistrust of the way a movie blended together illusion and reality. Movies could not be counted on for the facts. Films might be newfangled and entertaining, but they were also powerful, confusing, and intimidating, sometimes making the lives of ordinary folks seem even more unrewarding and lacking in imagination than they truly were.

In his novel *The Day of the Locust,* Nathanael West described the bitterness and hostility of a crowd waiting in line for a movie premiere at a "picture palace" that was modeled on Grauman's Chinese Theater, which had opened in Hollywood in 1927.

All their lives they had slaved at some kind of dull, heavy labor, behind desks and counters, in the fields and at tedious machines of all sorts, saving their pennies and dreaming of the leisure that would be theirs when they had enough. . . . Where else should they go but California, the land of sunshine and oranges?

Once there, they discover that sunshine isn't enough. They get tired of oranges, even of avocado pears and passion fruit. Nothing happens. . . . They watch the waves come in at Venice. There wasn't any ocean where most of them come from, but after you've seen them all. . . .

Their boredom becomes more and more terrible. They realize that they've been tricked and burn with resentment. Every day of their lives they read the newspapers and went to the movies. Both fed them on lynchings, murder, sex crimes, explosions, wrecks, love nests, fires, miracles, revolutions, wars. This daily diet made sophisticates of them. The sun is a joke. Oranges don't titillate their jaded palates.

The city fathers in Los Angeles shared the ambivalent attitude toward movies—an attitude that the world would one day adopt toward their entire city. They praised the studios for spreading gorgeously composed advertisements for the land that they hoped to develop, and then raged at them for their wanton disregard of private property. Whenever they tried to exert more control, the studio heads would threaten to move elsewhere.

Some merchants and manufacturers in L.A. came together to study the situation. They cut quickly to the chase and conveyed to the city that the film industry had about 25,000 employees and added about $5 million a year to the local economy. In most quarters, the bad feelings soon abated.

Hollywood and the movies were synonymous by the 1920s. The studios were bigger, better, and smarter, always ready to put a new spin on their product. Carl Laemmle, who owned the Independent Motion Picture Company, a precursor of Universal Studios, was instrumental in changing the course of the industry by widening the focus of his company's marketing to include the personalities of its actors under contract. He had learned from audiences and exhibitors that some actors generated more applause than others, and that movie fans yearned to know more about their lives off-screen and who they "really" were.

Biograph Studios had a very popular figurehead, Florence Lawrence, who was billed as the Biograph Girl and paid twenty-five dollars a week. Laemmle hired her away for a thousand a week and circulated a phony story to the Saint Louis papers that she'd died in a trolley accident. He followed that by placing a statement in a trade journal that accused his rivals of starting the rumor and denounced them for such low tactics.

No, no, insisted the wounded Laemmle, Florence Lawrence was not dead! To prove it, he dispatched her to Saint Louis with King Baggott, IMP's top male lead, and the two actors caused a mob scene and garnered even more publicity for the studio. In that instant, the star system could be said to have taken flight.

Mary Pickford and Charlie Chaplin were the first big stars in town. They made side bets about who could command the most money. Chaplin's brilliant films had an obvious appeal, but Pickford's popularity was harder to explain. At a time when feminism was on the rise, she seemed to comfort audiences by playing girl-women who were no danger to the sexual or political status quo.

Beneath her contrived innocence, though, she was a demon negotiator. Along with Chaplin, Griffith, and her husband, Douglas Fairbanks, she began a new company, United Artists, in order to grant them all more creative control over their movies, as well as to earn a larger share of the box-office gross.

The creation of Hollywood stars demanded an accelerated effort from the publicity departments at studios. They had to crank out reams of factual, quasi-factual, primarily fabricated, and grossly false releases to exalt the actors in their stables. It became expedient for a star to live on a scale befitting his or her astral stature, above all other mortals, whether or not he or she could afford it—in a Pickfair,

say, the faux Tudor hunting lodge that Fairbanks and Pickford built
in the Hollywood hills.

The first map to the homes of the stars hit the newsstands in
1924. Fans could now conduct their own tour of the kingdom and
judge for themselves how wretched they were by their distance from
the fabled aura. Some people were amused by the tour, but others
returned to their own homes feeling diminished, or fueled by crazy
ambition.

No life could be as fulfilling as a star's life. That was Hollywood's
message, so it made sense that the public applauded whenever a
famous actor took a fall from grace via drink, drugs, or a sexual
tangle. The mores of most Angelenos—and most Americans—were
still those of the middle-western Bible Belt, and a fall confirmed that
there was indeed something sinful afoot in the movies. Even the
beloved Mary Pickford dropped out of the firmament when she dared
to divorce her husband.

The attitude of most people toward Hollywood was firmly set by
then. It amounted to push-pull, or attraction-repulsion, and the movie
industry was quick to recognize this and would milk the antipodes
forever after.

Hollywood had turned into something very different from the
temperance community that Horace Henderson Wilcox had visual-
ized. It had turned into Oz, and it only remained for a pig-tailed
child star, Judy Garland, to consecrate the transformation by uttering
what amounted to both an in-joke and an undeniable truth after she
and her little dog went flying through the sky.

"We're not in Kansas anymore, Toto," Judy said.

AWAY FROM SANTA MONICA and the ocean, the skies were once again
rinsed in iodine. Where Sunset Boulevard began its descent into
Hollywood, I stopped to buy a map of the stars' homes from a twelve-
year-old Mexican boy from the *barrio*. Somebody had picked him up

in the morning and stationed him under a palm tree, and somebody would retrieve him again at night and shell out a miserly commission.

The map cost five dollars, and I could see immediately that I'd been had. It listed the present or *former* homes of a couple hundred movie stars, many of them in the graveyard with poor Wilcox. It even cannibalized the Ur-map of '24 and provided addresses for Chill Wills (17984 Boris Drive, Encino) and John Barrymore (6 Beverly Grove, Beverly Hills). There was an advisory note that stated, "Many Movie Stars prefer to live a secluded (secret) life." You can't be more secluded or secret, I thought, than in your burial plot at Forest Lawn.

I studied the map over a gin and tonic at Musso & Frank's on Hollywood Boulevard. The restaurant was so ancient that the menu, still typeset daily, went in for dishes like corned-beef hash and liver and onions—dishes from the Eocene of cookery, meals that could kill you on the spot. Musso & Frank's had never been a Chasen's or a Brown Derby, but you could ordinarily spot one or two almost recognizable actors in the house. The waiters were old and crusty and had probably served a few crab-stuffed tomatoes to Chill Wills.

On Hollywood Boulevard, tourists were gawking at the sidewalk stars on the Hollywood Walk of Fame. At that moment, they understood themselves to be absolutely in California and nowhere else. They jumped from star to star as though they were on a treasure hunt, ignoring the evangelist who was standing on Nina Foch and handing out salvation tracts.

"Clark Gable!" they cried, just as I had done ages ago. "Marilyn Monroe!"

There were no soda fountains at Hollywood and Vine anymore. I didn't find any agents lurking about or anybody being discovered, not even beauty queens from Tehachapi. As smog was to L.A., so, too, was beauty, omnipresent and virtually inescapable. You needed more than a pretty face to make it in the movies.

It could be hard on the beautiful when their luck or their savings ran out. Sometimes they took to strolling the boulevards and turning tricks, or worked as strippers or in peep shows, or commuted to San

Fernando Valley to perform in the porn videos that were fast becoming another thread in the brocade that defined California for outsiders, elevating mega-boobs and monumental penises into the hallowed ranks of beaches, surfers, and palm trees.

Beauty in Hollywood was just another commodity, really. Anyone could buy it. If the gene pool had cheated you, you could amend things by submitting to the scalpel and the sutures. The cosmetic surgeons around Los Angeles offered a dim sum of alterations big and small.

At a newsstand, I browsed through the ads in a local magazine and saw that hair replacers were as easy to find as auto mechanics. Radial keratotomists were set to adjust your eyesight and rid you of your hideously disfiguring glasses. Dentists of an aesthetic bent had the formula for bonding and whitening your teeth. The Leg Center could heal your varicose veins with sclerotherapy. Did your calves need enlarging or reshaping? Mel Bircoli in Beverly Hills was just a phone call away.

Cellulite removal, breast augmentation or reduction, scar revisions, penile implants, corrective tucks for protruding ears, forehead lifts, skin peels, and collagen injections for suckier lips—the phantasmagoria of options was rich enough to keep the nation's stand-up comics in business for years, and yet there was something touching about the frailty on display. Again, it amounted to a longing for physical perfection that might well be a modern California corollary to the ancient spiritual desire to be cleansed of sins.

Around Los Angeles, a city singularly uncommitted to the hereafter, the body truly was the temple. Corporeal demands had won out over any demands of the spirit, it seemed. Among the believers, a bald pate or a flat chest or chipped teeth or misshapen calves could be an awful stigma. Such flaws paraded in public announced that the maimed person was too poor to get fixed. And if you were poor, you had to be stupid, too, because money was everywhere, miles of money, money dropping from the clouds.

This narcissistic California, this California of tiny salads and bottled waters, a fartless, belchless, striving-to-be-pure California of monied Los Angeles, remained a riddle to me. The excesses were seriously embarrassing, but then I'd hear the voice of a believer in my surgically unenhanced ears.

"What's the harm?" the voice asked. "Why shouldn't people feel a little better about themselves if they can afford to?"

It made me wonder about my hoary, preapocalyptic attitude, some warmed-over moralizing imported on the *Mayflower*. There was nothing for it. I went back to Musso & Frank's for another drink and wrestled with the deeper philosophical issues, the barely graspables.

What if the scalpel- and hormone-enhanced perfection of the wealthy had the side effect of making less-fortunate souls feel even worse about *themselves*? Would a battle cry of "Nose jobs for everybody!" someday spearhead a revolution? Or were the poor and the stupid merely waiting in the wings for their own shot at affordable surgery, a California program on the order of Head Start to bring more and better beauty to the masses?

O, the confusions of L.A.! It seemed only right that I should be pondering the imponderables in the vicinity of Frederick's of Hollywood, where the windows were filled with crotchless panties and push-'em-up bras, and just a stone's throw away from the Church of Scientology, dispenser of self-involved religion in the country of the self-obsessed.

THE AGENT DROVE A LEXUS. She had a cellular phone and personalized license plates. She did not work for either Creative Artists or International Creative Management, the two big talent agencies in town, but for a boutique agency that did extremely well for a select roster of clients. She was petite, fit, smart, pretty, and rich.

It was a measure of her power that she felt secure enough to wear the oversized black eyeglasses favored by titans like Lew Wasserman and Irving "Swifty" Lazar—eyeglasses that looked at hideous disfigurement without blinking and stared it down.

The Agent had agreed to dish me the dirt on Hollywood over lunch at Langan's Brasserie in Century City. Our order was the standard one, two salads with the dressing on the side and a bottle of mineral water from some springs high in the Caucasus Mountains, near a grotto blessed by the Holy Virgin.

We started with some gossip. The Agent's was fresher than mine. I tried the story about Aaron Spelling and the seashells, but she topped me. She told about a birthday party that the Spellings had given for their daughter, and how the curtains on a home-entertainment stage had parted to reveal the party's special guest, Michael Jackson.

Next, she told about a director known for his low-budget features, who was so stingy that his son was suing him and his gardener had chopped down his hedges in a dispute over wages. Then there were the usual sexual rumors and innuendos to be explored, the ordinary speculation about who might be homosexual or bisexual or into S & M or fooling around with gerbils.

This insider gossip had a purpose, I saw. It was Hollywood's backhanded way of laying claim to some real life, canceling out all the sanitized pseudo-gossip that was retailed in the media. You had only to glance at *The Hollywood Reporter* to witness the vapidity with which the movie colony fostered an image of the industry as wholesomely American and beyond reproach. They wanted us to believe that they *were* still in Kansas.

In his influential column, "The Great Life," George Christy had recently covered a benefit premiere and had offered an account of it that was astonishing for its marshalry of petty details and its rigorous observance of status:

> ... among the 1,400 guests dining on Along Came Mary's grilled shrimp and stuffed chicken were Columbia's CEO Victor Kaufman and his wife Lorraine, St. John's Hospital's Virginia Zamboni, CAA's Mike Ovitz, Carol and Bill Haber, Ron Meyer, Barbara and Martin Davis, Julie and John Forsythe, Candy and Aaron Spelling,

John Davis, David Geffen, Donna Dixon, Lilly and Brandon Tar-
tikoff, Joel Silver, ICM's Jeff Berg with Denny. . . .

Christy had wheezed on through sixty-three more names, spicing the
pot with two plugs for restaurants, before concluding the paragraph.

The column would not have been out of place in a country-club
newsletter in Emporia. It pointed up Hollywood's middle-western
roots and its earnest desire to paint a bright face in public. Most
insiders recognized the absurdity, but they had to go along with it,
because in the film industry the Cartesian chestnut about existence
had been reformulated—*I was mentioned, therefore I am.*

About the movie business, the Agent said: "The first thing you
have to understand is that Hollywood, for all its influence, really is
a small town. Everybody knows everybody else, what they're worth
and where they stand. Everybody knows what everybody else is
working on. They know who isn't working, and they know why.
There are no secrets. Deals get made in living rooms. They get made
on golf courses and on tennis courts. They get made in bed.

"The second thing is that Hollywood is deathly conservative,
like most small towns. It is sexist and it is racist. It is conformist. It
can be incredibly unkind to anyone who isn't young or hot anymore.
There are no roles for older actresses, even somebody as good as
Meryl Streep. An older actress has to build a production company,
acquire properties, hire writers to tailor a script for her, and then
cross her fingers and hope.

"Third, the primary motivating factor in Hollywood is fear. Fear
of losing your job, fear of displeasing your boss, fear that the boss
you please is on the way out. Fear of not getting a good table at
Spago or at Morton's, fear of not being invited to Swifty Lazar's
Oscar party. There is an unconscionable fear of trying anything new
or different.

"You learn fast that it doesn't pay to be brave. You learn never
to try anything that hasn't been tried before. The unwritten rule is,
'When in doubt, imitate a success.' If it fails, you have a built-in

excuse. Say you do a *Terminator* knock-off and it doesn't open. Say it dies in three weeks. The boss calls you in on the carpet, and all you have to do is wail, 'But *Terminator* did so well!'

"Fear breeds cowards. Let's suppose you have a really first-rate script—a detective story, say—but another detective movie—*Dick Tracy,* say—has just flopped. Nobody will touch the property, regardless of how good it is. For two years, you'll hear the same thing over and over again. 'I love the script, but *Dick Tracy* was a flop.' Then people start to forget *Dick Tracy,* and maybe, if you're lucky, the picture might get made.

"Fourth, this thing you have about movie stars? Forget it. There are only a few real stars in town. Bobby de Niro's a wonderful actor, but he can't open a picture. Tom Cruise, Mel Gibson, Arnold Schwarzenegger, those guys and a couple more. That's about it. That's the short list.

"Stallone, you ask? Only if he stays in character and doesn't pretend to be smart. Women? Maybe Barbra Streisand, because she can't be stopped. And there's always somebody like Julia Roberts who's hot for a while and then disappears. Hollywood is a threshing machine for women. You can find people who'll tell you that it's deliberate.

"Being a star has nothing to do with acting. A star has to be able to open a picture on the basis of his or her name, no matter how crummy the movie is. The window of opportunity is small. That first week can mean everything. Staying on top is extraordinarily tricky. The public is fickle. They want to see you do the same thing and then they want to see you do it again. They don't like surprises. They know what they like, and it's the same thing that they liked last time."

I interrupted her. "So the movies are like McDonald's, right?"

"Sure, they're like McDonald's. What isn't like McDonald's nowadays?

"Anyway, being a star takes perseverance. It takes devotion, ego, intelligence, guidance, good fortune, and hard, hard work. You can never let up for a second. It's certainly true that you're only as good as your last picture. Katzenberg at Disney has made a mint hiring respected flops at rock-bottom prices—Bette Midler, Goldie Hawn, more directors than you can count on your fingers.

"The business has changed in the past few years. It used to be hard to find studio heads who read books, but now it's impossible. Everybody is twenty-seven years old, and they do not know about anything except the box-office grosses. They don't want to offend anybody. They want movies that are ordinary and familiar.

"There's more money around than ever before, but it seems to go to fewer people. Cruise could probably get fifteen million for a picture right now—accent on the 'right now.' Another rule—money breeds caution and inversely affects the element of risk. Fewer movies are being shot in Los Angeles. It's gotten too expensive. Producers search for cheaper locations and less red tape.

"It used to be that if a picture flopped in the States, you'd pray to get some money back through a sale to TV. Now you look to the foreign market, which has really grown. You look to the videocassette market, which has saved many asses in this town. Take *Batman,* a lousy picture. It grossed maybe two hundred fifty million in theatrical release, but it did about four hundred million on cassette. An average film now does about a third of its gross in theaters and the rest in other markets. Movies have gone global.

"You know what Hollywood stands for right now? Hollywood stands for TV. Almost all the network shows are done in L.A. Television is our bread-and-butter. You should know that. TV is what sells California to Americans.

"The final word on movies is this—we're dealing with a mainstream art that tries to pick the pockets of as large an audience as possible without totally discrediting itself. That's why movies are so bland."

I had a couple of questions. "What about the Japanese? How are they regarded?"

"When Sony bought Columbia, you got the predictable paranoia.

But the studios have been quietly chasing Japanese money for ages. You want to know what has the boys worried? The Japanese are taking over the private golf courses around L.A. An American guy quits or dies, and they jack up the cost of membership infinitely and sell it to a Japanese."

"How is it that somebody like Mickey Rourke still gets a million a picture when he's never had a hit?" I asked.

"That's about the going price for a B-grade leading man. His movies do well overseas. And besides, a million dollars is not a lot of money anymore."

Miles of money, money dropping from the clouds. The millionaire, an inspirational figure from my youth, was dead in California.

The Agent closed by saying, "I don't want you to go away with the impression that Hollywood's a bad town, because it isn't. But it's very real, and the old cliché is true—nothing matters but the bottom line. With all the money that's at stake, the competition is fast, tough, and fierce.

"How do you think it was in the gold mines, kiddo? You think those miners were sweethearts who looked out for one another? You think they were into sharing and caring? You've got another think coming. I'll give you another cliché that also happens to be true."

"Shoot."

"In Hollywood, it isn't enough to succeed. Your best friend must also fail."

IMMENSELY FAR from the aura cast by Hollywood, there was a penumbral Los Angeles that was crooked and raw. Nobody who lived there cared about the guest list for a benefit premiere or would ever taste the catered food of Along Came Mary. The penumbra was segregated and nonwhite, and the only movies that had legs among its citizens were blockbuster action films infused with lots of violence.

Teenagers in the penumbra were staunch fans of Bruce Willis and Chuck Norris and Sylvester Stallone when he wasn't trying to be smart. They saw *Die Hard* and *Terminator 2* as many times as they could afford, because the movies were loud and bloody and reflected the destructive force of life in California as they knew it.

The teenagers had little else to do. They had no jobs. They lived with their siblings and their cousins and their parents in crumbling, rat-infested apartment buildings around the city core, unimaginably deteriorated tenement slums that recalled the outrages of another century. Dummy corporations milked those cash cows for every penny, while the windows went unrepaired and the toilets spilled and flowed and the dealers of crack and smack walked the bulbless hallways.

The families were Latino, they were Asian and black. The recent immigrants among them were afraid to complain to anybody, afraid of cops and authorities. The adults were afraid that they'd lose what work they had. Their jobs were likely to pay them less than $11,000 a year and keep them well below the poverty line. About 18 percent of all the jobs, legal jobs, in Los Angeles paid less than $11,000.

The prospects for people in the penumbra were not good. They were worse than they used to be, in fact. Twenty years ago, a Latino male had earned ninety cents to an Anglo male's dollar, but now he earned seventy-eight cents. An American-born Latina earned forty-seven cents of that same dollar, and a Latina immigrant earned thirty cents of it.

It used to be, too, that the public schools could pave the way into a brighter world, but in the penumbra the schools were frequently just holding cells. The kids did as they pleased as long as they didn't cause any trouble. Among the nation's large cities, Los Angeles ranked thirty-second in terms of the maximum salary paid to a teacher with a master's degree. Jersey City paid its similarly credentialed teachers eight thousand dollars more a year.

California as a whole had the third-highest high-school dropout rate in the United States.

When a minority student in Los Angeles managed by dint of

supreme effort to make it through the system and get a diploma, he or she often had the educational skills of an average eighth- or ninth-grader. Such students did not go to college, except through affirmative-action programs. If they chose to work instead, they soon found that the traditional blue-collar employers around Los Angeles County, defense contractors and car manufacturers, Hughes Aircraft and General Motors, were laying off people, not hiring them.

In the eyes of struggling students, then, those who were still hanging on in school and trying to believe that it might be beneficial, the value of an education fell another notch, while the rewards of doing drugs or selling drugs, of gangsterism, of a stuporous resistance to the prevailing con, gained an added luster.

Sometimes it seemed that everyone in the penumbra was armed. There were shootings of every stripe almost every day. "Man Killed by Gang as He Admires View at Palisades," read a headline in the *Times*. "Gunman Kills 4 at LA Birthday Party," read another headline. "Tucson Man Held in Killing of Actress," read another, while yet another read, "L.A. Police Stymied by Church Killings."

The story went on to tell how a hooded gunman had burst into Mount Olive Church of Christ, had opened fire on about fifty parishioners who were singing hymns, and had murdered two of them.

Reporters always talked to eyewitnesses in the penumbra. They always filed the same report, the one in which a bystander in shock appears to be mystified by the violence, blurting something like, "How can that happen inside a church? The people there are nice and everything," as if a church still stood for something, as if it were a fortress.

Miles of money, money dropping from the clouds.

In Beverly Hills, in Bel-Air, in Pacific Palisades, in the other half of segregated Los Angeles, the dispatches in the *Times* were studied carefully, with the scrutiny that soldiers in old Hollywood Westerns gave to bulletins about hostile Indian tribes on the fringe. Among the wealthy, there was ample evidence of a severe lack of

faith in the social contract—the badges and the emblems of private
security firms, Armed Patrol, Armed Response, that were supposed
to afford protection when the cops could not.

The citizens, too, were preparing to take action, outfitting themselves in vigilante fettle, buying up guns against the gunners. They
were ready for the Armageddon that everyone in Los Angeles secretly
believed would come someday, the penumbra casting its shadow ever
wider as the oppressed stopped murdering one another and rode up
into the hills.

ON A SPRING NIGHT IN 1968, very late, Dennis Wilson of the Beach
Boys drove home from a recording session to an ersatz log cabin that
he had just rented on Sunset Boulevard. The cabin had once belonged
to Will Rogers. Wilson was in a floaty phase of his life, recently
divorced from his first wife and launched on a long slide into serious
drug and alcohol abuse that would eventually kill him.

Wilson was a friendly, accessible man not given to seclusion. It
was not unusual for a fan to track him down and come knocking
at his door, but he was flabbergasted by the sight that confronted
him that night, his new home awash with light and a full-scale party
going on inside.

Among the revelers, who were mostly young and female, he
recognized two hippie chicks that he'd offered a ride to earlier in
the day. He had brought them by his place to show them his gold
records and had made love to them both—Wilson was a world-class
cocksman. He could recall them prattling on about some mentor or
other, Charlie something, a great songwriter and a would-be messiah,
maybe Jesus and maybe not, but talk like that could be heard daily
around L.A.

When Wilson entered the log cabin, a dwarfish, long-haired man
with wild eyes walked toward him, sank to his knees, and kissed his
feet. Charlie Manson was fond of the ploy. He had used it before to
curry favor, and he needed a favor now.

Winter had come to Death Valley, and Manson had mounted up the troops and had driven the school bus to Canoga Park and found a house, but the Family was running out of money, and Charlie was tired of eating out of Dumpsters. He was searching for a patron or a mark, and his girls had made a fortuitous connection, because Wilson reveled in the kind of scene that had been orchestrated for him, a tableau of topless babes dancing to a booming stereo while joints and liquor bottles made the rounds.

He enjoyed it so much, in fact, that he wanted it repeated and invited Manson and the Family to bunk with him. Charlie would act as Wilson's orgy master, a pimp and a pal to a rock-and-roll star whose influence would help him to get his music recorded—or so Manson assumed.

Wilson seemed satisfied with the bargain in the beginning, even though it was costing him a fortune in penicillin to treat the gonorrhea that the Family kept passing back and forth. He let them "borrow" his clothes and his cash, fed them, and made no outcry when somebody totaled an uninsured Mercedes. Manson's school bus, *Hollywood Productions* lettered upon it, stayed parked beneath the trees.

For Wilson, the only drawback to the setup was that Charlie continued to push his songs, eager for a recording session. Whether out of fear, appeasement, or admiration, Wilson did introduce Manson to some people in the music business, among them Terry Melcher, Doris Day's son, who'd sung on a few Beach Boys' tracks.

Melcher worked as a producer sometimes and expressed an interest in Charlie. He also ran a salon for trendy young L.A. at his house on Cielo Drive in Beverly Hills, and though Manson never infiltrated it, he knew where the house was and what went on in it.

Nothing ever came of the contact, so instead Wilson arranged for Manson to lay down some tracks at a new studio at his brother Brian's place. The sessions were held at night and went fairly well until Charlie freaked out the engineer by flashing around a knife.

Maybe to smooth things over, Dennis Wilson bought the rights to one of Manson's songs, "Cease to Exist." Charlie claimed to have

written it to heal the ruptures among the increasingly fractious Beach
Boys. Brian had bailed out entirely and now remained in bed at home
for days at a time. The group recorded the song on their *20/20* album
as "Never Learn Not to Love." The lyrics were changed, too, so that
the refrain became "cease to *resist*."

Manson was apoplectic about someone tampering with his genius,
and Wilson had the good sense to avoid him. He was on the road
for most of the summer and never really did cut his ties to the Family.
Rather than face them directly, he merely rented another house in
Pacific Palisades and left it to the authorities to evict Manson from
the log cabin.

Charlie's mood was growing sour. Never before had he been so
close to pulling off a big score. It was becoming clear to him that he
might never be a star himself and might never be as famous as the
Beatles. For all his energetic self-inventing, all the dipping into Scientology and the laboring to perfect a rap, California had failed him
in the end.

Forced to move again, he retired with his Family to a dilapidated
ranch in Chatsworth, a Los Angeles suburb. The ranch had been
used in the past as a set for movie Westerns. Its owner, George Spahn,
was eighty-one. Decrepit and almost blind, he had sired ten children
by different women and had named them in honor of his horses.
Manson ordered Lynette "Squeaky" Fromme, who was nineteen, to
seduce the old man and keep him in her sexual thrall.

All the slights and the wounds that Manson had endured in a
lifetime were suppurating. He had been expelled from his own peculiar Eden, his credentials rudely revoked. In his fruity anger, he
predicted that the race war he'd been longing for was at hand. He
even hoped to help ignite it. If he couldn't live in paradise, neither
would anyone else.

He made careful preparations. To get some weapons, he got
involved with a bunch of outlaw bikers and traded them sex and
dope for guns. In need of more cash, he hit on a scheme whereby

his girls would become topless dancers at a bar, but when they auditioned they were rejected for being too flat-chested. He received it as another blow.

On the ranch, Charlie conducted warped maneuvers. He taught the Family how to creepy-crawl. They would invade a wealthy neighborhood at night, maybe Bel-Air or Beverly Hills, and steal into a house past the electrified fences, the canine patrols, the locked doors, and the windows honeycombed with alarms. They never robbed anything or made a mess. They just moved an object or two, shifted a lamp or a rug an inch or so to show that they'd been there—and that they *could* be there again, at any time.

On August 9, 1969, the Family creepy-crawled their way into the home of the betrayer, Terry Melcher, who had failed to transform Charlie into a rock idol. Melcher had rented the place on Cielo Drive to others, but he could still be taught a lesson. Melcher dead would never produce a Manson album, but Melcher alive and frightened might.

The new tenants on Cielo Drive were Roman Polanski, the director of *Rosemary's Baby,* and his pregnant wife, Sharon Tate, an actress whose most significant role to date was as a suicide in *Valley of the Dolls*. Polanski was on location in Europe, and Tate had invited in some friends for a quiet evening, Jay Sebring, Abigail Folger, and Voytek Frykowski.

Manson and his motley crew of assailants surprised them. Ever the orchestrator, Charlie choreographed an orgy of bloodletting, supervising the ritual murder of all four people—rich people, white people, the privileged of Los Angeles. With knives, handguns, and rope, the Family did his bidding enthusiastically. Tate alone would be stabbed sixteen times. Her blood was used to scrawl *PIG* on the front door.

To drive the nightmare deeper into the psyche of the city, Manson returned to Beverly Hills the very next night and orchestrated a double murder. It caused the barely repressed fear and hatred bubbling below the surface in L.A. to burst into the open. There were reports of soaring ammunition sales, and of movie stars carrying weapons and taking sudden, transatlantic vacations.

Manson must have been keenly hysterical after watching his scariest fantasy become a reality. On the lam, he searched out Dennis Wilson again and insisted that he be given $1,500 so that he could head for the desert, for Death Valley and the Panamints. It took the police nearly three months to apprehend him and put him behind bars, where, as he had once argued so strenuously, he ought to have been all along.

Even with Manson in prison, fear still gripped certain special enclaves in Los Angeles. Dwellers in them still jumped at the sound of a key turning in a lock or a dog barking at night. They were people who would spend the next few years looking over their shoulders, who would come to know panic intimately, who would learn to live with an ever-present sense of menace.

Somewhere in the recesses of the Beach Boys' archives, in a basement or a drawer or a vault, there were still some tapes of Charlie Manson's songs, but Dennis Wilson would not permit them to be played, ever, because "the vibes connected with them don't belong on this earth," in this California.

DENNIS WILSON, a Scorpio, was broke at thirty-nine, ragged, bearded, raspy-voiced from cigarettes and surgery on his vocal chords, strung out on coke, heroin, and alcohol, drinking vodka by the quart, homeless, red-eyed, trembly, and married unhappily for the fifth time to the nineteen-year-old illegitimate daughter of his first cousin, fellow Beach Boy Mike Love.

Wilson had used it up. He had fucked all the girls, sampled all the highs, and ridden all the waves. There was no more California left for him, no California at all.

Just after Christmas, in 1983, he could be found wandering from bar to bar in Santa Monica, scabbed and bloody from a recent fight, having fallen out of detox yet again.

A friend who lived aboard a yawl in Marina del Rey took him in. He tried to contain the boozing, but Wilson soon drank everything around and decided to go swimming. He was fixated on a boat he'd owned, the *Harmony,* that had once been docked nearby. The boat meant many things to him—a safe harbor, a safe passage, a better time.

Ignoring the winter chill, Wilson plunged into the ocean clad only in a pair of cut-off jeans. He scoured the ocean floor for souvenirs of the *Harmony,* lost batteries and even bits of twine. He went under again and again, diving and bringing up trinkets, until he went under a last time and drowned.

CHAPTER 23

FIRE SEASON was coming to Los Angeles. You could feel it in the hot, dry Santa Ana winds that occasionally blew down from the canyons to rattle the fronds of the skinny palm trees across from the Sovereign. The fronds tore loose and spiraled toward earth, where they smacked against the cars parked at curbside, leaving little dents and scratches on the gleaming fleet.

Soon the Santa Anas would blow more often. They would be more raw and blistering and would keep people off the beaches and begin to eat at their nerves. Wives would become so edgy, said Raymond Chandler, that they'd pick up their kitchen knives and study their husbands' necks.

In the Raymond Chandler Suite, I was packing my clothes and getting ready for a move. The Gigliottis were off to Europe and had invited me to stay at their house for a week or so before I left for the Mexican border. Already I felt a little dizzied by the prospect. In my months on the road I'd grown unfamiliar with the comforts of a home. The green gloom of Smith River seemed part of another lifetime, a souvenir snapshot from the early days of my journey when I was still blessed with boundless energy.

Aaron Gigliotti was to be my housemate. He had reached an

age of assertive selfhood and didn't think it was the least bit cool to accompany his family on trips. Cool mattered enormously to him, as it did to most teenagers around L.A., and he went to great lengths to court it.

Aaron was dark-haired and handsome, bright but not much of a student, sensitive and desperate to hide it. He affected the rebellious attitude of his favorite band, the Red Hot Chili Peppers, and liked to wear his baseball cap backward and go shirtless when his parents weren't around. He was a clandestine smoker of cigarettes and a sometime graffiti bomber who spray-painted slogans on walls.

He had never been in real trouble, but he'd flirted with it. His father worried about his future, but Aaron saw no cause for that, no cause for it at all.

I had never shared a house with a teenager before and had certain things to learn. Any food that I put into the fridge, say, was regarded as community property. A six-pack of beer could miraculously become a two-pack overnight. I realized almost immediately that Aaron and I needed to forge a pact to promote our peaceful coexistence. I felt bad for barging in on him and robbing him of his much-hoped-for solitude, but once he saw that I had no interest in being a surrogate parent, we got along fine.

Secretly, too, Aaron was hungry for adult company. He loved his father as much as his father loved him, but he believed that he ought to be running wild and free, trying to outpace the responsibilities that lay ahead of him. There wasn't much innocence left in Los Angeles, and somehow he must have known that.

The second evening I was at the house, he came to sit with me by the pool while I was writing in my notebook. He had on shorts and was bare-chested. On his right bicep was something I'd never noticed before, an elaborate, multicolored tattoo of an Indian's skull resting on some feathery peace pipes.

A tattoo artist in Hollywood had done it in two hours, Aaron said, at a cost of one hundred dollars. The worst part wasn't the sting of the needle but the slow process of healing. He'd had to apply creams and unguents like Noxema frequently and also had to devise many ruses to keep his scabbed-over skin hidden from everybody. In a family of eight, that had been a challenge.

The tattoo was really big. "Your parents don't know about it?" I asked.

"No," he said, grinning cockily. "They'd kill me."

I imagined all the hidden selves that were dying to burst out in teenage California, all the nipple rings and pierced nipples that were still concealed in bedrooms.

"How did you pick that design, Aaron?"

He had told himself a wonderful story and now told it to me.

"It's from when I was a baby. My dad used to sing me these Indian lullabies." He glanced at the tattoo doubtfully, as if he weren't entirely sure how it had got there. "Anyhow, it can be removed with laser technology," he said, with a youthful confidence that there was always a way to rectify your mistakes.

Aaron talked about his graduation from Santa Monica High School—Samo, he called it. He had liked the school very much for the diversity of the student body, but it had bothered him that the kids were so invested in cliques. They were divided along the divided lines of the city, grouped by race or by gang affiliation or by their identification with a subcult such as surfers or punkers.

It had surprised Aaron how few of his black classmates had actually graduated. It wasn't as though they had flunked out or anything. They just didn't show up for the graduation ceremony. Guys he'd known for four years, guys who'd visited him at his house—they simply weren't there. The same thing was true of the Hispanic students, he said, although to a lesser degree. Some of them did attend the ceremony to accept their diplomas.

With a keen eye for social logistics, Aaron described how the various cliques deployed themselves around the school grounds, with the jocks holding forth at the center, the blacks clinging to the margins, and the Hispanics hanging around by a Dumpster. The Dumpster business upset him. It seemed so obvious and so unfair.

"It's like they know they're treated like garbage," he said angrily. Aaron was still young enough to expect some justice from the world.

He brought out his yearbook to show me. It differed profoundly from the yearbook I had looked at in Wasco, at the Crettols' place. The Samo yearbook had a strange quality of aspiration about it. Sometimes the photos of the students and the teachers resembled the eight-by-ten glossies that agents sent to casting directors. It was as if the students weren't really students, and the teachers weren't really teachers. The dean had posed in a baseball cap worn backward, forever hip. There were no Hispanics on the faculty and only one black.

Aaron thumbed through the pages and remembered things. He would smile at a picture and relate an anecdote about the person or the situation. Then he came to some pictures of the faculty and said quietly that two teachers had died that year of AIDS.

How much more troubling his adolescence was than mine, I thought, and what sad facts he had to master. It would make anybody wonder about the value of growing up in California. Better to stay on your skateboard, as Aaron often did, rocketing past the palm trees directly to the beach.

FRED SANDS HAD HIS HEADQUARTERS in a ten-story building in Brentwood shielded by opaque windows of blackish smoked glass that kept out the storied light of Los Angeles. The windows made you think that something dark and insidious must be going on inside, but Fred Sands was clearly doing something right. He owned forty real estate offices around the city, dealt in commercial properties as far north as Sacramento, and held the highest honor that the Boy Scouts had to give, the God and Country Exemplar Award.

One reason for Sands's success was his ability to look toward the future. He was in the vanguard of southern California realtors in his efforts to sell blue-ribbon houses and land in the state to the Japanese.

He had recently entered into an affiliation agreement with Sumitomo Real Estate to market his residential listings in Japan, and his "Preview of Homes" videos would soon be shown on Japanese TV.

The Pacific Rim Division of Fred Sands was currently recording transactions at a monthly rate of $12 million. Its director, Christine Lee Watt, supervised several teams of realtors, each devoted to a specific market overseas, be it Korea, Taiwan, Japan, Hong Kong, Singapore, or Australia. The teams were staffed with native speakers as necessary and had the expertise to negotiate a deal in a way that was culturally acceptable and gave no offense.

Christine Lee Watt met with me while I was waiting out the minutes to my appointed hour with Fred Sands. She was a petite, fine-boned woman in her early thirties about to become a mother, eight months down and counting. She had been born in Tokyo to Chinese parents and had come to California to go to UC Berkeley, where she had majored in business. She had enjoyed her time at Berkeley very much, but after graduating she had gone back to Japan to take a job in investment banking.

Life was much simpler for her there, she said. She earned a better salary, had better health care, never fretted about her safety, and got better perks, such as reimbursement for her expenses as a commuter. She might never have returned to America if she hadn't married a Californian, in fact.

Her career with Fred Sands had started two years earlier. The bulk of her trade in the Pacific Rim Division was done with the Japanese. Everyone knew that they were ardent players in commercial real estate, but they were also quite active in the residential market, Christine told me, because the prices here were so low compared to what they paid at home.

She gave me an example. A nice apartment in the Ginza district in Tokyo could cost a buyer $6 million, while for $2 million that same buyer could buy an okay house, a *whole* house, in Beverly Hills, a neighborhood that the Japanese loved. The amount of desirable

Beverly Hills property was limited, so its market value was insured. Then, too, "Beverly Hills" stood for something special in Japan, something of inalterable quality, like Fresno cotton or John Wayne.

The Japanese always shopped for location, Christine went on, and avoided any neighborhood where there was a hint of danger. They loved the weather and the golf in southern California. At home, they would never dream of having so much space and so much privacy. A man might have a luxury car and belong to an exclusive club, but he would never own any land in a city, not ever.

They also found it cheaper to live in Los Angeles. The fruit and the vegetables available in Beverly Hills cost a pittance, they thought. In Tokyo, a ripe cantaloupe had the status of a rare gift and could run them a hundred dollars. They were becoming more comfortable, as well, because more and more Asians were settling around the city, making it less and less foreign to them.

At the most basic level, the Japanese who dealt with Christine saw residential property in L.A. as a superior investment. It helped them to bury money that they might otherwise lose in taxes. The inheritance tax in Japan was farcical. There was a saying that a family could be stripped of its fortune in three generations.

A Japanese buyer did not have to occupy a house purchased in California, Christine pointed out. It could be rented or used to put up visiting corporate executives. Often the houses were turned into residences for children who were getting an education in the United States.

I asked Christine if she had any particular problems when she worked with investors from Japan, but she said she didn't. Americans doing business on the Pacific Rim were more difficult, she thought, because they had so many misconceptions about the Japanese and their country. It was true that Japan was a democracy, at least in theory, but Christine believed that it was much more rigidly structured and controlled than the United States. People didn't feel as free.

"The system works better in some ways and less well in others," she said. "There are always trade-offs. Californians need to be more aware of the differences and more tolerant of them."

FROM THE PACIFIC RIM DIVISION, I walked to the lobby and boarded an elevator whose doors opened again on a plain outer office on the ninth floor, where a single, harried receptionist in a headset was both fielding telephone calls and signing in visitors. Had I made a wrong turn somewhere? The outer office didn't look anything like the imperial gateway that I had expected of Fred Sands. It seemed ill-suited to a man who had shaken hands with presidents and had been a frequent guest on TV and radio talk shows.

At any rate, I was right on time. After giving my name to the receptionist, I sat alone and in silence on a half-moon sliver of gray suede couch and read through the materials that the Fred Sands people had sent me, copies of profiles in such magazines as *Beverly Hills 213* that had photos of Fred and his wife, Cindy, and interesting quotes about how they had "hectic schedules" and tried to "prioritize and ration" their time.

Fred and Cindy had three kids and were building a house in Bel-Air to go along with their beach house in Malibu. They felt fortunate to have a great lifestyle and didn't take it for granted, the magazine article said.

After I'd been sitting on the sliver of gray suede for about ten minutes, a woman who identified herself as a publicity assistant darted out from the inner sanctum and sat next to me. She wanted to know what sort of questions I planned to ask Fred Sands. This was news to me, this preinterview. I ran through my mental list, *midget with a motorcycle, nature of the dynamo,* and answered as simply as I could.

"Questions about real estate," I said.

She nodded approvingly. "It will just be a minute."

Another thirty minutes went by before I rose from the couch to inform the receptionist that I would not be able to wait any longer for Fred Sands because I had to leave for my next appointment. Obviously, Sands had failed to prioritize me into his hectic schedule.

The brinksmanship sparked her into a flurry of activity. She spoke some hushed words through her headset to the inner sanctum and then the publicity assistant and a new player, Sands's secretary, intercepted me at the elevator, to tell me that Fred could see me now.

"It's too late," I said, pausing for effect. "I have to get to my next appointment."

Riding down in the elevator, I cursed Fred Sands and carried on about his bad manners and abominated him for being a venal and successful realtor, but I had to quit the ranting when the voice of Los Angeles broke into my tirade.

"You chump!" said Los Angeles, with a laugh. "Haven't you been paying any attention at all? Whatever made you think you counted?"

AARON GIGLIOTTI HAD a part-time minder, Teddy Zambetti, who lived down the block and looked in on him now and again as a favor to his parents. Zambetti's name was like the lush slide of brushes over the drums that he played as a musician. He had toured with Jackson Browne and had worked as a sideman on many rock albums, and one night he stopped by the house after ten o'clock looking really beat, a guy worn out from a long recording session and still willing to extend himself on behalf of friends.

Nobody had introduced me to Zambetti or explained to him what I was doing in the house, and he figured that maybe he should try to find out, just in case.

"I'm a drummer," he said, in a friendly way. "I've been in the studio for hours, you know? So, like, what are you—just bopping around?"

"No, I'm a writer."

"A writer?"

"Yes. The world is my studio."

In the morning, I felt stupid and small-minded. Los Angeles was turning me into the smartass that I'd always had the potential to become. There was a perverse rhythm to the city, a strange kind of accounting. Fred Sands fucked you over, I said to myself, so you had to fuck over Teddy Zambetti. The fucking-over just got passed along in L.A., like a malicious strain of influenza.

I took to the freeways, another aimless driver out to forget everything that had happened to him in the last few hours. I had learned that the freeways, however crabbed, had the power to induce a mood of calm once you'd taught yourself to look beyond the crashes and the mayhem and the flotsam of crumpled chrome and manikin limbs.

The comforting message of the freeways was that you would always be behind and so would always have an excuse. You would never accomplish what you'd hoped to accomplish, would never arrive where you had hoped to arrive at the time that you had hoped to arrive there, and would fail to accumulate the money or the fame that was deservedly yours because someone else, probably Aaron Spelling, had got to it first, jumping your claim.

The message brought a curious relief. Soon the freeway alpha waves began to flow, and I was as weightless as a dolphin in saltwater until I had to leave my car.

In Beverly Hills, where I parked near Rodeo Drive, I heard a man ask for directions to the Harbor Freeway and say, "Thanks, I'll be fine once I'm in the system."

Rodeo Drive served up a scary panorama of cosmetically enhanced women and extraterrestrial lounge lizards whose ponytails were stuck inside their slouchy sport coats. Like Susanville, Beverly Hills had a sister city—Cannes, France. At Tribeca Restaurant, a Los Angeles gloss on New York, two female shoppers discussed cholesterol while sipping Chardonnay.

"I give Adam turkey burgers all the time," one of them confessed to the other, *sotto voce*. "I put on the tomatoes and the lettuce, and he doesn't know the difference!"

An extraterrestrial blew in, a regular. The bartender asked, "Beer?" Came the reply, "Nah, just a Kaliber. I'm doing the wagon thing."

I got back on the freeway. The downside of driving and meditating was that you were exposed to four times as many cancer-causing chemicals than usual, even with your windows rolled up. You breathed carbon monoxide, of course, and benzene and toluene. You breathed xylene and ethylene dibromide and dichloride, formaldehyde, acetaldehyde, perchloroethylene, a little chromium, a dollop of nickel, and a ration of lead as a garnish.

At the house in the evening, I grabbed some recent copies of the *Times* and ransacked them for the latest bloodbaths. In addition to becoming a smartass, I was also developing into a shootings buff. My incredulity was constantly being tested. Each new slaughter seemed an attempt to stretch the limits of the genre and give a new spin to the concept of violent death, investing it with fresh imaginative energy to create a sequel with legs, Shootings II, Shootings III, and Shootings IV.

A drive-by in Pacoima. Three men killed as they walked from a soccer field after a game. Ordinary.

Here was something better. An eighty-four-year-old had murdered his estranged wife in the cafeteria at Universal Studios because she refused to take him back.

And something even better. A disturbed man had emptied a shotgun on a sound stage at Lorimar Studios in Culver City, where an episode of a TV series was being filmed, because he felt that one of the stars had fucked him over in a business deal pertaining to a popcorn company. Then he had committed suicide.

Elsewhere in Los Angeles County, a drifter from Arizona, who had last worked as a janitor at a Jack-in-the-Box, shot Rebecca Schaeffer, a starlet, because he was obsessed with her. The man had mental problems. He was apprehended in Tucson, where, the *Times* noted with its infinite attention to such details, the chief of police was Linda Ronstadt's brother.

A Jack-in-the-Box janitor-drifter with mental problems.

In the *Times,* I came upon a headline that read, "Mental Health Care: A System on the Verge of Collapse." A citizens' health-research group had rated L.A. County as the worst place in the United States in terms of the outpatient services that it afforded to the mentally ill. Yet more layoffs and budget cuts were looming. Social workers at a clinic in Santa Monica were reported to be demoralized in the aftermath of a recent attack during which a patient had shot a staff member.

"Poverty Gap Growing in L.A., Report Finds," read another headline in the *Times,* but I already knew the story. Miles of money, money dropping from the clouds.

I turned on the TV. Reba McEntire said to a talk-show person, "K. T. Oslin is so unique, she's an individual!"

Flip the channel.

Somebody was telling a talk-show person this funny story about how Ronald Reagan had once roomed with a Munchkin, Mickey Carrol, during his days as an actor. The Munchkin had testified that Dutch was clean and a good cook.

I turned off the TV, closed my eyes, and thought about what still lay ahead of me to the south—Orange County, the Colorado Desert, San Diego, and then the border.

What was it that Richard Ramirez, the Night Stalker, a mass murderer, had said after being sentenced to die at the close of his trial?

"Big deal, death always went with the territory. I'll see you in Disneyland!"

BARRY YOURGRAU'S HEART had mended some. He was feeling better. His movie would soon be released, and he was performing his stories at Cafe Largo, a fashionable little venue in the Fairfax District. The performing had gone so well that he'd been asked to read something at Cafe Largo's weekly poetry bash, where stars, starlets, ingenues, models, and celebrities tried their hand at being Ranier Maria Rilke and Sara Teasdale.

Poetry was big with the Hollywood crowd. It came in books and had no economic value whatsoever. A poem was a free spirit, like a butterfly. If you wrote a few, you proved that you were also a free spirit and entitled to wear black clothing and hideously disfiguring eyeglasses. Poetry was above the fray.

A valet parking attendant claimed my car at Cafe Largo—the first valet ever to work a poetry reading in the history of the world. All the tables inside were occupied or marked "Reserved," so I took a spot at the bar and listened to the murmuring about the poets who might show up to read that night, maybe Sean Penn or Ally Sheedy.

Yourgrau joined me momentarily in a state of perturbation. In front of Canter's Deli, in a benign ambience of derma and gefilte fish, a fellow motorist had taken issue with his driving skills and had threatened to crack his skull. Only a fateful blink of a traffic light, the distance from stop to go, had saved him from a thrashing.

All in all, it had been an unusual day for Yourgrau, another step forward in the evolutionary process by which he was becoming a Californian. That afternoon, he had visited a psychic in San Fernando Valley for a consultation about his future. He had got the man's name from the casting director on his movie.

The psychic lived in a simple tract house, but Yourgrau sensed that he wasn't like other human beings. He had refused a handshake because he'd just washed. Who knew what manner of interference Yourgrau's grit and germs might have had on the transmission?

Seating himself, the psychic had accepted fifty dollars and had eyeballed his visitor. He saw fame in Yourgrau's aura. Only once before had that happened, with one other special person.

"Who?" Yourgrau inquired.

"Vanna White," the psychic responded.

The psychic made several predictions about Yourgrau's love life, but they were radically off-base. Still, the trip to San Fernando Valley had been an adventure, and Yourgrau was glad that he'd gone. He wouldn't be at a loss anymore if a cocktail-party conversation swerved toward the pananormal, he said.

For now, though, he had to choose what to read on-stage. He was torn between two pieces. The first was a wacky, audience-friendly story about a cow, while the other was a much more deeply felt story that was exquisitely turned. Yourgrau asked for my opinion. Glancing at the youngish audience, men and women in their twenties and early thirties, I counseled him to go with the second piece. Youth would respond to its subtlety and its emotion.

The poet-boss of the Cafe Largo series was our emcee. He was from New York and had the kind of radiant flush that envelops somebody who has jumped from an airplane and landed unexpectedly on his feet. He introduced the first two readers, actorish men of a sentimental bent, each capable of being moved to extremes by the drama of his own life. Then he introduced Yourgrau.

In a matter of seconds, after Yourgrau had read just a few words, I began to cringe. Disaster lay ahead. The subtlety of the story was too subtle, and the emotions were too finely put. Here was an example of real literature, and the crowd didn't have a clue what to do with it, so they started chattering, ordering drinks, and looking at their watches.

For five slowly decomposing minutes, Yourgrau died an unnatural death on-stage before returning to the bar. "Thank you very much for your advice," he said.

The next reader was a starlet in a mini-skirt and patterned tights. Her poems, such as they were, had to do with bad relationships. The men that she knew were fucks, bastards, and assholes, always letting her down and leaving a pair of beat-up Tony Lama cowboy boots under her bed.

The word *fuck* brought down the house. Deafening applause greeted the brand-name reference to Tony Lama.

She was followed by a man who punctuated his existential dilemma by slapping himself in the face. Poetry was being transformed in Los Angeles, turned into a Three Stooges routine.

Yourgrau suggested a late supper at a famous hamburger joint in Westwood. We had to wait in line for twenty minutes to get inside. The menu advertised "Quality Forever," a heavy burden on the cooks. The two featured burgers were the Steakburger ("Our original, 1928") and the Hickoryburger ("Our original, 1945"). I couldn't tell the difference.

"Chili sauce," Yourgrau said, pointing to some fine print. "Homemade."

SOMETIMES I WOULD SIT by the swimming pool at the Gigliottis' house and listen to the birds singing and try to believe that I had really been to the Far North, that it really existed. It seemed to belong not only to another lifetime but to another century. I saw all the felled trees of the Far North traveling south to become tract houses, and all the water of the Far North flowing through the pipes and the toilets of those houses, and wondered what the Far North was getting in exchange.

Then I remembered all the little video shelves in hardware stores and Indian gift shops, and all the Hollywood videos stacking up in them like Big Macs, and I saw the Wolfgang Puck nouveau pizzas going into the freezer case in Hoopa Valley and saw the teenage daughters of loggers in their patterned tights and their mini-skirts chasing millworkers in Tony Lama boots and writing poems about them, and I thought, Well, maybe it's a fair deal. Or maybe not.

AND YET IN THE MORNING the sun rose in triumph again, rose beautifully, achingly, reductively, still collecting its residuals. After packing my bags for my last month on the road, I assumed my accustomed position by the pool and watched Aaron and some friends playing a vigorous game of paddle tennis. They had a bristly overabundance of energy that seemed to lap and flow around them, something sharp and animal pushing against the shape that was meant to contain it.

That evening, Aaron planned to host a big barbecue. This would be a signal event, I was given to understand, because a few girls had been invited and might actually show up.

In the late afternoon, freshly showered, Aaron began his advance prep. One friend had stayed behind to help him, a plumber's apprentice who'd suffered a hernia and was living on disability pay. He was a little older than the other boys in the posse and always had a terrible crimson sunburn, as if he could never quite remember when it was time to get off the beach. His main function, I thought, must be as the designated beer buyer, his legal I.D. in hand.

The Red Hot Chili Peppers roared from the stereo while Aaron laid out the steaks and tore some lettuce for a salad.

"I know everybody in the band," he said with authority to his pal.

"Cool," the plumber said. He seldom said much more than that.

Aaron had forgotten to buy some charcoal, so the boys zipped to the corner store on their skateboards, scooting along in a gnarly twilight zone between childhood and manhood. When they got back, they developed a case of the party jitters and kept checking the clock at five-minute intervals, wondering where their guests were. I could feel the helium escaping from their balloon. A half-hour went by, and then another boy finally knocked on the front door. He was the first and the last guest to arrive.

The defection of the girl guests was a major disappointment. After Aaron had the barbecue fire going and had thrown the steaks on, he phoned one of the backsliders, a friend named Thor, and vented his anger.

"What do you *mean,* man? You're cooking dinner for your *Dad?*" he shouted into the receiver. "You're eighteen years old, Thor! You're supposed to be *rebelling* against him. Don't tell me you *have* rebelled. Your rebellion got squashed, dude. You got squashed like Tiananmen Square!"

In the dusky shadows, the three boys sat at a table outside to partake of a desultory meal—another barbecue in California. They picked at the food and made halfhearted jokes about the missing girls. What a complicated world they were inheriting. They had to survive in Los Angeles, where illusions and realities were hopelessly entangled and expectations were astounding, where even a hamburger had to be more, much more, than a simple patty of ground beef.

CHAPTER 24

So WITH A SIGH of relief tempered only by the melancholy understanding that I had failed to become rich, famous, or transcendentally
beautiful in Los Angeles, I dodged the usual freeway spillage and
made it to Long Beach, twenty-three miles away, where the motto
was *Urbs Amicate,* the "Friendly City," and the circus had just left
town.

Long Beach felt like an anticlimax after L.A. It also felt like a
refuge. The smell of things burning was gone from the air, and the
locals would need a dictionary to find the meaning of apocalypse.
They were people who could be counted on to attend the farewell
tour of Gunther Gabel-Williams, the fabled trainer of big cats, whose
relic circus posters were still plastered to walls and billboards.

Long Beach was the fifth-largest city in the state, with a population of about 425,000, but it was virtually untouched by sophistication. Its chief tourist attractions were the *Queen Mary* and the *Spruce
Goose,* Howard Hughes's 200-ton flying boat, which was now a Walt
Disney production. Brochures reminded you that Disneyland itself
was just across the Orange County line.

The 1950s were not forgotten in Long Beach. All along the ocean,
I saw little beachfront motels offering weekly rates for suburbanites

on vacation. The motels frequently had a maritime motif and showed anchors and ships' bells in neon. Aging sailors presided over them, navy pensioners with daunting brush cuts and a marked distaste for anything modern.

The city came by its conservatism honestly. Earlier in the century, it had been known as "Iowa on the Pacific" because so many elderly Hawkeye farmers had retired there to die. They lived on their savings in efficiency apartments and were so numerous that a corn-on-the-cob picnic at Bixby Park might attract fifty thousand of them.

The newspapers back home were captivated by the farmers' migration and dispatched their writers to Long Beach to file reports about such esoterica as the practice of sunbathing. In 1937, Harlan Miller of the *Des Moines Register* had this to say about his journey to the Coast:

> At seven A.M. the clang of horseshoes begins. The retired farmers are at their chores, pitching ringers. . . . Day has begun in the coastal paradise where thousands of Iowans go before they die. . . . Behind the beach stretches the gaudy "Pike," the amusement artery line with open-fronted refreshment rooms and counters, its games of skill or chance, souvenir bazaars, liquor shops open even on Sunday. . . . Here a retired elder whose mortgages have gone a little sour can romp with discreet lavishness. . . .

Although the sunlight in California could be blinding, Miller said, the farmers didn't need any movie-star "smoked glasses" to protect them. They had toiled in the fields of Iowa and had no fear of wrinkles. He heard them complain about the quality of western beef and cast aspersions on the fried chicken, but they loved the warm weather and wouldn't trade it for anything. What a thing it was to feel welcome on earth at last!

The Hawkeye spirit still lingered in Long Beach, armored and wary. The beaches in town were sometimes as modest as the sandy, lakefront strips at midwestern fishing resorts, and hardly anyone wore a bikini. Sometimes the beaches looked out on manmade islands where oil was stored. The islands were named for dead astronauts, Chaffee Island and Grissom Island.

A lid was clamped on the downtown area after dark, Main Street again capped and shuttered and losing out to the life of shopping malls. The skyscrapers and hotels fronting on the ocean, monuments to redevelopment, had a sepulchral isolation at night and seemed huddled together to keep some unseen threat at bay.

The U.S. Navy was a major employer in Long Beach, with three active battleships home-ported to the naval shipyard, but the off-duty sailors didn't stick around to carouse and play as they used to do. They couldn't afford the housing prices in the city, so at the end of their shifts, they became commuters and went home to such suburbs as Lakewood, Carson, or Torrance instead of spending their money in honky-tonks.

The few honky-tonks that were left in town had been banished to the urban fringe, hidden as they might be in Iowa. Soon I came to recognize a familiar litany painted on stucco buildings in faceless neighborhoods: *Cocktails, Beer, Wine*. Often *Girls* was appended to it, and then the front door was not wide open but instead guarded by a muscular, long-haired greaser whose schooling had stopped somewhere shy of the eighth grade.

One night, cruising, I was drawn into Angel's, where the girls danced almost naked and did what they could to shake their rigid silicone breasts. The breasts had a remarkable shape and design. Maybe it was the navy presence that caused me to search for a military analogy, but they looked as indomitable as nuclear warheads. Bump into a nipple by accident, and you ran the risk of blinding yourself.

At Angel's, the specialty of the house was hot-cream wrestling, a variant of mud wrestling during which the strippers coated themselves in what looked to be slightly heated Gillette Foamy and did some sloppy Greco-Roman posing for a rowdy crowd of college kids, a few navy lads upholding tradition, and workers from the many oil refineries around.

Oil had always figured prominently in the life of Long Beach. At Signal Hill, a township nearby, geologists had discovered a huge oil field in 1921, tapping into gushers that had yielded about 250,000 barrels a day at their zenith. Some pumps were still dipping into the ooze of the hill with those curious, birdlike motions I'd seen around Bakersfield.

Big tankers brought crude oil to the city from Alaska and abroad, discharging more than 145 million barrels of it annually at the ports of Long Beach and Los Angeles on San Pedro Bay. All the important oil companies had storage tanks there. They funneled their stock to refineries such as Atlantic-Richfield's in Carson, where about 5 million gallons of gasoline were refined every day.

The refineries also handled oil piped in from the San Joaquin, and whenever the wind failed to blow, or whenever it blew the wrong way, you could taste and smell a thick petroleum haze. It was a fact of life in Long Beach, and though the haze sometimes made for a pungent olfactory experience, it had the beneficial side effect of keeping trendy Angelenos from those midwestern beaches, preserving the flavor of another era.

LONG BEFORE THE *Queen Mary* became a Disney tourist attraction, it used to carry passengers across the ocean, and Matthew Faulkner, late of Cornwall, England, could remember arriving in the United States aboard it as a child. Faulkner had stayed where he had landed and now found himself in the same boat as me, unable to deny that he'd turned into a Californian, however reluctantly. Whenever he went back to England for a visit, the folks regarded him with both admiration and suspicion, but he was not unhappy to have surrendered his birthright in exchange for a life in Long Beach and a position as a vice-president with the Chamber of Commerce.

When anybody asked Faulkner about Long Beach, he was never at a loss for words, and the boosterish words most often on his lips nowadays were *Pacific Rim*. I had no doubt that he would agree with

Henry Huntington, who had addressed southern California's prospects in foreign trade in the 1880s.

"I believe that Los Angeles is destined to become the most important city in the country, if not in the world. It can extend in any
direction as far as you like. Its front door opens on the Pacific, the
ocean of the future. Europe can supply her own wants; we shall
supply the wants of Asia."

Huntington was prescient, but he had erred in omitting Long
Beach from the equation. Quietly and efficiently, the city had been
stealing some of Los Angeles' business.

Among its new waterfront skyscrapers was a highly visible World
Trade Center that was destined to be second only to the World Trade
Center in New York, the biggest on the planet. The plans called for
four office towers, a hotel, and many shops and restaurants in a 2.2-
million-square-foot complex—a living, breathing hothouse for the
generating of capital.

The project was a true Pacific Rim venture, undertaken jointly
by Kajima International of Japan and IDM Corporation of Long
Beach. IDM, a consortium, had some American partners, but it also
included several Japanese banks.

In Faulkner's office at the World Trade Center, I learned that
Long Beach had been limping along as a dying navy town until the
Alaskan oil boom had started around 1975. By chance, the Port of
Long Beach had proven unusually suited to handling the cargo on
tankers, and it had added to its capacity ever since, bringing in more
container terminals and giant gantry cranes. The nearby Port of Los
Angeles, which was annexed to L.A. through the harbor towns of
Wilmington and San Pedro, was similarly equipped and also
expanding.

The Port of Long Beach afforded shippers another advantage in
that it was located in the only foreign trade zone in southern California, which meant that certain imported goods could enter the
United States and not be hit with a customs tax.

Both ports did a lion's share of their trading with Pacific Rim countries. The trade accounted for as much as three-quarters of each port's annual gross receipts. Automobiles headed the tally of imports, to the tune of some $30 million a year. Next came shoes and other footwear, followed by data-processing machines, motor vehicle parts, and tape players and recorders.

Oil was the primary outgoing cargo. The last sawlogs from our dwindling forests were shipped from Long Beach, too, and cotton, wheat, hides, and corn were exported in some quantity.

The economic prospects in Long Beach seemed bright, indeed, but Faulkner didn't want me to think that the redevelopment scheme was trouble-free. He directed my attention to the Long Beach Airport. It was smack in the middle of the city and had no room to grow.

Land everywhere in Long Beach was at a premium—that was why there weren't any new subdivisions around or any affordable houses. Only two large parcels were still available within the city limits, Faulkner said, and the Disney organization was studying one of them.

"What for?" I asked.

Faulkner shrugged. "They're very secretive, you know." But he assumed that they must be thinking about attracting the captive audience at the *Queen Mary* and the *Spruce Goose* nearby. He made the Disneys sound like the Rosicrucians.

Faulkner's main concern was that Long Beach might become too bland as the port grew and the redevelopment continued. Money had a way of driving out diversity. Some chamber members were already demanding a united front to put a best foot forward.

From Faulkner's office, I rode down to the lobby in one of those silent, high-speed elevators that have the impenetrable integrity of a space capsule. Several dark-suited American and Asian men, the millennium's strange bedfellows, were waiting outside it to be transported to their appointments high, high above the streets.

♦   ♦   ♦

SOMETIMES WHEN THE WIND FAILED to blow in Long Beach, or when it blew in the wrong direction, I thought I could smell a trace of fish in the petroleum haze, a whiff of mackerel essence, but I must have been imagining it. More fish used to be landed at San Pedro Harbor than anywhere else in the country, but now the commercial fleet was down to about thirty boats, and navy subs on maneuvers ripped through the fishermen's nets.

"All they had to do was look," John Emirzian told the Long Beach newspaper after losing a $3,800 net.

The paper was in trouble. Its circulation was in decline. In southern California, below Los Angeles, nobody wanted to be informed. They just wanted to be entertained.

Long Beach had a symbol of what life might be like away from the petroleum haze. It was Lake Tahoe. The cool, clear lake, the snowcapped Sierra Nevada, and the air-conditioned casinos were pictured often on billboards and advertised in the media.

At a Chinese restaurant one evening, a man across from me was chatting up a waitress, trying to seduce her with the lake, with its icy cleanliness, saying, "Close your eyes and try to imagine it, baby. It's twenty-six miles long and eleven miles wide. . . ."

You could see her going to Lake Tahoe in her head, sniffing at the comforting mountain air and watching this man, this stranger, put dollars on a counter to pay for a hotel room.

My waiter, a Vietnamese youth, was listening, too. He was ready for Lake Tahoe. He lived in Alhambra now and wanted to go to college, but he couldn't save enough money.

"Used to be, I think, you work hard and you get ahead," he told me, accurately handicapping the angles. "Now you need ideas!"

Still, he didn't take it personally, the absence of ideas in his brain, and was glad just to be in the United States, *big free country*. It was harder for a Vietnamese to get in than it used to be, he said, and easier to get stuck at a refugee camp in Hong Kong.

Used to be, used to be. Another evening, at Pine Avenue Grill, where a department store used to be, the cashier, Lily, noticed my surname and said that I was her second Slav in a row. You looked for such small conjunctive treats when you worked an eight-hour shift behind a cash register.

Lily was a Slav, too, from Queens, New York. Her parents had brought her to California when they'd retired to Orange County, but Lily wasn't ready to retire. She was twenty-one, red-haired, punked out, speedy, rebellious, and about to join the navy. Maybe. Lily was confused.

"I have some bad news for you, Lily," I said, teasing her. "It doesn't get any better."

"Please don't say that."

"The positive side is that it doesn't bother you so much."

Lily pouted. "If I join the navy, I'll get to travel, at least."

"You'll see the world, Lily."

At my motel, I opened the windows to smell the ocean air and tried to block the petroleum haze. Colored lights were blinking on the dead-astronaut oil islands. I thought about the Slovenian Hall in Delano, platters of beef, Iowan picnics, Japanese investors, and knock-off Italian shoes made in Taiwan coming through the Port of Long Beach.

Then I lay in bed and tried to hold California together in my head, but I couldn't, so I drifted instead and in half-sleep began ticking off a checklist of items you'd need to survive in the state once the calendar rolled over into the next century—goat cheese, arugula, condoms, yen. . . .

OUT ON SANTA FE AVENUE one afternoon, Keith Williams and Brittney Powers were painting a mural on a four-foot-high stucco wall that ran for thirty or so feet around the border of an older neighborhood. They were true artists and threw everything they had into their work. Passing motorists slowed down as if they'd been stunned by a bolt of sunlight and raised a hand in salute.

The artists were proud of their reception. They called the mural

"Irie Park." In the language of reggae, *irie* meant "to feel good."

They were reggae fans, young black men in their early twenties. Powers wore a painter's cap with the brim flipped up and had two earrings in one ear, a stud and a little hoop. His trousers and his sneakers were covered with paint, and his eyes shone intensely with pleasure, while Williams was cooler and more studied, a former hoopster in dreadlocks stepping back to examine the mural at a distance.

"It's fresh," he said, after a bit.

Powers cackled in joy. "It's fresh, all right."

They went at it again. I watched them, leaning against my car. They worked for the city in a program to paint over graffiti in rough neighborhoods and replace it with murals. Often they had the local kids pitching in. Williams was the captain of the team and always stuck an upbeat message or two onto a wall. He had done some painted backdrops for reggae bands and carried a looseleaf portfolio of photos and sketches and also some press clippings about his art.

Powers had his own notebook. He filled it with private musings, stuff that came at him when he was tired, late at night, rushing past his defenses—portraits of Prince and Mike Tyson, a whimsical drawing of Hitler going to hell in disco clothes.

The city gave the artists a van for their job. Paint cans and art supplies crammed the interior, but they still took their breaks sitting in back because they liked the shade.

They told me during a break about the seriocomic aspects of being an urban muralist. Finding a place to pee was a constant in the battery of problems that faced them. It could be acute in neighborhoods where trees or gas stations were rare.

The hose problem could also be severe. Brushes had to be rinsed, so it was up to you to befriend somebody who'd give you water. That wasn't as easy as you'd think. People made excuses. They invoked a drought or wondered aloud if you might be a thief or a murderer who'd broken out of prison.

"So you've been everywhere in California?" Williams asked me, wanting to hear more about my trip.

"Not everywhere," I said. "But I've seen a lot of it." And I told them some of what I'd seen.

Williams had done some traveling. "You know where I'd go if I could? Someplace up north. Mill Valley, the Berkeley Hills." He smiled dreamily. "All that green."

I thought then that Californians must be unusual in their ability to imaginatively inhabit a place, sailing off in their heads into the great geographical diversity of the state. Maybe we were all Else-wherians in the end, committed to a terrain that only half-existed on earth.

Williams's family roots were in Texas. Powers's grandfather was a Louisiana preacher who'd come West with a dollar in his pocket. Williams had an apartment in Long Beach, while Powers lived at home with his mother. She was a teaching assistant in comparative literature at Cal State, Long Beach, where he went to school, majoring in video arts.

Powers was concerned that his own neighborhood was becoming less stable. An absentee owner had leased a house to a crack dealer, so zombies floated by at all hours. It distressed Powers that they always seemed to stop for a time in front of his house.

"You got that nice lawn," Williams suggested.

"Yeah," said Powers dryly. "They must be drawn to it."

Powers believed that the press had exaggerated the amount of gang activity in Long Beach. He knew of a couple of big dealers who'd moved to Oregon and Arizona respectively because the police there were much easier to outfox. Some younger kids were in training and worked as lookouts and errand boys, but what else could you expect with the public schools the way they were?

The economy wasn't much help, either. Powers shook his head at the idea of a minimum-wage job, flipping burgers at some fran-chise. Still, he was fond of Long Beach, and so was Williams.

"It's a pretty good town," Williams said. "It's been good to me."

"I've been here twenty-one years, so it must have some hold on me," Powers chimed in. The intensity of his eyes brightened by a degree. "And when I'm visiting in Louisiana, being from California is like American Express Gold. The girls won't leave me alone!"

That cracked up Williams. "I'm surprised you ever come back!"

Powers considered this in silence for a moment. It required a response. "I don't like driving twenty miles to go to a party," he said, putting the excuse out there like a trial balloon and hoping that Williams wouldn't prick it with a pin.

Then their break was over. They closed up the van and did some random stretching to prepare for their next stint on the pavement. Williams opened a can of paint and started filling in the white space around some leaping basketball players.

The artists had impressed me with their lack of rancor. Williams and Powers were walking a hard road and knew that they were walking it, but they did it with joy and with spirit. They were both worried about money, though, since the funding for their program was in jeopardy in a way that funding for the World Trade Center was not.

As I was going, Williams came over and asked shyly if I made my living as a writer. I allowed that I did, sort of, with the usual pinching of pennies, and he confessed that he hoped to do the same as a painter someday. He'd had a recent show at a gallery downtown and had got some nice reviews.

"It's one thing to be a starving artist," he said, laughing at his predicament. "But it's a whole other thing to be a starving *black* artist."

Williams walked me to my car, and I had a wishful moment picturing him painting in a little cabin high up in the greenery of Mount Tamalpais.

•   •   •

BEAVER STREET in Wilmington used to be a tawdry strip that embodied the quintessence of every nasty dream born at sea, a sailors' playground with bars, burlesque shows, and bordellos all competing for a chance to steal a fellow's money. The action had died there years ago, and now Wilmington was a poor, blue-collar town, an Oildale-by-the-sea that was a short drive from Long Beach. The population was about two-thirds Mexican, and many of the Mexicans were foreign-born.

Wilmington had some refineries and some scrap-metal yards. In a decaying building hemmed in by crashing winos and the salvation missions that served them, I found the International Longshoremen's Union. Rene Herrera, the local's president, had agreed to talk to me about how dockworkers were faring at a modern port.

I waited for twenty minutes in a lobby hung with old maritime photos, visions of Fred Sands dancing in my head, before Herrera finally summoned me. He was a burly, bearded man who looked as if he could carry a ton of bricks up a gangplank. A little gold cross dangled from a chain around his neck. Some cronies were listening in as he spoke on the phone, dealing heatedly with a grievance.

The arguing continued for a while. It was like watching a scene from an old movie that was paying homage to an ancient dialectic. Herrera hung up at last and stared at me in a distasteful way. I could have been a scab.

"So what can I do for you?" he asked.

"You were going to tell me about how it is for a longshoreman in Long Beach today."

"Can't talk about it. We're in negotiations with the port."

There wasn't much Herrera *could* talk about. He had lots of excuses—it was a bad day, he was very busy. He suggested that I contact the union's historian, but I was interested in the present, not the past. Maybe if we set up another appointment in a couple of days?

"Sure. You give me a call." And I did give him a call, but Herrera was always in conference or on another line or out of the office, and he never got back to me.

Probably all the unions had to talk about, I thought, was the past. They represented just 16 percent of workers nationwide. The working stiff was dying in California, and the unions were dying with him.

THE COASTAL PLAIN between Long Beach and Los Angeles was a wilderness of tracts that were divided, one from another, by a haphazard sprinkling of strip malls and also larger malls where franchises competed for the dollars deposited in such unredeemable banks as Bellflower Savings & Loan or Lakewood Trust. Duplication and replication were the order of the day, and every new idea was quickly beaten into submission and copied not once but a trillion times, squeezed until nothing was left of its essence.

Weird start-up companies dedicated to the dream of someday becoming a chain, inchoate Von's and Ralph's and Wendy's, were marketing every useless item under the sun, bassinets for pooches and mood rings made from wishbones, and they left behind them a trail of unhappy creditors in the wake of their inevitable demise.

This was the Land of No Return, of empty heads and turned-out pockets, a slice of the state that New Yorkers always held up to scorn in their overarching paranoia about California.

Again, the story was familiar. The plain had once supported dairies. There used to be bean fields, fields of grain, and some orange and lemon groves. There used to be a paradise. Now you saw industrial parks with chainlink fences. You saw architecturally redundant plants built by military contractors such as McDonnell Douglas, where riveters fortunate enough to still be employed worked overtime to meet their monthly mortgage payment.

You saw many refineries because the plain was suffused with oil. The refineries belched their petroleum haze, and it blended with tailpipe effusions and the spent diesel fumes from Los Angeles International Airport to produce a truly creative smog.

So putrid was the air in Torrance, a suburb not terribly far from the ocean, that more than a hundred people had just filed a class-action suit against a Mobil refinery, charging that its emissions were responsible for causing respiratory problems, skin rashes, blisters, and cancers of the nose and throat.

The coastal plain was fraught with wonders. In Torrance, a little three-bedroom house twenty yards from a refinery had an asking price of $219,500. In Paramount, the city manager was swaggering because a new refinery there would furnish enough new revenue in taxes to add a sergeant and a detective to the task force fighting gangs.

Over in Compton, the gang kids were plugging one another with the sportive alacrity of hunters after quail. In Carson, there was a Choose-'N-Cut Christmas tree farm next to a Rockwell International plant. And in Lynwood, the citizens were trying to recall some city council members who'd changed the name of a street to honor Martin Luther King, Jr.

"Let's face it," said one of the accused defensively. "Would anybody have cared if we called it John Wayne Boulevard?"

All these things were really happening in California.

THE OCEAN, yes, brings us sanity. At the pier in Redondo Beach, a seaside town, the new Californians were reliving the great, unpackaged American boardwalk-and-arcade adventure and recapturing the lost innocence of a public space in the process. Honest life was bubbling and spurting everywhere as they kissed beneath lampposts and mugged by a statue of George Firth, the hero surfer.

They were eating crab, fried clams, pizza, kimchi, tacos, and steamed rice while they held hands and argued and giggled and fell in love. There was scarcely a white face among them.

A Korean woman was teaching her four-year-old son to play

Skee-Ball. Honest life! The boy didn't have a clue what to do. It
was late August, but he was bundled in layers of clothes. He would
roll a ball, and the ball would roll back at him. Finally, he picked
up a ball and flung it at the target. His mother didn't mind. She
yanked at the zipper on his snowsuit to keep the breezes at bay.

Out on the pier, anglers were hoping to catch some dinner. A
stout Mexican in a flowered shirt reeled in a tiny octopus that was
clamped to his hook. He treated it as gently as a kitten, easing it free
and letting it crawl over his forearm. The octopus lurched forward
on its little tentacles, its blob of a noggin bobbing.

"Let me tell you, this is some kind of strange feeling," the
Mexican said, displaying his arm and chuckling over the mysteries
of the deep.

There was a Vietnamese family fishing nearby—a mom, two
grandparents, and five children. The oldest boy, who was seventeen,
had come to Redondo Beach alone from his home in Cerritos early
that morning. He had wanted to land a big halibut and have a
Polaroid of himself and the trophy fish posted in the bait-shop window, but he'd been unlucky so far and had decided that it was time
to drop the pretense and torment his smallest brother.

"Look!" he shouted, snagging his hook on an underwater ledge
and straining against the bend that it put in his rod. He struggled
for a couple of minutes, then let the line go slack. "That was it! That
was some big halibut!"

His brother had obviously been through the drill before and
wasn't having any. "It could be anything that lives in the sea," he
said.

The grandmother smiled and patted him on the head.

Soon the older boy had a strike for real and brought in a small,
flat fish that would not have made a trophy even in a world where
fish were rare.

"Number ten," his mother said dismissively.

I asked her, "Is it a flounder?"

"No, halibut. But too small. He must throw it back."
"Flounder are smarter than halibut," the small brother told me.
"How do you know?"
"Nobody catches 'em so much."
In the observable fact, there is always wisdom.

A SUMMER MORNING in Long Beach, the blue of San Pedro Bay and the sky hazy with petroleum. Ships coming to port from all across the globe.

The *Admiralty Bay,* a tanker from Valdez. The *Kauai* from Honolulu bringing pineapples. The *Hyundai Challenger* out of Yokohama. The *Samoan Reefer* from Porto Armuelles loaded with Chiquita bananas. The *Novo Mesto* from Inchŏn with a cargo of shoes and purses.

Around Point Fermin they went, past the lighthouse and Cabrillo Beach to cut through the San Pedro breakwater and enter the harbor at Angels Gate. Or they rounded in from the east and entered through Queens Gate, a gap between the Long Beach and Middle breakwaters.

Ships laden with fish pulled into Fish Harbor, off Terminal Island, where trucks parked on Bass Street, Tuna Street, and Sardine Street awaited them. Ships in need of repair glided along the Main Channel and under Vincent Thomas Bridge to the Turning Basin, then swung west to Todd Shipyards.

Passenger ships docked at passenger terminals. There were terminals for bananas, autos, gypsum, and borax.

Container ships made up the bulk of the fleet after tankers. They were serviced at container terminals at both ports. Giant gantry cranes did the unloading. They stacked the rectangular containers like children's blocks. There was no mess. Nothing spilled out, nothing slopped over.

It used to be said that a longshoreman never had to bring his lunch to work because he could eat off the docks. Here an apple, there a banana. Life slopped over then, it spilled out uncontained.

Longshoremen still worked the port, but there weren't many of them. Nobody ever got laid off, but nobody ever got hired. The longshoremen looked at the gantry cranes and knew their future.

On the docks, you heard the grinding of machinery and the muffled roar of traffic. Seabirds circled on the wing. Gulls, cormorants, brown pelicans. The air smelled of gasoline.

CHAPTER 25

ORANGE COUNTY, the home of Disneyland, had a history of giving rise to fantasies. Helena Modjeska, a Polish actress renowned for her Shakespearian roles, was among those who had succumbed to its allure. Before emigrating to Anaheim with her husband, Count Charles Chlapowski, and some friends in 1876, she had rhapsodic visions of what her new life would be like. Poland was under the Russian boot at the time, and intellectuals in Warsaw and Cracow looked on California as a country of light, air, and magic, where the forces of repression did not exist.

In a memoir, Modjeska recorded her feelings as she was about to embark:

> Oh, but to cook under the sapphire-blue sky in the land of freedom! What Joy! I thought. To bleach linen at the brook like the maidens of Homer's *Iliad*! After the day of toil, to play the guitar and sing by moonlight, to recite poems, or to listen to the mocking-bird! And listening to our songs would be charming Indian maidens, our neighbors, making wreaths of luxuriant wildflowers for us. . . .

Anaheim was the county's pioneer town. Its settlers were German Jews from San Francisco who'd been recruited by John Froehling, a vintner in the city, to grow grapes under contract on the coastal plain. In 1857, they had traveled to a newly purchased tract of 1,165 acres on the Santa Ana River and made their home *(heim)* on the stream.

For a payment of seven hundred and fifty dollars, each member of the newly formed Los Angeles Vineyard Society got a twenty-acre lot. The society was a mixed group and included in its ranks some carpenters, blacksmiths, and merchants, as well as an engraver, a musician, a poet, and a bookbinder. They hired Mexicans to plant their rootstock, dig an irrigation system, and fence the property with forty thousand willow poles, and soon their vines were bearing so heavily that Froehling bought enough grapes from them every year to produce about 120,000 gallons of wine and brandy.

The Poles, on the other hand, were a frankly utopian crew. They hoped to model their community on Brook Farm in Massachusetts, although they knew nothing at all about farming, a dilemma that they tried to solve in an intellectual way. Sailing from Bremen, they docked briefly in New York and made a foray to Washington to pick up some government pamphlets on agriculture to study while they were steaming through the second leg of their journey, around Panama to San Francisco.

In Anaheim, they found waiting for them a two-bedroom frame house scarcely big enough to accommodate them all, but they were not easily daunted. With a burst of communal energy, they began tilling the soil, but they discovered to their displeasure that the physical labor made their muscles sore. Moreover, they didn't like the blood and guts of certain barnyard chores. It took three of them to butcher a single turkey. They were artists, not farmers, and they retreated, predictably, into art.

The odd thing about the Poles was that they seemed to accept their failure without complaint. They never howled or beat their breasts. One colonist, Henryk Sienkiewicz, the author of *Quo Vadis?*

and a Nobel laureate in 1905, simply dragged a table into the shade
of some trees and sat there smoking his pipe and writing in his
notebook while the entire enterprise was going down the tubes.

"You ought to have seen how jolly they used to be," a neighbor
once remarked, "when everything on the farm was drying up in the
sun and the animals were all sick and dying."

The communards went through about fifteen thousand dollars
in six months, a vast sum back then, and reckoned, as Modjeska put
it, "that our farming was not a success." Nobody would milk the
cows, so they had to buy their milk and butter. Dogs ate the eggs
that their chickens laid, and other farmers stole the muscat grapes
from their vines. Range cattle devoured their barley fields in spite of
Modjeska's firing at them with her revolver.

After less than a year in Anaheim, the Poles sold the farm and
sank the proceeds into return tickets to Poland—all but Modjeska,
who stayed on to make her mark in the American theater, playing
opposite such great actors as Edwin Booth. She retired at last to a
mansion in the Cleveland Mountains, not far from her old homestead.

The vineyards were gone from Orange County now, of course,
and so were the orange groves and most other traces of agriculture.
There was nothing beautiful to engage my eye as I drove toward
Anaheim on the Santa Ana Freeway, just the same old march of cars
and houses.

The absence of promise, the dullness of the undifferentiated
malls, the containerization, the way Orange County seemed to stick
a knife into your brain and drain it of ideas—the landscape might
be oppressive to me, but those who lived in the county were enchanted
by it. According to a recent poll in the *Times,* they were among the
happiest and most optimistic of all Californians.

Almost all the people in the survey had declared that they were
"very happy" or "somewhat happy" in Orange County. The single
factor determining a person's happiness appeared to be his or her
relative wealth. The more money that you made, the more likely you

were to be "very" rather than "somewhat" happy, but even among
the county's disadvantaged, those earning less than twenty thousand
a year, only 4 percent admitted to being "not too happy."

Fully a third of the respondents agreed that "living in Orange
County is the closest thing to paradise in America."

In the paradise of Orange County, real estate was a central
concern. The median price of a house was among the highest in the
state, and the homeowners, said the *Times* poll, were very attached
to their property. They were also attached to their automobiles and
enjoyed them as objects, status symbols, and private universes. They
liked to wax, buff, decorate, and personalize them. They liked how
they looked in them, and they liked to see how other drivers looked
in *their* cars, engaging in an act of mass voyeurism on wheels—but
they were worried about the traffic on the freeways.

In theory, they believed in car pooling and in mass transit, but
they confessed that they would never join a car pool, or ride a bus,
a trolley, or a subway.

"What it comes down to," the *Times* pollster had commented,
"is that people are hoping for a miracle that won't cost them anything
and that will allow them to commute the way they always have,
which is driving to work."

The citizens of Orange County had expressed some other concerns in the poll. They felt that the chief social problem among adults
was alcohol, with "lack of values" finishing second. Among the young,
drugs replaced alcohol at the top, but "lack of values" again garnered the second spot. Promiscuity fell near the bottom of both
charts.

The Bible was still an important text to most people, with 30
percent of the survey group taking it as the literal truth, but they
were not as rigidly conservative as you might imagine. They supported a woman's right to abortion and the right to rent pornogra-
phic videos. A majority rated the "moral climate" of the county
as "somewhat permissible" and endorsed an unwritten rule that
mutually consenting parties could do whatever they wanted to each

other as long as they did it in the privacy of their own container.

That was progress, really, in a county where the John Birch Society had thrived, where the airport was called John Wayne International, and where, in Yorba Linda, there was a museum honoring Richard Nixon, who'd also had his Western White House at San Clemente on the coast.

Harbor Boulevard in Anaheim paved the way to Disneyland, the very capital of happiness in Orange County. Walt Disney had called it the "happiest place on earth," in fact, but as I looked at the many cheesy gift shops and motels selling Disneyana, I wondered if I could handle happiness in such measure. Already I was beginning to question the wisdom of my mission, thinking that to tackle the park without an obligatory child or two in tow might do me significant damage.

AT THE ANAHEIM PUBLIC LIBRARY, I did some browsing and learned that the Disney family had ancient ties to California. Walt's paternal grandfather, Kepple, was the first to break for the Coast, leaving his farm on Lake Huron in 1878 for a belated junket to the gold mines. He brought along his two older brothers and his oldest son, Elias, a devoutly religious youth of nineteen. Elias could spout Bible passages whole and was a firm believer in hellfire and brimstone and probably in the literalness of the Holy Book.

During a stopover in Kansas, Kepple and the boys made Elias the butt of a cruel joke. They hired a bordello whore to relieve him of his virginity while they watched through a peephole in a closet door. Elias fended the woman off and angrily refused to continue the trip. Once Kepple had sobered up, he felt guilty about what he'd done and gave his son a grubstake before going on.

Elias was a troubled, unstable, restless soul. He bought a farm with his stake, but he didn't stay put. Instead, he bounced around working as a machinist and an apprentice carpenter and finally landed in Denver playing his fiddle outside saloons. Too shy to court his sweetheart, Flora Call, in Kansas, he followed her to Florida when she moved there with her family, and they were wed in 1888.

Elias kept struggling for the next few years. He failed at being a cattle rancher, managed a resort hotel in Daytona Beach, and enlisted in the militia, only to desert it when a war with Spain did not materialize. Flora invested her savings in a Florida orange grove, but the oranges died in a killer frost.

In the humid, swampy climate, Elias contracted malaria, so the Disneys moved to Chicago, where Walt was born in 1901, a child of the new century and the fourth of five kids. The city soon rankled Elias with its sinfulness and once again he fled, buying another farm, this time in Marcelline, Missouri, deep in the Bible Belt.

Walt would later remark that his years in Marcelline were his most satisfying. He gave all the barnyard animals names and liked to draw sketches of them, a hobby that bore fruit in his cartoons and his movies. So attached to the farm did he become that after his success in Hollywood he built a workshop on his estate that was a replica of his childhood barn in Missouri—a barn that was not a barn but merely a cleansed and sanitized version of one.

The Disneys didn't last in Marcelline, either. Swine fever ravaged all their hogs, and the ever-susceptible Elias caught typhoid fever. Now in his early fifties, frail, humorless, and embittered, he moved the family to Kansas City and put Walt and his brother, Roy, to work delivering newspapers for a franchise that he operated, skimming their wages in the process.

Roy was the first to rebel. He took an apartment of his own and got a job as a bank clerk. Then, in 1918, Walt broke free by adding a year to his age and joining a Red Cross unit bound for France. He was assigned to the same company as Ray Kroc, the founder of McDonald's, stretching the laws of probability to their very limit. Kroc would remember him as "a strange duck, because whenever we had time off and went to town to chase girls, he stayed in camp drawing pictures."

Walt also had a quiet business on the side. He made phony Kraut

Sniper Derbies, or KSDs, the rare, battle-scarred helmets that American soldiers prized as souvenirs. He'd take an ordinary helmet and
doctor it, shooting bullets at it and then tarnishing the holes and the
burn marks so that they'd look old. It was the sort of tactic he would
later perfect. Instead of banging his head against the hard facts, as
his father did, Walt learned to be playful—to alter the facts, transforming them to suit his taste.

   After the war, Walt went back to Kansas City and began car-
tooning with a vengeance. He was clever and gifted, a natural story-
teller, ebullient, dedicated, ambitious, and willful enough to surmount
the many hurdles that were placed in his path.

1919: With his friend Ub Iwerks, Disney hangs out a shingle as a
      commercial artist.

1920: Kansas City Film Ad Company hires him to draw cartoon
      features at forty dollars a week.

1921: Walt's going to the movies five times a week and animating
      Laugh-O-Grams (topical humor) for his boss.

1922: Takes Laugh-O-Grams indie and produces two cartoon
      shorts, "Puss and Boots" and "Red Riding Hood."

1923: Goes bankrupt trying to complete an *Alice in Wonderland*
      movie that combines cartoon figures and a live little girl. In
      July, he boards a train for California, traveling first class
      despite being broke.

1924: Forms Disney Brothers Studio with Roy to make live action/
      animated "Alice" short subjects.

1925: Weds Lillian Bounds, an inker at his studio and the only
      woman he ever dates seriously as an adult.

1926: A new studio in Silver Lake. Disney Brothers becomes Walt
      Disney Studio, with Walt in charge.

1927: Develops "Oswald the Lucky Rabbit" cartoons. Big success.
      He and Roy build identical, prefab homes on Lyric Avenue.

1928: Universal Pictures and Charlie Mintz, a distributor, connive
      to steal Oswald from Walt, who retaliates with a new cartoon

star, Mortimer Mouse. Mortimer is transformed into the beloved Mickey.

1929: Cuts a deal with another distributor, Pat Powers, for some
Mickey cartoons. Another whopping success.

1930: Powers is accused of withholding money from the Disneys
and also of trying to steal Mickey the way Oswald was stolen.
Walt falls into a major depression and takes an overdose of
sleeping pills.

1931: A million members in the Mickey Mouse Club. Mickey's done
in wax at Madame Tussaud's. Mary Pickford says, "Mickey
is my favorite star."

1932: A licensing agreement to merchandise Disney characters and
their likenesses. Mickey Mouse watches sweep the nation.
Walt wins a unique Academy Award for creating him.

1933: *The Three Little Pigs,* Disney's first really big animated hit.
Porker, a Marcelline hog recollected in tranquillity, serves as
a model. The American public adopts the song "Who's Afraid
of the Big Bad Wolf?" as an anthem.

By 1934, the Disney studio had almost two hundred employees.
Walt had lost his carefree manner and was cracking the whip. If you
were employed at Disney, you were likely to be underpaid and
overworked. The studio even had a dress code, jackets and ties for
men and a ban on trousers for women. Walt distrusted Jews and
never hired a black technician. His fundamentalist background was
beginning to assert itself in middle age.

Although Walt's views and his behavior became increasingly
conservative, he remained a bold and inventive gambler on the creative side. He was willing to invest a half-million dollars in his first
full-color, animated feature, *Snow White and the Seven Dwarfs,* when
nobody thought it would succeed. He even participated in the brainstorming sessions where the names of the seven dwarfs were dreamed
up. Among the discarded ones were Shifty, Flabby, Awful, Crabby,
Snoopy, Nifty, and Woeful.

Snow White went over budget by $1 million, but it netted $8 million in 1938, the year of its wide release. Walt's cartoon characters were invested with more emotion than ever before, and at the premiere in Los Angeles, Hollywood's biggest stars wept openly when the princess was laid upon a stone slab in mock death.

Walt proceeded to do a string of similar pictures, and they had a penetrating impact on most children who were raised in the 1940s and the 1950s. The movies derived their power from the strong, unequivocal feelings that they unleashed. It was impossible *not* to cry when Bambi's mother got trapped in a forest fire. A Disney film of the period was always urgent, primal, and mythic, about art and not packaging.

Yet for all his success, Walt was showing signs of another suicidal depression by 1947. He hit the Scotch whisky regularly and kept up his lifelong cigarette habit, two packs a day, that gave him a rousing smoker's hack and undermined his health. He billed himself as a devoted family man, but he worked long hours at the studio and hated to see the weekend come. He owed a small fortune in loan payments to the Bank of America.

Almost every day, he ate lunch at his desk, usually mixing a can of Gebhardt's chili with a can of Dennison's chili to achieve the proper ratio of meat to beans. His beverage of choice was V-8 juice. He took a new interest in politics and cultivated right-wing causes, contributing heavily to the Republican war chest and socializing with the likes of John Wayne.

Walt had inherited his father's restlessness, but in Walt's case it manifested itself intellectually. He didn't need to jump from one geographical place to the next, only from project to project. He despised being bored, and it annoyed him that he couldn't keep tinkering with a movie once it was done. He wanted to make something organic that would grow and change and never die. He had a farmboy's dream of the eternal.

Disneyland was the cure for Walt Disney's midlife crisis. The inspiration for it came, he said, from the trips that he had made to amusement parks with his daughters after their Sunday school classes. The parks were always filthy and unfriendly, and the parents in them were ill at ease. Mickey Mouse Park, as it was first called, would be nothing like that.

To accomplish his goal, Walt turned into a tireless student of amusement parks around the world. Tivoli Garden in Copenhagen was among his favorites because the grounds were immaculate. Cleanliness seemed to matter more to him than anything. From the start, against the prevailing wisdom, he had insisted on charging admission to keep out the riffraff.

"If I don't," he said once, "there can be drunks and people molesting people on the dark rides."

Getting the project funded wasn't easy. For some seed money, Walt borrowed against his life-insurance policy and then hit on a notion to market his park to a TV network. He sent Roy to New York with some hastily done architect's drawings and a six-page letter elaborating his vision, and a deal was cut with ABC-TV. In exchange for doing a one-hour television series, Walt would receive a half-million dollars in cash and a guaranteed line of credit for another $4.5 million. ABC's payoff was the series plus a 35 percent share of the park.

Walt commissioned Stanford Research Institute to scout for locations. Its researchers pinpointed a 160-acre orange grove in Anaheim that would be close to the center of southern California's population when the Santa Ana Freeway was finished. The landscapers tagged a number of specimen orange trees to be saved as part of the park, but a color-blind bulldozer operator destroyed them by accident.

The most cunning stroke in the Disneyland saga was Walt's intuitive grasp of the impact that TV was having on most Americans. For the first time, he could speak directly to his audience without any interference. On camera, Walt looked harmless, avuncular, and trustworthy. Most viewers *would* buy a used car from him and tended to believe anything that he said.

He used the first program in his series to run "Disneyland Story" in October of 1954, a documentary about the park's construction that was essentially a commercial. He did the same thing on his second show, plugging a new movie, *20,000 Leagues Under the Sea*. The pitch now seemed to be as important to him as the product.

As Disneyland got ready to open, Walt's attention to detail and to scale grew obsessive, as did his fanatical cleanliness. He decreed that no chewing gum could be sold, because people stuck it under benches. Peanuts were also banned unless they'd been shelled. Costumed employees with brooms and dustpans would be constantly patrolling to sweep up debris. Life would not be allowed to spill over. It would be contained.

The grand opening of Disneyland was carried live on ABC in July of 1955. The hosts were three clean, white Republicans, Art Linkletter, Bob Cummings, and Ronald Reagan.

Walt Disney loved his amusement park and loved to tinker with it. Often he had breakfast at Aunt Jemima's pancake house and dinner at Disneyland Hotel. He and Lilly spent nights in an apartment above the firehouse on Main Street. In the morning, he could sometimes be observed walking in his bathrobe to the Sunkist store for a glass of orange juice.

In his later years, Walt threw himself into a curious plan for a "city of the future" in Florida that would be even cleaner and more distant from reality than Disneyland—Experimental Prototype Community of Tomorrow, or Epcot. He did not live to see it built. His health went downhill through the 1960s, and he died of lung cancer on December 15, 1966.

DISNEYLAND ON A MORNING in late August was abuzz with paying customers about to be transformed into "guests," Walt's quaint locution for those who passed through the portals of the number one tourist attraction in the state. For many guests, Disneyland would *be* California, its summation and its *raison d'être*.

The parking lot was filling rapidly at nine o'clock. There were rental cars from Canada, vans packed with hyperactive brats from the Deep South, and an old Bluebird bus loaded with Explorer Scouts from Chihuahua, Mexico. I found a spot on Pluto Street and looked enviously at the dads, uncles, and grandpops who held a child by the hand, wishing that somebody had opened a Rent-a-Kid shop for people like me.

It seemed obvious that an unaccompanied adult was not going to have a great time inside. He would not think that the park was the happiest place on earth. Disneyland might once have been fun for grown-ups, but it had devolved over the years into a cultural rite of passage. A child, especially a California child, could no doubt file a suit in court if his parents hadn't taken him there by the time he was ten.

I pictured how the scene would play on the evening news, with some postliterate, yellow-haired TV reporter kneeling to get the scoop.

"We're here with young Peter Piper of Gardena," he'd say. "Pete, can you you tell us why you're suing your mom and dad?"

"I've never been to Disneyland."

"How old are you, Pete?"

"I'm eleven!"

Disneyland had only one entrance because Uncle Walt had wanted it that way, the better to control and manipulate his guests. You could walk to it easily, but almost everybody lined up to ride there in an open-air tram, surrendering their willpower at the earliest opportunity. Then, at the ticket booths, you got to spend another twenty minutes in line waiting to fork over your thirty dollars.

Waiting would prove to be the order of the day. In my notebook, I wrote, "Getting into the park is like being inducted into the army." I had a feeling that everybody had been briefed but me. Those Hmongs from Fresno would shine here, I thought. They'd chew up Disneyland and spit it out for breakfast.

The young woman in the ticket booth was very polite, but that was part of her job. Walt had been a stickler about demanding courtesy from his hirelings and had lectured them, sometimes scornfully, if they fell short. They were told to think of themselves as actors, not as wage slaves, and to believe that they had a role in a grand theatrical pageant.

Disney had laid down other rules to protect the sanctity of the park. Employees were forbidden to bring a car inside because it might destroy the illusion. Administration buildings were banned for the same reason. And for the same reason, nobody was allowed to take a photo of Disneyland when it was empty, without any guests to give it some life.

At last, I was moving through the entrance. Almost all the guests headed directly for the souvenir shops to buy some Disney memorabilia before they'd done anything worth remembering, but I was fixed in my tracks by the look of the park. It bore an uncanny resemblance to the interchangeable subdivisions of California, with familiar businesses spoking out from its hub—Coca-Cola, Carnation, Kodak, and Bank of America, among others.

When you glanced down the pathways and lanes off the hub, you caught glimpses of attractions that were intended to excite you. The tease was deliberate. Walt hoped to stir the juices of his guests and referred to the glimpses as "weenies," after the hot dogs that animal trainers dangle on a stick.

The lines inside the park were worse than those outside. You could wait for an hour to get on a crack ride such as Splash Mountain—a ride that only lasted for a couple of minutes. In a way, the waiting expanded the scope of Disneyland and made it seem even grander and more insurmountable. If you could see everything on a single visit, you might feel cheated.

The waiting also fostered a weird sort of greediness. Once you'd decided not to squander an hour on Splash Mountain, you started grabbing at any old attraction so that your trip wouldn't be a total waste. That was how I came to be in line for the ten o'clock showing of *Captain EO,* a 3-D movie in which I had not the slightest interest.

Waiting, ever more waiting. A battery of TV sets overhead bombarded us with commercials for Disney films and the Disney Channel. By the time we were seated in the theater, we were at the mercy of our environment, very nearly brainwashed and desperate for something, *anything,* to happen. The Disney planners were aware of that, of course, and they delivered in *Captain EO* the equivalent of a shot of crystal meth into the mainline.

The movie wasn't about anything but sensations. It had no story that you'd relate to a friend, even if you were a child. The music was loud, and the visuals were smashing. *Captain EO* simply overpowered you. It bullied you into submission. The long lines had put us to sleep, and now we were locked into a room with an alarm clock that we couldn't shut off. All around me, I could sense numbed nerves leaping into action, and strange hormones starting to flow.

Our release from the cool, dark theater into full sunlight was another shock to the system. The strategy of Disneyland became apparent—little shocks of a minute or two interspersed with cottony periods of waiting. It grieved me to think that somebody had spent countless hours devising the formula, that market researchers had been set to measuring just how much manipulation a human being could tolerate before he or she went over the wall.

What next? I did some shooting on Boot Hill at the Frontierland Arcade and rode the Mark Twain paddlewheel steamer and saw some Indians, a burning cabin, and some robot deer and elk. In Adventureland, I had a glass of pineapple juice at the Tiki Juice Bar, where the host was Dole Pineapple. For lunch, I went to Big Thunder Barbeque, where the host was Hunt's Ketchup and Barbeque Sauce.

And then, at one in the afternoon, I went over the wall.

Disneyland was a magnificent achievement, I thought. Whether consciously or not, Walt Disney had managed to anticipate the exact feel of life as it would later be manifested in much of suburban California. He had kept things neat and tidy and had given his park the appearance of virtue. For that, he owed a debt to his Bible-thumping father, Elias, who had always craved a world where there were no dark rides.

As Ronald Reagan was the Ultimate Californian, so, too, was Disneyland the Ultimate Suburb.

The organization that Disney built had survived him, and it had prospered through the 1980s. Its stock jumped from $12.50 a share in 1984 to $113.75 toward the end of the decade. Its CEO, Michael Eisner, earned a total compensation of $40.1 million in 1988, more than any other executive at a publicly held corporation in the United States.

In interviews, Eisner was modest about the company's profits. He attributed them to a favorable exchange rate that had attracted foreign tourists, a reemphasis on family values, and an indefinable something that he called "a quest for things past."

IN ANAHEIM, packing up for Palm Springs, I bid farewell to my traveling companions, Edwin Bryant and William Brewer. They had not explored the meridians to the east or to the south, or the far reaches toward the border. Their California existed only in flickers now, in preserves and museums, in the depths of rivers, and in memory.

Bryant had lived out the balance of his life shuttling between Kentucky and the West. For a time in 1847, he served as *alcalde,* or chief magistrate, of San Francisco, and got caught up in the real estate craze and sold town lots until 1853, when he went back to Kentucky again. In 1869, he made a final trip to San Francisco and died there in a hotel, possibly a suicide.

Brewer met with a cheerier fate, accepting a chair in agriculture at Yale when his tour with Professor Whitney was over. He married for a second time and had four children, Nora, Henry, Arthur, and Carl, and taught for thirty-eight years before retiring.

Despite his commitment to teaching, he never lost his taste for travel. He joined an expedition to Greenland in 1894 and journeyed to Alaska five years later when he was seventy-one. The University of California rewarded him with an honorary Doctor of Laws degree in 1910, the year of his death.

Brewer's life was long and full and good. He was a great appreciator. On a Sunday evening in 1861, while camped in the Santa Ana Mountains, he looked up at the sky and wrote dreamily, "We have the most lovely sunsets I have ever seen."

CHAPTER 26

SAN JACINTO TOWN on the way to Palm Springs was dry and bleached and almost empty of citizens on a Sunday morning. Roadrunners darted through it on their way to Arizona. The mayor, Trammell Ford, had left some business cards around that gave his home phone number. It made you want to call him up and say, "Here I am in San Jacinto, Trammell," to see what he could possibly produce in the way of entertainment.

The cards also showed some potatoes rolling out of a cornucopia into verdant fields. Potato farms and dairies were links to San Jacinto's past. In its future, there were Republicans, golf courses, and two thousand new houses.

San Jacinto was in *Ramona* Country, a region of California that Helen Hunt Jackson had put on the map with her novel of that name. She was the child of a Brahmin minister from Massachusetts. Her friend Emily Dickinson had counseled her to take up writing when she was about thirty-five, as an emotional release after her husband had died.

Jackson went to work with a vengeance and quickly poured out a flood of poems, stories, and travel sketches. She became a famous literary figure before she was fifty, hobnobbing with the likes of Nathaniel Hawthorne and the Jameses, Henry and William.

After she married for a second time, she went with her new husband to live in Colorado. Her life underwent a profound change in 1879, when she was on holiday in Boston and heard some touring Indians from the Ponca tribe address a public meeting at which they outlined their grievances against the U.S. government for trying to move them from their ancestral territories in Nebraska to a reservation in Oklahoma.

Jackson was incensed and turned into a staunch defender of the rights of Indians. Two years later, she published *A Century of Dishonor,* a pamphlet that was an indictment of the government for its crimes against Native Americans. That led to her being appointed a commissioner of Indian affairs by President Chester A. Arthur, who asked her to compile a report of the Mission Indians of southern California.

In 1883, she and a fellow commissioner traveled through the domain of such tribes as the Serranos, Cahuillas, San Luiseños, and Dieguiños. Sometimes Jackson spooked the Indians by wearing a hat made from the entire head of an owl. She recorded a pattern of abuse wherein white settlers were forcing the tribes from their lands, trashing their fields, and stealing their houses.

In San Jacinto Valley, she came to a Soboba village at the foot of the San Jacinto Mountains. The Indians were "greatly dispirited and disheartened at the prospect of being driven from their homes," she said. They had always supported themselves as farmers and by hiring out to shear sheep and do vineyard labor, and they had no desire to change.

A Soboba schoolchild, Ramon Cavavi, had written a letter to President Arthur, and Jackson had inserted it into her report.

Dear Sir: I wish to write a letter for you, and I will try to tell you some things. The white people call San Jacinto ranch their land, and I don't want them to do it. We think it is ours, for God gave it to us first. Now I think you will tell me what is right, for you have been so good to us, giving us a school and helping us. Will you not come to San Jacinto some time to see us, the school, and the people of Soboba village? Many of the people are sick, and some have died. We are so poor that we have not enough food for the sick, and sometimes I am afraid that we are all going to die. Will you please tell what is good about our ranches, and come soon to see us.

Your friend,
Ramon Cavavi

Cavavi's handwriting, said Jackson, was "clear and good."

After finishing her report to the president, she set about composing a "sugar-coated pill," *Ramona,* whose intent was to create a sentimental fiction that would drive home the fact that Indians were being mistreated throughout the nation. The story was a spin on *Romeo and Juliet,* telling of a doomed love affair between a beautiful halfbreed, Ramona Ortegna, and her full-blooded Indian husband, Alessandro.

Ramona was a cause célèbre, the *Uncle Tom's Cabin* of its day. It touched the emotions of readers and nudged Congress into action. Three movies were patched together from it, one of them directed by D. W. Griffith, and it also generated a popular love song.

The reservation, Soboba Springs, could still be found in San Jacinto Valley, across the dry bed of the San Jacinto River. The first thing I saw there was a brown mongrel with its tongue hanging out. The second thing was an immense Bingo parlor, as big as a K mart, where an Indian guard in a security uniform was on patrol.

Then the dusty road ran on over bleak, unyielding earth past a Catholic church, a day-care center, two backyard auto-body shops, and a Little League field that had weeds growing in the cracked basepaths and a refreshment stand collapsing into timbers. A hard grounder hit there would roll on forever, all the way to Orange County.

Young Indians left the reservation for nearby Hemet whenever they could, I was told in San Jacinto, and only returned for family emergencies, or if they were ill or had lost a job.

Some of the new houses being built in the valley were not far away, in a development called The Villages at Soboba Springs. The homes were clustered around a golf course that was the only patch of green for miles around. White golfers in peacocky clothes were riding around in carts and smacking at balls.

Maybe you needed the heart of a wealthy Republican to survive down south, I thought, an organ cast in concrete and fitted with pacemakers and plaque-free plastic tubing to let you last through the millennium or the next eighteen holes, whichever came first.

Just another Sunday in the Colorado Desert....

DOWN THE ROAD in Gilman Hot Springs, in a parallel universe, some Scientologists were holding an open house, squeezing it in before the end of the world. Their bait was a trimasted clipper ship, *Star of California,* that appeared to be sunk up to its hull in the ground. Young men and women in quirky naval uniforms scampered over the deck with a paramilitary fervor. The ship and its surroundings had the compelling isolation of a cult compound fortified against a threat, real or imaginary.

Apparently, I had stumbled into a corner of the state where weirdness was king. A few miles away, under a burning sun, Republicans were playing golf on the bones of Soboba Indians, while here the disciples of the late L. Ron Hubbard were making promotional and educational films and tapes about the Churches of Scientology at their compound, Golden Era Productions.

I saw the "gold" in Golden Era and remembered how Charlie Manson's school bus, with *Hollywood Productions* written on its side, had been parked under the trees at Dennis Wilson's house. Manson, who professed to be a theta clear.

In the early 1970s, I'd been stopped a couple of times in San

Francisco by recruiters for Scientology, who carried clipboards and elaborate questionnaires and wondered if I were interested in bettering myself by getting rid of irrational behavior. I found them scarier and more intense than any of the Moonies or Hare Krishnas who'd intercepted me. Once, I had even taken home a questionnaire and grappled with it until the degree of self-reference that it required defeated me.

I was still interested in bettering myself in those days. Now all I wanted was a concrete heart.

Star of California was a tribute to L. Ron Hubbard, who had a passion for nautical imagery and had dubbed his inner core of adepts the Sea Organization, or Sea Org for short. Hubbard himself was "the Commodore" and knew the Colorado Desert well. After publishing *Dianetics: The Modern Science of Mental Health* in 1950, a nationwide bestseller whose merits were touted in such magazines as *Astounding Science Fiction,* he had holed up in a Palm Springs apartment to work on his second book, *Science of Survival.*

The Churches of Scientology had bought 520 acres of land and several buildings at Gilman Hot Springs from Massacre Canyon Inn, a resort, in 1978 to create a haven for Hubbard, reportedly paying $2.7 million for the property. According to a former associate of Hubbard's, the Commodore ordered a house built for himself nearby, outside Hemet, insisting that it be constructed on bedrock in a neighborhood where no blacks lived. It had to be free of dust, defensible, and on higher ground than anything around it.

Armageddon was coming in the form of a nuclear war, the Commodore suggested in a bulletin to his inner circle, but his true enemies were the FBI and the IRS.

The clipper ship was meant to offer Hubbard some comfort in his declining years, when he was rumored to be ill, sometimes grossly overweight, and often incapacitated. It had cost about a half-million dollars to build, but the money had gone mostly for materials, with Sea Org carpenters contributing the labor.

Hubbard seems not to have made much use of the *Star of Cali-*

fornia. Instead, he lived reclusively in a motor home on a 160-acre ranch in Creston, about thirty miles from San Luis Obispo, where yet another house was under construction. Six akitas guarded the ranch's perimeters, and there were also horses, cattle, some llamas, four buffaloes, and Bubba, a prize bull, in residence. At Creston, attended to by his personal physician, the Commodore died of a "cerebral vascular accident" in 1986.

The open house at Golden Era Productions was "open" only a crack. After I signed in at the gate, I was admitted to the compound, where there was a nice Olympic-sized swimming pool with palm trees all around it. The ship was a beautifully crafted piece of work done in rich mahogany and polished brass. Belowdecks, in the captain's quarters, it did feel comforting and enclosed, a space that was safe from any harm.

A journalist had visited the ship shortly after Hubbard's death and had noticed that the Sea Org cadets kept things exactly the way he'd liked them, as if the Commodore might drop in again at any minute. Glasses of drinking water were set out, along with the pads and pencils that Hubbard used to jot down ideas. A pair of his favorite black Thom McAn clogs were positioned in each bathroom, ready to be slipped into after a bath or a shower.

While I was in the captain's quarters, a woman from Golden Era Productions introduced herself to me and said that she would accompany me for the rest of the tour. Free-range browsing would no longer be an option. She was pleasant and ingratiating and had a fixed smile. She would give me the pitch every step of the way, I feared, and try to hook me on betterment again and probably make me pay for it, so I left the compound and missed my chance to listen to the tapes that celebrities such as John Travolta and Karen Black had recorded.

Dianetics was not for me, even though the Commodore had stated in *Dianetics and Scientology Technical Dictionary* that Scientology "is used to increase spiritual freedom, intelligence, ability, and to produce immortality." To my way of thinking, he was really just

another miner who'd struck it rich in California, finding some gold
in the broken hopes of those who'd migrated to the Coast in search
of transcendence and had seen the elephant instead.

IN THE EVENING, feeling overjoyed, as though I'd survived a trip
through the Bermuda Triangle, I reached Palm Springs at last. The
sky above the city was an immaculate blue, and the temperature
hovered near one hundred degrees, a dry and searing heat.

Palm Springs was a celebration of water where water didn't
belong, a liquid flaunting that bubbled in fountains, coursed down
the sides of hotels, rippled in ponds and in swimming pools, and
sprinkled in rainbow arcs over greens and fairways.

The water came from the Colorado River and from snow melting
on the peaks of the San Jacinto Mountains. It came from aquifers
that were in such good shape that the Agua Caliente Indians, the
region's first settlers, claimed that there was enough water underground to last through seventeen years of drought.

The Colorado was a civilized desert. Trash didn't collect in it
as it did in the Mojave. Nobody was driving around equipped with
nuclear capability. It was hotter and more arid, with just three inches
of rainfall in an average year. The main vegetation was creosote bush,
not sagebrush. The mountains, a peninsular range running down
into Baja California, were high and broad and rocky. They rose like
a bulwark between the dire demands of daily life and your privileged
vacation.

Raymond Chandler, a desert rat, knew Palm Springs well. He
called it Poodle Springs "because every third elegant creature you
see has at least one poodle."

Beginning in the 1920s, it was *the* resort for affluent Angelenos
and Hollywood stars. The town's very name was like an imprimatur
of class, and in winter, in high season, a visit could entail a misery-
inducing round of social obligations. You had to attend cocktail
parties and charity balls and never, ever, show that you were aging.

Now there were many desert resort towns, and the competition among them was intense. Palm Springs still had a classy element, but Indian Wells and Bermuda Dunes challenged it for toniness. Rancho Mirage had a less formal, country-club atmosphere and was much favored by retired, Republican golfer-presidents like Gerald Ford.

Dinah Shore Drive ran through Palm Springs, and so did Gene Autry Trail. Gerald Ford Drive and Frank Sinatra Drive guided you east toward Indio. The lanes in South Palm Desert, a subdivision, were named for tennis greats, Bill Tilden, Rod Laver, and Pancho Segura. The roads in Sahara Park honored Aladdin, Araby, and Mecca.

Some roads bisected the Agua Caliente Reservation, and the Agua Calientes collected a toll.

Palm Springs was the native habitat of silver-haired devils. They had uncorruptible tans and skin as taut as lizards. They wore pastel shirts and white slacks and costly loafers without any socks. On their arms were women sometimes half their age and half a head taller, leggy in tennis skirts and always perfectly groomed. There was nothing mortal about them. Money had built another bridge.

I had a sense that nothing in Palm Springs was ever finished or completed. Completion implied a kind of death, and death was to be avoided. Every house I saw was being renovated or added to, fitted with Roman shades, burlap side drapes, or an Ambiance luxury tub that could be commanded to fill automatically at a signal from your cellular phone. Gardens were tiered and transitional, sand verbena and brittlebush flowing between the mountains and the desert.

Faces and bodies were being renovated, too, on a scale that shamed Beverly Hills. No woman and few men over forty went untouched. The battling among cosmetic surgeons could be intense. A surgeon scored points for each procedure done on a president, a star, or a celebrity. Two prominent doctors, Borko Djordjevic and M. Reza Mazaheri, had even feuded in public over which of them had really "done" Betty Ford's face.

Behzad Mohit, M.D., FAACS, saw himself as a toiler in the tradition of Michelangelo. "Medical schools and cosmetic surgery training programs will, by necessity, have to select artistic talents and train them in the fundamentals of art and sculpture," he had once said, in public.

Toward the end of the 1920s, some Hollywood stars were tiring of Palm Springs, feeling put upon and overexposed, so they chose to ride in chauffeured town cars for another twenty miles to the outpost of La Quinta Hotel—Greta Garbo, Delores Del Rio, Ginger Rogers, Bette Davis, Clark Gable, Errol Flynn, Frank Capra, the list went on.

Summer was "value season" in the desert, a time when the heat forced resorts to cut their rates in half, so I drove the extra miles to La Quinta, where the buildings were light and airy, like a sun-washed village in Greece. My *casita* had a deck that looked out on the mountains and a big, comfortable bed that I sank into early, with the profoundest gratitude.

IN THE COLORADO DESERT, a paradise of golf, there were links for everyone. The pastel legions began their assault on the front nine at first light, striding briskly forward to get in a round before ten o'clock, when the sun would be too strong for all but the most dedicated players. In every part of the desert, you heard the *thwock* of clubs against balls and saw if you looked up hundreds of little white asteroids against that immaculate blue sky.

Marriott's Desert Springs in Palm Desert, between Rancho Mirage and Indian Wells, was among the newer resorts to open. On its four hundred acres, it had two 18-hole courses that rolled through a "Fantasy Island" landscape of ponds and lagoons where ducks, swans, geese, and flamingos were sporting. Even in the heat of value season, the fairways were emerald green and smoothly flowing, and they would stay that way until the first winter frost.

Jim Lopez was a veteran of the Marriott chain. He had started as a doorman in Houston eighteen years ago and now held a position as director of marketing at Desert Springs. He was a genial, easygoing fellow, who had an athletic bearing and enjoyed the pastimes that he promoted, the golf and the tennis and the swimming.

Lopez assured me that golf courses were vital to every resort around. The links at Desert Springs were being planned and developed long before construction began on the hotel proper. The architect, Ted Robinson, had done some other courses in the valley and knew the terrain and how to make use of the native vegetation.

Sometimes a golf-course architect could make or break a place, Lopez said. The most famous of them, a Pete Dye or a Robert Trent Jones, attracted guests simply by putting his autograph on the turf.

The soil in the desert was quite fertile, Lopez told me. Grass took to it with surprising ease. The Desert Springs fairways were a blend of Bermuda grass and ryegrass. The ryegrass grew straight up, and the Bermuda grass ran across its grain. Ryegrass was sturdy and tougher to swing a club through, while Bermuda grass was greener and lusher and did better in the heat.

To build the lakes on the course, workers had scooped out beds and lined them with polyurethane to prevent seepage. A layer of sand went on top of that. All the lakes had to be filtered. The resort pumped about a million gallons of water a day through its filtration system.

The Desert Springs courses seemed to be a hit with golfers so far, Lopez went on. The eighteenth hole on one course was the trickiest in the valley. The hotel was booked to about 80 or 90 percent of its capacity on summer weekends. The Marriott tried to bring in conventions during the week—for that, the hotel absolutely had to have a golf package.

Lopez traveled to Tokyo at least once a year to sell the resort to the Japanese. They were discriminating buyers, he felt. They worried about crime and about terrorists and played thirty-six holes on every day of their vacation, eighteen in the morning and eighteen in the afternoon, regardless of the temperature.

Television was the chief merchandiser of the golf courses around Palm Springs, though. Big tournaments like The Bob Hope Desert Classic, The Dinah Shore Invitational, or the Skins Game were brilliant advertisements that reached millions of viewers—advertisements for California, like the Rose Bowl Parade.

In snowbound Maine, in the dead of winter, duffers in their armchairs gaped at the perfect sky and the perfect grass and imagined themselves in the tasseled shoes of their favorite pro. The chance to play a world-class course like PGA West was as savory to them as taking batting practice at Yankee Stadium might be to the weekend softball hero.

I wandered around Desert Springs astonished at how the raw desert had been transformed. Around the main swimming pool, guests who had already turned the color of peanut butter basted themselves with lotions that were the very scent of dwindling summer. Koi in the ponds shimmered in reds, oranges, and gold. The flamingos, Central American in origin and brokered through the San Diego Zoo, stood sleeping in their lake.

EVENING WAS THE PAYOFF TIME in the Colorado Desert. I sat on my deck at La Quinta pleasantly tired from walking and swimming, as others were tired from tennis or golf, and had a drink and watched the light fall across the mountains. There was nothing beyond the moment, nothing but a sensation that my body was surrendering to the elements, bathing in them.

I became a Republican drifting toward the libidinous dark and thought of women in hotel bathrooms, their skin flushed from the shower, touching a soft towel to the damp between their legs. I thought about the damp and saw them run a brush through their wet hair and touch the towel to their nipples.

They put on G-string panties and wriggled into leather miniskirts and applied red lipstick to their beestung lips, all for me.

Republicans knew their secrets and what they were whispering. Republicans knew the right things to do.

Then I set off into the dusky valley, where the air was cooling but still warm on my skin, and the lights along the boulevards were coming on. It gave me that old feeling of being among the chosen in California. It was as if all the exercise and the sunshine and the oat bran and the mineral water were merely a prelude to this, bringing us all to a peak in the evening. My blood began to beat. Tiny motors began to whir.

Rudy knew about the evening. He knew about the light and the air and the sex. He earned a living by parking cars at various restaurants and hotels. He had a ponytail and good teeth and sometimes worried that he was wasting his life. He came from a farm town in the San Joaquin and wished that he had finished college and gone into business, but here he was parking cars instead. He was almost thirty.

Resort life had taught Rudy something, though, and he shared it with me once—money was not the same as class. Class, he told me, was "doing what's appropriate." He hated it when a beautiful girl fucked a guy just because he had a Learjet.

In Palm Springs, Rudy and two friends rented a house. It had four bedrooms and a swimming pool. Sometimes when he got home from work and the worries about his future put a knot into his back, he would turn on the stereo, fire up a joint, and slip naked into the pool. He would take the rubber band from his ponytail and let his hair flow all around him.

Suspended in the blue, he would close his eyes and feel his worries dissolving, made immaterial and insubstantial. At that moment, he knew that he wasn't going anywhere, not ever, because nowhere else could be so good.

THE GRAND RESORTS of the Colorado Desert vanished beyond La Quinta, and the landscape turned agricultural. Along Highway 111, in the first week of September, I came to Shields Date Gardens in Indio, in Coachella Valley. Date palms grew in rows, their fronds snapping in a breeze. Water stood in the ditches between rows. The trees needed the equivalent of 120 inches of rain a year to produce a crop. They were irrigated every ten days.

An old saying went, "A date palm must have its feet in the water and its head in the fires of heaven."

Mission fathers had brought the first date palms to California, and Bess M. and E. Floyd Shields had gone on from there. They'd been in business since 1924. Sometimes in photos E. Floyd could be seen standing proudly in the grove, wearing a pith helmet and showing off a special palm, such as the great-great-grandmother date that the Shields had imported from Algeria. The tree was in its eighties now.

Many of the Shields' trees were from Algerian stock. They had about 1,200 date palms and 700 citrus trees—oranges, lemons, and grapefruit. They had dates in 119 varieties. One variety, Shields Black Beauty, was so rare that its sale was limited, one to a customer.

The Shields had an air-conditioned theater where a slide show, "The Romance and Sex Life of the Date," played continuously. It told the story of date propagation in a comic way. To appreciate it, you had to be really hot and sweaty and so desperate for a break from the desert that slides of male and female date blossoms appealed to you.

I went on into Indio. The town was new and cheap, home to more retired people in trailer parks and Mexicans who worked at the resorts around Palm Springs and on farms in Coachella Valley. Sometimes Indians from the Cabazon Reservation blew through.

In Indio, the last soda fountain had just closed. A developer, Mirage Homes, had houses for sale at Avenue 48 and Arabia. I slept in a noisy motel and nearly wept with nostalgia for my room at La Quinta, for the high, broad, dusky mountains and the women fresh from their showers.

In the morning, I sat in my car in a business park drinking bad coffee that I'd bought at a donut shop. Before me were the offices of Doctors Badri and Arha Nath. I decided that Indio was not a town I had to spend time in. It couldn't tell me anything about California that I didn't already know.

THROUGH THE LITTLE VILLAGES of Thermal and Mecca on Highway 111, Coachella Valley grew very wide. The earth was sandy and a pale brown color. There were olive trees, willows, fan palms, and citrus groves. Some table grapes were staked and trellised in fields. The light was delicate, even fragile, and very beautiful. In a split second, California had fooled me again by turning into Jerusalem.

I was on my way to the Salton Sea. It was 108 degrees when I left Indio. My radio was tuned to the hits on K-PALM, and I could feel the aridity in my nostrils and looked at my forearms and saw how tan I'd become without even trying.

The Salton Sea was a freak, an accident. At the very end of the nineteenth century, George Chaffey, an engineer, had teamed with Charles Rockwood, who'd been with the railroads, to form the California Development Company and bring water from the Colorado River to the desert. The CDC was a real estate setup to sell irrigated land to farmers, in an area that the partners agreed to call Imperial Valley.

Chaffey designed a canal to bring the river water to the valley. The system didn't deliver enough water in dry years, however, so Rockwood took it upon himself to cut a bypass, the Rockwood Cut, around the canal and its gate. When the Colorado flooded in 1905, it overflowed the revamped system and poured into an old lakebed, the Salton Sink, which was about 250 feet below sea level. For nearly two years, the river kept pouring into the sink, leaving a "sea" that had no outlet, except for some irrigation ditches.

The Salton Sea was about 45 miles long and some 83 feet deep. I could smell it before I could see it—the heat had incited a powerful stink of algae and murk. It was saltier than the Pacific Ocean because

Coachella and Imperial Valley farmers flushed the salts from their soil with irrigated water, and the water all drained downhill into the sea. So did high concentrations of selenium, a naturally occurring element that can cause birth defects and nesting failure among waterfowl and shorebirds.

At Salton Sea State Recreation Area, a ranger gave me a pass and some materials about the park. They advised anglers to dine judiciously on their catch, because the fish were likely to be tainted with selenium. So spectacular was the birding during migratory season, the materials said, that birders from abroad sometimes made a special pilgrimage.

Up close, the stink of the sea was hard to take, but some children were eagerly splashing in it, anyway. Their families had brought them down from Riverside for a day at the beach. The sea had a greenish tint and was swarming with plant life. Rangers kept it stocked with tilapia, who were algae eaters. Tilapia were rumored to be the fish that Jesus used to feed the multitudes.

You could also catch corbina and croaker in the sea. I watched two black couples scaling and gutting a mess of croaker that ran to the size of sunfish or crappies. The couples were from Riverside, too, and had driven down in a van. They came all the time, they said. They were fleshy and middle-aged. The oldest of the men seemed to be in a private funk out of which he rose to regard me with baleful, bloodshot eyes.

"They're easy fish to catch," he told me. "We only fished for about two hours."

"Were you using bait?" I asked.

"Mmm-hmm. Anchovies." He accented the second syllable, an*cho*vies.

They sipped from cans of Meister Bräu and went about their job in silence, moving their knives over the croaker to scrape away the scales and then digging in the tip to slit the fishes' bellies and scoop out the entrails. They held the cleaned croaker under a tap and washed off the blood and the few clinging scales before stowing them in a plastic bucket, maybe two dozen of them lying there in a silvery pile.

SATURDAY NIGHT ON THE ROAD, twilight, and I was in Brawley, a cattle town in Imperial Valley about twenty miles from the border. In the Mexican quarter, men sat in folding chairs, on car hoods, and on steps drinking beer. The temperature had dropped into the nineties, and it was much cooler outside than in their little houses, where the blades of electric fans were turning.

Brawley was slow and stolid. The town looked flat-out poor. The cops were driving VW Bugs, and many buildings were boarded up. The marquee of the defunct local picture palace was blank but for two letters, *BR*, not yet fetched away by the desert wind.

The Planter's Hotel was a big, old, rattly place that had been decorated and redecorated countless times. There were just three customers at the bar, Phillip and Robert, who were welders, and a cowboy from some ranch. The cowboy was talking about going to Mexico to get some fancy boots.

"I doubt I could walk in anything but boots," he told us all, whether or not we wanted to know.

"Last night, I dreamed about an earthquake," the bartender, Charlene, said as she brought him another beer.

The cowboy nodded. "You never can tell," he said. "You get an earthquake in Brawley, the earth just rolls. It doesn't shake the way it does in San Francisco. I saw a documentary about it on PBS. Plate tectonics."

Phillip and Robert were corn-fed boys from Oklahoma. Phillip had played defensive tackle in high school and took up a lot of space. He and Robert, his assistant, were working at a geothermal plant by the Salton Sea. Phillip told me that he had no choice but to go where the work was, hauling his rig from job to job while his wife and his daughter waited for him on a forty-acre spread in Oklahoma.

"I'd drive home in a minute if my little girl needed me," he pledged. He came from country where daughters revered their daddies, and vice versa. "I've got a fuzzbuster in my four-wheeler, and I'd be there in a minute, all right."

"I had a daughter, but she died." The speaker was a new fellow who'd joined us uninvited, a skinny dude from Texas dressed in his best shirt and smelling of cologne. This part of California seemed to slide into the Southwest and into Mexico.

The skinny dude's story was sad. His wife had left him and his daughter had died. He was down to his last twenty-four dollars. He had looked at a room in an even worse hotel across the way, but it was full of dust and roaches. The manager wouldn't rent to him, anyhow, because he didn't have any references.

"I said to him, 'References? Do those cockroaches have references?'"

"Maybe you ought to just go on home," Phillip suggested to him.

"Ain't no work in Texas, bub," the skinny dude informed us. "And I'd do about any old thing! I'd be a damn roustabout."

"You could try up in Bakersfield," I said, recalling the oil fields.

"No way in hell am I going to Bakersfield!" he yelled, as if I'd asked him to pull out his fingernails with a pair of pliers.

While Phillip was doing some further career counseling with him, I discussed literature with Robert. He wanted to write a book for children, but he couldn't spell very well. He'd write a page in his notebook, and then he would read it over, find some misspellings, get angry, and rip it up.

"What's your advice?" he asked.

There he was, a bad-spelling welder from Oklahoma trying to cope with Brawley by writing a book for children. "Live with your mistakes," I advised him.

"Okay," Robert said. "From now on, I will."

I drank two beers and picked an opportune moment to leave. The bar was getting crowded and smoky, and a very large, bearded cowboy in a Stetson approached Phillip with a conniving smile on his face.

"Well, sir," he said, rocking on his heels, "you look to be about the biggest guy in here tonight."

Phillip allowed that it was true. "I do seem to be."

"Guess you and me will be the ones fighting later on."

"I guess so," Phillip said, not budging an inch.

Robert said, "When I get home tonight, I'm going to write a page and let it be. I promise it. I really will."

I congratulated him and made for the door of the Planter's Hotel.

In Imperial Valley, baled hay was stacked in fields. There were sheep and cattle being finished, herded in from the open range and fattened up for the slaughter. Cantaloupes were ripening on the vine, almost bursting at the seams. I saw some cotton, some sugar beets, and many little vegetable plots where truck crops grew. The telephone wires were heavy with hawks.

El Centro had a population of more than thirty thousand and was the valley's big town. It liked to bill itself as the "largest city below sea level in the Western Hemisphere."

At a pharmacy, a clerk told me that Brawley did have some money, but it all belonged to white ranchers.

"They even have a country club up there," he said, as if in El Centro a country club had the probability of a blizzard. More economic growth could be expected, he thought, when the new prison was finished in Calipatria, fifteen miles to the north.

I drove on to Calexico on the All American Canal. Arizona was about sixty miles to the east, toward some sandy hills and the Cargo Muchacho Mountains.

At the Mexican border, INS agents were supervising the comings and goings of people to and from Mexicali. On a Sunday afternoon, thousands were passing through turnstiles and gates, carrying shopping bags and straw baskets. They were almost all Hispanic and did not appear to be under any close scrutiny.

I walked through a gate into Mexico. The transition was simple and undramatic. The border seemed meaningless. Mexicali had some chain stores such as Leeds, National, and Pay Less, some cantinas, a couple of hotels, and many Chinese restaurants. There was life in the noisy streets, a heartening press of flesh that was good to see after witnessing all the main streets in California rolled up and packed away, from Smith River to Brawley.

Mexicali also had 131 *maquilas,* the assembly plants where Mexican workers labored for a very low hourly wage putting together everything from computers to elevator parts for U.S. and foreign corporations, doing the work that Californians used to do.

THAT EVENING, I camped in the Anza-Borrego Desert and woke around midnight to a whipping wind and a sky cracking with electricity. I heard thunder and saw streaks of lightning, but no rain ever fell. The lightning flashed like a strobe and threw bolts into the desert and illuminated the spiny, crippled arms of ocotillos. The wind blew hard through the tent to bring scatterings of sand.

I crawled back into my sleeping bag and listened to the thunder. I could hear creatures moving about in the dark making sounds. It was as if the storm had roused every living thing and had started them all skittering across the sandy earth. I lay there unable to sleep, alone and listening to the noises and feeling the immensity of the desert all around me until I finally nodded off toward dawn and woke later to a clear sky and sheep grazing on distant hills.

FROM EL CENTRO I traveled east through Seeley, Dixieland, and Plaster City, where gypsum was mined and off-road vehicles were tearing up the ground. The landscape turned extraordinary again near Jacumba on the border with huge boulders strewn about for miles, a poetry of plate tectonics. The vegetation was various and had an internal sense of order, as composed in its way as a terrarium.

Farther on, I came to the Desert Tower, a work of folk art built of rock and commanding a view to the north of Anza-Borrego and the Coyote Peaks. An old rockhound sat at a table covered with polished gems and minerals. He was talking to a tourist couple from Washington State.

"We're from Seattle," the woman was saying. "We thought we'd come down here because everybody from California's going up there."

Walking around the tower, I saw two scorpions locked in an arachnoidal embrace.

Foul brown air drifted up from the *maquilas* in the town of Tecate, at the Tecate Divide on Interstate 8. Between six and nine new assembly plants opened in Tecate every month. The workers were making such things as patio furniture, wine racks, kitchen cabinets, and rubber Halloween masks in the image of Freddy Kreuger.

Then I was climbing into the Cleveland National Forest past Live Oak Springs, Pine Valley, and many Indian reservations—Manzanita, La Posta, and Capitan Grande.

El Cajon marked my return to civilization. Here again was the panoply of strip malls and franchises, the jumble of immigrant communities—Cambodian, Vietnamese, Korean—and the card parlors, check-cashing facilities, and adult bookstores. El Cajon was the gateway to San Diego, the last big city in California and also the last paradise before Mexico.

CHAPTER 27

IN HIS CELEBRATED BOOK, *California for Health, Wealth and Residence,* (1872), Charles Nordhoff told of a visit to southern California during which he encountered lovely mountain scenery and bright sunshine wherever he went. The sublimity of the climate peaked in San Diego, he said, where the sun shone so constantly that people took it for granted.

Unaccustomed to such splendor, Nordhoff had once made the mistake of remarking on the perfect weather to a San Diegan.

"It's a fine day," he'd said, innocently enough.

The man had looked at him aghast and had replied, "Of course, it's a fine day. Why not? Every day is a fine day here!"

More than a century later, the editors of *Twin Plant News,* a trade journal that chronicled the *maquiladora* industry in California, Texas, and Mexico, where the legal working age is fourteen, conveyed a similar picture of San Diego to its readers:

Visiting San Diego is like stepping into paradise. With an average year-round temperature just below 70 degrees and with none of the oppressive heat of the desert or the wilting humidity of the tropics, San Diego seems just about perfect. There is so much to see and do that visitors usually find themselves short of time and residents never lack for entertainment.

San Diego, the last paradise. Realtors had built it, too, during the boom of the 1880s, selling off the land so fast that the city's population had jumped from about 5,000 in 1884 to nearly 32,000 in 1888. Speculators bought on credit and turned their holdings around for a profit in less than twenty-four hours. It could cost you up to $500 just to stand in line to bid for a lot.

The real estate fever hit its highest pitch with the marketing of Hotel del Coronado, in 1888. The owners advertised that the grounds were free of malaria and hay fever, and that languor was absent from the air. Guests would never have to contend with thunder, cyclones, or mad dogs, either. A cage full of monkeys appeased visiting kids, who also got to ride across the lawn on the backs of giant sea turtles.

San Diego was Ray Kroc's hometown, a McDonald's kind of town. It was a paradise without affect, thick with Republican virtues. You could count on having a good time in the city, I thought, but you'd never have a great one. The first few days I was around, I kept pinching myself to be sure that I was still alive. Purgatory could be like San Diego, really, with each moment and each day repeating the one before it, and nothing ever changing.

On the downtown streets, I saw so many blond, well-groomed, conservatively dressed men and women that I became convinced there must be a convention of former quarterbacks and cheerleaders going on somewhere. They had the high spirits of students who'd passed a tricky geometry exam and had just been told they would not have to miss the prom, after all. So much blondness, so much sun-washed light—I felt as though I were being tugged kicking and screaming into the pages of *Sunset*.

San Diego was for the young in spirit and the young at heart. The median age in the city was 28.7, and everything seemed half-formed and still tinged with a blush of adolescence. People were clinging to their naïveté and keeping at least ten yards between themselves and any serious information.

San Diegans might not be bookish or intellectual, but they were religious in their way and all worshiped at the First Church of Recreation, conducting their devotionals on 78 golf links and 1,200 tennis courts, in countless parks and fitness centers, and aboard 50,000 boats. They had to work, yes, but they did it reluctantly. The prevailing fantasy was to become a successful entrepreneur, not for the money but for the time it would buy you, more time to recreate. About three-quarters of the city's businesses were small and independent and had fewer than ten employees.

The economy of San Diego had once been pegged to agriculture and the U.S. Navy, but now manufacturing and tourism were equally important. The big fortunes were still being earned in real estate, on subdivisions, and on strip malls. The hills around town had all been shaved and leveled for new construction—"condo-farming," the practice was called.

Not every San Diegan was in favor of growth. A vocal minority objected strongly to the tracts and the condos and complained that San Diego was spreading too fast and without proper planning. The city lagged far behind its needs in building schools, roads, and firehouses. Its budget was stretched paper-thin, and its suburbs were an eyesore sprawl.

So what else is new in California? I asked myself.

Some alarmists subscribed to a hellish scenario whereby San Diego would blend gradually into Los Angeles to form a monster megalopolis. They yanked at their hair and cried that the distance between the cities was slowly being eroded, mourning the loss as they might a closing of the gap between sanity and madness.

Only Camp Pendleton, a training camp for the U.S. Marines, stood in the path of developers, commanding the terrain that separated San Diegans from their threatening neighbors.

Jokes about how to keep Angelenos and Los Angeles away were rampant in the city. One writer had suggested setting up a checkpoint where guards would search cars for such L.A.-style contraband as Evian water, self-hypnosis tapes, and cellular phones. The guards would also ferret out interlopers by asking questions like, "What's the difference between a treatment and a screenplay? Between a screenplay and a novelization?"—questions that no self-respecting San Diegan would be able to answer.

While a few San Diegans were trying to shut the gate behind them, many others were kicking it open again. The Convention and Visitors Bureau was even advertising the merits of the city over the radio in Los Angeles. In one commercial, a man and a woman stalled in a traffic jam were heard talking about what they did to stay calm. They both closed their eyes and thought about moving to San Diego.

SAN DIEGO MIGHT BE THE LAST PARADISE in California, but it was a paradise under siege. While Los Angeles was pinching it from the north, Mexico was pinching it from the south. Thousands of Mexicans—and Central and South Americans—crossed the border every day, some of them legal and some of them not, and made the city their first stop and often never left.

Immigrant women gave birth at public hospitals, families went on welfare, and children were educated in public schools, and the taxpayers in San Diego County had to pick up the tab. They did not pick it up with enthusiasm.

San Diegans, although closer to the border, were not unlike other Californians in their schizophrenic attitude toward Mexico. They wanted the shoppers and the laborers and the bargain-priced goods manufactured in *maquilas,* but they didn't want Mexicans to stay in their city. All the maids and the gardeners, the pourers of concrete, they should go back home on the evening trolley.

Irma Castro ran the Chicano Federation out of an older house in Barrio Sherman in San Diego. She had the same sort of coffee cups and furniture that Alejandro Montenegro had up in San Rafael. She was a fiery, dynamic woman who cared deeply about the rights of Latinos and the federation's mission to attend to them and see that every person got their due. Almost all the clients of the agency came from low-income families and lacked the language skills to cope with the forms and the offices of government, even when they were legal residents of the state.

In many respects, Irma Castro told me when I visited her, San Diego was just as segregated as Los Angeles. Hispanics lived in *barrios* in the inner city and in the towns south of Interstate 8 that rolled toward the border. National City, Chula Vista, and San Ysidro were gritty and prone to drugs, gang life, and crime.

The next generation of Hispanic children might not be much better off than their predecessors, Irma Castro felt. The elementary schools in the *barrio* were designed to hold about six hundred kids, but they took in twice that many. The buildings were old and the playgrounds were dirt. The San Diego School Board had one black person on it, but there were no Latinos, even though they made up about a quarter of the city's residents.

"The leadership here thinks this is the Midwest," Irma Castro said. "They reject the whole notion of diversity."

San Diego had never welcomed immigrant Hispanics with open arms, she explained, and that was still true, except that the situation had gotten more complicated. Sometimes legal Hispanics were as hard on the new arrivals from Mexico as white people were. They thought that the newcomers reflected badly on them, that they were lumped together with them in the public mind and forced to pay for their mistakes.

In the past, it had been almost impossible to make any progress in the city, Irma Castro said, because of blatantly dirty politics. Among the recent triumphs of the Chicano Federation was the role it had played in forging an important settlement agreement with San Diego that would help to change that.

The federation had joined in a class-action suit, *Perez* v. *City of San Diego,* that had taken issue with the way that districts were gerrymandered for electoral purposes. Because of the gerrymandering, no Hispanic had ever been elected outright to the city council. Furthermore, no nonincumbent black had ever defeated a nonminority candidate.

After lots of litigation and arbitration, the class plaintiffs and the defendant, San Diego, had reached a compromise agreement. It admitted that the political structure of the city was a violation of the 1965 Voting Rights Act and had denied minorities fair representation. The settlement agreement ordered a redistricting that would allow minority candidates an equal chance to be elected.

I had always heard that San Diego was not a good town to get caught in if you were a Mexican, but I still found it hard to believe that no Latino had ever been elected to the city council. Irma Castro assured me that it was so, but she added that one Latino had been appointed, Jess Haro, who chaired the federation's board of directors.

"You should talk to him," she said, and grabbed a phone and arranged a meeting for the next morning.

JESS HARO WAS A STRAPPING, strong-featured, opinionated man who looked every bit the former U.S. Marine. He met me for breakfast at the Hob Nob, a downtown restaurant that catered to government workers, where the waitresses knew everybody by name and the people occupying the booths spoke in whispers about the impending affairs of state.

Haro's parents had come to the United States from Jalisco, Mexico, in 1910. His father started as a farmworker in Texas and later moved the family to California and took a job with Columbia Steel in Pittsburg, in Contra Costa County. He and his wife had nine children, and Jess was the youngest of them.

After graduating from high school, Jess Haro had attended Stockton Junior College and Sacramento State, studying economics and foreign languages. He'd had an attitude back then, a chip on his shoulder.

"As a young man, I thought I was smarter than anybody else," he said, amused by the notion and what time had done to it. "I might show up late for an appointment, and if you called me on it, I'd just tell you to go fuck yourself."

From college, he went on to join the marines and became a pilot, and when he returned home, a friend from the corps hired him to work for a brokerage firm in San Diego, but the job wasn't to his liking.

"It was so superficial," Haro said, waving a hand in dismissal. "I was always touting clients on stuff I didn't know a thing about. I couldn't even read a financial statement. We were just selling intangibles. Truly, I learned nothing in two years."

So he left the brokerage firm and went to work as a lumber salesman for Georgia-Pacific, but he ran into trouble with his boss, believing that the man had it in for him and resented Haro's success and the good time that he was having. One day, on the spur of the moment, he quit, although he had no idea how he would pay his rent. He began buying and selling lumber on his own, managing to stay afloat by turning around a load of mahogany, say, in twenty-four hours.

"It can be better to do things out of ignorance sometimes," he said. "You can be too analytical, you know?"

Now Haro owned a big lumber and building materials company in the city. He did a lot of business in Mexico, about fifteen percent of his gross. Mexicans knew that it was wise to trade with Californians, he told me, and to keep relations cordial, but most Californians had yet to learn that lesson.

When a vacant seat opened on the city council 1975, one of his buddies from the marine corps urged him to try to get himself appointed. This friend and others like him did not approve of the choice that Pete Wilson, who was the mayor then, had put forth. Haro rose to the challenge. He still had the presence of a person who was born to such things, stubborn and a little hotheaded and not easily dissuaded from reaching a goal.

He won the appointment handily and served for almost four

years. The coalition that picked him looked at his credentials as a businessman and assumed quite wrongly that they were acquiring another conservative member.

"It's funny how life works out," he reflected, sipping his coffee, "how you get from here to there. If I think back, I can see that I always had a social conscience. My dad was a union man and a Democrat before me. With my background, what else *could* I be?"

Haro had always felt that politics in San Diego were discriminatory, and his time in office confirmed it for him. He saw the greased wheels turning. The local papers, for example, never had a bad word to say about Pete Wilson. As for minorities, they were always outside the process of ascension. They had no sense of continuity in government and so had no connections and no patronage.

In Haro's opinion, successful Latinos were partly to blame. They made their money and moved away to the suburbs instead of pumping something back into the community.

"What's the future going to be like?" I asked him. "What effect will the settlement agreement have?"

Real political power for Hispanics was at least a decade away, he thought. They needed to produce candidates who were not simply identified with ethnic issues, candidates who could addresss a much broader constituency.

"The whole thing is about hope," Haro said, with intensity. "If you give me some hope, I'll bust my ass for you. I'm not impatient because we're not in the top positions. I'm impatient because we're not in the *bottom* positions. The pyramid is not being built." He paused for a minute. "With all the immigrant-bashing that's going on, every Hispanic politician has to stand up. The debate is just not rational."

When the waitress brought our check, I mentioned to Haro that I would soon be in Mexico, my journey ended at last, and his entire demeanor changed. His jaw no longer seemed so set, and the discipline and the intensity dropped away. He looked as though he were ready to jump in the car and go with me. He had some happy memories, all right.

He took my pen and wrote in my notebook "Hotel El Rosa," where the swimming pool was spectacular. He wrote "Rey Sol," where the French food was exquisite. He wrote "Puerto Nuevo," a little town known for serving lobster. You wrapped the lobster in a tortilla with some beans, some rice, and some salsa.

"You wait until you get in that swimming pool," Haro said, with a big grin, all thoughts of politics fled. "You'll never want to get out."

UP THE COAST in San Diego County, in Carlsbad, some Mixtec Indians from Oaxaca were camped in a dry streambed, below the strawberry fields where they worked. Roberto Martinez took me there to meet them. He was the regional director of American Friends Service Committee in San Diego and kept a record of the abuses that were heaped on migrant laborers.

Martinez was a chunky man who complained about being deskbound. He preferred to be out in the open air. He drove north on Interstate 5 along the curve of the ocean. On every leveled ridge, in all directions, a monotony of newer subdivisions, Quail Ridge and Huntington Gate and Senterra Elite, looked out toward the Gulf of Santa Catalina.

It was another perfect day, sunshiney, with a temperature of seventy-two degrees.

Not much agricultural land was left around Carlsbad. There were a few farms for nursery stock, some truck farms for vegetables, and the strawberry fields, but the town was really a suburb now.

We walked down to the Mixtecs' camp through oaks, bay laurels, and eucalyptus. About sixty men were living in shacks cottered together from scrap lumber, newspapers, and chicken wire. They had no heat, no electricity, no running water, and no toilets. Their peak season had passed, so they weren't working steadily anymore. When they did work, they were paid $3.65 an hour.

The camp wasn't a bad one, Martinez said. He knew of others where the men lived in spider holes, digging a pit and covering the top with leaves and branches to stay warm in winter.

He had some old blankets and sweaters to distribute, and the Mixtecs gathered round. Nine out of ten were wearing baseball caps that said such things as "SWAT" and "Old Fart" and "California Highway Patrol." They were all from the same pueblo in Oaxaca and were saving their earnings to send back home, hiding it in their shoes or in their underwear.

I knelt to look inside some shacks and saw lumpy mattresses on bare earth. One Mixtec had used a U.S. government publication for immigrants as insulation, stuffing it between some wire and some cardboard. The first paragraph began, "The United States has fifty states. Rhode Island is the smallest state."

I asked the Mixtec, "Is Rhode Island our smallest state?"

"Okay," he said, with a smile.

Seldom did the Mixtecs leave their camp. Although most of them were documented, they were still afraid of the world outside. The strawberry grower had hired a private security firm to protect them from robbers and teenage gangsters, but the guards were surly and might as well have been holding them prisoner.

The Border Patrol hardly ever raided such camps, Martinez said, and neither did any of the San Diego County agencies that you'd expect to be concerned. He didn't know why that should be.

With little fieldwork to do, the Mixtecs were relaxing. They played a penny-ante card game and did their laundry in buckets of water that they hauled from the tract house of Dona Elvira, who lived nearby. There were houses all around them, fifty yards away. They had a rusty basketball hoop nailed to a tree, but their ball was punctured and deflated and kept them out of action.

Toward noon, a few Mixtecs ventured from the streambed to a

Carlsbad 7-Eleven, where they would wait for somebody from Sen-terra Elite or Huntington Gate to drive by and hire them to pull weeds or pound nails. The others bought overpriced groceries from a quilt truck that was parked on a street above the camp. They called the truck a *fayuca,* or a roach wagon, and worried that they were eating too much junk food and not enough fresh fruit and vegetables.

Dona Elvira had a mini-store in her house that the Mixtecs also patronized, Martinez told me. She made a profit on them, but she wasn't an insensitive person. At night, she let the men sit outdoors on the patio and watch their favorite programs on a black-and-white TV.

WHEN SAN DIEGANS wanted to be elsewhere, away from the unchang-ing ocean and the sun-washed light, they drove into the oak-and-pine foothill country of Cleveland National Forest. They could camp, fish, hike, or just park their RVs and blow off rounds of ammunition to their hearts' content, firing into canyons and at tree trunks and small mammals foolish enough to present themselves as targets.

Julian, a little mountain town, was one of the only foothill set-tlements of any size. The drive to it along Old Julian Highway took me through Ballena Valley and into the parched hills, where the green of apple orchards stood out against the straw-colored grasses.

In Julian, you could kick over the traces of a late-blooming Gold Rush that had started with a strike at George Washington Mine in February of 1870 and had raged briefly through San Diego County. The mines were all played out in ten years' time, so the miners packed up and crossed over to Tombstone, Arizona, for the next boom. The homesteaders had moved in and planted apple and pear orchards, run some cattle, and built apiaries to house bees for honey.

Julian did not look very different from the northern foothill towns. It had a rustic, western feel and a museum dedicated to mining history. It was not as isolated as Willow Creek, say, and not as rough.

It did not have the puzzled disappointment of those logging towns that were waking up from the nineteenth century with a terrific hangover.

Still, Julian wasn't an entirely peaceful place. Some foothill people were angry about the daytrippers from San Diego who came up to play. Foothill people could be as squirrely as Mojave Desert people in their need for privacy or secrecy. They staked out mining claims and plunked about for flakes and nuggets, finding just enough gold to give rise to paranoiac fantasies about flatlanders out to raid their Eldorado.

Some foothill codgers idling about downtown told me of a recent incident involving two of their own, Chris Zerbe and Joe Lopes, an affable old boxer who was well liked. The men had gone off one afternoon to chase some flatlanders from a mining claim that Zerbe had been hired to protect.

Zerbe was a decent sort, the codgers said, a hippie and a loner who walked around barefoot with a bandanna wrapped around his head. He liked nature and rabbits and would only cut timber from a tree that had fallen and not from anything live.

The flatlanders were suburbanites from El Cajon. They, too, had filed a claim with the BLM and were enjoying a family picnic. By law, they had every right to be on the land, regardless of any existing claim, as long as they were not interfering with an ongoing mining operation. The codgers understood that, but they disapproved. It was not the way in the foothills.

Everybody was armed. The suburbanites blew away Zerbe and Lopes and killed them dead. The killings didn't sit well with the foothill people. The codgers felt that Zerbe was a good marksman with a rifle and could not have been shot unless he was ambushed.

"They come up here with their guns like nobody's business," one angry codger said. "On the weekends, it's Rambo time. How'd you like those idiots to be shooting at things in your backyard?"

All that afternoon as I drove the backroads around Julian, I could hear the occasional report of arms being fired. The air smelled of apples, and of the chemical fumes from the illegal methamphetamine labs that the county police were busting at the rate of four a month, down from a dozen a month last year.

THE PERFECT WEATHER WAS ALSO RESPONSIBLE for drawing the U.S. Navy to San Diego in 1907. The navy had valued the available land along the bay, as well, and the proximity of the city to the Panama Canal. Military operations would spread and grow after World War I until they evolved into the largest naval complex in the Western world, with a submarine base, a couple of air stations, a training center, and a base at the foot of Thirty-second Street.

Point Loma was the navy's focal point. There you saw the sailors promenading in their dress whites and the retired sailors who owned the 1950s ranch houses on the hills above the ocean. You heard the navy buffs talking in coffee shops about their latest sitings and how they had seen such destroyers as the U.S.S. *Lynde McCormick* or the U.S.S. *John Young,* or had seen a hospital ship or a dock-landing ship or an attack submarine.

The buffs had an amazing grasp of military terminology and seemed to depend on it to keep them steady.

Cabrillo National Monument was on Point Loma, a commemorative to the first European explorer of California. On the brilliantly perfect morning that I visited, there were some backsliding youths in Conservation Corps uniforms pulling weeds from the lawn, and some Japanese tourists, all men, marching in soldierly single file to their bus. Ships were maneuvering on the bay, cargo ships bound for port and navy ships on training missions. Military planes and helicopters were soaring through the sky, Goshawks and Greyhounds and Fighting Falcons.

I looked out at the deep-blue water and at the flapping sails of boats and recognized again the primal beauty of the state. I tried to imagine the land as Cabrillo had seen it, a calm, low-lying harbor both vulnerable and inviting.

You never should have pressed on, Juan Cabrillo, I thought. The real treasure, the true gold, was here, right here, along the privileged and sheltered shore where Diegueño Indians had lived, surviving on buckwheat, sage, and yucca, on rabbits and squirrels and the ocean's bounty.

SAN DIEGO WAS THE GRAVEYARD of the shipbuilding industry in California, regardless of the U.S. Navy. The once-prosperous shipyards could not compete with Japan, South Korea, and West Germany, where builders received direct and indirect government subsidies, or with Poland and China, where the industry was government-controlled. All they could do to stay afloat was repair work, patching the holes in such ships as the *Exxon Valdez*.

The *Valdez* was in dry dock at National Steel and Shipbuilding Company (NAASCO). A flotilla of tugs had hauled it there from San Clemente Island about sixty miles away, where the ship had been drifting for four months. The *Valdez* was responsible for the worst oil spill in U.S. history, dumping 11 million gallons of crude along a previously unspoiled strip of the Alaskan coast.

While being dragged to National Steel, the *Valdez* supposedly had left an eighteen-mile-long oil slick on the California waters. It was not a ship to be trusted, not ever.

Fred Hallett, a NAASCO vice-president, took me around the yard. He was a tall, friendly, polite man in a hurry. His company was solvent but struggling. Its employees had bought it not long ago to save their jobs and had instituted a profit-sharing system. Hallett did not hold much hope of ever challenging the subsidized operations abroad. Their stools had four legs, he said, while NAASCO's had only three.

The NAASCO yard was a welter of steel, rust, and heavy machinery. It was as though I'd wandered by accident onto a forgotten set from an old war movie, the kind where a handsome skipper in a peerless uniform shields his slightly misty eyes with a hand to watch the jets taking off.

The contract to repair the *Valdez* was a godsend to NAASCO. It would bring in more than $25 million and would create about three hundred new jobs. NAASCO had built the *Valdez* and its sister ship, the *Exxon Long Beach,* between 1986 and 1987 at a cost of $250 million. They were the last ships to be built at the yard.

Hallett showed me the *Valdez*. I was not prepared for its majesty. It was like an expansion bridge or Hoover Dam, something monumental that human beings had dreamed up and then managed to build. The tanker was 166 feet wide and almost a thousand feet long. It had a deadweight of 211,000 tons. Most of its cargo tanks were badly banged up. The workers on it seemed as puny as the Lilliputians on Gulliver. Their repairs would go on for about nine months.

NAASCO was actively hiring, Hallett said. The company paid $5.50 an hour for an entry-level position. That went up to $6.00 after training. A journeyman earned $11.00 an hour, but that was probably not enough to live on in the inflated real estate climate of San Diego.

A few days after my tour of NAASCO, a statement from Exxon Shipping Company appeared in the paper. Its president, Frank Iarossi, said that the company was thinking about changing the *Valdez*'s name after it was rebuilt.

IF SAN DIEGO WAS THE LAST PARADISE, why was I so eager to leave it? It had killed my desire to explore. I felt that even if I went looking for intrigue, I wouldn't find it. Intrigue did not exist in San Diego.

There was so much to do in the city—the San Diego Padres, Sea World, Baby Shamu the Killer Whale, shark fishing on charter boats, rides in hot-air balloons, the golf courses and the tennis courts and the superb jogging trails in Mission Bay—and I didn't want to do any of it. I began to believe that somebody had stolen my happiness.

As I walked through the city, I kept saying to myself, Sunshine is not enough, sunshine is not enough.

Yet I knew in some part of me that San Diego might well be the model for our California of the future, that twenty-first-century state from which all the heroic and epic elements of manifest destiny had finally been edited.

And yet, and yet . . .

There came an evening in La Jolla, Raymond Chandler's last stop, when everything turned around for a moment, when my defenses were down after a day's hiking in Torrey Pines, a state park, and I was high on the negative ions and the deep breaths of sea air and was transported again.

La Jolla was rich, beautiful, and manicured, a Republican town right on the Pacific, thirty minutes from downtown San Diego. Chandler had owned a house there in the past and had returned again toward the end of his life to rent an apartment on Neptune Place, even though he claimed to dislike the placidity and the conservatism of the town and had said once that it made him want to run through the streets yelling four-letter words.

Chandler was in his early seventies. He had done little writing of late, except for some newspaper sketches for the *San Diego Tribune*. He was drinking heavily and bouncing back and forth between his digs, a La Jolla convalescent hospital, and a clinic in Chula Vista. He had tried living in England for a while, taking a flat in London, but California had reeled him in again, and now he was dying in California, where he had never wanted to be at all.

On a September evening, out for a walk, Chandler might have come upon a scene like the one that confronted me at twilight in La Jolla.

I stood above a cove where swimmers were splashing about in the gentlest tide imaginable, their bodies streaks of white in the ink-dark ocean. The sky behind them was fading slowly to a pinkish ribbon. The grass on the lawn of a nearby shuffleboard club was an unsurpassable green. Pelicans flew by in twos and threes, while cormorants posed on marbly rock ledges. Again, the air was a gift. There was nothing to fight and nothing to resist.

A diapered baby, towheaded and joyous, all innocence and vapors, cried out at the sky and the birds and the swimmers.

In the end, I thought, when all the redwoods had been logged and the rivers were just a trickle, when the fish were but a memory and the earth had been leached of all its minerals, when the farms were dust and all the prisons had been built, when every last bit of recalcitrant flesh had been toned and tanned and corrected, when the realtors had completed their subdividing and the wilderness was no more, maybe California would be reduced, simply, to this—this light, this air, this feeling on the skin.

CHAPTER 28

WHEN I CAME to the dusty boneyard of San Ysidro in the last days of September, I believed that I had reached the end of California. Ahead lay the border and beyond it lay Tijuana and Mexico.

I had always imagined the line between the countries as a highly charged zone protected by a high fence and patrolled by hardcore Border Patrol agents in mirrored sunglasses and polished leather boots. It had never occurred to me that the border did not exist, that it was a useful fiction.

San Ysidro was a shadowy, abstract place where ordinary suburban life mingled with the abrupt and secretive transactions that governed illegal immigration. It had a curious doubleness. I would go by a schoolyard and see children playing, and then look up to find the sky filled with ravens and vultures.

The two largest buildings in town were a K mart and a blood bank. Sometimes men and women from Tijuana went through the port of entry, sold some blood, and indulged themselves in a shopping spree at a new mall, loading up on cut-rate Reeboks at a factory-outlet store. They might top off the visit with a meal at a Denny's restaurant, where the food never differed from its picture on the laminated menu.

The San Ysidro port of entry was the busiest border crossing in the world. About 43 million people passed through it every year. They passed through on foot, in buses and in vans, and in cars and on bicycles. They were the legal travelers.

Nobody knew how many people entered the state illegally each day. The Border Patrol caught about 1,500 illegal aliens every twenty-four hours, but another 5,000 or so probably slipped over *la frontera* and eluded capture.

In its San Diego sector, the Border Patrol was understaffed and underfunded. The dispatches from its chief patrol agent had the plaintive tone of somebody who feels misunderstood and misrepresented and wants badly to correct all that.

> The severe depression of the economies in many developing countries, overpopulation, and underemployment, combined with the lure of jobs and access to benefits in the United States, have precipitated a massive movement of people to our back door ... Violence against aliens, agents, and citizens has escalated to crisis proportions. Smuggling of contraband across land boundaries continues to increase at an alarming rate ... We welcome the opportunity to show you our operation and the challenges we face in accomplishing our mission.

In San Ysidro, it was easy for illegal aliens to vanish. They crossed the border in clothes meant to disguise them as Californians, wearing jeans, L.A. Dodgers caps, and bogus sweatshirts from the Hard Rock Cafe, and they blended smoothly into the town's mostly Hispanic population.

San Ysidro had safe houses where a migrant could hide out. It had dealers who sold phony documents. A trolley ran straight to San Diego, and there was little chance that you'd be pulled from it unless you had the bad luck to meet with a rare INS sweep.

At the port of entry, criminals and would-be criminals were always hanging around the pay phones. They had a cottage industry that earned them and their less-visible partners millions. They performed such valuable services as laundering money, steering drugs in profitable directions, and arranging rides to Los Angeles or farther.

Drivers were always circling in San Ysidro, going slowly, stopping, maybe looking for something or someone, their movements a curious echo of the dark birds wheeling in the sky above them.

I did find a chainlink fence at the border. It ran for about fifteen miles from the Pacific Ocean to Otay Mesa, another port of entry, where the industrial parks seemed to double almost daily to keep pace with the *maquiladoras* on the Mexican side. In most spots, the fence was trampled or had fallen down, or had been snipped with shears or simply torn. It presented no obstacle.

All along its length, I saw the trash left behind by travelers—gum wrappers, diapers, syringes, soda cans, and even the comic book *novelas* that often featured cautionary tales about the perils of a journey to *El Norte*.

San Ysidro made me uncomfortable. Nothing about it was ever absolute. A man who had glanced at you the right way yesterday might glance at you the wrong way tomorrow. A car might pull from a curb to tail you for a few blocks before dropping back. Was it a cop? A case of mistaken identity? Somebody fucking with your mind? Paranoia was the border's stock-in-trade.

The border, I learned, was also a dumping ground. Stolen pesticides were dumped there and carried deeper into Mexico for resale. A quart of Rally from the San Joaquin could fetch up to sixty dollars, while Roundup fetched fifty by the quart. It was fruitless to speculate on how or where the pesticides were applied. There were few environmental controls and fewer still that could not be got around with a bribe.

Maquiladoras dumped their toxic wastes in toxic cemeteries—pits in the ground that were swiftly covered over. The contaminated chemical drums were then hauled to wretchedly poor *colonias* and sold as reservoirs for drinking water. Otay Mesa was a vision of rusting trucks, cars, and motorcycles that had been dumped hastily in the heat of an escape from a Border Patrol pinch.

Still, oddly, there was the fact of ordinary life in San Ysidro. Commuters to San Diego bought tract houses and tried to shut their eyes to the illegals who dashed across their yards or stopped for a drink of water from their garden hoses. Everybody understood the deal and did their best not to stand in its way. That was how it went along the border, all the way to Arizona.

ALL DAY IN SAN YSIDRO, every day, I watched people crossing illegally into California. The numbers were preposterous, and the means of entry were various, bold, and sometimes stagy. Illegal immigration had been boiled down and refined over the years until it was nothing more than an elaborate game of cat and mouse that was often conducted in broad daylight at a cost to taxpayers of untold billions.

On Dairy Mart Road one afternoon, a country road, I had to slam on my brakes when seven teenagers sprinted in front of me out of a dry creekbed concealed by bamboo and sagebrush. They seemed to have materialized out of nowhere, dropped from the clouds and set to running full speed upon the desert earth.

There were four girls and three boys, all about sixteen. Each of them carried a plastic grocery sack or a balled-up towel that held their most treasured belongings. A mirror, a comb, an electric hair dryer. I remembered Luis Martinez in the Alexander Valley and how proud he was of his battered suitcase.

As quickly as they had appeared, they disappeared into the brush on the other side of the road. They ran without apparent fear, never panting nervously or looking back over their shoulders. Instead, they had the high-spirited, athletic grace of people doing laps around a track.

They had nothing to lose, really. In the unlikely event that they met with a Border Patrol agent, they would just be processed and returned to Tijuana, where they could mount a new try in the morning.

Monument Road off Dairy Mart Road afforded me even more amazing scenes. Against a concrete levee of the Tijuana River, a dribble of raw sewage that was posted *Peligroso!* and marked with a skull and crossbones, people who were preparing to cross began to gather in the early evening. They ripped up the shrubbery to build small fires against the autumn chill and bought beer, cigarettes, tacos, and tamales from venders circulating among them with carts and coolers. The terrain before them was rugged and potholed, an expanse of hard ground and crusty arroyos dotted with vegetation.

The smugglers known as *coyotes* moved among the travelers to solicit business, promising a safe trip for a specified price. I could see the coyotes collecting customers and drilling them as a team, standing in front of ten or twenty migrants, pointing out landmarks, and discussing strategies in the way of coaches giving chalk talks.

There were hundreds of routes into the state—easy routes, taxing routes, even brazen routes.

At the levee, for instance, everyone was out in the open, their purpose announced to all and sundry, but the run to California was short and the runners were many, so *la migra* never caught more than a third of them. At the embankment, you were gambling on the odds.

The floodlights of the Border Patrol came on at dusk to shine on the playing field. Agents riding all-terrain vehicles motored over the concrete and through the vegetation. Helicopters from the naval station at Imperial Beach, just north of San Ysidro, were poised overhead, their chopper blades roaring. Beacons slashed at the sky.

I thought of tired commuters in their backyards lighting the charcoal in their grills—a barbecue in Vietnam. I could see them flipping on the TV and could hear an ESPN commentator saying, "Rodriguez feints to the right, then goes left and darts by Agent Whipple. Yes, yes, Rodriguez is going to go all the way, he's going to make it to California. . . ."

Soon after dark, there was a frantic scurrying of shapes and forms, and human beings took off singly or in groups. Every possible emotion was on view. I saw terrified old men, befuddled Indians from the interior, young mothers clutching infants to their breasts, and little girls in freshly laundered communion dresses.

Many teenagers like those on Dairy Mart Road broke headlong and hellbent toward the future, sometimes acting on an impulse. Staggering tequila drunks fell down in the river slime.

The agents assigned to chase the migrant horde had a hapless job. They were often faked out or jostled or led astray by decoys. They would manage to corner three migrants only to see six more slide by them, inches away. They were like men trying to contain a flood tide by improvising a dike from a few old bricks held together with chewing gum.

So insistent was the action that it seemed at times as if Mexicans must be engaged in an unconscious effort to reclaim the territory they had surrendered long ago. They were everywhere.

In Imperial Beach, I watched some agents arrest four young men as they wandered up the sand from Tijuana, carefree in their bathing suits and affecting the air of American lads on holiday. I watched a train go by San Ysidro and saw migrants spreadeagled and plastered to the tops of boxcars.

At the port of entry, I watched an acrobatic fellow clamber over the hoods of cars and squeeze between them in a blatant and successful dive toward dollars.

On Interstate 5, I watched couples dart past the hurtling traffic. The freeway was a deathtrap, and people were frequently killed as they crossed it—112 illegals in the last three years. The Border Patrol had done a recent tally of migrants stranded on traffic islands per twenty-four hours and had counted 650 on an average weekday and twice as many on weekends.

I saw a boy of about eight emerge from the bushes along I-5 on yet another afternoon. He had thin, black hair, and his cheeks were dirty and streaked with tears. He was feral-looking, an ugly child and all alone. His T-shirt bore a picture of Snoopy and was stained with grass, as though he'd been crawling under barriers.

I wondered why he had crossed. Maybe he'd got cut off from his family and was searching for them. Maybe a teacher had scolded him. Maybe his old man had whacked him once too often.

He ran by the rushing cars and barely missed being hit. His eyes were wild and frantic. A Hispanic man approached him with a look of concern, but when the boy asked a question, the man shoved him away, not wanting to be implicated. The boy was obviously in trouble. He would be unlucky for certain.

All at once, the boy seemed to know that, admitting to himself how furiously lost he was, and he sat down in a motel parking lot and began crying in earnest.

On a night when the moon was full above San Ysidro, I rode with Joe Nuñez, a Border Patrol veteran, as he scoured Otay Mesa near Brown Field Airport for illegal immigrants. He drove a Chevy Blazer that had dents in it from the rocks that truants had flung at it. In the San Diego sector, the agency spent about fifty thousand dollars a year just replacing the windshields in its vehicles.

Nuñez was a relaxed and good-humored fellow. Boredom was his main enemy on the job. Night after night, he went through the same routine, making one arrest after another, but nothing ever changed. There were always new people to arrest. Only once in eleven years had he endured a dangerous incident, when a migrant had tried to stab another agent with a knife. Nuñez had wrestled it away.

"The knife was made of wood," he told me, as if the essence of his work could be summed up in such illusions.

Sometimes Nuñez became so bored that he considered applying for a transfer to an investigative unit in the *barrios* of Los Angeles. He never let himself dwell on whether or not the chaos at the border was intentional. That was a forbidden subject and could cause mental depression.

The migrants that Nuñez caught around Brown Field Station were usually from Mexico or Central America. He had taken a few Chinese once and had also nabbed some Yugoslavs.

OTMs—Other Than Mexican—were not uncommon in the San Diego sector. Over the past year, agents had netted 347 Colombians; 266 Brazilians; 53 South Koreans; 20 Indians; 16 Turks; 11 Filipinos; 7 Canadians; 3 Israelis; and one person apiece from Nigeria, Somalia, Gambia, Algeria, and France.

We had not been on the mesa for more than five minutes before Nuñez spotted some prey.

"Look there," he said, and I looked and saw five people crouched at the edge of Otay Mesa Road.

Nuñez killed the Blazer's headlights, downshifted into first, and glided toward them. He was absolutely calm. The maneuver was as familiar to him as brushing his teeth.

The migrants were so preoccupied that they didn't see the Blazer until it was almost upon them. Then one of them yelled, and they all spun on their heels and ran.

"Halt!" Nuñez shouted.

They did. No show of force was needed. The migrants complied immediately, slumping to their knees and putting their hands on their heads with perfect expertise, as their *coyote* had doubtlessly instructed them to do.

The *coyote* was a burly professional. He had been caught before and would be caught again. The bust was a minor inconvenience to him, something he would shake off at a cantina tomorrow, a bit of misfortune that was bound to come sooner or later to anybody who played the game.

His clients were three men and a woman in their early twenties. They were far less sanguine about their predicament. They had never crossed the border before. The moonlit mesa must have seemed immense to them, and California still as distant as a star.

Nuñez called for a van to pick them up. Then he frisked them all. He found a handkerchief tied to one man's leg, hidden under his trousers. The man made a keening noise, as though the handkerchief held precious gems. Nuñez unrolled it and out fell ten faded dollar bills.

"Where are you from?" Nuñez asked in Spanish. He projected sympathy. The circumstances were embarrassing, really.

The oldest migrant cleared his throat. He kept looking at the *coyote,* wanting to strangle the bastard.

"Oaxaca," he said.

Oaxaca was about sixteen hundred miles away. I thought of the bus rides and the scrimped meals and the nights spent sleeping in alleys or on floors. Oaxaca, where the soil was so depleted that it scarcely supported a corn crop anymore. Sixteen hundred miles, sore legs, an empty belly, and there you were slumped on your knees on Otay Mesa. Eldorado was nothing but dust and a black sky.

"Why did you cross?" Nuñez asked.

The man shrugged. "To work," he said.

Trabajar, to work. Throughout the night, whenever Nuñez asked his question, "Why did you cross?," he got the same reply. People crossed the border to work, and they didn't care what the work was like. They would do all the things I'd seen them doing—swab floors, swim in pesticides, harvest sea urchins, and pick grapes. They'd pour hot tar for roofs, handle beakers in meth labs, mow lawns, deliver circulars, and clean sewers. They would do anything at all.

The night dragged on. About eleven o'clock, Nuñez got a radio call about some Salvadorans who were being rounded up. He sighed. Central Americans were a pain in the ass. They required about forty-five minutes of paperwork each.

The Salvadorans would all insist that they were victims seeking political asylum, and by the time a court date was arranged, they would all be working somewhere. If they couldn't find any work, they would go home.

Nuñez's shift would stretch into the wee hours. He had accepted such hitches as part of his job, but some agents couldn't tolerate the tricky metaphysics of their situation. They had signed up to be heroes, but they were just spinning in a revolving door and developed stress-related illnesses and marital problems and problems with booze.

Out on the mesa, they sometimes got terrible headaches when they realized that no one could tell for sure where California ended and Mexico began.

OTAY MESA was a different story in the morning. There were no illegals to be seen. Earthmovers were digging up the ground near Pacific Rim Boulevard and Maquiladora Court, two streets that had fire hydrants and electrical cables but no buildings yet.

Trucks in a steady caravan went through the port of entry, more than a thousand a day, carrying freight into Mexico and to the Zona Industrial of Tijuana. Businessmen reported for work at the American and Japanese corporations that operated assembly plants on the other side—Casio, Sanyo, Sony, Maxell, General Motors, Honeywell, and so on.

A hundred years ago, German settlers had dry-farmed barley on the mesa. Siempre Viva was the first town. It had a post office, a saloon, and a horse-racing track that pulled in customers from as far away as San Francisco, but it died in a recession, in 1893. Speculators drilled a useless oil well in 1928, and miners took bentonite clay from open pits through the 1940s.

An amusement park called "Captain Nemo's Twenty Thousand Leagues Under the Sea" had once been targeted for the mesa, but it never made it past the planning stage.

Only now was Otay Mesa being fully exploited. Its developers had lobbied to have it included in a U.S. Foreign Trade Zone that gave all sorts of economic incentives to firms willing to locate there and take part in the *maquiladora* scheme, and they had succeeded.

Tijuana had more than five hundred *maquiladoras* at present. The workers earned much less than an American or a Japanese worker would earn for doing the same job. They were primarily young women, and they spent about half of their wages on a place to live and another sixth on transportation. The average *maquiladora* had a high rate of employee turnover, up to 25 percent a month.

In the Zona Industrial, the air smelled of exhaust fumes and was so thick with dust rising from dirt roads that I felt I could grab a handful of it. At the Maxell plant, the *maquila* girls were coming out of their fenced compound on a lunch break. They bought food from quilt trucks and carts—sandwiches, fruit, cold drinks. They were done up as though for a night on the town, lavishly powdered and lipsticked, their hair teased and pomaded and a fetching look in their eyes.

A handsome boy selling melon slices was about to wilt under their attentions. They were killing him with their perfume. Romance was dangerous in the *maquila* world and could strike at any minute.

I talked with a Japanese supervisor, who was sipping coffee and sucking on a cigarette. He had been transferred to Tijuana from L.A. He didn't mind it at all, he said. His wife was petite like many Mexican women and had enjoyed great success in shopping for clothes.

Then the break was over, and I drove over washboard streets back to Otay Mesa on the California side. There was no Joe's by any of the industrial parks, only a Chevron Station and a McDonald's. I bought a Big Mac and sat on a lawn outside a corporate building to eat it. You win, Derrel Ridenour, Jr., I thought, stretching out on the lush grass and looking up at the circling birds.

AY, ¡CARAMBA! I couldn't stop traveling. I followed California into Mexico, crossing the border again at San Ysidro port of entry on a Saturday afternoon, in the company of some moon-faced Lambda Chis already halfway drunk and some nuzzling couples soon to be enveloped in the margarita haze at Rosarito Beach Hotel. There were gigantic coeds flexing their volleyball muscles, secretive bald men after bargain-basement Rogaine, and dorky little poontang hounds who kept the strip joints in the Zona Rosa in business.

Now I understand the blandness of San Diego. For a century, its citizens had looked to Tijuana as the place to act out their passions. Mexico embodied all the honest life that was missing from their city. They craved its spicy cuisine and the fire in its loins. They, too, needed an occasional taste of blood.

Thousands of cars poured over the line. Californians were riding in donkey carts on Avenue Revolución and having their pictures taken in serapes and sombreros. At Hussong's and Popeye's they were pounding beers and tequila shooters and dancing in joyous stupidity to mariachi bands. Their hips moved as never before. The demons were coming out of their closets. Tongues would touch other tongues, and untoward liaisons would occur. Guilt could wait until tomorrow, resurrecting itself on the other side.

By midnight, the streets were wacky with reeling collegians all sunburned to a crisp and throwing up in unison. The *maquila* girls were just hitting their stride, arriving at discos with the flare of starlets on the verge of a breakthrough and trailing their killer perfume. I pitied the poor youths who were the target of their lingerie. Someday they might wake up as husbands in a new house in a yet-to-be-built subdivision, Mismo Acres, up Chula Vista way.

Sunday morning, there were church bells and atonement. I kicked at garbage as I walked through the *centro*. A kid with a shoeshine box gave me a shine. The *maquila* girls had finished their dreaming and had put on mantillas.

Tijuana was a city of 4 million people. There were at least three thousand applicants for any job. Grand homes sat on a hillside above the dusty air and were favored with views of a golf course, just as in *El Norte*. I saw pizza parlors, video rental stores, fancy dress shops, and fine Italian and French restaurants, but most people lived in *colonias* such as El Florido on the blanched earth at the edge of canyon country.

El Florido had not existed five years ago. Now it was home to fifty thousand, many of them *maquiladora* workers. They built their houses slowly, brick by brick and board by board. Compared to other provinces in Mexico, Baja California was the land of opportunity. Tijuana was at the center of a Mexican Gold Rush.

I bought a Coke from Lino Gonzalez Alvarez, a refugee from Guadalajara. He kept the sodas on ice in a metal drum. His *tienda* had a plywood counter and the usual complement of flies that could not be avoided in the city. *Maquiladora* workers were his main customers, and he made the equivalent of ten thousand American dollars a year, more than he'd ever made before.

Street musicians from Oaxaca played on the boulevards. The tourists were packing up to depart, forming a long line at the port of entry and squandering their last pesos on hideous ceramic dwarfs and neon-bright piñatas that would serve them forever after as a reminder of the time they were a little crazy down in Mexico and did some things they'd never do again.

JESS HARO HAD MADE A SMALL MISTAKE. Hotel El Rosal in Ensenada was Las Rosas Hotel by the Sea. It was Mexico sanitized, a playground for San Diegans and Angelenos, but I didn't care. I took a room with a balcony overlooking the Pacific and kept writing in my notebooks and eating fish tacos and drinking Coronas.

The swimming pool was spectacular, indeed. It was situated on an incline so that the negative edge appeared to flow into the ocean. Whenever I swam in it, I felt as if my body were weightless and floating into a new and unblemished world. That was my new dream.

Afternoons I sat at the bar saying, *"Mas Corona, por favor,"* and watching the San Francisco *Gigantes* and their pennant race on TV. I was postponing the inevitable, of course, the demise of my own little paradise.

Ensenada stank of fish-processing plants. I thought about Crescent City—so long ago, on another planet. The city had its share of *maquiladoras,* too, and also a Louisiana-Pacific mill.

One day, I drove aimlessly into the countryside to Agua Caliente, a hot springs resort seven miles down a dirt road into a canyon. An old man was sitting on a chair outside a bungalow at the resort, implacably patient, as if he knew I would come, as if my arrival were preordained.

"You like to go into the baths, *señor*?" he asked.

I looked at the pools, but the water in them could not be said to beckon. Old car seats were arranged around them, and there were motel units that the Joads might have been hesitant about staying in. I had a sense that creatures really owned the place, rats and mice and scorpions. Or maybe time did.

I said to the old man, "Just a cold *cerveza, por favor.*"

The next day, still aimless, I took another dirt road to the settlement of Ojos Negros. There were some farms, some horses in pastures, and some onion fields. Hawks rested on the graying wood of fence posts. On the horizon, I saw two figures about a half-mile away and watched them grow bigger as I got closer, going five miles an hour over the ruts and the bumps.

An old woman and her granddaughter. The old woman had kind eyes and an Indian face. The little girl clutched at her grandma's fingers, not knowing what to make of a gringo in a Taurus. I slowed to a crawl to keep from burying them in dust, and the old woman flagged me down and made gestures indicating that she'd like a ride back to the houses at Ojos Negros.

"Get in," I said, and they did.

They sat together in the backseat, my two mysterious passengers. I could see the old woman in my rearview mirror, smiling contentedly at this unexpected gift. The little girl wouldn't let go of her hand. The car was as big as the world to her, and she loved it and was frightened by it and hoped only that it would take her home.

The old woman asked to be let out in front of a house. She shooed the little girl inside it, then came around and leaned against my door. She was still smiling. I thought that she'd probably been smiling like that for eighty years, smiling because she knew a secret.

"*Gracias, señor,*" she said, touching my arm, and I watched her go into the house and then drove home myself, to California.

PART SIX

EARTHQUAKE WEATHER

Rightly, in every age it is assumed we are witnessing the disappearance of the last traces of the earthly paradise.
—*E. M. Cioran,*
Anathemas and Admirations

CHAPTER 29

THE AFTERNOON of October seventeenth was unusually warm and muggy in San Francisco, and the Giants, our miracle children, were about to host the Oakland A's in a World Series game at Candlestick Park. On Twenty-fourth Street, I heard somebody say, "Earthquake weather," but I paid it no mind. In the city, people were always talking about an earthquake, the epochal one that was going to rip apart the turf and raise up Nostradamus with his final predictions.

At about five o'clock, the phone rang at our house. I chatted for a while with a neighbor down the block, filling her in on my travels and telling her that I was still restless and hadn't yet been able to settle down. She interrupted me quite suddenly to exclaim, "Oh, my! I believe we're having an earthquake!"

I felt nothing at first, but I could hear the distant tinkling of glassware, and then, all at once, the hardwood floor began to shift from side to side beneath my feet in a giant, rolling motion, like the deck of a boat in a rough sea.

Our hill seemed to be liquefying, turning to Jell-O. There were sounds of plaster ripping and joists creaking—cries of pain on the part of an old house as its brittle bones got rearranged. I watched in awe as a filigree of fine cracks appeared on the living room walls and ceiling.

The rolling motion subsided in about a minute, only to be followed by several sharp aftershocks, hard little jolts that were akin to the pinpoint jabs that a good boxer throws to keep an opponent off-balance. My wife, who'd been taking a nap, emerged from the bedroom, and together, still jumpy, we inspected the house and found that we had been lucky. The only damage that we'd suffered was some broken plates.

A few minutes later, a friend arrived in a trembly condition. He'd been driving to our place, idly thinking about the ball game, when the earthquake hit and the road before him started buckling and rippling, folding in on itself. He had never seen anything like it, he said. Craters were opening in front of him, and he had to swerve to avoid them and also the other swerving drivers.

We sat outside on the front steps. I could feel my heartbeat returning to normal, and I had a sense, too, of collecting a self that had been dislodged and shattered into fragments. The fragments had flown randomly into the air and were now being reintegrated into my system—a picture curiously celestial, like one of exploding galaxies.

It was oddly calm and pleasant outside. There was no electricity, the telephone lines were down, and the cars were few and far between. Evening was coming on, and candles burned in windows against a dusky, blue sky. We were seeing the city as it must have looked more than a century ago, at a time when the wheels of existence turned more slowly. The many hills were cupped in a pastoral silence.

We had the contentment of survivors, but our feelings changed when we dug up some batteries for a radio and listened to the early news reports from around the Bay Area—the ball game canceled, houses falling down, freeway ramps collapsing, and sporadic incidents of looting. We learned that people had died. Scientists had measured the earthquake at 7.1 on the Richter scale, a magnitude of shaking that none of us had ever experienced before.

The bulletins were like dispatches from a battlefront in a war that was not ours. Except for the power outages, Noe Valley was relatively unaffected. We went about cooking dinner in an alternating mood of hilarity and gloom, switching the radio to a call-in show where sundry "eyewitnesses" were supplying the testimony to prove that the earthquake was both a collective and an individual phenomenon, rattling each private universe to a greater or a lesser degree.

After dark, my brother showed up at the front door with his wife and his daughter. He was carrying a bottle of red wine and two cans of Dinty Moore beef stew, the only canned food that he could find on the ravaged shelves of his corner grocery. His family had the dour look of the dispossessed. They had just moved into a new condo across town, and their fireplace chimney had come unmortared and had crashed through a window. Their plaster had not just cracked. It had ripped free in chunks to reveal the lath behind it.

They were afraid that if a particularly strong aftershock were to strike, the entire structure might tumble down and kill them in their sleep, so we set them up in the spare bedroom, fed them, and uncorked the wine. The night was taking on a festive, end-of-the-world edge.

In the morning, with the electricity back and the telephone lines repaired, we could almost pretend that the earthquake hadn't happened, but scenes of destruction had been playing on TV across the nation, and we had to field a succession of calls from worried relatives and friends. Once again, California was being portrayed in the media as a danger zone, even a mortal threat, where the chance of striking it rich was equalized by the chance that a catastrophe would wipe you out.

I could hear the admonitions echoing in Oneida, in Orlando, and in Pittsburgh. *You see, Charlie? Aren't you glad you didn't move out there?* The fundamentalists had probably concluded that we were being punished for our sins.

The calls were a comfort to us, anyway. They reestablished connections. The desire to be connected to someone, *any*one, was overwhelming after the earthquake and clearly evident in our neighborhood, where there were twice as many people on the streets. If you'd got caught alone, the trauma had reinforced your loneliness, and you didn't want to experience that again.

In a few days, when the emergency measures were lifted, I visited the Marina District, where the devastation had been the most severe. Many plate-glass windows on Chestnut Street were splintered or demolished, and the pavement was riddled with small tears. Driveways had split in two, as though a huge ax had cleaved them, and curbs had torn away from sidewalks. Bricks lay everywhere in heaps.

Entire blocks were cordoned off in the Marina. Looking down one, I saw a row of about twenty apartment buildings that were drifting away from plumb, tilting forward and backward like a bunch of tipsy men in a lineup. On the Marina Green, a grassy park along the bay, army tents were bivouacked. Some of the grand houses with water views were deserted, all the furniture gone from inside them, as if thieves had run off with it.

Elsewhere, young renters were loading chairs and beds into a van. They were fleeing from San Francisco before the next calamity hit, surrendering their identity as Californians and hoping to turn themselves back into blameless Iowans or Pennsylvanians before it was too late.

The quiet in the marina was exceptional. It resembled the hush that you encounter among the faithful during a church service. The earthquake had made everything solid seem watery. It had drawn into question the very stability of our so-called terra firma. For a single minute, we'd been liberated from our orderly illusions and subjected to the chaotic laws of nature, our lives tossed into the sky, and a new set of transformations was beginning.

AN EARTHQUAKE SHAKES THINGS LOOSE. At my house, the stalemate got worse, not better, and soon I had moved into a furnished apartment by myself and had reluctantly acquired two more badges of a Californian, a therapist and a legal separation.

I say that flatly now, but then I was sick at heart. I cursed and railed and kicked at any handy object, wandering around in the evenings and looking for solace in useless bars from which every stitch of solace had vanished long ago. I felt as though I had joined a fallen world and was now obliged to hear the confessions of friends and acquaintances who were newly eager to share with me the details of their own season of pain.

Mostly, though, I was sad, deathly sad. Love is as scarce in California as it is everywhere else, and to have forfeited a portion of any that might have accrued was a tragedy.

The therapist, a Jungian, understood my blues. The soul, he said, rose up in middle age and tried to throw off its shackles, even if the shackles were self-imposed. The soul had its own irrepressible urges, and that could lead to unacceptable emotions that were in conflict with the feelings that you were supposed to have—wise, good feelings—and ultimately to despair.

In time, my wife and I spruced up our house and put it on the market. It sold on the very day that it was listed, an April Fool's Day, for double the money that we'd paid for it. In our seven years of tenancy, we had struck it rich backhandedly, losing in the process something far more precious to us.

For months, I walked around with my pockets full of greenbacks, crying, "I'll never buy another house! I'll be a renter forever!," until my potential tax liability sank in, and I began a hasty search for property. I thought that I would head for the country again, no doubt stirred by my memories of Alexander Valley, but I was on my own now and decided against the isolation. My head was still spinning, and my heart was still in shreds.

So, by chance, as a compromise, I wound up in the paradise of Marin County, buying a little, shingled cottage on a private tree-shaded lot in a small town. A young couple had built the cottage in

1906, to get away from San Francisco after the great earthquake and fire. Thick redwood timbers anchored it to an unbudgeable foundation, but I didn't become aware of the aptness of my choice until I signed the closing papers.

I slept badly during my first weeks in the cottage, waking to the scurrying noises of animals, coons and skunks and possums on the prowl. I put in some tomatoes where the daisies used to grow and mulched them heavily against a trip to Real Foods, but some deer slipped through an open gate one night and ate the plants.

Winter came. There was a good old boy in San Rafael who chopped down sickly or unwanted trees and sold them off as firewood, so I stacked my porch with oak and eucalyptus logs and burned fires right through to March. Ashes drifted across the mantelpiece, and I would dampen a rag to wipe them from the books and the framed photos of my niece, our family's first-born Californian, blond and blue-eyed Nora, a girl of the Golden West.

ANOTHER SPRING, and I laced on my boots and hiked around Mount Tamalpais, up over the trails by Phoenix Lake feeling the pull on leg muscles gone soft in winter and feeling, too, the strong beating of my blood. The mountain was alive with water, every creek and rill flowing, and again there was the seasonal gift of wildflowers, something so simple and elegant and yet so easily missed.

Often as I hiked I thought about all that I'd seen on my journey and about the future in California and what it would bring to my niece. The problems in the state were immense but not unsolvable, although the solutions might require a fundamental change in the human heart. I looked at the tall trees and the birds and passed blacktail deer and once a little red fox, hoping that some of what I loved about California, its fast-fading natural bounty, could still be preserved for her.

I sensed a fear upon land. As our resources became smaller, Californians were reaching and grabbing for what they could get, damning the consequences. Sometimes I pictured a future California where there were places as impoverished as the *colonias* in Tijuana, where the schools were even shabbier and all pretense of democratic caring had fallen by the boards. At other times, in a better mood, I believed that we might yet learn from our errors and begin assembling a vital, dynamic community whose potential was unlimited.

All the reimaginings and the reformulations, the infinite attempts at transformation, they were the psychic capital of California. As my accuser in Buttonwillow had known, we were all fly-by-nighters in the end, making ourselves up as we went along, simultaneously tolerant and intolerant of our mutual acts of self-invention.

Among certain Indian tribes in California, it used to happen that a man might rise up without a word and go off to wander for a while in the world, not knowing what he was looking for, or maybe not looking for anything in particular. Nobody could predict whether or not the man would return, or what he would have to say if he did return.

In many respects, I felt like such a man—somebody who had wandered in the world—and what I brought back with me from my grand tour of California were the most basic of truths, things so elementary that to utter them in public was to risk being handed a cap and bells. Love the earth, I would say. Find the beauty and protect it. Care for the sick and the outcast. Build schools to teach your children. Be gentle. Dream.

The essential map of the territory is James D. Hart's *A Companion to California* (New York: Oxford University Press, 1978), an indispensable guide that I relied on frequently to point me in the right direction. My primary source for historical background was David Lavender's *California: Land of New Beginnings* (New York: Harper & Row, 1972), although I consulted many other histories as well, such as the work of Kevin Starr. I was on the road from April to October of 1989, but I continued to follow the stories recounted herein after I got home and updated the figures cited in them whenever possible.

My main source for such data was *California Statistical Abstract,* which is published by the state's Department of Finance. The median prices quoted for homes come from *California Cities, Towns, and Counties* (Palo Alto, CA: Information Publications, 1993).

For my assessment of the lives of certain prominent Californians past and present, I was fortunate to have at hand several books whose authors had preceded me and had done a fine job of research and interpretation. Anyone interested in a fuller treatment of the various subjects could study them profitably.

Vincent Bugliosi, with Curt Gentry, *Helter-Skelter* (New York: W. W. Norton, 1974), about Charles Manson.

Lou Cannon, *President Reagan* (New York: Simon & Schuster, 1991); and Anne Edwards, *Early Reagan,* (New York: William Morrow, 1987).

Steven Gaines, *Heroes and Villains* (New York: New American Library, 1976), about the Beach Boys.

Frank MacShane, *The Life of Raymond Chandler* (New York: E. P. Dutton, 1976).

Bob Thomas, *Walt Disney* (New York: Simon & Schuster, 1976); Leonard Mosley, *Disney's World* (New York: Stein & Day, 1984); and Katherine and Richard Greene, *The Man Behind the Magic* (New York: Viking Penguin, 1991).

Frederick Turner, *Rediscovering America* (New York: Viking Penguin, 1985), about John Muir.

I am also indebted to the many local newspapers that I consulted along the way, most of them mentioned by name in the text. *Surfer* magazine was helpful in deciphering that subculture. For my treatment of the go-go years in Silicon Valley, I found much of use in *The Computer Entrepreneurs* by Robert Levering, Michael Katz, and Milton Moskowitz (New York: New American Library, 1984).

My edition of Edwin Bryant's *What I Saw in California* was published by Ross & Haines, Inc., of Minneapolis as part of its Western Americana series in 1967. William Brewer's *Up and Down California in 1860–1864* was first published by Yale University Press in 1930, but my copy was a paperback from the University of California Press, 1974.

Obviously, *Big Dreams* could not have been written without the kind participation of countless Californians who were willing to open themselves to a stranger and entrust him with their stories. I remain immensely grateful to them all. Luis Martinez in Sonoma County, Adam in Sacramento, and Rudy in Palm Springs are pseudonyms for those who did not want their real names used. The agent in Hollywood is a composite of two such agents of my acquaintance.

Abeloe, Willian N. *Historic Spots in California*. Stanford, CA: Stanford University Press, 1948.

Andrews, Ralph W. *Heroes of the Western Woods*. New York: E. P. Dutton & Co., 1979.

Atack, Jon. *A Piece of Blue Sky: Scientology, Dianetics and L. Ron Hubbard Exposed*. New York: Carol Publishing Group, 1990.

Baker, Elna. *An Island Called California*. Berkeley: University of California Press, 1971.

Brooks, George R., ed. *The Southwest Expedition of Jedediah S. Smith*. Glendale, CA: A. H. Clark Co., 1977.

Brownlow, Kevin. *Hollywood: The Pioneers*. New York: Alfred A. Knopf, 1979.

Conaway, James. *Napa*. Boston: Houghton-Mifflin, 1991.

Day, Mark. *Forty Acres*. New York: Praeger, 1971.

De Angulo, Jaime. *Indian Tales*. New York: Hill and Wang, 1953.

Drury, William. *Norton I: Emperor of the United States*. New York: Dodd, Mead, 1986.

Friedrich, Otto. *City of Nets*. New York: Harper & Row, 1986.

Heintz, William F. *Wine Country: A History of Napa Valley*. Santa Barbara, CA: Capra Press, 1990.

Henstell, Bruce. *Sunshine and Wealth*. San Francisco: Chronicle Books, 1984.

Hine, Robert V. *California's Utopian Communities*. Berkeley: University of California Press, 1983.

Holliday, J. S. *The World Rushed In*. New York: Simon & Schuster, 1981.

Hyink, Bernard; Brown, Seyam; and Thatcher, Ernest. *Politics and Government in California*. New York: Harper & Row, 1979.

Jackson, Helen Hunt. *Ramona*. 1884. Reprint. New York: Signet Classics, NAL, Dutton, 1988.

————. *Report on the Condition and Needs of the Mission Indians*. 1888. San Jacinto Museum.

Jackson, Joseph Henry. *Anybody's Gold*. New York and London: Appleton-Century Co., 1941.

Kent, Nicholas. *Naked Hollywood*. New York: St. Martin's Press, 1991.

Kirsch, Robert, and Murphy, William S. *West of the West*. New York: E. P. Dutton & Co., 1967.

Kotkin, Joel, and Grabowicz, Paul. *California, Inc.* New York: Rawson, Wade Publishers, Inc., 1982.

Kramer, William. *Norton I.* Santa Monica, CA: N. B. Stern, 1974.

Kroeber, Alfred. *Handbook of the Indians of California*. Washington, D.C.: Government Printing Office, 1925.

Lantis, David, ed. *California: Land of Contrasts*. Belmont, CA: Wadsworth Inc., 1963.

Lapp, Rudolph M. *Afro-Americans in California*. Danvers, MA: Boyd & Fraser, 1987.

Le Conte, Joseph. *A Journal of Ramblings*. San Francisco: Sierra Club Books, 1960.

Lennon, Nigey. *Mark Twain in California*. San Francisco: Chronicle Books, 1982.

Levy, JoAnn. *They Saw the Elephant: Women in the Gold Rush*. Hamden, CT: Archon Books, 1990.

Lewis, Oscar. *Sutter's Fort: Gateway to the Gold Fields*. Englewood Cliffs, NJ: Prentice-Hall, 1966.

McCoy, Esther. *Five California Architects*. 2nd ed. Los Angeles, CA: Hennessey & Ingalls, Inc., 1987.

McGowan, Joseph A., and Willis, Terry R. *Sacramento: Heart of the Golden State*. Chatsworth, CA: Windsor Publications, 1983.

Margolin, Malcolm, ed. *The Way We Lived*. Berkeley, CA: Heyday Books, 1981.

Matthiessen, Peter. *Sal Si Puedes*. New York: Random House, 1969.

Miller, Joaquin. *Overland in a Covered Wagon*. D. Appleton & Company, 1931.

Miller, Russell. *Bare-faced Messiah: The True Story of L. Ron Hubbard*. New York: Henry Holt, 1988.

Mirak, Robert. *Torn Between Two Lands: Armenians in America*. Cambridge: Harvard University Press, 1983.

Nelson, Byron, Jr. *Our Home Forever: A Hupa Tribal History*. Hoopa Valley Reservation: Hupa Tribe, 1976.

Norris, Frank. *The Octopus*. New York: Doubleday, Page & Co., 1901.

Orenduff, Robert. *Introduction to California Plant Life*. Berkeley, CA: University of California Press, 1974.

Powers, Stephen. *Tribes of California*. Contributions to North American Ethnology, vol. 3. Washington, D.C.: Government Printing Office, 1977.

Rice, Richard E. "The Uncounted Costs of Logging." *National Forests: Policies for the Future*. Washington, D.C.: The Wilderness Society, 1989.

Rintoul, William. *Drilling Ahead*. Lower Burrell, PA: Valley Publishers, 1981.

———. *Oildorado*. Lower Burrell, PA: Valley Publishers, 1978.

Rosenus, Alan, ed. *Selected Writings of Joaquin Miller*. Eugene, OR: Urion Press, 1977.

San Francisco League of Women Voters. *A Guide to California Government,* 1977.

Schell, Orville. *Brown.* New York: Random House, 1978.

Starr, Kevin. *Americans and the California Dream.* New York: Oxford University Press, 1973.

————. *Inventing the Dream: California Through the Progressive Era.* New York: Oxford University Press, 1985.

————. *Material Dreams: Southern California Through the 1920s.* New York: Oxford University Press, 1990.

Steinbeck, John. *The Grapes of Wrath.* New York: The Viking Press, Inc., 1939.

————. *The Harvest Gypsies.* Berkeley, CA: Heyday Books, 1988.

Turner, Henry A., and Vieg, John A. *The Government and Politics of California.* New York: McGraw-Hill, 1966.

Vincent, Stephen, ed. *O California!* San Francisco: Bedford Arts Press, 1990.

Watkins, T. H. *California: An Illustrated History.* Carlsbad, CA: American West Publishing, 1973.

West, Nathanael. *The Day of the Locust.* New York: New Directions, 1950.

Williams, Richard L. *The Loggers.* New York: Time-Life Books, 1976.

Young, Stanley. *The Missions of California.* San Francisco: Chronicle Books, 1988.